P9-CDK-355

Please remember that this is a library book,
and that it belongs only temporarily to each
person who uses it. Be considerate. Do
not write in this, or any, library book.

Theoretical Criminology

Fifth Edition

by the late
George B. Vold,
Thomas J. Bernard,
and
Jeffrey B. Snipes

New York   Oxford
Oxford University Press
2002

364.2
V914t
2002

Oxford University Press

Oxford   New York
Athens   Auckland   Bangkok   Bogotá   Buenos Aires   Cape Town
Chennai   Dar es Salaam   Delhi   Florence   Hong Kong   Istanbul   Karachi
Kolkata   Kuala Lumpur   Madrid   Melbourne   Mexico City   Mumbai   Nairobi
Paris   São Paulo   Shanghai   Singapore   Taipei   Tokyo   Toronto   Warsaw

and associated companies in
Berlin   Ibadan

Copyright © 2002 by Oxford University Press, Inc.

Published by Oxford University Press, Inc.
198 Madison Avenue, New York, New York 10016
http://www.oup-usa.org

Oxford is a registered trademark of Oxford University Press

All rights reserved. No part of this publication may be reproduced,
stored in a retrieval system, or transmitted, in any form or by any means,
electronic, mechanical, photocopying, recording, or otherwise,
without the prior permission of Oxford University Press.

Library of Congress Cataloging-in-Publication Data

Vold, George B. (George Bryan), 1896–1967.
    Theoretical criminology / by George B. Vold, Thomas J. Bernard, and Jeffrey B.
Snipes.—5th ed.
        p. cm.
    Includes bibliographical references and index.
    ISBN 0-19-514202-0 (alk. paper)
    1. Criminal anthropology. 2. Criminology. 3. Deviant behavior. 4. Social conflict. I.
Bernard, Thomas J. II. Snipes, Jeffrey B.

HV6035 .B47 2001
364.2—dc21

2001039095

Printing number: 9 8 7 6 5 4 3 2

Printed in the United States of America
on acid-free paper

Please remember that this is a library book,
and that it belongs only temporarily to each
person who uses it. Be considerate. Do
not write in this, or any, library book.

Contents

Chapter Four: Psychological Factors and Criminal Behavior   55

Intelligence and Crime: Background Ideas and Concepts—IQ Tests and
Criminal Behavior—Delinquency, Race, and IQ—Interpreting the
Association Between Delinquency and IQ—Policy Implications of the
IQ–Delinquency Link—Personality and Criminal Behavior—Antisocial
Personality Disorder—Psychiatric Predictions of Future Dangerousness—
Early Childhood Predictors of Later Crime and Delinquency—Impulsivity
and Crime—Policy Implications of Personality Research—Conclusions

Chapter Five: Crime and Economic Conditions   84

Research on Crime and Economic Conditions: Contradictions and
Disagreements—Crime and Unemployment: A Detailed Look at
Research—Problems Interpreting Research on Crime and Economic
Conditions—Implications and Conclusions

Chapter Six: Durkheim, Anomie, and Modernization   100

Emile Durkheim—Crime as Normal in Mechanical Societies—Anomie as a
Pathological State in Organic Societies—Assessing Durkheim's Theory of
Crime—Conclusion

Chapter Seven: Neighborhoods and Crime   117

The Theory of Human Ecology—Research in the "Delinquency Areas" of
Chicago—Policy Implications—Residential Succession, Social
Disorganization, and Crime—Sampson's Theory of Collective Efficacy—
Implications and Conclusions

Chapter Eight: Strain Theories   135

Robert K. Merton and Anomie in American Society—Strain as the
Explanation of Gang Delinquency—Policy Implications—The Decline and
Resurgence of Strain Theories—Strain in Individuals and in Societies:
Negative Emotions and Institutional Anomie—Conclusion

Chapter Fourteen: Marxist and Postmodern Criminology   248

Chapter Fifteen: Gender and Crime   267

Chapter 16: Age and Crime   283

Chapter Seventeen: Integrated Theories   301

Chapter Eighteen: Assessing Criminology Theories   318

Index   339

CHAPTER ONE

Theory and Crime

Criminology as a field of study has been well documented by a long line of excellent and distinguished textbooks going back many decades.[1] Most of these texts concentrate on presenting *facts* known about the subject of crime. For example, they discuss the extent and distribution of criminal behaviors in society; the characteristics of criminal law and procedure; the characteristics of criminals; and the history, structure, and functioning of the criminal justice system. The theoretical material presented in these texts is usually somewhat limited. Almost all texts review the major theories about the causes of criminal behavior, and some texts present other theoretical material such as sociology of law, philosophy of punishment, or theories of correctional treatment.

As a text in theoretical criminology, this book does not concentrate on presenting the facts known about crime, although at least some of those facts are presented in the various chapters. Instead, this book concentrates on the *theories* used to explain those facts. The theories themselves, rather than the facts about criminality, are the focus of this book.[2]

---

[1]A few of the very large number of textbooks in general criminology may be mentioned here: Freda Adler, Gerhard O. W. Mueller, and William S. Laufer, *Criminology*, 3rd ed., McGraw-Hill, New York, 1998; Larry J. Seigel, *Criminology*, 6th ed., West/Wadsworth, Belmont, CA, 1998; Stephen E. Brown, Finn-Aage Esbensen, and Gilbert Geis, *Criminology: Explaining Crime and its Context*, 3rd ed, Anderson, Cincinnati, 1998; John E. Conklin, *Criminology*, 6th ed., Allyn and Bacon, Boston, 1998; Frank E. Hagan, *Introduction to Criminology*, 4th ed., Nelson-Hall, Chicago, 1998; Piers Beirne and James Messerschmidt, *Criminology*, 2nd ed., Harcourt Brace, Fort Worth, TX, 1995; Sue Titus Reid, *Crime and Criminology*, 8th ed., Brown and Benchmark, Madison, WI, 1998; and Frank Smalleger, *Criminology Today*, Prentice-Hall, Englewood Cliffs, NJ, 1996.

[2]Some of the recent texts that focus on criminology theory include Franklin P. Williams III and Marilyn D. McShane, *Criminological Theory*, 3rd ed, Prentice Hall, Upper Saddle River, NJ,

A theory is a part of *explanation*.[3] Basically, an explanation is a sensible way of relating some particular phenomenon to the whole world of information, beliefs, and attitudes that make up the intellectual atmosphere of a people at a particular time or place. In the broad scope of history, there are two basic types of theories of crime. One relies on spiritual, or other-world, explanations while the other relies on natural, or this-world, explanations. Both types of theories are ancient as well as modern.

SPIRITUAL EXPLANATIONS

Spiritual explanations of crime are part of a general view of life in which many events are believed to result from the influence of otherworldly powers. For example, primitive people regarded natural disasters such as famines, floods, and plagues as punishments for wrongs they had done to the spiritual powers.[4] They responded by performing sacred rites and rituals to appease those powers.

In the Middle Ages in Europe a spiritual view of the world was joined to the political and social organization of feudalism to produce the beginnings of the criminal justice system.[5] Originally, crime was a largely private affair in which the victim or the victim's family obtained revenge by inflicting a similar or greater harm on the offender or the offender's family. The problem was that private vengeance had a tendency to start blood feuds that could continue for many years until one or the other family was completely wiped out. The feudal lords therefore instituted methods by which God could indicate who was innocent and who was guilty. The first such method was trial by battle, in which the victim or a member of his or her family would fight the offender or a member of his or her family. Because God would give victory to the innocent party, the family of the loser would have no grounds for exacting vengeance on the winner, and the blood feuds were ended.

1999; Ronald Akers, *Criminological Theories*, 2nd ed., Roxbury, Los Angeles, 1997; Werner Einstadter and Stuart Henry, *Criminological Theory: An Analysis of Its Underlying Assumptions*, Harcourt Brace College Publishers, Fort Worth, TX, 1995; J. Robert Lilly, Francis T. Cullen, and Richard A. Ball, *Criminological Theory: Context and Consequences*, 2nd ed., Sage, Newbury Park, CA, 1995; Stephen J. Pfohl, *Images of Deviance and Social Control*, 2nd ed., McGraw-Hill, New York, 1994; Larry Siegel, *Criminology: Theories, Patterns, and Typologies*, West, St. Paul, 1992; and Randy Martin, Robert J. Mutchnick, and W. Timothy Austin, *Criminological Thought: Pioneers Past and Present*, Macmillan, New York, 1990.

[3]Arthur L. Stinchcombe, *Constructing Social Theories*, Harcourt, Brace & World, New York, 1968, pp. 3–5.

[4]Graeme Newman, *The Punishment Response*, Lippincott, Philadelphia, 1978, pp. 13–25.

[5]Harry Elmer Barnes, *The Story of Punishment*, 2nd ed. revised, Patterson Smith, Montclair, NJ, 1972, pp. 7–10.

The problem with trial by battle was that great warriors could commit as many crimes as they wanted, secure in the knowledge that God would always give them victory. Thus, somewhat later in history, trial by ordeal was instituted. In this method the accused was subjected to difficult and painful tests, from which an innocent person (protected by God) would emerge unharmed while a guilty person would die a painful death. For example, a common method of determining whether a woman was a witch was to tie her up and throw her into the water.[6] If she floated she was considered innocent, but if she sank she was guilty. Other forms of ordeal included running the gauntlet and walking on fire. Trial by ordeal was condemned by the Pope in 1215 and was replaced by compurgation, in which the accused gathered together a group of twelve reputable people who would swear that he or she was innocent. The idea was that no one would lie under oath for fear of being punished by God. Compurgation ultimately evolved into testimony under oath and trial by jury.

Spiritual explanations of crime appeared in the New World in the Puritan colony on Massachusetts Bay. During the first sixty years of its existence, this colony experienced three serious "crime waves" thought to be caused by the devil. The most serious of these "crime waves" occurred in 1792, when the community was thought to have been invaded by a large number of witches.[7]

Our modern prison system also originated in association with a spiritual explanation of crime. Around 1790 a group of Quakers in Philadelphia conceived the idea of isolating criminals in cells and giving them only the Bible to read and some manual labor to perform. The Quakers thought criminals would then reflect on their past wrongdoings and repent.[8] They used the term *penitentiary* to describe their invention, a place for *penitents* who were sorry for their sins.

Today, some religious individuals and groups still attribute crime to the influence of the devil. For example, Charles Colson, who was special counsel to President Richard M. Nixon and who served seven months in prison for his part in the Watergate affair, attributes crime to sinful human nature.[9] He argues that religious conversion is the only "cure" for

---

[6]Newman, op. cit., p. 97.

[7]Kai T. Erikson, *Wayward Puritans,* John Wiley, New York, 1966.

[8]Harry Elmer Barnes and Negley K. Teeters, *New Horizons in Criminology,* Prentice Hall, New York, 1945; Negley K. Teeters, *The Cradle of the Penitentiary: The Walnut Street Jail at Philadelphia, 1773–1835,* Temple University Press, Philadelphia, 1955.

[9]Charles Colson, "Toward an Understanding of the Origins of Crime," in John Stott and Nick Miller, eds., *Crime and the Responsible Community,* Hodder and Stoughton, London, 1980. See also David R. Wilkerson, *The Cross and the Switchblade,* B. Geis, New York, 1963; Oral Roberts, *Twelve Greatest Miracles of My Ministry,* Pinoak, Tulsa, 1974, ch. 9; Gerald Austin McHugh, *Christian Faith and Criminal Justice: Toward a Christian Response to Crime and Punishment,* Paulist Press, New York, 1978.

crime and spends much of his time bringing that Christian message to prisoners.

NATURAL EXPLANATIONS

Spiritual explanations make use of otherworldly powers to account for what happens; natural explanations make use of objects and events in the material world to explain the same things. Like the spiritual approach, the natural approach to explanation is ancient as well as modern.

The early Phoenicians and Greeks developed naturalistic, this-world explanations far back in their history. For example, Hippocrates (460 B.C.) provided a physiological explanation of thinking by arguing that the brain is the organ of the mind. Democritus (420 B.C.) proposed the idea of an indestructible unit of matter called the atom as central to his explanation of the world around him. With Socrates, Plato, and Aristotle, the ideas of unity and continuity came to the fore, but the essential factors in all explanations remained physical and material.

By the first century B.C. Roman thought had become thoroughly infused with naturalism. For example, Roman law combined the spiritualism of the Hebrew tradition with the naturalism of the Greek tradition to provide a natural basis for penalties as well as for rights. The Hebrew doctrine of divine sanction for law and order merged with Greek naturalism and appeared in Roman law as a justification based on the "nature of things." Later, the rule of kings by divine right became a natural law looking to the "nature of things" for its principal justification.

In the sixteenth and seventeenth centuries writers such as Hobbes, Spinoza, Descartes, and Leibniz studied human affairs as physicists study matter, impersonally and quantitatively. Modern social science continues this naturalistic emphasis. The disagreements among social scientists are well known, but at least they have in common that they seek their explanations within observable phenomena found in the physical and material world.

SCIENTIFIC THEORIES

Scientific theories are one kind of natural explanation. In general, scientific theories make statements about *the relationships between observable phenomena.*[10] For example, some scientific theories in criminology make statements about the relationship between the certainty or severi-

---

[10]Stinchcombe, op. cit., pp. 15–17.

ty of criminal punishments and the volume of criminal behaviors in society. Other scientific theories make statements about the relationship between biological, psychological, or social characteristics of individuals and the likelihood that those individuals will engage in criminal behaviors. Still other scientific theories make statements about the relationship between the social characteristics of individuals and the likelihood that those individuals will be defined and processed as criminals by the criminal justice system. All these characteristics can be observed, and so all these theories are scientific.

Because they make statements about the relationships among observable phenomena, a key characteristic of scientific theories is that they can be *falsified*.[11] The process of attempting to falsify a scientific theory involves systematically observing the relationships described in the theory and then comparing those observations to arguments of the theory itself. This process is called research: That is, the assertions of the theory are tested against the observed world of the facts.[12] If the observations are inconsistent with the assertions of the theory, then the theory is falsified. If the observations are consistent with the assertions of the theory, then the theory becomes more credible, but it is not proved; there are always alternative theories that might also explain the same observed relationships.

A theory can gain a great deal of credibility if all the reasonable alternative theories are shown to be inconsistent with the observed world of facts. At that point the theory might simply be accepted as true. However, it is always possible that some new facts will be discovered in the future that are inconsistent with the theory, so that a new theory will be required. For example, Newton's laws of physics were accepted as true for 200 years, but they were replaced by Einstein's theory of relativity at the beginning of the twentieth century due to the discovery of some new facts.[13]

CAUSATION IN SCIENTIFIC THEORIES

Causation is one type of relationship among observable variables, and all scientific theories in criminology make causal arguments of one type or

---

[11]Ibid., pp. 5–6; Thomas J. Bernard, "Twenty Years of Testing Theories: What Have We Learned and Why," *Journal of Research in Crime and Delinquency* 27(4): 325–47 (Nov. 1990).

[12]Thomas J. Bernard and R. Richard Ritti, "The Role of Theory in Scientific Research," in Kimberly L. Kempf, ed., *Measurement Issues in Criminology*, Springer-Verlag, New York, 1990, pp. 1–20.

[13]Thomas S. Kuhn, *The Structure of Scientific Revolutions*, University of Chicago Press, Chicago, 1969.

another. Generally speaking, causation in scientific theories means four things: *correlation, theoretical rationale, time sequence,* and *the absence of spuriousness.*

Correlation means that things tend to vary systematically in relation to each other. For example, height and weight are correlated: People who are taller generally weigh more and people who are shorter generally weigh less. The relation is not perfect—some short people weigh more and some tall people weigh less. But the tendency still exists for more height to go with more weight and less height to go with less weight. This is called a "positive" correlation.

A "negative" correlation is where more of one thing tends to be associated with less of the other. For example, the more miles you have on your car, the less money it generally is worth. As with height and weight, the relation is not perfect because some old cars are worth a lot and some new cars aren't worth much. But for cars in general, mileage and price are negatively correlated.

Correlation, whether positive or negative, is necessary for causation. If two things do not vary together in some systematic way, such as height and IQ, then the one cannot cause the other. But correlation alone is not sufficient for causation. You also need a good reason to believe a causal relation exists. This is the *theoretical rationale,* the second element of scientific causation.

For example, some criminologists argue that harsh erratic discipline by parents increases the likelihood of delinquency in their children.[14] There must be correlation: Parents who use such techniques must be more likely to have children who are delinquent than parents who use moderate consistent discipline. But there also must be a theoretical rationale—a coherent explanation why these techniques by the parents may cause delinquency in the children.

An example of such a rationale would be that harsh discipline conveys anger rather than love and increases the chance that the child will rebel and engage in delinquency to get back at the parents. In addition, erratic discipline means that most of the time there is no punishment for misbehavior anyway. So in this example, a coherent theoretical rationale exists that, if coupled with evidence of a correlation, would support a conclusion that harsh erratic discipline causes delinquency.

But consider a very different scenario. Imagine loving parents who have a delinquent child. These parents use moderate and consistent discipline but it just doesn't work. Eventually they become angry and frus-

---

[14]Robert J. Sampson and John H. Laub, *Crime in the Making,* Harvard University Press, Cambridge, MA, 1993.

trated. Then when the child gets into trouble, they either do nothing at all (because nothing works anyway) or they use harsh discipline (because they are angry and frustrated). In this scenario, the child's delinquency causes the parents' harsh erratic disciplinary techniques.

The problem in this example is that correlation does not establish direction of causation: Does harsh erratic discipline cause delinquency or does delinquency cause harsh erratic discipline? The solution is to determine *time sequence,* the third element of scientific causation. If the discipline comes first and the delinquency comes later, then we can conclude that the discipline causes the delinquency. But if the delinquency comes first and the discipline later, then we can conclude that the delinquency causes the discipline.

The fourth and final element of scientific causation is called the *the absence of spuriousness.* Suppose that parents in low-income families, for whatever reason, are more likely to use harsh erratic discipline even when their children are not delinquent. And suppose that children in low-income families, for whatever reason, are more likely to engage in delinquency regardless of the parents' disciplinary techniques. If both of these suppositions were true, then it might look like harsh erratic discipline causes delinquency. But in fact, both the discipline and the delinquency could be caused, in one way or another, by the low family income.

In this example, the relationship between delinquent behavior and parental disciplinary techniques would be spurious. But suppose the researchers control for income—that is, suppose they compare low-income parents who use harsh erratic discipline with other low-income parents who use moderate consistent discipline. Then if they find that delinquency is associated with harsh erratic discipline, it can not be because of low family income. Then it is reasonable to conclude that a causal relation exists.

The conclusion that a causal relation exists, however, always is a statement about *probability,* never an assertion of certainty. To say that harsh erratic discipline causes delinquency is like saying that smoking causes cancer. Most people who smoke do not get cancer. Rather, smokers have a greater probability of getting cancer than non-smokers. Similarly, if our causal theory is correct, then children raised with harsh erratic discipline are more likely to become delinquent than children raised with moderate consistent discipline.[15]

---

[15]For example, see David P. Farrington, "Early Predictors of Adolescent Aggression and Adult Violence," *Violence and Victims* 4:79–100 (1989). This article reports the percentage of juveniles who engage in delinquency for each of a very large number of characteristics. Thus, it gives a good sense of how much (or how little) a particular characteristic affects the probability of engaging in delinquency.

The whole point of causal theories is to gain power over the world in which we live. When we want less of something (such as crime and delinquency) or more of something (such as law-abiding behavior), we try to find out the causes of what we desire. Then we try to influence those causes in order to get what we want.

Even though causal theories in social science deal only with probabilities, knowing about those probabilities can be quite useful for policy purposes. For example, if harsh erratic discipline actually does increase the probability of delinquency, even if by a small amount, then it may be useful to try to affect parenting styles. Special classes could teach parents, especially those with children at high risk of becoming delinquent, effective discipline techniques. If these classes succeeded at changing the disciplinary techniques used by parents, then we should end up with less delinquency in the future. In fact, such classes appear to reduce delinquency by significant amounts over the long run.[16]

All scientific theories in criminology make causal arguments, but there are very different and in some ways contradictory frames of reference, based on different ways of thinking about crime. To give a sense of the breadth of the field of criminology, three such frames of reference are identified and briefly described in the paragraphs that follow.[17] The first frame of reference describes criminal behavior as freely chosen, while the second describes it as caused by forces beyond the control of the individual. The third frame of reference views crime primarily as a function of the way that the criminal law is written and enforced. Thus, this third frame focuses on the behavior of criminal law rather than the behavior of criminals.

CLASSICAL CRIMINOLOGY

First, there is the view that intelligence and rationality are fundamental human characteristics and are the basis for explaining human behavior. In this view humans are said to be capable of understanding themselves and of acting to promote their own best interests. Societies are formed because people rationally decide to make them according to patterns that seem "good" to them—either monarchies or republics, totalitarian

---

[16]See, for example, Peter W. Greenwood, Karyn E. Model, C. Peter Rydell, and James Chiesa, "Diverting Children from a Life of Crime," Rand Corporation, Santa Monica, CA, 1996.

[17]For a discussion of underlying assumptions in criminological theories, see Einstadter and Henry, op. cit. For a complex discussion of philosophical methods in criminology involving some of the same issues, see Bruce DiCristina, *Method in Criminology: A Philosophical Primer*, Harrow and Heston, Albany, NY, 1995.

dictatorships or democracies. The key to progress is said to be intelligent behavior brought about by careful training and education. Each person is said to be master of his or her fate, possessed of free will rather than driven by spirits or devils.

This is the frame of reference of classical criminology, as well as of classical thinking in other fields such as philosophy, political science, and economics.[18] Crime is seen as a product of the free choice of the individual, who first assesses the potential benefits of committing the crime against its potential costs. The rational response of society is to increase the costs and to decrease the benefits of crime to the point that individuals will not choose to commit crime. Within this frame of reference, then, criminologists attempt to design and test a system of punishment that will result in a minimal occurrence of crime. That is, this frame of reference is concerned with theory and research on the question of deterrence.

POSITIVIST CRIMINOLOGY

Next is the view that behavior is determined by factors beyond the individual's control. This view implies that humans are not self-determining agents free to do as they wish and as their intelligence directs. More accurately, the view maintains that people can only behave as they have already been determined to behave. Thinking and reasoning are actually processes of rationalization in which individuals justify their predetermined courses of action, rather than processes by which individuals freely and intelligently choose what they want to do. Humans have changed and developed through a slow process of evolution, and not because intelligence has led to increasingly rational choices.

This is the frame of reference of positivist criminology, as well as of positivist thinking in other fields such as psychology, sociology, and philosophy. Within this frame of reference, criminologists attempt to identify the causes of criminal behavior. The original positivist criminologists looked mainly at biological factors, but later criminologists shifted their focus to psychological and then to social factors in their attempts to find these causes. At the present time, some criminologists hold that criminal behavior can be explained by one type of factor, while other criminologists take a multiple-factor approach, holding that there are many factors that increase or decrease the likelihood of a person engaging in

---

[18]Clarence R. Jeffery, "The Structure of American Criminological Thinking," *Journal of Criminal Law, Criminology and Police Science* 46: 663–64 (Jan.–Feb. 1956).

criminal behavior.[19] Consequently, most of the chapters in this book are concerned with various explanations of those causes.

THE BEHAVIOR OF CRIMINAL LAW

Finally, there is the view that criminal behaviors are essentially similar to legal behaviors and involve similar causal processes. Criminologists who take this view attempt to explain why some behaviors are legally defined as criminal while other similar behaviors are not. They also seek to explain why some people are officially defined as criminal while other people who behave in essentially similar ways are not. The theories that these criminologists propose have been described in a variety of ways but will be called "theories of the behavior of criminal law" in this book because they focus on how the criminal law itself is written and enforced.[20]

For example, consider the most serious of all crimes, murder. Criminologists might study systematic differences in the enforcement of laws that result in certain groups being disproportionately processed by the criminal justice system. They might argue, for example, that wealthy and powerful groups tend to be weeded out of the criminal justice system at successive decision points, so the end result is that poor and powerless groups are disproportionately convicted and imprisoned. Wealthy and powerful people who kill may be less likely to be arrested, tried, or convicted at all, or they may be convicted of a less serious offense and given a more lenient sentence.

These criminologists may also examine differences in the types of deaths that are defined as murders by the law. For example, *felony murder* laws make an offender liable for first-degree murder if a death results from the commission of certain "dangerous" felonies such as forcible rape, robbery, arson, or burglary. No intent to kill is required, as the intent to commit the lesser offense is transferred to the greater one.[21]

In contrast with the severity of this law are the extremely lenient laws associated with serious injuries and deaths resulting from the actions of corporate executives. Many serious injuries and deaths associated with

---

[19]Travis Hirschi and Michael Gottfredson, eds., *Understanding Crime: Current Theory and Research,* Sage, Beverly Hills, CA, 1980, pp. 7–19.

[20]This term is derived from Donald Black, *The Behavior of Law,* Academic Press, New York, 1976. Black's term is broader in that it includes all "governmental social control." The present term includes only the criminal law and excludes other forms of governmental social control since those other forms do not influence the distribution of official crime rates.

[21]Hazel B. Kerper, *Introduction to the Criminal Justice System,* West, St. Paul, 1972, pp. 111–12.

corporate decision making occur where there is the intent to commit a lesser offense (for example, to violate health or safety laws), combined with the full knowledge that the decision may result in serious injury and death to numbers of innocent people. If a law similar to the felony murder law were applied to corporate decision making, then many corporate executives might find themselves convicted of murder and sentenced to death.

Theories of the behavior of criminal law suggest that the volume of crime and the characteristics of criminals are determined primarily by how the law is written and enforced. Most people convicted of crimes are poor, but not because poverty causes crime. Rather, the actions typical of poor people are more likely to be legally defined as crimes, and the laws applying to such crimes are more likely to be strictly enforced.

THE RELATIONSHIP AMONG THE VARIOUS FRAMES OF REFERENCE

Science with its naturalistic approach has abandoned the satisfying argument of spiritual explanations. To those who believe in spiritual influences, this does not invalidate their frame of reference; it only points out that scientists are unable to recognize the true sources of crime when they encounter them. Individuals who believe in spiritual influences do not need, and have no interest in, the natural explanations of behavior. They are satisfied that they already have a more adequate explanation.

Something very similar also may happen with those who reject spiritual explanations and accept natural explanations but have different frames of reference. Classical criminologists may hold on to the view that crime can be judged in terms of deliberateness, intent, and understanding of right and wrong. These criminologists may view the search for the causes of crime as a fundamentally wrongheaded endeavor that produces no beneficial results. In contrast, positivist criminologists may reject both the spiritualism of some religious individuals and the free will of the classical criminologists. Within this frame of reference, however, some criminologists may focus on social factors and hold that there is little or no role for biological and psychological factors in the causes of criminal behavior. Others may argue that biological or psychological factors explain substantial amounts of criminal behavior, and social factors enter into the picture through their interaction with the biological or psychological factors. Finally, criminologists who propose theories of the behavior of criminal law may regard both classical and positivist theories as fundamentally misinterpreting the phenomenon of crime. In their view, the volume of crime in society and the characteristics of criminals are both reflections of the operations of the criminal justice system, not the behavior of individuals.

Within the naturalistic frame of reference, however, criminologists can do more than simply disagree with each other. All these theories are scientific, and so they all make assertions about relationships among observable phenomena. Criminologists therefore can systematically observe the world to see if the asserted relationships actually exist— i.e., they can conduct research. The results of research should indicate that some theories are consistent with observations in the real world, while other theories are inconsistent with them. This is the scientific process.

While this process probably works in the long run, in the short run it is often difficult to reach a conclusion about whether a particular theory is consistent with the observations. The research on a particular theory is rarely black or white—rather, there are innumerable shades of gray with some research providing support for the theory and other research tending to contradict it.[22] In that situation, different criminologists may reach very different conclusions about the same theories.

In the chapters that follow, the implications of some of these general propositions will be examined in much greater detail. The chapters have been organized primarily for the sake of convenience and clarity; no necessary separateness or mutual exclusiveness should be inferred. In general, the chapters are organized in the historical sequence in which the theories originated, so that the earliest theories are presented first. This is intended to provide the reader with a sense of how the field of criminology has evolved over time.

Chapter 2 focuses on the classical and positive schools of criminology. This chapter presents historical materials on how criminology emerged as a field of study during the eighteenth and nineteenth centuries. Chapters 3 through 16 present various specific types of criminology theories. These chapters are arranged in the order in which the types of theories emerged. For example, the earliest types of criminology theories focused on the biological and psychological characteristics of individual criminals, so the chapters covering these theories are presented first. Later types of theories tended to focus more strongly on social factors, so these are presented in later chapters. These chapters all contain modern as well as historical materials. That is, each chapter brings the

---

[22]As a practical matter, most criminology theories seem impossible to falsify. See Bernard, op. cit. As a result, the authors of the present text recommend that criminology abandon falsification itself as a criterion of scientific utility, and move to a risk factor approach (see Chapters 17 and 18.)

work of the early theorists up to date by presenting more recent theories and research that take the same general point of view.

After presenting all the different types of theories, Chapter 17 discusses recent attempts to integrate those different types of theories into broader approaches. Finally, Chapter 18 offers some concluding thoughts on the current state of theorizing in criminology and how to advance criminology as a science.

CHAPTER TWO

Classical and Positivist Criminology

The term "classical" and "positivist" refer to certain ideas and certain people who have been very important in the long history of trying to understand, and trying to do something about, crime.

"Classical" criminology is most often associated with the name of the Italian Cesare Bonesana, Marchese de Beccaria (1738–1794). Beccaria's work was based on a kind of free-will rationalistic hedonism, a philosophical tradition going back many centuries. He proposed a wide range of specific reforms for the criminal justice systems of his time, describing how they could achieve both justice and effectiveness. Beccaria's ideas have become the basis for almost all modern criminal justice systems.

About fifty years after Beccaria wrote, the French scholar Andre-Michel Guerry (1802–1866) and the Belgian scholar Adolphe Quetelet (1796–1874) began to study the social characteristics of political units such as provinces and nations in order to determine what might cause their high or low crime rates. About fifty years after that, the Italian physician Cesare Lombroso (1835–1909) began to study the biological, psychological, and social characteristics of criminals in order to determine the causes of their criminal behavior. Positivist criminology is usually associated with the names of Guerry, Quetelet, and especially Lombroso.

THE SOCIAL AND INTELLECTUAL BACKGROUND OF CLASSICAL CRIMINOLOGY

Classical criminology emerged at a time when the naturalistic approach of the social contract thinkers was challenging the spiritualistic approach that had dominated European thinking for over a thousand years. This broad spiritualistic approach included a spiritual explanation of crime that formed the basis for criminal justice policies in most of Europe. Classical criminology was a protest against those criminal justice policies and against the spiritual explanations of crime on which they were based.

One of the most important sources for these spiritual explanations of crime was found in the theology of St. Thomas Aquinas (1225–1274), who lived 500 years before Beccaria.[1] Aquinas argued that there was a God-given "natural law" that was revealed by observing, though the eyes of faith, people's natural tendency to do good rather than evil. The criminal law was based on and reflected this "natural law." People who commit crime (i.e., violate the criminal law) therefore also commit sin (i.e., violate the natural law). Aquinas held that crime not only harmed victims, but it also harmed criminals because it harmed their essential "humanness"—their natural tendency to do good.

This spiritual explanation of crime, and others like it, formed the basis for the criminal justice policies in Europe at the time. Because crime was identified with sin, the state had the moral authority to use many horrible and gruesome tortures on criminals. That was because the state claimed that it was acting in the place of God when it inflicted these horrible punishments on criminals. For example, Beirne quotes from the sentence that was imposed on Jean Calas in 1762, two years before Beccaria published his little book[2]:

. . . in a chemise, with head and feet bare, (Calas) will be taken in a cart from the palace prison to the Cathedral. There, kneeling in front of the main door, holding in his hands a torch of yellow wax weighing two pounds, he must . . . (ask) pardon of God, of the King, and of justice. Then the executioner should take him in the cart to the Place Saint Georges, where upon a scaffold his arms, legs, thighs, and loins will be broken and crushed. Finally, the prisoner should be placed upon a wheel, with his face turned to the sky, alive and in pain, and repent for his said crimes and misdeeds, all the while imploring God for his life, thereby to serve as an example and to instil terror in the wicked.

The extensive religious symbolism in the manner of execution clearly

---

[1] A brief review of Aquinas's ideas can be found in Thomas J. Bernard, *The Consensus-Conflict Debate*, Columbia University Press, New York, 1983, ch. 3.

[2] Piers Beirne, *Inventing Criminology*, State University of New York Press, Albany, 1993, pp. 11–12. Another widely quoted example from the same time period is the execution of Damiens, who had stabbed the king of France in 1757. See Michel Foucault, *Discipline and Punish*, Pantheon, New York, 1977, pp. 3–5.

suggests that crime is intertwined with sin, and that in punishing crime, the state is taking the part of God.

Beginning with Thomas Hobbes (1588–1678), "social contract" thinkers substituted naturalistic arguments for the spiritualistic arguments of people like Aquinas.[3] While Aquinas argued that people naturally do good rather than evil, Hobbes argued that people naturally pursue their own interests without caring about whether they hurt anyone else. This leads to a "war of each against all" in which no one is safe because all people only look out for themselves.

Hobbes then argued that people are rational enough to realize that this situation is not in anyone's interests. So people agree to give up their own selfish behavior as long as everyone else does the same thing at the same time. This is what Hobbes called the "social contract"—something like a peace treaty that everyone signs because they are all exhausted from the war of each against all. But the social contract needs an enforcement mechanism in case some people cheat and begin to pursue their own interests without regard to whether other people get hurt. This is the job of the state. According to Hobbes, everyone who agrees to the social contract also agrees to grant the state the right to use force to maintain the contract.

Other social contract philosophers such as Locke (1632–1704), Montesquieu (1689–1755), Voltaire (1694–1778), and Rousseau (1712–1778) followed Hobbes in constructing philosophies that included a natural and rational basis for explaining crime and the state's response to it. These theories differed from each other in many ways, but all were rational and naturalistic approaches to explaining crime and punishment, as opposed to the dominant spiritualistic approach. By the middle of the 1700s, just before Beccaria wrote his book, these naturalistic ideas were well known and widely accepted by the intellectuals of the day, but they did not represent the thinking of the politically powerful groups that ruled the various states in Europe. Those ruling groups still held to the spiritual explanations of crime, so that crime was seen as manifesting the work of the devil. Consequently, the criminal justice systems of the time tended to impose excessive and cruel punishments on criminals.

Beccaria was a protest writer who sought to change these excessive and cruel punishments by applying the rationalist, social contract ideas to crime and criminal justice. His book was well received by intellectuals and some reform-minded rulers who had already accepted the general framework of social contract thinking.[4] Even more important for

---

[3]A discussion of Hobbes and his relation to Aquinas can be found in Bernard, op. cit, ch. 4.

[4]Graeme Newman and Pietro Marongiu, "Penological Reform and the Myth of Beccaria," *Criminology* 28(2): 325–46 (May 1990).

the book's acceptance, however, was the fact that the American Revolution of 1776 and the French Revolution of 1789 occurred soon after its publication in 1764.[5] These two revolutions were both guided by naturalistic ideas of the social contract philosophers. To these revolutionaries, Beccaria's book represented the latest and best thinking on the subject of crime and criminal justice. They therefore used his ideas as the basis for their new criminal justice systems. From America and France, Beccaria's ideas spread to the rest of the industrialized world.

BECCARIA AND THE CLASSICAL SCHOOL

Cesare Bonesana, Marchese de Beccaria, was an indifferent student who had some interest in mathematics.[6] After completing his formal education, he joined Allessandro Verri, an official of the prison in Milan, and his brother Pietro Verri, an economist, in a group of young men who met regularly to discuss literary and philosophical topics. Beccaria was given an assignment in March 1763 to write an essay on penology, a subject about which he knew nothing. With help from the Verri brothers, the essay was completed in January 1764, and was published under the title *Dei deliti e delle pene (On Crimes and Punishments)* in the small town of Livorno in July of that year, when Beccaria was 26 years old.[7]

In common with his contemporary intellectuals, Beccaria protested against the many inconsistencies in government and in the management of public affairs. He therefore proposed various reforms to make criminal justice practice more logical and rational. He objected especially to the capricious and purely personal justice the judges were dispensing and to the severe and barbaric punishments of the time.

The following ten principles summarize Beccaria's ideas about how to make the criminal justice system both just and effective.

1. The role of the legislatures, according to Beccaria, should be both to define crimes and also to define specific punishments for each specific crime.[8]

---

[5]Beccaria's work was extensively quoted by Thomas Jefferson, John Adams, and other American revolutionaries. See David A. Jones, *History of Criminology,* Greenwood, New York, 1986, pp. 43–46.

[6]An account of the life and work of Beccaria may be found in Beirne, op. cit., ch. 2. See also Randy Martin, Robert J. Mutchnick, and W. Timothy Austin, *Criminological Thought: Pioneers Past and Present,* Macmillan, New York, 1990; and Elio D. Monachesi, "Pioneers in Criminology: Cesare Beccaria (1738–94)," *Journal of Criminal Law, Criminology and Police Science* 46(4): 439–49 (Nov.–Dec. 1955), reprinted in Hermann Mannheim, *Pioneers in Criminology,* Patterson Smith, Montclair, NJ, 1972, pp. 36–50.

[7]Cesare Beccaria, *On Crimes and Punishments,* translated by Henry Paolucci, Bobbs-Merrill, Indianapolis, 1963.

[8]Ibid., pp. 13–14.

This contrasted with the practice of Beccaria's time when legislatures passed very general laws and left the implementation up to the vast discretion of the judges.

2. The role of judges should be solely to determine guilt—i.e., whether the defendant had committed a crime. Once that determination was made, then the judge should follow the strict letter of the law in determining the punishment. Instead of vast discretion, Beccaria argued that judges should have no discretion whatsoever: "Nothing is more dangerous than the popular axiom that it is necessary to consult the spirit of the laws. It is a dam that has given way to a torrent of opinions, . . ."[9]

3. The seriousness of a crime should be determined solely by the extent of the harm that it inflicts on society. Beccaria argued that other factors were irrelevant in determining seriousness, including the intent of the offender: "Sometimes, with the best intentions, men do the greatest injury to society; at other times, intending the worst for it, they do the greatest good."[10]

4. Punishments should be proportionate to the seriousness of the crime and their purpose should be to deter crime: "It is to the common interest not only that crimes not be committed, but also that they be less frequent in proportion to the harm they cause society. Therefore, the obstacles that deter man from committing crime should be stronger in proportion as they are contrary to the public good, and as the inducements to commit them are stronger."[11] This argument contrasted with the view, illustrated above in the case of Jean Calas, that criminal punishments should convey religious symbolism, with the state acting in the place of God.

6. Punishments are unjust when their severity exceeds what is necessary to achieve deterrence: "For punishment to attain its end, the evil which it inflicts has only to exceed the advantage derivable from the crime; in this excess of evil one should include the certainty of punishment and the loss of the good which the crime might have produced. All beyond this is superfluous and for that reason tyrannical. . . ."[12]

7. Excessive severity not only fails to deter crime but actually increases it: "The severity of punishment of itself emboldens men to commit the very wrongs it is supposed to prevent; they are driven to commit additional crimes to avoid the punishment for a single one. The countries and times most notorious for severity of penalties have always been those in which the bloodiest and most inhumane of deeds were committed, for the same spirit of ferocity that guided the hand of the legislators also ruled that of the parricide and assassin."[13]

---

[9]Ibid., pp. 14–15.

[10]Ibid., pp. 64–65.

[11]Ibid., p. 62.

[12]Ibid.

[13]Ibid., pp. 43–44.

8. Punishments should be prompt: "The more promptly and the more closely punishment follows upon the commission of a crime, the more just and useful will it be. I say more just, because the criminal is thereby spared the useless and cruel torments of uncertainty. . . . I have said that the promptness of punishment is more useful because when the length of time that passes between the punishment and the misdeed is less, so much the stronger and more lasting in the human mind is the association of these two ideas, *crime and punishment.*"[14]

9. Punishments should also be certain: "The certainty of a punishment, even if it be moderate, will always make a stronger impression than the fear of another which is more terrible but combined with the hope of impunity; even the least evils, when they are certain, always terrify men's minds. . . ."[15]

10. Ultimately, laws should be structured so as to prevent crime from happening in the first place: "It is better to prevent crimes than to punish them. That is the ultimate end of every good legislation. . . . Do you want to prevent crimes? See to it that the laws are clear and simple and that the entire force of a nation is united in their defense, and that no part of it is employed to destroy them. See to it that the laws favor not so much classes of men as men themselves. See to it that men fear the laws and fear nothing else. For fear of the laws is salutary, but fatal and fertile for crimes is one man's fear of another."[16]

Beccaria also emphasized that the laws should be published so that the public may know what they are and support their intent and purpose; that torture and secret accusations should be abolished; that capital punishment should be abolished and replaced by imprisonment; that jails be more humane; and that the law should not distinguish between the rich and the poor. Beccaria summarized his ideas in a brief conclusion to his book:[17]

In order for punishment not to be, in every instance, an act of violence of one or of many against a private citizen, it must be essentially public, prompt, necessary, the least possible in the given circumstances, proportionate to the crimes, dictated by the laws.

Beccaria's ideas were quite radical for his time, so he published his book anonymously and defended himself in the introduction against charges that he was an unbeliever or a revolutionary. In fact, the Roman

---

[14]Ibid., pp. 55–56.

[15]Ibid., pp. 58–59.

[16]Ibid., pp. 93–94.

[17]Ibid., p. 99.

Catholic Church condemned the book in 1766 because its rationalistic ideas abandoned the spiritualistic frame of reference. The book
was placed on the church's *Index of Forbidden Books* where it remained for over two hundred years. But despite Beccaria's fears
and some opposition, his ideas were extremely well received by his
contemporaries.

Following the French Revolution of 1789, Beccaria's principles were
used as the basis for the French Code of 1791. Consistent with his arguments, the judge was only an instrument for applying the law, and the
law undertook to prescribe an exact penalty for every crime and every
degree of crime. The greatest practical difficulty in applying this code
came from ignoring differences in the circumstances of particular situations. The code treated everyone exactly alike, since only the act, not the
intent, was considered in determining the punishment. Thus first offenders were treated the same as repeaters, minors were treated the
same as adults, insane the same as sane, and so on. The set, impersonal
features of this code then became the point of attack for a new school of
reformers who complained about the injustice of a rigorous code and
championed the need for individualization and discriminating judgment
to fit individual circumstances. Ultimately, these reactions resulted in
revisions to the code so that judges were able to exercise discretion in
considering factors such as age, mental condition, and extenuating circumstances. These practical revisions of classical criminology constitute
what is often called the "neoclassical" school.

As such, the neoclassical school represented no particular break with
the basic doctrine of human nature that made up the classical tradition
throughout Europe at the time. The doctrine continued to be that people possess free will and that they are guided by reason and self-interest.
They therefore can be controlled by their fear of punishment: If the
pain obtained from punishment exceeds the pleasure obtained from
crime, then people will choose not to commit crime. In this form, the
neoclassical view is, with minor modifications, "the major model of human behavior held to by agencies of social control in all advanced industrial societies . . ."[18]

THE TRANSITION TO POSITIVIST CRIMINOLOGY

Beccaria's theory changed criminal justice policies, especially in France,
and led to the expectation that crime would soon decrease. But there

---

[18]Ian Taylor, Paul Walton, and Jock Young, *The New Criminology*, Harper & Row, New York, 1973,
pp. 9–10.

was really no way to find out whether this occurred, since there were no annual crime statistics to measure whether crime was going up or down.

The first annual national crime statistics were published in France in 1827, about sixty years after Beccaria wrote his book.[19] It soon became clear that these crime statistics were astonishingly regular. The rates of crime in general and of particular crimes such as murder and rape remained relatively constant from year to year. In addition, some places in the nation had higher crime rates while others had lower, and these differences remained relatively constant from year to year.

Today, we take such regularity in crime statistics for granted, but at that time, those who held a "free will" theory of crime expected random changes in the number of crimes, especially in the number of unpremeditated crimes such as passion murders. The regularity of crime statistics suggested that Beccaria had been right in his argument that, rather than being entirely the product of free will, crime must be influenced by factors in the larger society. It also supported Beccaria's hope that, by changing those factors, crime might be reduced.

But the new crime statistics also made it clear that crime rates were going up, not down. Earlier local statistics had suggested the same thing. Even more distressing, these statistics suggested that recidivism was going up: People who had received the prompt, proportionate punishments provided by the new French code were committing more new offenses rather than fewer. This suggested that Beccaria had been wrong to argue that changes in punishment policies alone could reduce crime.

The new crime statistics clearly revealed the failure of classical punishment policies, while at the same time suggesting that other social factors might influence the level of crime in society. This gave rise to a new brand of criminology, which eventually became known as positivism. Its goal was to study the causes of crime either in the larger society or in the individual.

GUERRY AND QUETELET

The development of national crime statistics in France reflected the larger development in Europe of relatively accurate official records as part of the development of stable social and political organization. Systematic registries of births and deaths, for example, developed in European cities and states in the 1500s.[20] In the 1600s various items in the

---

[19]This discussion and the following one about Quetelet and Guerry rely heavily on the work of Piers Beirne, op. cit., chs., 3, 4.

[20]Walter F. Wilcox, "History of Statistics," in *Encyclopedia of the Social Sciences*, vol. 14, Macmillan, New York, 1931, p. 356.

official records began to be counted and compared as part of an analysis of economic conditions and their consequences. In England such studies came to be called "political arithmetic,"[21] while in Germany they were called "moral statistik."[22] Edmund Halley (1656–1742), the astronomer for whom Halley's comet was named, compiled and published, in 1692–93, the first systematic "life expectancy tables."[23] Adam Smith used these same official data on social and economic conditions in his great work, *Inquiry into the Nature and Causes of the Wealth of Nations* (1776), as did Malthus in his controversial studies on population growth.[24]

Shortly after the publication of the first modern national crime statistics in France in 1827, Andre-Michel Guerry (1802–1866) published what is considered by many to be the first work in "scientific criminology."[25] Guerry was a French lawyer who, soon after he took an interest in these statistics, was appointed director of criminal statistics for the French Ministry of Justice. Guerry used shaded ecological maps to represent differing crime rates in relation to various social factors. After preliminary publication in 1829, his work appeared in expanded book form in 1833 under the title *Essai sur la statistique morale de la France.*

Guerry tested the commonly held belief that crime was associated with poverty, finding instead that the wealthiest region of France had a higher rate of property crimes but only about half the rate of violent crime.[26] However, Guerry had measured wealth and poverty by the amount of direct taxation, and he pointed out that the wealthiest sections had a great deal of poverty in them. Although he did not directly measure the poverty in those wealthier provinces, he concluded that poverty itself did not cause property crime. Rather the main factor was opportunity: In the wealthier provinces there was more to steal.

Guerry also attacked the widely held view that lack of education was associated with crime.[27] New statistics were available on the reading and

---

[21]Bernard Lécuyer and Anthony R. Oberschall, "The Early History of Social Research," *International Encyclopedia of the Social Sciences,* vol. 15, pp. 36–37.

[22]Yale Levin and Alfred Lindesmith, "English Ecology and Criminology of the Past Century," *Journal of Criminal Law and Criminology* 27: 801–16 (March–April 1937).

[23]Lécuyer and Oberschall, op. cit., p. 37.

[24]Cf. Thomas R. Malthus, *Essay on Principle of Population as It Affects the Future Improvement of Society,* London, 1798.

[25]Terence Morris, *The Criminal Area,* Routledge and Kegan Paul, New York, 1957, pp. 42–53.

[26]Beirne, op. cit., pp. 119–23.

[27]Ibid., pp. 124–27.

writing abilities of all young men subject to the military draft. Guerry used these statistics to determine the education levels of the various sections of France. The most educated sections were in northeast France, where almost 75 percent of young men could read and write, while the least educated sections were in western and central France, where only about 7 percent were literate. Guerry then showed that areas with the highest education levels had the highest rates of violent crime, while those with the lowest rates of such crime had the lowest education levels.

A second person to analyze these statistics was Adolphe Quetelet (1796–1874).[28] Quetelet was a Belgian mathematician and astronomer who had achieved considerable success in these fields while still quite young. In 1823, when he was 27, the Belgian Royal Academy sent him to Paris as part of a project to build an astronomical observatory in Brussels. While there, he studied new statistical techniques that were being developed as part of "celestial mechanics." He also became familiar with the new social data that were first being collected in France at that time, such as the numbers of births and deaths in a year. On his return to Brussels the following year, he used his newly acquired statistical techniques to analyze some of the social data—e.g., he showed that there was considerable regularity in the rates of death each year. He then argued that the regularities in this social data were analogous to the regularities found in "celestial mechanics." He therefore used the term "social mechanics" to describe this type of analyses of social data.

In 1828, he turned his attention to the newly published French crime statistics. He showed that there was considerable regularity throughout those statistics—e.g., in the number of people accused of crimes against property, in the number accused of crimes against persons, and in the ratio between these two numbers; in the number of those convicted, in the number acquitted, and in the ratio between those two numbers; in the ratio of males to females convicted of crimes, and in the distribution of convictions by age. He then suggested that it would be desirable to have similar statistics for other countries "to see if they follow a march as regular as the tables of mortality."[29] He went on to present his basic orientation toward these statistics:

. . . there must be an order to those things which, when they are reproduced with astonishing constancy, and always in the same way, do not change quickly

---

[28]The following discussion is taken largely from Beirne, op. cit., pp. 65–110.
[29]Quoted in Beirne, ibid., pp. 78–79.

and without cause. For the moment we are adopting the role of an observer. In the study of human affairs we rely on the same principles used to study other natural causes.

Quetelet then began to analyze this data more closely. He found that some people were more likely to commit crime than others, especially those who were young, male, poor, unemployed, and undereducated. Young males were more likely to commit crime under any circumstances, so that places with more young males tended to have more crime. But places with more poverty and more unemployment actually had less crime. As it turned out, the poor and unemployed tended to commit crimes in places where there were many wealthy and employed people. So crime was higher in places with *less* poverty and unemployment, but it tended to be committed by the poor and unemployed people who lived there.

Like Guerry, Quetelet suggested that opportunities might have something to do with explaining this pattern in that wealthier cities "might attract vagabonds who hope to find impunity by losing themselves in the crowd."[30] He also pointed to an additional factor: The great inequality between wealth and poverty in the same place excites passions and provokes temptations of all kinds.[31] This problem is especially severe in those places where rapidly changing economic conditions can result in a person suddenly passing from wealth to poverty while others still enjoy wealth. In contrast, provinces that were generally poor and had little wealth had less crime as long as people were able to satisfy their basic needs.

Also like Guerry, Quetelet found that increased education did not reduce crime. People with more education tended to commit less crime on the whole, but they also tended to commit more violent crime. Those with less education committed more crime but it tended to be property crime. Quetelet therefore argued that increased education itself would not reduce crime.[32]

Quetelet concluded that the propensity to engage in crime was actually a reflection of moral character. Relying on Aristotle's views, he identified virtue with moderation: "rational and temperate habits, more regulated passions . . . [and] foresight, as manifested by investment in savings banks, assurance societies, and the different institutions which

---

[30]Adolphe Quetelet, *Research on the Propensity for Crime at Different Ages*, translated by Sawyer F. Sylvester, Anderson, Cincinnati, 1984, p. 40.

[31]Ibid., pp. 37–38.

[32]Beirne, op. cit., pp. 83–84.

encourage foresight."[33] Young males often did not have these very virtues, and so they committed high levels of crime. Similarly, these virtues tended to break down among poor and unemployed people who were surrounded by wealth. Thus, his main policy recommendations were to enhance "moral" education and to ameliorate social conditions to improve people's lives.[34]

Quetelet's most famous and controversial statement described crime as an inevitable feature of social organization:[35]

The crimes which are annually committed seem to be a necessary result of our social organization. . . . *Society prepares the crime, and the guilty are only the instruments by which it is executed.*

This was an extraordinarily radical statement for the time, and Quetelet was forced to defend his theories against attacks by those who held free-will spiritual explanations of crime.[36] These critics saw his arguments as a deterministic heresy that necessarily implied atheism. Even worse, these critics claimed that Quetelet implied that nothing could be done to reduce crime. For example, Quetelet had argued that crime and punishment tended to be constants in a society:[37]

The share of prisons, chains, and the scaffold appears fixed with as much probability as the revenues of the state. We are able to enumerate in advance how many individuals will stain their hands with the blood of their fellow creatures, how many will be forgers, how many poisoners, pretty nearly as one can enumerate in advance the births and deaths which must take place.

In response to these criticisms, Quetelet repeatedly affirmed his belief in God and in the individual's ability to freely choose in the face of these causal factors. In addition, he argued that his theories really were very optimistic because they indicated that there were a limited number of causes of crime. He argued that governments should continue the types of punishment policies recommended by Beccaria, but he also argued that they should undertake a variety of social reforms that would im-

---

[33]Ibid., pp. 88–90. The idea of moderation as virtue is related to Quetelet's conception of the "average man," whose characteristics fall in the center of a normal distribution while "deviants" such as criminals are found at the tails. This in turn was an analogy from astronomy. See ibid., pp. 82–83.

[34]Ibid., p. 92.

[35]Quoted in Beirne, op. cit., p. 88.

[36]Ibid., pp. 92–97.

[37]Quoted in Beirne, op. cit., p. 82.

prove the conditions of people's lives and would allow the moral and intellectual qualities of citizens to flourish. In that way, the causes of crime
would be reduced, and a reduction in crime itself would follow.

Quetelet retained the view throughout his life that crime essentially
was caused by moral defectiveness, but increasingly he took the view
that moral defectiveness was revealed in biological characteristics, particularly the appearance of the face and the head.[38] To that extent,
his theories became increasingly as his critics had described them—i.e.,
deterministic and pessimistic in the sense that government policies
could do little to reduce crime. This also made him a direct predecessor
of Lombroso, whose major book was published only two years after
Quetelet's death.

CESARE LOMBROSO

Cesare Lombroso (1835–1909) was a physician who became a specialist
in psychiatry, and his principal career was as a professor of legal medicine at the University of Turin.[39] His name came into prominence with
the publication of his book, *L'uomo delinquente (The Criminal Man)*, in
1876. In that book Lombroso proposed that criminals were biological
throwbacks to an earlier evolutionary stage, people more primitive and
less highly evolved than their noncriminal counterparts. Lombroso used
the term *atavistic* to describe such people. The idea of evolution itself
was relatively recent at the time, having first been proposed by Darwin
in his book, *On the Origin of Species* (1859). That book had brought
about the final break with the spiritualist, free-will thought of the past.
Darwin presented evidence that humans were the same general kind of
creatures as the rest of the animals, except that they were more highly
evolved or developed. The ancestors of modern people were less highly
evolved and were part of a continuous chain linking humans to the earliest and simplest forms of life. Even the idea that some individuals might
be reversions to an earlier evolutionary stage had been originally suggested by Darwin, who had written: "With mankind some of the worst

---

[38]Ibid., pp. 90–91.

[39]Information about Lombroso's life and work can be found in ch. 2 of Randy Martin, Robert J.
Mutchnick, and W. Timothy Austin, *Criminological Thought: Pioneers Past and Present*, Macmillan, New York, 1990; and in Marvin E. Wolfgang, "Cesare Lombroso," pp. 232–91 in Hermann
Mannheim, ed., *Pioneers in Criminology*, 2nd ed., Patterson Smith, Montclair, NJ, 1972. For a
more critical view, see ch. 4 of Stephen Jay Gould, *The Mismeasure of Man*, Norton, New York,
1981, where Lombroso's theory of atavism is presented in its historical and scientific context. Gould
argues that scientists of the time, desiring to prove their own superiority and the inferiority of other racial and ethnic groups, cloaked their prejudices in the veil of objective science.

dispositions which occasionally without any assignable cause make their appearance in families, may perhaps be reversions to a savage state, from which we are not removed by many generations."[40]

Lombroso's theories will be further discussed in Chapter 3, but as a founder of the positive school of criminology he is something of an anomaly. Lombroso is known principally for the earliest formulation of his theory of the atavistic criminal. The real basis of the positive school, however, is the search for the causes of criminal behavior. That search is based on the conception of multiple factor causation, in which some of the factors may be biological, others psychological, and still others social.

Lombroso did much by way of documenting the effects of many of these factors. As his thinking changed over the years, he looked more and more to environmental rather than biological factors. This change and growth in his thinking was evidenced by the increases in the number of pages in successive editions of *L'uomo delinquente*. In its first edition in 1876, Lombroso required 252 pages to explain his theory of evolutionary atavism as the cause of crime. Twenty years later, in the fifth edition of his book, he needed over 1,900 pages to include all the items that appeared to be related to crime causation. Those included such things as climate, rainfall, the price of grain, sex and marriage customs, criminal laws, banking practices, national tariff policies, the structure of government, church organization, and the state of religious belief. Lombroso's last book, *Crime, Its Causes and Remedies*, was a summary of his life work specially prepared for American readers.[41] Published in 1911, two years after Lombroso's death, it includes discussions of many factors related to crime causation, of which by far the largest number are environmental rather than biological.

Lombroso's later, more mature thought therefore included many factors other than the physical or anthropological. He maintained that there are three major classes of criminals: (1) *born criminals,* to be understood as atavistic reversions to a lower or more primitive evolutionary form of development, and thought to constitute about one third of the total number of offenders; (2) *insane criminals,* i.e., idiots, imbeciles, paranoiacs, sufferers from melancholia, and those afflicted with general paralysis, dementia, alcoholism, epilepsy, or hysteria (strange bedfellows, to be sure); and (3) *criminaloids,* a large general class without spe-

---

[40]Charles Darwin, *Descent of Man,* John Murray, London, 1871, p. 137.

[41]Cesare Lombroso, *Crime: Its Causes and Remedies,* 1912 edition reprinted by Patterson Smith, Montclair, NJ, 1972.

cial physical characteristics or recognizable mental disorders, but whose mental and emotional makeup are such that under certain circumstances they indulge in vicious and criminal behavior. Lombroso conceded that well over one half of all criminals were "criminaloids," so that they were not "born criminals" or "insane" in the sense that he used those terms.

By the time of Lombroso's death in 1909 it was evident that his theories were too simple and naive. Anthropology abandoned the conception of uniform, linear evolution with humans as the most highly evolved animal (and the English gentleman as the most highly evolved human), whereupon his notion of the atavistic criminal as a less evolved person became quite meaningless. Psychiatry and psychology were already marshaling evidence to show that the relationship between crime and epilepsy, or between crime and insanity, was much more complex and involved than Lombroso assumed.

Despite these criticisms, Lombroso's theory of the atavistic criminal received enormous public attention at the time. This gave it great prominence in criminology, while Guerry's and Quetelet's earlier work more or less dropped out of sight. As a result, for most of the twentieth century, Lombroso was described in criminology textbooks as the first criminologist to search for the causes of crime and therefore as the founder of positivist criminology.

THE RELATION BETWEEN POSITIVIST AND CLASSICAL THEORIES

Positive criminology might seem opposed to classical criminology, but this is not necessarily the case. Rather, classical theories can be interpreted as implying a theory of human behavior that is quite consistent with positivism. In the past, classical criminologists have assumed that the certainty and severity of criminal punishments could affect criminal behavior, but that other variables in the environment could not. But in his defense of classical criminology, Roshier argues[42]:

In general, there was nothing inherent in Beccaria's intellectual position to preclude a consideration of the socio-economic context of crime, any more than there was to necessitate his sole concentration on deterrence. . . . Indeed, it is an oddity that he seemed to see the criminal justice system as being the only aspect of the environment that influences individual decisions about whether it is worthwhile to commit crime or not.

---

[42]Bob Roshier, *Controlling Crime*, Lyceum, Chicago, 1989.

Classical criminologists therefore could expand their theoretical frame of reference and examine how crime rates are influenced by a wide range of factors outside the criminal justice system, including biological, psychological, and social factors. All these factors could then be described as "causes" of crime. Reflecting this basic position, Beirne argues that the proper place for Beccaria's theory in the history of criminology lies "at the very beginning of the tradition to which it is commonly opposed, namely, positivist criminology."[43]

A similar point can be made about positive criminology. In the past, positivist criminologists have assumed that biological, psychological, and social factors can influence criminal behavior, but that the certainty and severity of criminal punishments could not. But in their defense of positive criminology, Gottfredson and Hirschi argue:[44]

No deterministic explanation of crime can reasonably exclude the variables of the classical model on deterministic grounds. These variables may account for some of the variation in crime. If so, they have as much claim to inclusion in a "positivistic" model as any other set of variables accounting for the same amount of variation.

Thus, positive criminologists can include the certainty and severity of criminal punishments among the many other factors that might influence criminal behavior.

Positivist and classical criminology therefore are really part of the same enterprise—they both seek to identify the factors that influence the incidence of criminal behavior. The basic controversy between them is empirical rather than theoretical: Which factors have more influence on criminal behavior and which have less?[45]

CONCLUSION

In the chapters that follow, the major theories on the causes of criminal behavior will be examined. Each of these theories suggests that certain factors, either at the individual or the societal level, may have a causal influence on crime. Research has disproven some of the earlier theories, in the sense of finding that the factors to which they point have no causal

---

[43]Piers Beirne, "Inventing Criminology: The 'Science of Man' in Cesare Beccaria's *Dei Delitti e Delle Pene* (1764)," *Criminology* 29(4): 777–820 (Nov. 1991).

[44]Michael R. Gottfredson and Travis Hirschi, "The Positive Tradition," pp. 9–22 in Gottfredson and Hirschi, eds., *Positive Criminology*, Sage, Newburg Park, CA, 1987.

[45]This innocuous sounding statement contains major implications about the authors' view of the nature of scientific theories in criminology (see Chapter 18).

influence on crime whatsoever. Extensive research has been done on the more recent theories, but there is considerable disagreement about which factors have greater and which have lesser influence on crime.

The fact that there are no conclusive answers to the question of the causes of crime does not mean that criminology is unscientific. It is precisely because criminology theories are scientific, in the sense that they assert relationships between classes of observable phenomena, that they can be tested with research at all. Nonscientific explanations of crime, such as spiritual explanations, cannot be tested with research because they include phenomena that are not observable.

In general, the earlier chapters follow the lead of Lombroso in that they focus on the question of why one person engages in criminal behaviors while another does not. Thus, the earlier chapters emphasize factors associated with individuals, especially biological and psychological factors. Later chapters increasingly take Quetelet's approach, seeking to explain high or low crime rates by looking at factors associated with societies. But there is no absolute division between these two types of theories. Rather, it is a question of where their emphasis lies. This was true even for Lombroso and Quetelet. By the end of his life, Quetelet had included in his theory many biological factors that explained why some individuals are more likely to engage in crime, so that his theory ended up being quite similar to Lombroso's later one. And by the end of his life, Lombroso had included in his theory many societal-level factors that seemed more appropriate for explaining rates of crime rather than the individual's propensity to engage in it. To some extent, Lombroso's theory had become like Quetelet's earlier one.

CHAPTER THREE

Biological Factors and Criminal Behavior

This chapter focuses on biological characteristics that are said to be associated with an increased risk of engaging in criminal behavior. Modern biological theories in criminology do not argue for biological determinism. Rather, these theories argue that certain biological characteristics increase the probability that individuals will engage in certain types of behaviors, such as violent or antisocial behaviors, that are legally defined as criminal or delinquent.[1] Only an increased probability is asserted, not an absolute prediction that everyone with these characteristics will commit crime. In addition, many of these theories focus on the interaction between biological characteristics and the social environment.[2] Certain biological characteristics may have little impact on crime in some situations while they have a large impact in other situations. Thus, these are best described as "biosocial" theories.

In this chapter, we review some, but not all, of the recent research on biology and crime. First, we examine biological factors that are hereditary, which result from the genes individuals receive from their parents at the time of conception. Second, we examine biological factors that originally may be hereditary but may change during the life course in response to environmental conditions. Third, we examine biological factors that originate in the environment.

---

[1]Diana Fishbein, *Biobehavioral Perspectives in Criminology*, Wadsworth, Belmont, CA, 2001, pp. 9–12.

[2]For examples, see ibid., pp. 13–17.

PHYSICAL APPEARANCE: DEFECTIVENESS

The earliest biological theories in criminology emphasized physical appearance as the distinguishing mark of the criminal. Criminals were thought to be somehow different, abnormal, defective, and therefore inferior biologically. This biological inferiority was thought to produce certain physical characteristics that made the appearance of criminals different from that of noncriminals. The real explanation of criminal behavior, however, was the biological defectiveness and inferiority—physical and other characteristics were only symptoms of that inferiority.

The belief that criminals have an unusual physical appearance goes back to ancient times. For example, Socrates was examined by a Greek physiognomist who found that his face revealed him as brutal, sensuous, and inclined to drunkenness. Socrates admitted that such was his natural disposition but said he had learned to overcome these tendencies.[3] In 1775, Johan Caspar Lavater (1741–1801), a Swiss scholar and theologian, published a four-volume work on physiognomy that received nearly as much favorable attention as Beccaria's work had only eleven years earlier. In this work, Lavater systematized many popular observations and made many extravagant claims about the alleged relation between facial features and human conduct.

Where physiognomy studied the face, phrenology studied the external shape of the skull. This concept was originally based on Aristotle's idea that the brain is the organ of the mind. Phrenologists assumed that the shape of the skull revealed the shape of the brain inside, and that different parts of the brain were associated with different faculties or functions of the mind. Therefore, the shape of the skull would indicate how the mind functioned. In 1791, the eminent European anatomist Franz Joseph Gall (1758–1828) started publishing material on the relations between head conformations and the personal characteristics of individuals. His student and onetime collaborator, John Gaspar Spurzheim (1776–1832), carried their doctrines to England and America, lecturing before scientific meetings and stimulating interest in their ideas.[4]

---

[3]Havelock Ellis, *The Criminal*, 2nd ed., Scribner, New York, 1900, p. 27. A rather popular discussion of the symbolic meanings of physical appearance, including the tendency to link beauty to goodness and ugliness to evil, can be found in Robin Tolmach Lakoff and Raquel L. Scherr, *Face Value: The Politics of Beauty*, Routledge & Kegan Paul, Boston, 1984.

[4]For a history of phrenology, as well as a defense of its use in modern times, see Sybil Leek, *Phrenology*, Macmillan, New York, 1970. For a discussion of Gall and Spurzheim, see Leonard Savitz, Stanley H. Turner, and Toby Dickman, "The Origin of Scientific Criminology: Franz Joseph

Cesare Lombroso (1835–1909) extended the tradition of physiognomy and phrenology by studying all anatomical features of the human body, not merely the features of the face or the shape of the skull. Lombroso was a doctor in the Italian army who was concerned about the problems, including crime, of soldiers who came from Southern Italy. At that time, the "Southern question" was a popular concern, with many allegations from the popular press and conservative politicians that "the Southerners are inferior beings . . . lazy, incapable, criminal, and barbaric."[5]

Lombroso had a flash of insight while performing a postmortem on a thief who came from Southern Italy:[6]

. . . on laying open the skull I found on the occipital part, exactly on the spot where a spine is found in the normal skull, a distinct depression which I named *median occipital fossa,* because of its situation precisely in the middle of the occiput as in inferior animals, expecially rodents. . . . At the sight of that skull, I seemed to see all of a sudden, lighted up as a vast plain under a flaming sky, the problem of the nature of the criminal—an atavistic being who reproduces in his person the ferocious instincts of primitive humanity and the inferior animals.

Lombroso went on to perform autopsies on sixty-six male criminals, and he found that these had a significant number of characteristics that were similar to primitive humans. He also examined 832 living criminals, both male and female, 390 noncriminal Italian soldiers, and ninety "lunatics." These studies were presented in his book, *L'uomo delinquente (The Criminal Man),* which appeared in 1876.

Some of the physical characteristics that Lombroso linked to crime included deviations in head size and shape, asymmetry of the face, large jaws and cheekbones, unusually large or small ears or ears that stand out from the head, fleshy lips, abnormal teeth, receding chin, abundant hair or wrinkles, long arms, extra fingers or toes, or an asymmetry of the brain.[7] Many of these characteristics were said to resemble lower animals, such as monkeys and chimpanzees.

Gall as the First Criminologist," in Robert F. Meier, ed., *Theory in Criminology,* Sage, Beverly Hills, CA, 1977, pp. 41–56.

[5]Antonio Gramsci, "Some Aspects of the Southern Question," in Quintin Hoare, ed., *Gransci: Selections from Political Writings,* International Publishers, New York, 1978, p. 444.

[6]Cesare Lombroso, *L'uomo delinquente (The Criminal Man),* 4th ed., Bocca, Torino, 1889, p. 273, as quoted by Enrico Ferri, *Criminal Sociology,* D. Appleton, New York, 1900, p. 12.

[7]This is a partial listing adapted from the basic work by Gina Lombroso Ferrero, *Criminal Man According to the Classification of Cesare Lombroso,* Putnam, New York, 1911, pp. 10–24; reprinted by Patterson Smith, Montclair, NJ, 1972.

Lombroso's theory generated strong reactions, both favorable and un-favorable, among his contemporaries. In response to criticisms of his theory, Lombroso offered to have an impartial committee study of 100 "born criminals," 100 persons with criminal tendencies, and 100 normal persons. Lombroso offered to retract his theories if the physical, mental, and psychological characteristics of the three groups were found to be identical. This challenge was never really met, since Lombroso's opponents said it was impossible to distinguish between the three groups accurately.

However, a study by Charles Goring, begun in England in 1901 and published in 1913, was to some extent a response to Lombroso's challenge.[8] Goring's study was strictly a comparison between a group of convicts—persons convicted of crimes and imprisoned—and a group of unconvicted persons who included university undergraduates, hospital patients, and the officers and men of units of the British army. Thus, no attempt was made to distinguish between "born criminals," persons with criminal tendencies, and normal persons. Also, Goring relied totally on objective measurements of physical and mental characteristics, where Lombroso had objected to such total reliance, maintaining that many anomalies were "so small as to defy all but the most minute research."[9] He argued that these could be detected by the eye of the trained observer, but could not be measured.

Lombroso had asserted that criminals, compared with the general population, would show anomalies (i.e., differences or defects) of head height, head width, and degree of receding forehead, as well as differences in head circumference, head symmetry, and so on. Goring, in comparing prisoners with the officers and men of the Royal Engineers, found no such anomalies. There were no more protrusions or other peculiarities of the head among the prisoners than among the Royal Engineers. Goring also compared other characteristics, such as nasal contours, color of eyes, color of hair, and left-handedness, but found only insignificant differences. He compared groups of different kinds of criminals (burglars, forgers, thieves, etc.) on the basis of thirty-seven specific physical characteristics. He concluded that there were no significant differences between one kind of criminal and another that were not more properly related to the selective effects of environmental factors.[10]

---

[8]Edwin D. Driver, Introductory Essay in Charles Goring, *The English Convict: A Statistical Study,* 1913 edition reprinted by Patterson Smith, Montclair, NJ, 1972, p. vii.

[9]Cesare Lombroso, *The Female Offender,* Unwin, London, 1895; quoted in Goring, op. cit., p. 16.

[10]Goring, *The English Convict,* pp. 196–214.

The one general exception to Goring's conclusion was a consistent "inferiority in stature and in body weight." The criminals were one to two inches shorter than noncriminals of the same occupational groups, and weighed from three to seven pounds less.[11] Goring was satisfied that these differences were real and significant, and he interpreted them as indicating a general inferiority of a hereditary nature. This interpretation agreed with his general thesis of hereditary inferiority (as measured by comparisons of mental ability and various other indices of hereditary influence) as the basis for criminal conduct.[12] Goring's theory of hereditary inferiority is discussed later in this chapter.

Assessments of Goring's work on physical appearance generally found more support for Lombroso's theories than Goring admitted.[13] But the weight of expert opinion was against the proposition that criminals are somehow physically different from noncriminals, and the general conclusions of Goring on the matter came to be accepted by most modern criminologists. Goring wrote:[14]

Our results nowhere confirm the evidence [of a physical criminal type], nor justify the allegation of criminal anthropologists. They challenge their evidence at almost every point. In fact, both with regard to measurements and the presence of physical anomalies in criminals, our statistics present a startling conformity with similar statistics of the law-abiding class. Our inevitable conclusion must be that *there is no such thing as a physical criminal type.*

PHYSICAL APPEARANCE: BODY TYPE

Some of the more interesting attempts at relating criminal behavior to physical appearance are the so-called body type theories. The body type theorists argue that there is a high degree of correspondence between the physical appearance of the body and the temperament of the mind. It should be recalled that Lombroso had attempted to establish some relation between mental disorder and physical characteristics. Many others, before and after Lombroso, have made similar attempts.

---

[11]Ibid., p. 200.

[12]Ibid., p. 287, especially Table 119.

[13]Driver, Introductory Essay, op. cit., p. v.

[14]Goring, op. cit., p. 173 (italics in the original). On the other hand, see the discussion of "minor physical anomalies," including some of the characteristics discussed by Lombroso, in Fishbein, op. cit, pp. 65–66. These are said to result from prenatal influences rather than from evolutionary atavism.

The work of William Sheldon,[15] especially his book on delinquent youth, is a good example of a body type theory. Sheldon took his underlying ideas and terminology of types from the fact that a human begins life as an embryo that is essentially a tube made up of three different tissue layers, namely, an inner layer (or endoderm), a middle layer (or mesoderm), and an outer layer (or ectoderm). Sheldon then constructed a corresponding physical and mental typology consistent with the known facts from embryology and the physiology of development. The endoderm gives rise to the digestive viscera; the mesoderm, to bone, muscle, and tendons of the motor-organ system; the ectoderm, to connecting tissue of the nervous system, skin, and related appendages. Sheldon's basic type characteristics of physique and temperament are briefly summarized in the following scheme:[16]

Physique

Temperament

1. *Endomorphic:* relatively great development of digestive viscera; tendency to put on fat; soft roundness through various regions of the body; short tapering limbs; small bones; soft, smooth, velvety skin.

1. *Viscerotonic:* general relaxation of body; a comfortable person; loves soft luxury; a "softie" but still essentially an extrovert.

2. *Mesomorphic:* relative predominance of muscles, bone, and the motor organs of the body; large trunk; heavy chest; large wrists and hands; if "lean," a hard rectangularity of outline; if "not lean," they fill out heavily.

2. *Somotonic:* active, dynamic person; walks, talks, gestures assertively; behaves aggressively.

3. *Ectomorphic:* relative predominance of skin and its appendages, which includes the nervous system; lean, fragile, delicate body; small, delicate bones; droopy shoulders; small face, sharp nose, fine hair; relatively little body mass and relatively great surface area.

3. *Cerebrotonic:* an introvert; full of functional complaints, allergies, skin troubles, chronic fatigue, insomnia; sensitive to noise and distractions; shrinks from crowds.

Each person possesses the characteristics of the three types to a greater or lesser degree. Sheldon therefore used three numbers, each between

---

[15]William H. Sheldon (with various associates), *Psychology and the Promethean Will*, 1936; *Varieties of Human Physique*, 1940; *The Varieties of Temperament*, 1942; *Varieties of Delinquent Youth*, 1949; *Atlas of Man*, 1954. All published by Harper, New York and London. Information about the life and work of Sheldon can be found in ch. 2 of Randy Martin, Robert J. Mutchnick, and W. Timothy Austin, *Criminological Thought: Pioneers Past and Present*, Macmillan, New York, 1990. A thirty-year follow-up on Sheldon's work can be found in Emil Hartl, *Physique and Delinquent Behavior*, Academic Press, New York, 1982.

[16]The schematic arrangement of basic types has been constructed from the discussion in Sheldon, *Varieties of Delinquent Youth*, pp. 14–30.

1 and 7, to indicate the extent to which the characteristics of the three types were present in a given individual. For example, a person whose somatotype is 7-1-4 would possess many endomorphic characteristics, few mesomorphic characteristics, and an average number of ectomorphic characteristics.

Sheldon presented individual case histories, uniformly written according to a rigorous case outline, of 200 young males who had had a period of contact, during the decade 1939–1949, with the Hayden Goodwill Inn, a small, somewhat specialized, rehabilitation home for boys in Boston. He found that these youths were decidedly high in mesomorphy and low in ectomorphy, with the average somatotype being 3.5-4.6-2.7. Sheldon had earlier studied 200 college students who were apparently nondelinquents, and had found that the average somatotype was 3.2-3.8-3.4. The difference between these two groups with respect to mesomorphy and ectomorphy is significant ($p = 001$).[17]

The association between mesomorphy and delinquency was also found in a study by the Gluecks, who compared 500 persistent delinquents with 500 proven nondelinquents.[18] The two groups were matched in terms of age, general intelligence, ethnic-racial derivation, and residence in underprivileged areas. Photographs of the boys were mixed together and then visually assessed for the predominant body type. By this method 60.1 percent of the delinquents, but only 30.7 percent of the nondelinquents, were found to be mesomorphs.[19] The analysis included a study of sixty-seven personality traits and forty-two sociocultural factors to determine which of these were associated with delinquency.[20] The Gluecks found that mesomorphs, in general, were "more highly characterized by traits particularly suitable to the commission of acts of aggression (physical strength, energy, insensitivity, the tendency to express tensions and frustrations in action), together with a relative freedom from such inhibitions to antisocial adventures as feelings of inadequacy, marked submissiveness to authority, emotional instability, and the like."[21] They also found that those mesomorphs who became delinquent were characterized by a number of personality traits not normally found in mesomorphs, including susceptibility to contagious diseases of childhood, destructiveness, feelings of inadequacy, emotional instability, and emotional conflicts.[22] In addition, three socio-

[17]Juan B. Cortés, *Delinquency and Crime*, Seminar Press, New York, 1972, p. 14.

[18]S. Glueck and E. Glueck, *Physique and Delinquency*, Harper, New York, 1956.

[19]Ibid., p. 9.

[20]For a complete list of these traits and factors, see Ibid., pp. 27–31.

[21]Ibid., p. 226.

[22]Ibid., p. 221.

cultural factors—careless household routine, lack of family group recreations, and meagerness of recreational facilities in the home—were strongly associated with delinquency in mesomorphs.[23]

FAMILY STUDIES

Explanations of human behavior in terms of heredity go far back in antiquity and are based on the common sense observation that children tend to resemble their parents in appearance, mannerisms, and disposition. Scientific theories of heredity originated around 1850 and were more extensively worked out over the next fifty or seventy-five years.[24] In connection with the development of the theory of heredity, new statistical methods were devised by Francis Galton and his students (notably Karl Pearson) to measure degrees of resemblance or correlation. Charles Goring[25] used these new statistical techniques in the analysis of criminality, arriving at the conclusion that crime is inherited in much the same way as are ordinary physical traits and features.

Goring assumed that the seriousness of criminality could be measured by the frequency and length of imprisonments.[26] He therefore attempted to find out what physical, mental, and moral factors were correlated with that measure. Goring found that those with frequent and lengthy imprisonments were physically smaller than other people and were mentally inferior. Although there could be an environmental component to these factors, Goring believed that they both were primarily inherited characteristics.

Goring also found that there were high correlations between the frequency and length of imprisonment of one parent and that of the other, between the imprisonment of parents and that of their children, and between the imprisonment of brothers. Goring argued that these findings could not be explained by the effect of social and environmental conditions, since he found little or no relationship between the frequency and length of imprisonment and such factors as poverty, nationality, education, birth order, and broken homes. He also argued that these findings

---

[23]Ibid., p. 224.

[24]A review of the development of theories of heredity can be found in most textbooks on genetics. See, for example, Eldon J. Gardner and D. Peter Snustad, *Principles of Genetics,* 7th ed., John Wiley, New York, 1984.

[25]Goring, op. cit. For discussions of Goring's work, see Thorsten Sellin, "Charles Buckman Goring," *Encyclopedia of the Social Sciences,* Macmillan, New York, 1931, vol. 6, p. 703; Edwin D. Driver, "Charles Buckman Goring," in Hermann Mannheim, ed., *Pioneers in Criminology,* Patterson Smith, Montclair, NJ, 1972, pp. 429–42; and Driver, Introductory Essay, pp. v–xx.

[26]Goring treated crime as a strictly legal category, and thus preferred the term *convict* to *criminal.* See Driver, "Charles Buckman Goring," pp. 431–33, and Introductory Essay, pp. ix–x.

could not be explained by the effect of example among people who were closely associated with each other. For example, the imprisonment of one spouse could not be explained by the example of the other spouse, since most of them were already engaged in crime at the time they got married. Goring therefore concluded that criminality (i.e., frequent or lengthy imprisonment) was associated with inherited, but not with environmental, characteristics and recommended that to reduce crime, people with those inherited characteristics not be allowed to reproduce.[27]

There are serious problems with each of Goring's arguments.[28] The most important problem concerns the fact that Goring attempted to establish the effect of heredity by controlling for and eliminating the effect of environment. To accomplish that, it is necessary to have accurate measurements of all the environmental factors involved, which he obviously did not have. Goring dealt with only a few environmental factors, quite imperfectly, and these were roughly measured. Though these particular ones may have shown low correlation with his measure of criminality, other environmental factors might still be very important. By his method of reasoning, the failure to measure environmental influence adequately has the result of overemphasizing the significance of the influence of heredity.

Later studies of the families of criminals have encountered a similar problem. In general, there are many similarities among family members in their tendencies to commit crime.[29] The problem is that it is impossible to control for the effects of similar environment within the family itself. If family members resemble each other in their tendency to commit crime, it may not be because they share a similar heredity. Rather, it may be because they all live in the same environment and the similar environment causes the similar tendency to commit crime.

TWIN AND ADOPTION STUDIES

Studies attempting to address the hereditary bases of criminality by examining traditional families found it impossible to disentangle the effects of nature (such as genes) from those of nurture (environment). This prompted researchers to study twins and adoptees. Instead of attempting to eliminate environmental factors, one may control the hereditary factor. The study of the relative criminality of twins suggests

---

[27]Driver, "Charles Buckman Goring," pp. 439–40.

[28]See Edwin H. Sutherland and Donald R. Cressey, *Criminology*, 10th ed., Lippincott, Philadelphia, 1978, p. 120.

[29]For example, see David C. Rowe and David P. Farrington, "The Familial Transmission of Criminal Convictions," *Criminology* 35(1):177–201 (1997).

this possibility, since in genetics there is a clear-cut distinction between identical and fraternal twins. Identical twins (monozygotic) are the product of a single fertilized egg and have identical heredity; fraternal twins (dizygotic) are the product of two eggs simultaneously fertilized by two sperms, and therefore have the same relation as ordinary siblings.[30] Differences in the behavior of identical twins therefore may not be attributed to differences in heredity, and presumably similarities of behavior could be attributed to their identical inheritance. Obviously this need not be true, since the similarities could be due to similarities in training. But any general tendency to greater similarity of behavior when heredity is identical sets up a strong presumption that the similarity is due to the influence of heredity.

A number of studies have used this approach in trying to determine the role of heredity in criminality. All tend to show greater similarity of criminal behavior among identical than among fraternal twins.[31] Each of these studies begins with criminals who are known to have twins and determines whether the twins are also criminals. Such a procedure is open to subtle bias, however, since the investigator may attribute criminality in borderline cases only when it is convenient to do so.[32] To avoid the possibility of bias Christiansen used the official *Twins Register* of Denmark to study all twins born in the Danish Islands between 1881 and 1910 when both twins lived at least until the age of 15.[33] They totaled about 6,000 pairs. He then used the official *Penal Register* to determine whether either twin, or both, had been found criminal or delinquent. He found sixty-seven cases in which at least one of a pair of male identical twins was registered as a criminal, and in twenty-four of these cases (35.8 percent) the other twin was also registered. For male fraternal twins he found this to be true in only fourteen out of 114 cases (12.3 percent). For females he found "criminal concordance" in three out of fourteen cases of identical twins (21.4 percent) and in one out of twenty-three cases of fraternal twins (4.3 percent). Christiansen later

[30]Most humans share 99 percent of their genes with other humans. Dizygotic twins share 50 percent of the remaining 1 percent, whereas monozygotic twins share all of the remaining 1 percent. See Adrian Raine, *The Psychopathology of Crime*, Academic Press, Inc., San Diego, 1993, p. 54.

[31]See a summary of such studies in Juan B. Cortés, op. cit., pp. 31–35; David Rosenthal, *Genetic Theory and Abnormal Behavior*, McGraw-Hill, New York, 1970, pp. 225–36; and Karl O. Christiansen, "A Review of Studies of Criminality among Twins," in Sarnoff Mednick and Karl O. Christiansen, eds., *Biosocial Bases of Criminal Behavior*, Gardner Press, New York, 1977, pp. 45–88. See also Fishbein, op. cit., pp. 27–29.

[32]Cf. Sutherland and Cressey, op. cit., p. 116.

[33]K. O. Christiansen, "Threshold of Tolerance in Various Population Groups Illustrated by Results from the Danish Criminologic Twin Study," in A. V. S. de Reuck and R. Porter, eds., *The Mentally Abnormal Offender*, Little, Brown, Boston, 1968.

demonstrated that concordance was higher for more serious criminality than for less serious.[34]

The principal difficulty with this method is that the greater similarity of behavior noted in the case of the identical twins may be due to the greater similarity of training and environmental experience just as well as to their identical hereditary makeup.[35] There is no certain way of separating environment and heredity as contributing factors in this situation. Referring to his own study, Christiansen pointed out:[36]

Nothing in these results, however, can be interpreted as indicating that a higher twin coefficient in [identical] than in [fraternal] twins, or in pairs with more serious than in pairs with less serious forms of criminality, is due to what Lange called the quite preponderant part played by heredity in the causation of crime.

One way to control for the possibility that identical twins share a more common environment than fraternal twins would be to study twins who were reared apart. Grove and his colleagues looked at thirty-two sets of identical twins who were separated shortly after birth,[37] and Christiansen looked at eight pairs of identical twins raised apart.[38] Although these studies were based on a small sample of twins, they both found evidence that antisocial behavior can be inherited. Finally, Walters performed a meta-analysis of fourteen twin studies published from 1930 to 1984, attempting to assess whether these studies on the whole find evidence of a gene-crime relationship.[39] He took into account such factors as the sample sizes of the studies, the quality of the research designs, the

---

[34]K. O. Christiansen, "Seriousness of Criminality and Concordance among Danish Twins," in Roger Hood, ed., *Crime, Criminology, and Public Policy,* The Free Press, New York, 1974.

[35]As Raine (op. cit.) points out (p. 58), there are also problems in the accuracy of labeling twins as monozygotic or dizygotic. The most accurate method is DNA fingerprinting, which is not usually employed. Other methods have varying degrees of reliability.

[36]Ibid., p. 77. For a similar conclusion, see also Steffen Odd Dalgaard and Einar Kringlen, "A Norwegian Twin Study of Criminality," *British Journal of Criminology* 16: 213–32 (1976). They found that when twins were grouped according to their mutual closeness, all differences between identical and fraternal twins disappeared. They concluded that "the significance of hereditary factors in registered crime is non-existent." For a criticism of this study, see R. A. Forde, "Twin Studies, Inheritance and Criminality," *British Journal of Criminology* 18(1): 71–74 (Jan. 1978). See also Saleem A. Shah and Loren H. Roth, "Biological and Psychophysiological Factors in Criminality," in Daniel Glaser, ed., *Handbook of Criminology,* Rand McNally, Chicago, 1974, pp. 133–34.

[37]W. M. Grove, E. D. Eckert, L. Heston, T. J. Bouchard, N. Segal, and D. T. Lyken, "Heritability of Substance Abuse and Antisocial Behavior: A Study of Monozygotic Twins Reared Apart," *Biological Psychiatry* 27: 1293–1304 (1990).

[38]Christiansen, "A Review of Criminality Among Twins," in S. A. Mednick and K. O. Christiansen, eds., *Biosocial Bases of Criminal Behavior,* Gardner Press, New York, 1977, pp. 89–108.

[39]Glenn D. Walters, "A Meta-Analysis of the Gene-Crime Relationship," *Criminology* 30(4): 595–613 (1992).

gender and nationality of the twins, and the year of the studies. Walters concluded that on the average these studies show evidence of a hereditary basis of criminality.

Another method for determining the effects of heredity on criminality is to study the records of adoptees. For example, Hutchings and Mednick examined the records of all nonfamily male adoptions in Copenhagen in which the adoptee had been born between 1927 and 1941.[40] First, the authors grouped the boys according to whether they had criminal records, and then looked at the criminal records of the biological fathers. A total of 31.1 percent of the boys who had no criminal record had biological fathers with criminal records, but 37.7 percent of the boys who had committed only minor offenses and 48.8 percent of the boys who themselves had criminal records had biological fathers with criminal records.[41] These figures indicate adopted boys are more likely to commit crime when their biological fathers have a criminal record.

Next, the researchers grouped the biological and adoptive fathers according to whether they had criminal records, and then looked at the criminal records of the boys. They found an interactive effect between the criminality of the biological and the adoptive fathers.[42] When only one was criminal, the effect was not as significant as when both were criminal. In addition, the effect of the criminality of the adoptive father was not as great as the effect of criminality of the biological father.

Hutchings and Mednick then selected all the criminal adoptees whose fathers (both biological and adoptive) had been born after 1889 to maximize the reliability of police records. The 143 adoptees who met this criterion were matched with 143 noncriminal adoptees on the basis of age and occupational status of adoptive fathers. The criminal adoptees were found to have a higher percentage of criminal adoptive fathers (23 percent vs. 9.8 percent), of criminal biological fathers (49 percent vs. 28 percent), and of criminal biological mothers (18 percent vs. 7 percent).[43]

This sample of Danish adoptees was expanded to females and the entire country of Denmark, and re-analyzed by Mednick and his colleagues.[44] These researchers found that the adoptee's probability of be-

---

[40]Barry Hutchings and Sarnoff A. Mednick, "Criminality in Adoptees and Their Adoptive and Biological Parents: A Pilot Study," in Mednick and Christiansen, op. cit., pp. 127–41.

[41]Ibid., p. 131, Table 4.

[42]Ibid., p. 132, Table 6. See also ibid., p. 137, Table 8.

[43]Ibid., p. 134.

[44]Mednick, W. H. Gabrielli, and Hutchings, "Genetic Influences in Criminal Convictions: Evidence from an Adoption Cohort," *Science* 224: 891–94 (1984). For a review of all adoption analyses see

ing convicted of a crime was influenced by the number of court convictions of their biological parents, but not their adoptive parents. This was true for property offenses but not for violent offenses. Later re-analyses of the same data found that the socioeconomic status of adoptive and biological parents, personality disorders of the biological parents, and the number of placements before final adoption all influenced adoptee convictions.[45] Again, these relationships held mostly for property offenses but not for violent offenses.

Walters performed a meta-analysis of thirteen adoption studies published between 1972 and 1989, finding significant evidence for heritability of crime and antisocial behavior.[46] However, two limitations of adoption studies may be mentioned. First, in several of the studies, adoptive parents engaged in criminal behavior at much lower rates than the normal population.[47] This makes it difficult to generalize about the effects of family environment, and to examine the interaction between environment and genetics in its potential joint influence on behavior. Second, several studies found hereditary effects for petty and property offenses, but not for more serious and violent offenses. But this result may reflect the fact that petty and property offenders are more likely to be frequent offenders. Thus, hereditary effects would be much easier to find with those offenders than with serious and violent offenders, who commit crimes very infrequently.

NEUROTRANSMITTERS

Neurotransmitters are chemicals that allow for the transmission of electrical impulses within the brain and are the basis for the brain's processing of information. As such, they underlie all types of behavior, including

---

Gregory Carey, "Genetics and Violence," in Albert Reiss, Klaus Miczek, and Jeffrey Roth, eds., *Understanding and Preventing Violence*, vol. 2, National Academy Press, Washington, DC, 1994, pp. 34–39.

[45]K. T. VanDusen, Mednick, Gabrielli, and Hutchings, "Social Class and Crime in an Adoption Cohort," *Journal of Criminal Law and Criminology* 74: 249–69 (1983); L. A. Baker, "Estimating Genetic Correlations among Disconcordant Phenotypes: An Analysis of Criminal Convictions and Psychiatric Hospital Diagnoses in Danish Adoptees," *Behavior Genetics* 16: 127–42 (1986); Baker, W. Mack, T. E. Moffitt, and Mednick, "Etiology of Sex Differences in Criminal Convictions in a Danish Adoption Cohort," *Behavioral Genetics* 19: 355–70 (1989); Moffitt, "Parental Mental Disorder and Offspring Criminal Behavior: An Adoption Study," *Psychiatry: Interpersonal and Biological Processes* 50: 346–60 (1987).

[46]Walters, op. cit., pp. 604–5. The overall effect in the adoption studies was somewhat stronger than that in the twin studies, but this is probably because the adoption studies had larger samples than the twin studies, making it easier to achieve statistical significance.

[47]Carey, op. cit., p. 43.

antisocial behavior.[48] About thirty studies have examined the linkage between neurotransmitters and antisocial behavior. These studies at least tentatively suggest that the levels of three different neurotransmitters may be associated with antisocial behavior: serotonin, dopamine, and norepinephrine.

Scerbo and Raine performed a meta-analysis of studies on the relationship between neurotransmitter levels and antisocial behavior.[49] They reported that twenty-eight studies, on average, found that antisocial people have significantly lower levels of serotonin than normal people. Studies of norepinephrine and dopamine did not show any overall differences in these transmitter levels across the groups of subjects, but when only studies using a direct measure of neurotransmitter functioning were considered, an effect of norepinephrine on antisocial behavior was also found.[50] The authors concluded that it is important to control for alcohol abuse when examining the effects of neurotransmitters, since alcoholism itself is associated with differences in neurotransmitter levels.[51]

Although neurotransmitter levels initially are determined by genetics, it is possible to manipulate them with drugs, such as lithium carbonate (for serotonin), reserpine (for norepinephrine) and various antipsychotic drugs (for dopamine). The research on whether these manipulations can actually reduce antisocial behavior is mixed, but includes some encouraging results.[52] Neurotransmitter levels can also be affected by changes in the environment. For example, changes in diet can significantly increase the levels of serotonin, dopamine, and norepinephrine, which could possibly reduce the tendency to engage in violent or antisocial behavior. In addition, living in very stressful conditions (such as inner-city areas) can dramatically lower serotonin levels and increase the tendency to engage in these behaviors.[53]

HORMONES

In addition to neurotransmitter levels, much research has been generated relating to the effect of hormone levels on human behavior, including

---

[48]P. A. Brennan, S. A. Mednick, and J. Volavka, "Biomedical Factors in Crime," in James Q. Wilson and Joan Petersilia, eds., *Crime*, ICS Press, San Francisco, 1995, p. 82. For an introduction to neurotransmitters see also Raine, op. cit., pp. 83–84; and Fishbein, op. cit., pp. 35–41.

[49]A. Scerbo and A. Raine, "Neurotransmitters and Antisocial Behavior: A Meta-analysis," reported in Raine, op. cit., p. 87.

[50]Ibid., p. 91.

[51]Ibid., pp. 92, 98–99.

[52]For a review see D. A. Brizer, "Psychopharmacology and the Management of Violent Patients," *Psychiatric Clinics of North America* 11: 551–68 (1988).

[53]Fishbein, op. cit., p. 15.

aggressive or criminal behavior. Interest in hormones dates back to the mid-1800s, when biochemists were first able to isolate and identify some of the physiological and psychological effects of the secretions of the endocrine glands (hormones). Most recent attention paid to hormone levels and aggressive or criminal behavior relates to either testosterone or female premenstrual cycles.[54]

The role of testosterone in the aggressiveness of many animal species has been well documented,[55] but a question remains as to whether testosterone plays a significant role in human aggressive and violent behavior. Raine reviews some of this literature, finding mixed results.[56]

A major problem with this research is that there are several possible causal paths between testosterone and aggressive behavior.[57] In general, researchers want to know whether high testosterone levels cause increased aggression. But it is possible that the causal path is in the opposite direction: certain types of aggressive behavior may cause an increase in testosterone production.[58] A third possibility is that some individuals may generally have normal levels of testosterone, but they may respond to certain types of situations with very large increases in testosterone. These people may have an increased tendency to engage in aggressive behavior due to their high testosterone levels, even though their testosterone levels measure as normal most of the time. Finally, social variables may intervene in the relationship between testosterone and antisocial behavior. Booth and Osgood examined the relationships between testosterone, social integration, prior involvement in juvenile delinquency, and adult deviance.[59] They found that although there is a strong initial association between testosterone and adult deviance, the magnitude of this effect is reduced substantially when controlling for social integration. In other words, testosterone may reduce social integration, and reduced social integration is associated with higher deviance levels. In addition, testosterone is associated with juvenile delinquency, and when

---

[54]Ibid., pp. 41–45.

[55]For an excellent overview, see Paul Brain, "Hormonal Aspects of Aggression and Violence," in Reiss, Miczek, and Roth, eds., *Understanding and Preventing Violence*, vol. 2, op. cit., pp. 173–244.

[56]Adrian Raine, *The Psychopathology of Crime*, op. cit. For another review of recent research on testosterone and aggression, see David Benton, "Hormones and Human Aggression," in Kaj Björkqvist and Pirkko Niemelä, eds., *Of Mice and Women: Aspects of Female Aggression*, Academic Press, San Diego, 1992, pp. 37–48.

[57]See Julie Aitken Harris, "Review and Methodological Considerations in Research on Testosterone and Aggression," *Aggression and Violent Behavior* 4(3): 273–91 (1999).

[58]Brain, op. cit., p. 221. See also Albert J. Reiss and Jeffrey Roth eds., *Understanding and Preventing Violence*, vol. 1, National Academy Press, Washington, DC, 1993, p. 119.

[59]Alan Booth and D. Wayne Osgood, "The Influence of Testosterone on Deviance in Adulthood: Assessing and Explaining the Relationship," *Criminology* 31(1): 93–117 (1993).

controlling for delinquency, the relationship between testosterone and adult deviance diminishes further. Research such as this highlights the need for more biosocial theories of criminal behavior and deviance.

Although most research on hormones and crime has focused on males, some work has examined the role that hormones play in female crime, especially in connection with the menstrual cycle. Biological changes after ovulation have been linked to irritability and aggression.[60] Research is mixed on the strength of this linkage, but at least a small percentage of women are susceptible to cyclical hormone changes that result in a patterned increase in hostility.[61] This patterned increase is associated with fluctuations in female hormones and a rise in testosterone, to which some women appear to be quite sensitive.

THE CENTRAL NERVOUS SYSTEM

The central nervous system contains neurons and systems that exist within the brain and spinal cord. Of particular importance in research on aggression and violence is the outer portion of the brain, the cerebral cortex. This consists of two hemispheres divided into four lobes: frontal, temporal, parietal, and occipital. Most attention paid by investigators studying antisocial behavior is to the frontal and temporal lobes, since these lobes are involved with goal-directed behavior, impulses, and emotions. Disturbances or irregularities within the frontal lobe generally influence neuropsychological performance, while the temporal lobe in general appears to involve behaviors more directly emotional in expression.[62]

One common way of measuring brain abnormalities is through the use of the electroencephalograph (EEG). The EEG measures electrical brain activity, and can detect abnormalities in brain wave patterns. Hundreds of studies have examined EEG activity in various types of criminals.[63] Most reviewers agree that repeat violent offenders are characterized by EEG abnormalities, but the relationship between psychopathy

---

[60]See R. F. Haskett, "Premenstrual Dysphoric Disorder: Evaluation, Pathophysiology and Treatment," *Progress in Neuro-Psychopharmacology and Biological Psychiatry* 11: 129–35 (1987); and E. P. Trunell and C. W. Turner, "A Comparison of the Psychological and Hormonal Factors in Women with and Without Premenstrual Syndrome," *Journal of Abnormal Psychology* 97: 429–36 (1988).

[61]Diana Fishbein, "The Psychobiology of Female Aggression," *Criminal Justice and Behavior* 19: 99–126 (1992).

[62]For a review of neuropsychological indicators of brain dysfunction and abnormal behavior, see Raine, op. cit., pp. 103–27.

[63]Ibid., p. 175.

and EEG indicators is more uncertain.[64] Raine points out that most of this research is too broad in focus, and while it may point to some general relationship between dysfunctional behavior and EEG abnormalities, we need to know much more specific information about the processes by which brain wave activity may affect behavior.[65]

More recently, however, more direct measures of the central nervous system have become available: brain imaging techniques. These techniques include computerized tomography (CT), magnetic resonance imaging (MRI), positron emission tomography (PET), and single photon emission tomography (SPECT). These new brain imaging procedures have been used to detect structural and functional abnormalities in both the frontal and temporal lobes.[66] After a comprehensive review of brain imaging studies, Raine concludes that:[67]

An integration of findings from these studies gives rise to the hypothesis that frontal dysfunction may characterize violent offenders while temporal lobe dysfunction may characterize sexual offending; offenders with conjoint violent and sexual behavior are hypothesized to be characterized by both frontal and temporal lobe dysfunction.

THE AUTONOMIC NERVOUS SYSTEM

In addition to the central nervous system, there is a relatively separate part of the nervous system, called the autonomic nervous system (ANS), which controls many of the body's involuntary functions such as blood pressure, heart and intestinal activity, and hormone levels. The ANS is especially active in a "fight or flight" situation, when it prepares the body for maximum efficiency by increasing the heart rate, rerouting the blood from the stomach to the muscles, dilating the pupils, increasing the respiratory rate, and stimulating the sweat glands. Lie detectors measure these functions and use them to determine whether the subject is telling the truth. The theory is that, as children, most people have been conditioned to anticipate punishment when they tell a lie. The anticipation of punishment produces the involuntary fight or flight response, which results in a number of measurable changes in heart, pulse, and breathing

---

[64]Ibid., pp. 175–76.

[65]Ibid., pp. 177–80. EEG abnormalities and EP (evoked potential) responses may be indicative of several possible problems, including CNS instability, underarousal, or subcortical epilepsy. Lumping all EEG abnormalities together is a mistake, since they may refer to different problems that may have different effects on behavior.

[66]Ibid., p. 130.

[67]Ibid., p. 155.

rate, and, because sweat itself conducts electricity, in the electric conductivity of the skin.

The anxiety reaction in anticipation of punishment has been described by some researchers as the primary socializing agent for children.[68] Children are conditioned by their parents to anticipate punishment in certain types of situations, and the anxiety they then feel (usually called conscience or guilt) often leads them to avoid those situations. Because the anxiety reaction in anticipation of punishment is essentially an autonomic nervous system function related to the fight or flight response, the level of socialization in children may depend at least in part on the functioning of that system. Specifically, if the fight or flight response is activated slowly or at low levels in situations in which punishment is anticipated, or if it fails to deactivate quickly when the situation changes, then the child will be difficult to socialize.

A number of studies of autonomic nervous system functioning have measured the same peripheral functions that are measured by a lie detector. For example, Mednick[69] maintains that the rate of skin conductance response (SCR) recovery—the time between when the skin conducts the most electrical current and when that conductance returns to normal levels—can be taken to measure the general rate of recovery in the autonomic nervous system. If so, SCR recovery would measure the rate at which fear is reduced following removal of the threatening situation. Mednick points out that fear reduction is the most powerful reinforcer known to psychology. When fear is reduced quickly, the individual receives a large reinforcement for avoiding the punishment, and conditioning is more likely to occur.

The results of research on this whole line of reasoning, however, are quite mixed. In general, research has found that antisocial individuals have lower levels of skin conductance, as well as lower heart rates, when they are in resting situations.[70] These physiological measures may indicate that antisocial people have lower levels of ANS functioning. But Mednick has argued that a crucial indicator of this lower ANS functioning is skin conductance response recovery—i.e., its return to normal levels after the person is presented with an aversive stimulus such as pun-

---

[68]H. J. Eysenck, *Crime and Personality*, Houghton Mifflin, Boston, 1964, pp. 100–119; Gordon Trassler, "Criminal Behavior," in H. J. Eysenck, ed., *Handbook of Abnormal Psychology*, Putnam, London, 1972; Sarnoff A. Mednick, "A Biosocial Theory of the Learning of Law-Abiding Behavior," in Mednick and Christiansen, op. cit., pp. 1–8.

[69]Mednick, "A Biosocial Theory," op. cit., pp. 2–4.

[70]Pauline S. Yaralian and Adrian Raine, "Biological Approaches to Crime," in Raymond Paternoster and Ronet Bachman, eds., *Explaining Criminals and Crime*, Roxbury, Los Angeles, 2001, pp. 57–72.

ishment. Earlier studies generally support Mednick's argument that antisocial individuals would show slow recovery of skin conductance response after presentation with punishment; however, later research generally has failed to support this finding.[71]

However, the point of Mednick's argument is that antisocial people may be more difficult to condition than other people. Some studies have directly attempted to compare conditioning in antisocial and normal people. These studies are similar to Pavlov's famous experiments with dogs: Pavlov would ring a bell just before he gave the dogs food, and conditioning was said to occur when the dog salivated at the sound of the bell. Raine reviewed six similar studies that generally supported the notion that antisocial people are harder to condition than regular people.[72] This finding would be similar to a finding by Pavlov that some dogs are slow to learn to salivate at the sound of the bell. On the other hand, this finding only applied to people from poor social backgrounds.[73] This would suggest that, even if low ANS functioning can explain some crime, it cannot explain lower-class crime. Overall, there is some evidence that ANS functioning may be related to criminal behavior, but it is difficult to draw firm conclusions at this point.

ENVIRONMENTALLY INDUCED BIOLOGICAL COMPONENTS OF BEHAVIOR

Up to this point we have discussed research on hereditary factors that influence antisocial and criminal behavior (such as the family, twins, and adoption studies), and research that addresses factors which may be hereditary but may also change over time due to environmental influences (such as hormones, neurotransmitter levels, and skin conductance responses to stimuli). Now we examine research on several biological factors that may influence criminal behavior but are clearly environmental in the sense that they have nothing to do with the person's hereditary or genetic make-up. These factors include drug and alcohol abuse, diet and toxin intake, head injury, and pregnancy and delivery complications.

There are many possible relationships between *drug and alcohol abuse* and violent behavior: biological, psychosocial, social, cultural, and economic. For example, violence and crime may result from an addict's need to get money to buy drugs, or from wars between rival drug gangs

---

[71]Ibid., p. 59.

[72]Ibid., pp. 59–60.

[73]Ibid., p. 60.

over the right to sell drugs in certain areas. Because the range of literature is so broad in these areas, we do not summarize it here.[74] Instead,
we present a few brief comments on the strictly biological links between
violence and alcohol or drug use.

Alcohol is known to temporarily increase aggressive behavior in lower
doses (when people get nasty), and temporarily decrease aggressive behavior in higher doses (when people pass out).[75] Many people believe
that the increased aggressiveness at lower doses is because of alcohol's
"dis-inhibiting" effect—alcohol tends to release people from their inhibitions—but there is little evidence for this. An alternative explanation is
that alcohol increases the production of the endocrine system, especially testosterone, but again, there is little evidence for this. Other possible
neurobiological explanations involve serotonin functioning and EEG abnormalities, but experiments have yet to confirm any of these possible
explanations. Some researchers believe that there may be a genetic basis
for the relationship between alcohol and violence, but there is no confir-
mation of this to date. So while the relationship between alcohol and violence is probably the strongest of any drug, especially for males,[76] the
reason for this relationship remains unclear.

Other drugs that may have a biological association with violence are
opiates, amphetamines, cocaine, hallucinogens, and steroids. Opiates
are known to temporarily reduce aggressive and violent behavior, although chronic use may increase the possibility of violent behavior.
Withdrawal from opiates is related to aggressive behavior as well.[77]
There is still no direct evidence of a biological effect of cocaine use on
violent behavior,[78] although the association between crack cocaine and
violence in inner cities is very well established.[79] Marijuana use most
likely decreases or does not affect violent human behavior, while PCP,
when used over a long term, may increase aggressive behavior. Chronic
amphetamine use may provoke violent outbursts in humans, but usually

---

[74]For a broad review of the drug and violence literature, see Alfred S. Friedman, "Substance
Use/Abuse as a Predictor to Illegal and Violent Behavior: A Review of the Relevant Literature," *Aggression and Violent Behavior* 3(4): 339–55 (1998). See also Diana H. Fishbein and Susan E. Pease,
The Dynamics of Drug Abuse, Allyn and Bacon, Boston, 1996, and Reiss and Roth, eds., *Understanding and Preventing Violence,* vol. 1, op.cit., chapter 4.

[75]The discussion of alcohol and violence is summarized from Reiss and Roth, ibid., pp. 189–191.

[76]Friedman, op. cit., but see Helene Raskin White and Stephen Hansell, "The Moderating Effects
of Gender and Hostility on the Alcohol-Aggression Relationship," *Journal of Research in Crime and
Delinquency* 33(4): 450–70 (1996).

[77]Reiss and Roth, op. cit., p. 192.

[78]Ibid, p. 194.

[79]Friedman, op. cit.

only when the individuals already are prone to violent behavior.[80] Similarly, the use of LSD and steroids may intensify violent behavior in those already prone to violence.[81]

Various studies have found correlations between *nutrition or toxin* intake and antisocial or aggressive behavior, but the methodological shortcomings of these studies make it difficult to conclude that causal relationships exist. Most commonly studied are sugar and cholesterol consumption and lead toxicity.[82]

Research in the 1980s showed hypoglycemia (low blood sugar), which is caused in part by excess sugar intake, to be common in habitually violent criminals. Numerous methodological problems with these studies are cited by Kanarek[83] and cast significant doubt on whether sugar intake causes antisocial behavior. Sugar has also been associated with hyperactivity in children, but again, there is reason to doubt the validity of most of the research that supports the association.[84] More research that is methodologically solid, examining potential negative consequences of sugar, is needed before any conclusions should be drawn on the sugar-violence link. Research has also purported that there is a link between blood cholesterol and violent behavior, but these studies suffer from the same sorts of problems as the research on sugar and violent behavior.[85] Finally, exposure to lead in diet and environment has been shown to negatively affect brain functioning, bringing about learning disabilities and hyperactive attention deficit disorder in children, and may increase the risk for antisocial behavior.[86] Future research is certain to continue examining the linkages between lead exposure and negative behavioral consequences.

Several studies have found a correlation between *head injury* and criminal and antisocial behavior; whether the relationship is causal is another matter.[87] Such head injury can be detected by medical tests such as X-rays, CAT scans, and spinal taps. A variety of studies have found

---

[80]Ibid.

[81]Reiss and Roth, op. cit., p. 195; Ingemar Thiblin, Marianne Kristiansson, and Jovan Rajs, "Anabolic Androgenic Steriods and Behavioural Patterns Among Violent Offenders," *Journal of Forensic Psychiatry* 8(2): 299–310 (1997).

[82]This discussion is taken primarily from Robin B. Kanarek, "Nutrition and Violent Behavior" in Reiss, Miczek, and Roth, eds., *Understanding and Preventing Violence*, vol. 2, op cit., pp. 515–539.

[83]Ibid., pp. 523–26.

[84]Ibid., pp. 530–31.

[85]Ibid., pp. 533–34.

[86]Diana H. Fishbein, "Biological Perspectives in Criminology," *Criminology* 28(1): 27–72 (1990).

[87]Mednick et al., "Biology and Violence," pp. 52–58.

that prisoners and violent patients report a large number of head injuries that involve loss of consciousness. Mednick found some support for a relationship between brain damage and violent behavior among juveniles in a study of children born at a hospital in Copenhagen between 1959 and 1961.[88] Those who later became violent delinquents had generally good medical, physical, and neurological reports during pregnancy and delivery, despite relatively poor social conditions. However, they had significantly worse physical and neurological status at one year of age. Similar findings were reported by Dorothy Lewis and her colleagues.[89] Lewis also found a strong association between parental criminality and the presence of serious medical problems in their children. She suggested that delinquency among children with criminal parents may reflect the combined physical and psychological effects of parental neglect and battering, rather than any genetic factors.[90]

Raine discusses some possible scenarios that would account for the association between head injury and criminal behavior. For example, in abusive homes children are more likely to incur head injuries, and these homes may also be more conducive to criminal behavior among offspring raised in them.[91] Still, Raine cites evidence that the link between head injury and criminal behavior may be at least partially causal.[92] Some processes by which head injury may influence negative behaviors are: (1) increasing sensitivity to effects of alcohol; (2) decreasing cognitive and social skills; (3) headaches and irritability which increase the possibility of violent outbursts; and (4) damage to the frontal and temporal lobes of the brain that increases anxiety, anger, and hostility.[93]

Another possible source of CNS deficits (which have been linked to aggressive behavior) is *pregnancy and delivery complications*.[94] A recent study by Kandel and Mednick examined data on 216 children born

---

[88]Ibid., p. 55.

[89]Dorothy Otnow Lewis et al., "Perinatal Difficulties, Head and Face Trauma, and Child Abuse in the Medical Histories of Seriously Delinquent Children," *American Journal of Psychiatry* 136 (4): 419–23 (April 1979). See also Lewis et al., "Violent Juvenile Delinquents: Psychiatric, Neurological, Psychological, and Abuse Factors," *Journal of the American Academy of Child Psychiatry* 18(2): 307–19 (1979); and Lewis, et., *Vulnerabilities to Delinquency*, Spectrum, New York, 1981.

[90]Dorothy Otnow Lewis et al., "Parental Criminality and Medical Histories of Delinquent Children," *American Journal of Psychiatry* 136(3): 288–92 (March 1979).

[91]Raine, op. cit., p. 193.

[92]Ibid., pp. 193–94.

[93]Ibid., pp. 194–95.

[94]For reviews, see Fishbein, *Biobehavioral Perspectives in Criminology*, op. cit., pp. 65–70 and Yaralian and Raine, op. cit., pp. 67–68.

between 1959 and 1961 in Copenhagen.[95] The group of 216 was selected from an original cohort of 9,125 children because their parents were schizophrenic, psychopathic, or character-disordered; the children were therefore considered to be at high risk of becoming delinquent. The research examined pregnancy complications (such as infections, chemotherapy, and jaundice) and delivery complications (such as ruptured perineum, weak secondary labor, and ruptured uterus), and measured criminal behavior with arrest records for property and violent offenses when the subjects were 20 to 22 years old. Pregnancy complications were not significantly related to offending rates, but delivery complications were related to violent offending: 80 percent of violent offenders had greater than average delivery complications, compared to 30 percent of property offenders and 47 percent of nonoffenders.[96] A subsequent study found that violent offending occurs most often among individuals with both a high number of delivery complications and parents with psychiatric problems.[97] Another study found that delivery complications, combined with rejection by the mother before age one, were associated with serious violent crime at age 18.[98]

IMPLICATIONS AND CONCLUSIONS

Biological theories are necessarily part of a "multiple factor" approach to criminal behavior—that is, the presence of certain biological factors may increase the likelihood but not determine absolutely that an individual will engage in criminal behaviors. These factors generate criminal behaviors when they interact with psychological or social factors. Mednick, for example, has suggested a possible interaction between biological and social factors:[99]

Where the social experiences of an antisocial individual are not especially antisocial, biological factors should be examined. The value of the biological factors

---

[95]Elizabeth Kandel and Sarnoff A. Mednick, "Perinatal Complications Predict Violent Offending," *Criminology* 29(3): 519–29: (1991).

[96]Ibid., p. 523.

[97]P. Brennan, S. A. Mednick, and E. Kandel, "Congenital Determinants of Violent and Property Offending," in D. J. Pepler and K. H. Rubin, eds., *The Development and Treatment of Childhood Aggression,* Erlbaum, Hillsdale, NJ, 1993, pp. 81–92.

[98]Adrian Raine, Patricia Brennan, and Sarnoff A. Mednick, "Interaction Between Birth Complications and Early Maternal Rejection in Predisposing Individuals to Adult Violence," *American Journal of Psychiatry* 154(9): 1265–71 (1997).

[99]Mednick et al., "Biology and Violence," op. cit., pp. 55, 68. A similar conclusion is reached in Mednick et al., "An Example of Biosocial Interaction Research," in Mednick and Christiansen, op. cit., pp. 9–23.

is more limited in predicting antisocial behavior in individuals who have experienced criminogenic social conditions in their rearing.

In the past, biologically oriented and sociologically oriented criminologists have often been at odds with each other. Both sides have overstated their own positions and refused to acknowledge partial validity in their opponents' views. This is changing, as criminologists on both sides are recognizing the need for biosocial theories that examine not only the separate contribution of sociological and biological phenomena to criminal behavior, but the interaction of these perspectives as well. This emerging synthesis of perspectives will probably benefit biological criminology, since extreme biological views often raise images of determinism among some audiences, who subsequently react negatively to the furthering of such research and to any policies based on it.

CHAPTER FOUR

Psychological Factors and Criminal Behavior

This chapter examines theories that explain criminal behavior primarily in terms of the psychological characteristics of the individual. Low intelligence probably has been the psychological characteristic most often used to explain criminal and delinquent behavior. It was an important type of theory in the early years of the twentieth century, but it fell out of favor when research using IQ tests showed little or no difference in intelligence between criminals and noncriminals. Since the 1970s, however, there has been renewed support for this hypothesis, particularly with respect to juvenile delinquents.

Other psychological theories explain criminal behavior in terms of the enduring personality characteristics of the individual. The term personality refers to the emotional and behavioral attributes that tend to remain stable as the individual moves from situation to situation. Some research on the personality uses a type of psychological test called the personality inventory. This type of test is similar to the IQ tests used to measure intelligence. Other research focuses on specific personality characteristics thought to be associated with crime and delinquency, such as the antisocial personality and impulsivity.

Psychological theories also consider biological and situational factors in their explanations of criminal behavior. Much of the biological research presented in Chapter 3 has been done by psychologists and psychiatrists and can be considered part of psychological or psychiatric theories of crime. Those theories also consider the impact of the situation on the individual, and they explain behavior by interrelating the situation with the individual's biological and psychological characteristics. Situational factors, however, will be discussed in the chapters on sociological theories of criminal behavior. Psychological theories which argue that criminal behavior is the result of normal learning processes are discussed in Chapter 9.

INTELLIGENCE AND CRIME: BACKGROUND IDEAS AND CONCEPTS

The language and literature of all peoples have words to describe and stories to illustrate the conduct of "dull-witted" or "slow" individuals whose intelligence is no more than that of a young child. From a spiritualistic point of view, such mentally deficient or retarded people sometimes were thought to be possessed by the devil. They were sometimes banished as "unclean" and forced into exile and almost certain death.

With the transition from spiritual explanations to naturalistic ones, ideas about this affliction were modified. Instead of being explained as curses of God, they were explained as curses of nature. Inheritance and family line of descent became the naturalistic way of accounting for such misfortunes. This view was associated with the evolutionary theories of Charles Darwin and others in the late nineteenth century. Darwin argued that the evolution of a species proceeds through natural variations that occur among the offspring.[1] The weaker and the less capable offspring die off or fail to reproduce, while the stronger and more capable survive and flourish. Through this process of "natural selection" by "the survival of the fittest," the characteristics of the more capable offspring come to dominate the species, and the species itself evolves to a more advanced state.

These were the ideas of the time, and it was natural that they would be applied to the problems of crime. One person who did this was Lombroso, as discussed in Chapters 2 and 3.

Another was Richard Dugdale, who used this basic idea to explain the history of a family he called the "Jukes."[2] As part of his work for the Prison Association of New York, Dugdale found six members of this family in a county jail in 1874. He traced the genealogy of the family back over 200 years and found a history of "pauperism, prostitution, exhaustion, disease, fornication, and illegitimacy." He attributed this melancholy history to the "degenerate" nature of the family. His study had a striking impact on the thinking at the time, despite the fact that it

---

[1]Charles R. Darwin, *On the Origin of Species*, Penguin, New York, 1968 (originally published in 1859).

[2]Richard L. Dugdale, *The Jukes: A Study in Crime, Pauperism and Heredity*, Putnam, New York, 1877; reprinted by Arno, New York, 1977.

was based on unreliable, incomplete, and obscure information and was filled with value judgments and unsupported conclusions. For example, Henderson, writing in 1899, cited the Jukes as typical of families of degenerates and argued that private charitable work to alleviate the suffering of these people was actually allowing them to reproduce in great numbers, resulting in "the rising tide of pauperism, insanity, and crime which threatens to overwhelm and engulf our civilization."[3] He argued that this "deterioration of the common stock" must be resisted by segregating such inferior people in institutions and not allowing them to reproduce.

These studies of degenerate families supported the popular opinion that criminals are what they are because they do not know enough to understand the hazardous nature of criminality or the satisfying rewards of a law-abiding life. But critical scientific judgment requires more exact and systematic procedures than were possible in such case studies before any considered conclusions can be drawn. Accurate comparisons call for exact measurements, and therefore the critical investigation of the relationship between crime and mental ability could come only after the development of intelligence tests and their applications to this problem.

IQ TESTS AND CRIMINAL BEHAVIOR

In 1880 a German psychologist, H. Ebbinghaus (1850–1909), devised a test of the ability to memorize so that the differences observed among individuals in this respect could be expressed on a numerical scale. This is the essential idea of an intelligence test, the object of which is to express numerically differences among persons in their ability to perform a variety of "mental" operations that, taken together, are considered "intelligence" or an indicator of intelligence.[4]

---

[3]C. R. Henderson, "The Relation of Philanthropy to Social Order and Progress," *Proceedings of the National Conference of Charities and Correction* 26: 1–15 (1899); partially reprinted in Frederic L. Faust and Paul J. Brantingham, eds., *Juvenile Justice Philosophy*, 2nd ed., West, St. Paul, 1979, pp. 48–57.

[4]For a short factual account of the development of intelligence tests, see the article by Robert L. Thorndike, "Intelligence and Intelligence Testing," in *International Encyclopedia of the Social Sciences*, Macmillan and The Free Press, New York, 1968, vol. VII, pp. 421–29. Also see textbooks on psychological testing and chapters on this subject in general psychology texts, such as Lee J. Cronbach, *Essentials of Psychological Testing*, 3rd ed., Harper & Row, New York, 1970, pp. 197–226; Philip H. DuBois, *A History of Psychological Testing*, Allyn and Bacon, Boston, 1970; David A. Goshin, *The Search for Ability*, Russell Sage, New York, pp. 19–44; Frank S. Freeman, *Theory and Practice of Psychological Testing*, Holt, Rinehart, and Winston, New York, 1962, pp. 1–23; Gardner Lindzey, Calvin S. Hall, and Richard F. Thompson, *Psychology*, 2nd ed., Worth Publishers, New York, 1978, ch. 12, pp. 351–78.

The distinguished French psychologist Alfred Binet (1857–1911) first took intelligence testing out of the laboratory and applied it to the persisting problem of retardation in the Paris schools. In 1892 he became assistant director of the then recently founded psychological laboratory at the Sorbonne (he became director in 1894, holding that position until his death) and began his lifelong quest for a way to measure intelligence, conceived of as native ability rather than learned behavior.[5] He first tried to assess intelligence by measuring the volume of the skull, following the method of his countryman Paul Broca, but quickly became convinced that such methods were useless. After writing a report on his findings, he abandoned the effort.

In 1904 Binet became a member of a commission to formulate policy for the administration of special classes in the public schools of Paris and returned to the effort to measure intelligence. This time, however, he decided to take a practical approach. He assembled a large number of small tasks related to everyday life but which involved the basic reasoning processes. These were then arranged in ascending difficulty so that the first tasks could be performed by very young children while the last could be performed only by adults. In this task he had the valuable assistance and collaboration of Theodore Simon, the medical officer of the Paris schools. Their first scale of tests appeared in 1905 and was called the *Binet-Simon Scale of Intelligence*.

This scale was revised in 1908, when the concept of *mental age* was added.[6] Binet decided to assign an age level to each task on the test. The typical 9-year-old, for example, would be able to perform the tasks graded for age 9 or younger but not for age 10 or older. The age level of the last tasks the child could perform would then be described as his or her mental age and could be compared with his or her chronological age. In 1912 the psychologist W. Stern suggested that mental age be divided by chronological age and the results multiplied by 100. This would then be called the *intelligence quotient*, or IQ (a quotient being the answer in a division problem). Thus the typical 9-year-old who had a mental age of 9 would have an IQ of 100, smarter 9-year-olds would have IQs above 100, while duller ones would have IQs below 100.

This test was revised again shortly before Binet's death in 1911. At that time Binet expressed his reservations about the ways in which his

---

[5]The following account is derived principally from Stephen Jay Gould, *The Mismeasure of Man*, Norton, New York, 1981, pp. 146–58.

[6]This method of determining IQ has now been discarded in favor of one employing means and standard deviations. For a discussion of the present method, as well as a discussion of the problems of the mental age method, see Cronbach, op. cit., pp. 215–18.

test might be used. The test had been designed to identify children who were doing poorly in school so that they could receive special help. Binet argued that the test should not be used to identify children of superior intelligence, since it was not designed for that purpose. He also warned against using the test to label slower students as unteachable so that, instead of being helped, they would be ejected from the schools. Binet was strongly committed to the view that these slower students could improve their performance if properly helped, and he set up special classes in the Paris schools for the children who did poorly on his tests. He wrote with pleasure of the success of these classes, arguing that the pupils increased not only their knowledge but their intelligence as well: "It is in this practical sense, the only one accessible to us, that we say that the intelligence of these children has been increased. We have increased the intelligence of a pupil: the capacity to learn and to assimilate instruction."[7] Thus Binet rejected the idea that intelligence is a fixed and inborn quantity that cannot be changed.

With the success of the Binet-Simon scale in Paris, numerous revisions, extensions, and adaptations were made in many lands. In the United States Binet's tests and articles were translated into English and popularized by H. H. Goddard of the New Jersey Training School for the Feeble Minded at Vineland. Somewhat later Lewis M. Terman of Stanford University published what became the best-known and most widely used form of the test, called the *Stanford Revision and Extension of the Binet-Simon Scale.* Binet's 1908 scale consisted of fifty-four individual tests arranged in order of difficulty so that the easiest test might be passed by a 3-year-old child, with the most difficult requiring the ability of an average adult. The Stanford Revision consisted of ninety tests, similarly arranged in order of difficulty from the 3-year-old level to that of the "superior adult."

Unlike Binet, the Americans were convinced that intelligence was a fixed and inborn quantity, so that their primary purpose in giving intelligence tests was to sort people into appropriate social roles.[8] Those with IQs above 115 or 120 were said to be appropriate for the professions, while IQ 75 to 85 was appropriate for semiskilled labor. Terman, for example, mentioned that "anything above 85 IQ in a barber probably represents dead waste."[9]

---

[7]Quoted in Gould, op. cit., p. 154.

[8]Lewis M. Terman, *The Measurement of Intelligence,* Houghton Mifflin, Boston, 1916, p. 17; cited in Gould, op. cit., p. 181.

[9]Terman, op. cit., p. 288; quoted in Gould, op. cit., p. 182.

The Americans were particularly concerned with identifying those whose intelligence was "subnormal." Their purpose, however, was the opposite of Binet's: They wished to institutionalize these people and prevent them from reproducing, much like Henderson had suggested earlier. This required that some IQ score be determined to be the dividing line between normal intelligence and feeblemindedness. Goddard gave intelligence tests to all the inmates at his institution at Vineland and to all new inmates on admission. This testing program disclosed no inmate with a mental age over 13. Goddard therefore concluded that mental age 12 (IQ 75 on the then commonly held assumption that full mental ability is reached at chronological age 16) marked the upper limit of feeblemindedness, so that mental age 13 marked the lower limit of normal intelligence.

With that standard as the basis for comparison, Goddard and many other psychologists gave intelligence tests to the inmates of prisons, jails, hospitals, and various other public institutions. Goddard examined a large number of such studies on the intelligence of criminals.[10] The proportion of criminals diagnosed as feebleminded in these studies ranged from 28 to 89 percent, with the median study finding that 70 percent of criminals were feebleminded. Goddard therefore concluded that most criminals were feebleminded.

Goddard also discovered a large group of "defectives" living in the pine barrens of New Jersey and traced their heritage back to a man who had had an illegitimate child by a "feebleminded" barmaid.[11] Of 480 descendants of this union, Goddard claimed that 143 were feebleminded, 36 illegitimate, 33 sexually immoral, 24 confirmed alcoholics, 3 epileptics, 3 criminals, and 8 keepers of houses of prostitution. The man later married a righteous Quaker woman, a union ultimately resulting in 496 "normal" descendants who "married into the best families of their state."

Goddard mourned the "havoc that was wrought by one thoughtless act"[12] and concluded that criminality and feeblemindedness were two aspects of the same degenerate state, so that all feebleminded people

---

[10]H. H. Goddard, *Feeblemindedness: Its Causes and Consequences*, Macmillan, New York, 1914; reprinted by Arno, New York, 1972.

[11]H. H. Goddard, *The Kallikak Family, A Study in the Heredity of Feeble-Mindedness*, Macmillan, New York, 1912. Goddard called this family the "Kallikaks" because the name combined the Greek words for "beauty" (*kallos*) and "bad" (*kakos*). Gould, op. cit., pp. 168–71, points out that Goddard had diagnosed feeblemindedness among this family by sight and did not administer any intelligence tests to them. Goddard also included pictures of them in his book that had been retouched to make them appear evil and retarded.

[12]Goddard, *The Kallikaks*, p. 103.

were potential criminals. Feeblemindedness was said to be caused by a recessive gene that obeyed the normal rules of inheritance originally formulated by Gregor Mendel.[13] Thus Goddard argued that feeblemindedness could be eliminated through selective breeding. This led to his recommendation that the feebleminded be institutionalized and not allowed to reproduce.

These ideas dominated the thinking of mental testers for a time but were directly challenged by the results of intelligence testing administered to draftees during World War I. Following Goddard, the Army Psychological Corps at first made the conventional assumption that those of mental age 12 or below were feebleminded and therefore not fit for military service. This procedure led to a diagnosis of feeblemindedness for 37 percent of the European Americans and 89 percent of the African Americans tested.[14] The patent fallacy of assuming that nearly one half of the population was feebleminded was generally recognized. Thus Goddard wrote, soon after the war, "The most extreme limit that anyone has dared to suggest is that one percent of the population is feebleminded."[15] He later concluded that feeblemindedness might be remedied by education and that it was not necessary to segregate the feebleminded in institutions and to prevent them from reproducing.[16] Goddard was frank about his own change of mind: "As for myself, I think I have gone over to the enemy."[17]

Publication of the results of World War I testing also provided a new perspective on the relationship between intelligence and crime. A number of studies were done comparing the performance of prisoners with that of draftees on intelligence tests. These studies generally found insignificant differences between the two groups,[18] and several studies found that prisoners actually scored higher than draftees.[19] As a result of

---

[13]Goddard, *Feeblemindedness*, p. 539. See the discussion in Gould, op. cit., pp. 158–64.

[14]Robert M. Yerkes, ed., "Psychological Examining in the United States Army," *Memoirs of the National Academy of Sciences*, U.S. Government Printing Office, Washington, DC, 1921, vol. 15, p. 791.

[15]H. H. Goddard, "Feeblemindedness and Delinquency," *Journal of Psycho-Asthenics* 25: 173 (1921).

[16]H. H. Goddard, "Feeblemindedness: A Question of Definition," *Journal of Psycho-Asthenics* 33: 225 (1928).

[17]Ibid., p. 224.

[18]For example, see Simon H. Tulchin, *Intelligence and Crime*, University of Chicago Press, Chicago, 1939; reprinted 1974.

[19]For example, see Carl Murchison, *Criminal Intelligence*, Clark University Press, Worcester, Mass., 1926, ch. 4.

such studies feeblemindedness largely disappeared as a basis for explaining criminal behavior.

DELINQUENCY, RACE, AND IQ

Although it is no longer believed that large numbers of criminals are feebleminded, the IQ of criminals and delinquents has become embroiled in a more recent controversy concerning the relationship between intelligence and race. African Americans, on average, score about 15 points lower than European Americans on IQ tests. Some scholars have used the difference in IQ scores to explain the difference in crime and delinquency rates between the races. Their arguments have generally focused on the issue of delinquency rather than crime in general, and it is there that the stronger case has been made.

However, these arguments must be considered in the context of the overall controversy about the meaning of IQ scores. First, there is a controversy about whether IQ measures intelligence or whether it measures such other factors as academic achievement, reading ability, or "test-wiseness." If one assumes that IQ actually does measure intelligence, then there is a controversy about whether the tests are "culturally biased" so that the intelligence of minority groups is underreported. Finally, if there is a real difference between the intelligence of African Americans and European Americans, then there is a controversy about whether this difference is the result of genetic or environmental influence.[20]

The seeds of this controversy are found in a 1967 speech before the National Academy of Sciences by William Shockley, a winner of the Nobel Prize for physics for his role in the invention of the transistor.[21] Shockley speculated that the differences in IQ between African Americans and European Americans might be solely the result of genetic differences and that these genetic differences might also explain the differences in poverty and crime rates between these groups. He also suggested that "IQ test results may actually be a deeper measure, at least on a statistical basis, of a distribution of some more fundamental

---

[20]A review discussing this controversy can be found in R. A. Weinberg, "Intelligence and IQ: Landmark Issues and Great Debates," *American Psychologist* 44: 98–104 (1989).

[21]W. Shockley, "A 'Try Simplest Cases' Approach to the Heredity-Poverty-Crime Problem," *Proceedings of the National Academy of Sciences* 57(6): 1767–74 (June 1967). Shockley founded a sperm bank for geniuses, with himself as the first donor, as part of his efforts to increase the genetic endowment of the human race.

social capacity." He did not actually argue that the all-genetic model was correct, but urged that a National Study Group be set up to research the problem and to make recommendations if the IQ-Poverty-Crime problem was found to be related to genetic differences.[22]

In 1969 Arthur Jensen published a lengthy article in which he positively argued many of the points on which Shockley had only speculated.[23] Specifically, he contended that IQ tests do measure a factor that is important for performance in Western industrialized societies, and that about 80 percent of the individual differences on this score are determined by genetic rather than environmental differences. He concluded that remedial education programs had failed for precisely this reason. This article set off the large IQ controversy just mentioned.

Jensen's article was used by Gordon to argue that variations in delinquency rates are best explained by variations in IQ.[24] Gordon cited Jensen to the effect that IQ is largely a biological factor, and quoted several studies that support the hypothesis that delinquency is related to the biology of the individual. He pointed to the similarity between the distribution of IQ scores and the distribution of delinquency, and demonstrated that court record data from Philadelphia and national rates for commitment to training schools could be duplicated merely by assuming that all youths (both African American and European American) with IQs below a certain level, and no youths above it, became delinquent. He did not argue that such a relationship between IQ and delinquency actually exists, but that this coincidence "virtually necessitate(s) that there be some more reasonable functional relationship within sex between IQ and delinquency that is common or nearly common to both races." He went on to argue, without supporting data, that the delinquency rates of several other racial groups are also related to IQ. Japanese, Chinese, and Jewish Americans have maintained low delinquency rates despite their minority group status and generally low eco-

---

[22]Several such committees were set up. They concluded that this problem merited study, but denied that it was especially urgent. See "Recommendations with Respect to the Behavioral and Social Aspects of Human Genetics," *Proceedings of the National Academy of Sciences* 69: 1–3 (1972). By 1977, however, the question had become so volatile that one scholar, Herbert C. Kelman of Harvard, argued that it would seem advisable "to forgo research at this time on genetic differences in intelligence among racial groups." See Herbert C. Kelman, "Privacy and Research with Human Beings," *Journal of Social Issues* 33(3): 169–95 (1977).

[23]A. R. Jensen, "How Much Can We Boost IQ and Scholastic Achievement?" *Harvard Educational Review* 39: 1–123 (1969).

[24]Robert Gordon, "Prevalence: The Rare Datum in Delinquency Measurement and Its Implications for the Theory of Delinquency," in Malcolm W. Klein, ed., *The Juvenile Justice System,* Sage Publications, Beverly Hills, CA., 1976, pp. 201–84.

nomic position, and these groups are said to have somewhat higher IQs than European Americans. Mexican Americans are said to have both delinquency rates and average IQs somewhere in between those of African Americans and European Americans.

In a later article, Gordon responded to the frequent criticism that his results reflect differences in social class between African American and European American youth, and that they do not prove anything about a relationship between delinquency and intelligence.[25] If that were the case, Gordon reasoned, then direct measures of social class would predict delinquency better than indirect measures such as IQ. Gorden identified several measures of social class, including male income, family income, educational attainment, and occupational status. He then demonstrated that these direct measures of social class could not do what the IQ data had done: duplicate the Philadelphia juvenile court record data and the national training school commitment rates merely by assuming that all youths below a certain "class," and no youths above it, became delinquent. The social class measures that came closest to duplicating those rates were those that, according to Gordon, most closely approximated intelligence.

Additional support for the association between IQ and delinquency was presented by Travis Hirschi and Michael Hindelang, who reviewed a number of studies on the subject.[26] They found that low IQ was at least as important as social class or race in predicting official delinquency and that it was more important in predicting self-reported delinquency;[27] that delinquency is consistently related to low IQ within races and within social classes so that, for example, lower-class delinquents are more likely to have low IQs than lower-class nondelinquents;[28] and that the principal sociological theories of delinquency "have been saying for

---

[25]Robert A. Gordon, "SES versus IQ in the Race-IQ-Delinquency Model," *International Journal of Sociology and Social Policy* 7(3): 30–96 (1987).

[26]Travis Hirschi and Michael J. Hindelang, "Intelligence and Delinquency: A Revisionist Review," *American Sociological Review* 42: 572–87 (1977).

[27]The term *official delinquency* refers to delinquent behaviors that have been recorded in the official records of criminal justice agencies and thus have become part of official delinquency statistics. *Self-reported delinquency* refers to delinquent behaviors reported by juveniles anonymously on questionnaires, and includes much behavior that is not known to criminal justice agencies.

[28]The studies cited with respect to delinquency within social classes are A. J. Reiss, Jr. and A. L. Rhodes, "The Distribution of Juvenile Delinquency in the Social Structure, *American Sociological Review* 26: 720–32 (Oct. 1961). Travis Hirschi, *Causes of Delinquency*, University of California Press, Berkeley, 1969. Marvin Wolfgang, Robert M. Figlio, and Thorsten Sellin, *Delinquency in a Birth Cohort*, University of Chicago Press, Chicago, 1972; and D. J. West, *Who Becomes Delinquent?*, Heinemann, London, 1972. The studies cited for delinquency within races are Wolfgang et al., op. cit.; Hirschi, *Causes of Delinquency*; James F. Short, Jr., and Fred L. Strodtbeck, *Group Process and Gang Delinquency*, University of Chicago Press, Chicago, 1965; and Jackson Toby and

some time that IQ should be related to delinquency for the same reason social class is, or should be, related to it."[29] They argue that IQ as an explanation of crime and delinquency has been ignored in criminology because a strong bias against it arose in the early part of this century. At that time IQ as an explanation of crime and delinquency was strongly associated with the physicians (such as Goring and Goddard) who had dominated the field of criminology since the time of Lombroso. The sociologists who were beginning to take over the field were eager to focus attention on the effects of social conditions and away from the characteristics of the individual. Over the previous twenty years decreasing proportions of criminals and delinquents had been reported as feebleminded because of the repeated lowering of the "normal" mental age. Hirschi and Hindelang state that Sutherland "called attention to this twenty-year trend—which, in fact, continued for another 30 years—and allowed his readers to conclude that it would continue until the initial claims of difference between delinquents and nondelinquents had no foundation in fact."[30] But Hirschi and Hindelang point out that the difference between these two groups never entirely disappeared and seemed to stabilize at about eight IQ points.[31] Later studies have also found that more serious offenders have even lower IQ scores than minor offenders,[32] and that low IQ scores among small children are associated with later offending when these children become adolescents and adults.[33]

Marcia L. Toby, "Low School Status as a Predisposing Factor in Subcultural Delinquency," Mimeo, Rutgers University, New Brunswick, NJ, 1961.

[29]Hirschi and Hindelang, op. cit., p. 579. Support for this statement is derived largely from a review of Albert Cohen's *Delinquent Boys*, The Free Press, New York, 1955. Cloward and Ohlin's theory (*Delinquency and Opportunity*, The Free Press, New York, 1960) is said to predict that higher-IQ youths are more likely to become delinquent; labeling and conflict theories are said to be consistent with the low-IQ argument, since the system is seen as discriminating against these youth; Sutherland's "differential association" theory (Edwin H. Sutherland and Donald R. Cressey, *Criminology*, Lippincott, Philadelphia, 1978, pp. 80–83) is "strictly silent" on the matter; and "social control" theories are consistent with this view, although they have not emphasized it in the past.

[30]Hirschi and Hindelang, op. cit., p. 580. The reference is to Edwin H. Sutherland, "Mental Deficiency and Crime," pp. 357–75 in Kimball Young, ed., *Social Attitudes*, Henry Holt, New York, 1931; partially reprinted in Stephen Schafer and Richard D. Knudten, eds., *Criminological Theory*, D. C. Heath, Lexington, MA, 1977, pp. 157–60.

[31]This difference does not seem to be caused by problems in the administration of the tests. See Ronald Blackburn, *The Psychology of Criminal Conduct*, John Wiley, Chichester, England, 1993, pp. 186–89.

[32]Alfred Blumstein, David P. Farrington, and Soumyo Moitra, "Delinquency Careers," pp. 187–219, in Michael H. Tonry and Norval Morris, eds., *Crime and Justice: A Review of Research*, University of Chicago Press, Chicago, 1985; Deborah W. Denno, *Biology and Violence*, Cambridge University Press, New York, 1990.

[33]Paul D. Lipsitt, Stephen L. Buka, and Lewis P. Lipsitt, "Early Intelligence Scores and Subsequent Delinquency," *American Journal of Family Therapy* 18: 197–208 (1990).

More recently, attention has focused on the verbal abilities of delinquents, as measured by IQ tests, and on the difference between the
"verbal IQ" and the so-called "performance IQ." The verbal IQ measures the person's comprehension of language while the performance
IQ measures the degree of nonverbal contact with environment and the
capacity to work in concrete situations. For most people, the verbal and
performance IQ scores are quite close to each other. But delinquents
consistently show a large gap between the two scores, with lower verbal
IQ scores but basically normal performance IQ scores.[34]

Quay suggests several reasons why low verbal IQ may be associated
with delinquency.[35] First, low verbal ability may lead to school problems, and the school problems may then lead to delinquency. Second,
low verbal abilities may be associated with a variety of other psychosocial problems, and those other problems may then lead to delinquency. Finally, low verbal abilities may lead to a failure to develop higher-
order cognitive processing such as moral reasoning, empathy, and
problem solving. The lack of these cognitive processes may then lead to
delinquency.

Other theorists, however, point out that verbal IQ is affected by educational achievement while performance IQ is not.[36] This suggests that
the pattern of low verbal but normal performance IQ among delinquents may simply reflect the fact that they tend to underachieve in
schools, particularly if they are from the lower socioeconomic class.

INTERPRETING THE ASSOCIATION BETWEEN
DELINQUENCY AND IQ

It seems clear that, whatever it measures, low IQ scores are associated
with crime and delinquency. But it is still necessary to explain why people with low IQ scores commit crimes more frequently than those with
high scores. The explanation one accepts will depend to a large degree
on one's view of what IQ measures.

The most common approach among those who study the IQ-
delinquency relation is to assume that *IQ measures some form of abstract
reasoning or problem-solving ability and that this ability is largely in-*

---

[34]R. J. Herrnstein, "Criminogenic Traits," in James Q. Wilson and Joan Petersilia, eds., *Crime,* Institute for Contemporary Studies Press, San Francisco, 1995, pp. 49–53.

[35]Herbert C. Quay, "Intelligence," pp. 106–17 in Quay, ed., *Handbook of Juvenile Delinquency,* Wiley, New York, 1987.

[36]Gary Groth-Marnat, *Handbook of Psychological Assessment,* Van Nostrand Reinhold, New York,
1984, p. 76.

herited. Gordon, for example, assumes this perspective and suggests that ineffective child-rearing practices by low-IQ parents might be the cause of delinquency among their low-IQ children.[37] Hirschi and Hindelang also believe that IQ measures innate ability, but argue that IQ influences delinquency through its effect on school performance: Low-IQ youths do poorly in school, which leads to anger at the school and to truancy, which then leads to delinquency.[38] This argument is consistent with research that shows that the school characteristics associated with educational failure are the same school characteristics associated with delinquency: high student-teacher ratios, low student attendance, high student turnover, and poor academic quality.[39] More recently, Gottfredson and Hirschi have suggested that youths with low intelligence tend to seek short-term immediate gratifications, where these actions often turn out to be criminal.[40] A similar argument was made by Wilson and Herrnstein, who suggest that those with low IQ are inclined to commit "impulsive crimes with immediate rewards."[41] All of these interpretations assume that IQ scores measure some form of innate ability.

In a second approach, it could be argued that *IQ does not measure innate ability, but instead measures qualities that are related to the dominant culture.* Jane Mercer illustrated the meaning of cultural bias by constructing a test of simple behavioral tasks related to intelligence, such as being able to tie one's own shoes by the age of 7.[42] The test was given to samples of lower-class African Americans and Mexican Americans, and middle-class European Americans, all of whom had IQs below 70. Of the African Americans, 91 percent were able to pass the test, of the Mexican Americans, 61 percent passed, whereas none of the European Americans did. This would indicate that many African Americans and Mexican Americans may be more intelligent than would appear from their IQ scores.

---

[37]Gordon, op. cit., p. 269.

[38]Hirschi and Hindelang, op. cit.

[39]D. A. Hellman and S. Beaton, "The Pattern of Violence in Urban Public Schools," *Journal of Research in Crime and Delinquency* 23: 102–27 (1986). See also Kenneth Polk, "The New Marginal Youth," *Crime and Delinquency* 30: 648–59 (1984); and W. T. Pink, "Schools, Youth, and Justice," *Crime and Delinquency* 30: 439–61 (1984).

[40]Michael R. Gottfredson and Travis Hirschi, *A General Theory of Crime*, Stanford University Press, Stanford, 1990.

[41]James Q. Wilson and Richard J. Herrnstein, *Crime and Human Nature*, Simon & Schuster, New York, 1985.

[42]Jane Mercer, "IQ: The Lethal Label," *Psychology Today*, Sept. 1972, pp. 44–47ff. For a critique of Mercer, see Robert A. Gordon, "Examining Labelling Theory: The Case of Mental Retardation," in Walter R. Gove, ed., *The Labelling of Deviance: Evaluating a Perspective*, Halsted-Wiley, New York, 1975, pp. 35–81.

A third approach would be to argue that *IQ measures general abilities, but that those abilities are largely determined by the person's environment.* Simons criticized Hirschi and Hindelang's interpretation of the relationship between IQ and delinquency by citing this literature.[43] He cited a number of studies that reported IQ gains averaging about 15 points when low-IQ, lower-class children were placed in special classes, where most of those gains were produced in about one year's time. Hirschi and Hindelang had reported an average gap of only 8 points between delinquents and nondelinquents. Simons concluded that IQ is best viewed as "a broad set of verbal and problem-solving skills which are better labeled academic aptitude or scholastic readiness." He pointed out that the questions on standard verbal intelligence tests are virtually indistinguishable from those on reading comprehension tests, and that the score distributions from the two types of tests are virtually identical. He also cited a study that showed that children in the early grades of lower-class African-American schools and of middle-class African American schools had similar reading comprehension test scores, but by the eighth grade there were large differences between the two groups. That suggests that the lower-class children's interactions with their schools stagnated their growth, and that they were not mentally inferior to begin with. Finally, Simons pointed out that delinquents are almost always described as unmotivated students, and asked why anyone would think that these students would be motivated to perform to the best of their ability on the day the IQ tests are administered when they are not motivated to do so on any other school day.

POLICY IMPLICATIONS OF THE IQ–DELINQUENCY LINK

If low intelligence directly causes delinquency and if intelligence itself is largely determined by inborn biological characteristics, then some people might think, as did Goddard and Henderson, that the only option would be to prevent low-IQ people from reproducing. But in fact that would not be true. Instead, the situation with low IQ would be similar to the situation with biologically based learning disabilities. Such learning disabilities make it difficult for children to learn in a normal classroom environment, but that does not mean these children cannot learn.

---

[43]Ronald L. Simons, "The Meaning of the IQ-Delinquency Relationship," *American Sociological Review* 43: 268–70 (April 1978). See also Scott Menard and Barbara J. Morse, "A Structuralist Critique of the IQ-Delinquency Hypothesis: Theory and Evidence," *American Journal of Sociology* 89(6): 1347–78 (May 1984). They argue that IQ exerts no causal influence on delinquent behavior but is a criterion used for differential treatment in certain institutional settings.

Rather, it means some relatively straightforward steps need to be taken to accommodate the children's special needs. Similarly, if low intelligence were found to have a direct causal effect on delinquency, then some relatively straightforward steps would have to be taken to ensure that these children are properly socialized.

But beyond that, most researchers today do not argue that low intelligence directly causes delinquency. Rather, they argue that there is some intervening factor that is associated with low intelligence, and that the intervening factor actually causes delinquency. For example, Gordon suggests that ineffective child-rearing practices by low IQ parents might be the cause of delinquency in their low-IQ children. If this is the case, then poor parenting is the cause of delinquency, not low intelligence. Special classes to teach effective parenting skills to low-IQ parents therefore should reduce the risk of delinquency in their low-IQ children. Similarly, Hirschi and Hindelang suggest that low intelligence causes school failure, and that school failure then causes delinquency. But delinquent children, on the average, score only eight IQ points lower than their non-delinquent peers, so providing these children with extra help in school should eliminate their greater risk of school failure, and therefore eliminate their increased risk of delinquency. Similarly, Quay has suggested that low intelligence affects delinquency through the failure to learn higher cognitive skills, such as moral reasoning, empathy, or problem solving. But again, delinquent children on the average score only eight IQ points lower than nondelinquent children, so they could be taught these skills with a little extra effort much as children with learning disabilities are taught reading and math. This instruction should eliminate their increased risk of delinquency.

Finally, it is important to remember that intelligence itself cannot be directly measured, and the principle measure of intelligence—IQ scores—may instead measure reading ability or the motivation to succeed at academic tasks. If this is the case, then the overall difference in IQ scores between delinquents and nondelinquents probably reflects environmental rather than genetic factors.

PERSONALITY AND CRIMINAL BEHAVIOR

The term *personality* refers to the complex set of emotional and behavioral attributes that tend to remain relatively constant as the individual moves from situation to situation. Commonsense notions of what constitutes personality generally have focused on qualities of the individual other than intellectual ability. Words such as *aggressive, belligerent, suspicious, timid, withdrawn, friendly, cooperative, likable, argumentative,* and *agreeable* have long been used to describe or express impressions of some of these qualities. Psychological tests to measure personality differences have been developed more or less parallel to intelligence tests. Inevitably, delinquents and criminals have been tested with these "personality inventories" to discover how their personalities differ from those of nondelinquents and noncriminals.

In 1950, the Gluecks published an intensive study that compared 500 delinquent and 500 nondelinquent boys.[44] They argued that "the delinquent personality" is not so much a matter of the presence or absence of certain characteristics, but is more a matter of the interrelatedness of these characteristics. The Gluecks summarize their impression of this interrelationship of characteristics as follows:[45]

On the whole, delinquents are more extroverted, vivacious, impulsive, and less self-controlled than the non-delinquents. They are more hostile, resentful, defiant, suspicious, and destructive. They are less fearful of failure or defeat than the non-delinquents. They are less concerned about meeting conventional expectations, and are more ambivalent toward or far less submissive to authority. They are, as a group, more socially assertive. To a greater extent than the control group, they express feelings of not being recognized or appreciated.

There are a number of desirable features in this description of the delinquent, which can be confusing from the point of view of theory. Often, theories about the "delinquent"or "criminal" personality are based on the implicit assumption that delinquents are somehow defective and therefore inferior to nondelinquents. This, of course, is the same assumption found in earlier theories related to biology and intelligence. But the gluecks' description would suggest that a delinquent may be, and often is, as attractive and socially acceptable as a nondelinquent.

Even if these findings are confusing from the standpoint of theory making, the differences between delinquents and nondelinquents nevertheless lend themselves to making statistical predictions. The Gluecks developed three prediction tables,[46] one based on factors in the social background, one based on character traits as determined by the Rorschach test, and one based on personality traits as determined in the psychiatric interview. All three are said to give impressive results. For example, only about 10 percent of juveniles in the best-score class may

---

[44]Sheldon Glueck and Eleanor Glueck, *Unraveling Juvenile Delinquency*, Commonwealth Fund, New York, 1950.

[45]Ibid., p. 275.

[46]Ibid., pp. 257–71 for detailed tables.

be expected to become delinquent, as opposed to about 90 percent in the worst-score class.[47]

Similar results have been obtained with the Minnesota Multiphasic Personality Inventory (MMPI), which is a list of 550 statements developed to aid in psychiatric diagnosis.[48] People who take the MMPI indicate whether the statements in the test are true or false about themselves. Ten different scales are then scored and assumed to measure different aspects of the personality. These scales were originally identified by the names of the psychiatric symptoms or pathologics they were assumed to measure, such as hypochondriasis, depression, or hysteria. Since the MMPI is now often used with normal individuals, the scales are now identified by number only (Scale 1, Scale 2, etc.). The ten scores a person gets on the ten scales are then arranged into a "profile," so that no single score indicates a person's performance on the MMPI.[49]

Waldo and Dinitz examined ninety-four personality studies performed between 1950 and 1965 and found that about 80 percent of these studies reported statistically significant differences between criminals and noncriminals.[50] The most impressive results were found with Scale 4 of the MMPI, previously called the "psychopathic deviate" scale, which consistently produced significant results. These studies generally concluded that delinquents and criminals were more "psychopathic" than nondelinquents and noncriminals.

Scale 4, however, includes statements such as "I have never been in trouble with the law," "Sometimes when I was young I stole things," "I like school," and "My relatives are nearly all in sympathy with me." On the average, nondelinquents and noncriminals responded to four of

---

[47]Ibid., Table XX-3, p. 262. The predictive validity of a revised table was supported in studies by M. M. Craig and S. J. Glick ("Ten Years' Experience with the Glueck Social Prediction Table," *Crime and Delinquency* 9: 249–61 [1963]; and "Application of the Glueck Social Prediction Table on an Ethnic Basis," *Crime and Delinquency* 11: 175–78 [1965]) and N. B. Trevvett ("Identifying Delinquency-Prone Children," *Crime and Delinquency* 11: 186–91 [1965]). Kurt Weis ("The Glueck Social Prediction Table: An Unfulfilled Promise," *Journal of Criminal Law, Criminology and Police Science* 65: 397–404 [1974]), however, argued that its results are only slightly better than chance.

[48]For a full discussion of the use of the MMPI, see S. R. Hathaway and P. E. Meehl, *An Atlas for the Clinical Use of the MMPI*, University of Minnesota Press, Minneapolis, 1951; for an account of its application and use in the study of delinquency, see S. R. Hathaway and E. D. Monachesi, *Analyzing and Predicting Juvenile Delinquency with the MMPI* (1953) and *Adolescent Personality and Behavior* (1963), both published by the University of Minnesota Press, Minneapolis. A more recent review of studies using the MMPI on criminals can be found in Edwin I. Megargee and Martin J. Bohn, Jr., *Classifying Criminal Offenders*, Sage, Beverly Hills, CA, 1979.

[49]For a full discussion of the profiles, see Hathaway and Meehl, *An Atlas;* a short account may be found in Hathaway and Monachesi, *Analyzing and Predicting*, pp. 19–23.

[50]Gordon P. Waldo and Simon Dinitz, "Personality Attributes of the Criminal: An Analysis of Research Studies, 1950–1965," *Journal of Research in Crime and Delinquency* 4(2): 185–202 (July 1967).

these statements differently than did delinquents and criminals. This may simply reflect differences in the situations and circumstances of their lives, rather than any increased "psychopathy" among delinquents and criminals.[51] It seems best to conclude that the differences that appear between criminals and noncriminals on personality tests do not have any theoretical relevance to understanding the causes of criminal behavior or to treating it.[52]

ANTISOCIAL PERSONALITY DISORDER

In addition to appearing on personality inventories, the term psychopath is used by psychiatrists to describe individuals who exhibit a certain group of behaviors and attitudes.[53] When used in this way, the term psychopath can be considered synonymous with the more recent terms sociopath and antisocial personality disorder. The three terms are used interchangeably in this section.

The fourth edition of the official *Diagnostic and Statistical Manual* (DSM-4) of the American Psychiatric Association states that "the essential feature of Antisocial Personality Disorder is a pervasive pattern of disregard for, and violation of, the rights of others that begins in childhood or early adolescence and comes into adulthood."[54] The diagnosis may be made when there are at least three of the following six characteristics: (1) repeated violations of the law that are grounds for arrest; (2) repeated lying, use of aliases, or conning others for personal profit or pleasure; (3) impulsivity or failure to plan ahead; (4) repeated physical fights or assaults; (5) repeated failure to sustain consistent work behavior or honor financial obligations; and (6) lack of remorse.

The DSM-4 distinguishes "antisocial personality disorder" from "adult antisocial behavior," which is criminal behavior that occurs with-

---

[51]In fact, Scale 4 had originally been constructed by listing statements that "normal" persons said were true about themselves and that "psychopaths" said were not. The original "psychopathic" group consisted largely of young delinquents, so that a person who scores high on Scale 4 makes responses to the statements that are similar to the responses of a group consisting primarily of young delinquents. It should not be surprising if that person is also a delinquent.

[52]Blackburn, op. cit., pp. 185–86; Jack Arbuthnot, Donald A. Gordon, and Gregory J. Jurkovic, "Personality," in Herbert C. Quay, ed., *Handbook of Juvenile Delinquency*, John Wiley, New York, 1987, pp. 139–83.

[53]See Blackburn, op. cit., pp. 80–86; Harold I. Kapland and Benjamin J. Sadock, *Synopsis of Psychiatry*, 6th ed., Williams and Wilkins, Baltimore, 1991, pp. 532–33.

[54]*Diagnostic and Statistical Manual of Mental Disorders*, 4th ed., American Psychiatric Association, Washington, D.C., 1994, pp. 645–50.

out the presence of any personality disorder. A person should be diagnosed as having "antisocial personality disorder" when these characteristics are "inflexible, maladaptive, and persistent, and cause significant functional impairment or subjective distress." The DSM-4 also states that the antisocial personality disorder "has a chronic course but may become less evident or remit as the individual grows older, particularly by the fourth decade of life."

The DSM-4 attempts to provide a fairly precise definition of the term "antisocial personality," especially so that it can be distinguished from criminality. In practice, however, Cleckley points out that "the term psychopath (or antisocial personality) as it is applied by various psychiatrists and hospital staffs sometimes becomes so broad that it can be applied to almost any criminal."[55] He argues, however, that the majority of psychopaths are not criminals, and the majority of criminals are not psychopaths. Psychopaths may be found in any profession, including business, science, medicine, and psychiatry.[56] Typical psychopaths differ from typical criminals in that their actions seem less purposeful, they cause themselves needless sorrow and shame, and they usually do not commit major crimes or crimes of violence.[57]

These terms "psychopath" and "antisocial personality" are not merely descriptions of behavior patterns, but also imply that those behaviors originate in the personality of the individual. It is possible, however, that the behaviors may be explained by factors other than personality. For example, Yablonsky argued that "core" members of violent gangs were sociopaths who led the gang in moblike violence as a way of acting out their own hostility and aggression.[58] Other gang researchers described the behavior of core gang members in a similar way, but argued that the behavior resulted from the need to create and maintain a leadership position in the gang.[59] Thus, the origin of these behaviors may not lie in personality characteristics.

Because psychiatrists tend to assume that antisocial actions originate in the personality of the offender, some psychiatrists have recommended that people with "antisocial personality disorder" be locked up until

---

[55]Hervey Cleckley, *The Mask of Sanity*, Mosby, St. Louis, 1976, p. 263.

[56]Ibid., pp. 188–221.

[57]Ibid., pp. 261–63.

[58]Louis Yablonsky, *The Violent Gang*, Penguin, New York, 1970, pp. 236–47.

[59]James F. Short, Jr., and Fred L. Stodtbeck, *Group Process and Gang Delinquency*, University of Chicago Press, Chicago, 1974, especially pp. 248–64. This material had been previously published in *Social Problems* 12: 127–40 (fall 1964).

they reach middle age,[60] and even that they be executed.[61] This is because psychiatrists have no effective methods for treating this disorder,
so they assume that the person will continue to commit antisocial actions if allowed to remain free. But this assumption is not supported by
a study by William McCord, who has done extensive work on psychopaths and crime.[62] McCord found that delinquents who had been diagnosed as psychopathic at two juvenile institutions had only slightly
worse recidivism rates than other delinquents at the same institutions,
and that several years after release the recidivism rates were identical.

Walters reviewed research on what he called the violence-prone personality.[63] In particular, he examined the extent to which such a personality might be inherited, and the extent to which it is stable across time
and across situations. For a whole variety of reasons, he rejected this
concept and argued that it should be replaced with eight more specific
concepts. At this point, it seems reasonable to conclude that the search
for a general personality type which can be considered a cause of crime
and violence has come to an end.

PSYCHIATRIC PREDICTION OF FUTURE DANGEROUSNESS

Some psychiatrists recommend that offenders with antisocial personality disorder be locked up for extended periods of time. While this may be
a reasonable policy for frequent and serious offenders, psychiatrists go
further by arguing that they are able to identify these offenders through
psychiatric means. If that is their claim, then their track record so far has
been poor.[64]

For example, a ten-year study in Massachusetts by Kozol and associates[65] involved the use of extensive psychiatric and social casework services in the attempt to predict the future likely dangerousness of a group

---

[60]E.g., Samuel B. Guze, *Criminality and Psychiatric Disorders*, Oxford University Press, New York, 1976, p. 137.

[61]Charles Patrick Ewing, "Preventive Detention and Execution: The Constitutionality of Punishing Future Crimes," *Law and Human Behavior* 15(2): 139–63 (1991).

[62]William McCord, *The Psychopath and Milieu Therapy*, Academic Press, New York, 1982. See also William McCord and Jose Sanchez, "The Treatment of Deviant Children: A Twenty-Five-Year Follow-Up Study," *Crime and Delinquency* 29(2): 238–53 (April 1983).

[63]Glenn D. Walters, "Disposed to Aggress? In Search of the Violence-Prone Personality," *Aggression and Violent Behavior* 5(2): 177–90 (2000).

[64]For a review, see Blackburn, op. cit., pp. 328–35.

[65]Harry L. Kozol, Richard J. Boucher, and Ralph F. Garofalo, "The Diagnosis and Treatment of Dangerousness," *Crime and Delinquency* 18: 371–92 (1972).

of high-risk offenders prior to their release from prison. As it turned out, the researchers were unable to predict nearly two thirds of the violent crime that ultimately occurred (thirty-one crimes out of forty-eight), and nearly two thirds of the persons whom they predicted would be violent (thirty-two persons out of forty-nine) were not. Because of the probable occurrence of such errors, Morris argues that it is fundamentally unjust to detain anyone on the basis of a prediction of his future behavior.[66] In addition, the idea that a person can be punished for what he *might* do rather than for what he has actually done seriously threatens the basic notions of freedom of the individual from unwarranted governmental control.[67]

Monahan extensively reviewed the clinical techniques for predicting violent behavior and concluded that it can only be done within very restricted circumstances.[68] Specifically, he concluded that it is possible to estimate the probability of a violent act in the immediate future when the person is going to remain in a situation that is essentially similar to ones in which he or she had committed violent acts in the past. Monahan presented a complex procedure for estimating this probability, which included: (1) a comparison of the circumstances the offender was likely to encounter in the near future with the circumstances in which the offender had committed violent acts in the past; (2) the recency, severity, and frequency of violent acts the individual had committed in the past; and (3) general statistics on the probability of violence for individuals who are similar in age, sex, race, class, history of drug abuse, residential and employment stability, and educational attainment. Monahan stated that it is not possible to predict violence over a long period of time, or to predict it when a person was moving from one situation to a very different one (e.g., on being released from prison). He also maintained that this type of prediction is entirely separate from the diagnosis of mental disease, and that if mental disease is also of interest, a separate examination must be undertaken. Finally Monahan argued that psychologists should confine themselves to estimating the probability of a violent act and should not recommend whether any official action should be taken in a given case. According to Monahan, criminal justice officials are responsible for deciding whether or not to take official actions while

---

[66]Norval Morris, *The Future of Imprisonment,* University of Chicago Press, Chicago, 1974, pp. 71–73.

[67]Ibid., pp. 83–84.

[68]John Monahan, *Predicting Violent Behavior,* Sage, Beverly Hills, CA, 1981.

the role of psychologists and psychiatrists is to provide accurate information on which to base those decisions.

EARLY CHILDHOOD PREDICTORS OF LATER CRIME AND DELINQUENCY

Psychological and psychiatric researchers have now turned away from the question of trying to predict whether particular *individuals* will commit acts of violence in the future. Instead, researchers now are attempting to identify *factors* that are associated with an increased or decreased likelihood that an individual will commit crime in the future. With respect to particular individuals, then, the prediction becomes probabilistic: This individual has many factors and so has a high risk of committing crime in the future, while that individual has few factors and so has a low risk. In addition, most of this research has focused on delinquency rather than adult criminality, and on less serious crime rather than more serious violence, since these are easier to predict.

The strongest predictor of later delinquent and criminal behavior is earlier childhood problem behaviors such as disruptive classroom conduct, aggressiveness, lying, and dishonesty.[69] This means that the same individuals who caused the most problems when they were young children will also cause the most problems when they are adolescents and adults. Other factors in early childhood that are associated with later delinquency and crime include poor parental child management techniques, offending by parents and siblings, low intelligence and educational attainment, and separation from parents.[70] These findings suggest that the later crime and delinquency may be associated with or caused by early childhood experiences. For example, based on a broad review of the research and on interviews with young men in prisons, Garbarino argues that "senseless" youth violence can be explained in terms of early traumatic childhood experiences.[71]

---

[69]E.g., Rolf Loeber, David P. Farrington, Magda Stouthamer-Loeber et al., "The Development of Male Offending: Key Findings from the First Decade of the Pittsburgh Youth Study," *Studies on Crime and Crime Prevention* 7(2): 141–71 (1998); Lynn Kartzer and Sheilagh Hodgins, "Adult Outcomes of Child Conduct Problems," *Journal of Abnormal Child Psychology* 25(1): 65–81 (1997).

[70]For reviews, see David P. Farrington, "Predictors, Causes, and Correlates of Male Youth Violence," pp. 421–75 in Michael Tonry and Mark H. Moore, eds., *Youth Violence* (vol. 24 of *Crime and Justice: A Review of Research*), University of Chicago Press, Chicago, 1998; Rolf Loeber and David P. Farrington, eds., *Serious and Violent Juvenile Offenders: Risk Factors and Successful Interventions,* Sage, Thousand Oaks, CA, 1996; and David P. Farrington, "Introduction," in Farrington, ed., *Psychological Explanations of Crime*, Dartmouth, Aldershot, England, 1994, p. xv.

[71]James Garbarino, *Lost Boys: Why Our Sons Turn Violent and How We Can Save Them*, The Free Press, New York, 1999. For a discussion of longer-range effects of early childhood traumatic expe-

Research on the predictors of future delinquency has generally led to an optimistic view about our ability to influence those factors. For example, Loeber and Farrington argue that it is "never too early" and also "never too late" to successfully intervene even with the most serious and violent juvenile offenders.[72] This optimism is in stark contrast to the earlier pessimism about the ability of psychiatrists and psychologists to treat antisocial personality disorder.

IMPULSIVITY AND CRIME

A rather diverse group of researchers have recently suggested that impulsivity is the key personality feature associated with antisocial behavior.[73] In general, these researchers assume that impulsivity is manifested in high levels of activity (especially where the person acts without thinking), a tendency to become impatient and to seek immediate gratification, and a tendency to become distracted.[74]

One theory that focused on this characteristic was by Wilson and Herrnstein.[75] Farrington describes this as a "typical psychological explanation of crime, incorporating propositions seen in several other psychological theories."[76] In general, those propositions include the assumption that crime is inherently rewarding, so that everyone would commit it unless we were restrained by internal inhibitions. These internal inhibitions are associated with what is normally called "conscience," and are developed primarily in early childhood by parents

---

riences, in the context of case studies of adult murderers, see Dorothy Otnow Lewis, *Guilty by Reason of Insanity*, Ballantine, New York, 1998.

[72]Rolf Loeber and David P. Farrington, "Never Too Early, Never Too Late: Risk Factors and Successful Interventions for Serious and Violent Juvenile Offenders," *Studies on Crime and Crime Prevention* 7(1): 7–30 (1998). For other optimistic policy recommendations for preventing "senseless" violence"" among young males, see Garbarino, op. cit.

[73]See, for example, the collection of articles in Alan R. Felthous, ed., "Impulsive Aggression," *Behavioral Sciences & the Law* 16(3): 281–389 (1998); David P. Farrington, "Have Any Individual, Family, or Neighbourhood Influences on Offending Been Demonstrated Conclusively?" in Farrington, Robert J. Sampson, and P. O. Wikstrom, eds., *Integrating Individual and Ecological Aspects of Crime*, National Council for Crime Prevention, Stockholm, 1993, pp. 3–37; E. E. Gorenstein and J. P. Newman, "Disinhibitory Psychopathology," *Psychological Review* 87: 301–15 (1980); Jennifer L. White et al., "Measuring Impulsivity and Examining Its Relationship to Delinquency," *Journal of Abnormal Psychology* 103(2): 192–205 (1994); Marvin Zuckerman, "Personality in the Third Dimension," *Personality and Individual Differences* 10: 391–418 (1989); Jeffrey A. Gray, "Drug Effects on Fear and Frustration," in Leslie L. Iversen, Susan D. Iversen, and Solomon H. Snyder, eds., *Handbook of Psychopharmacology: Drugs, Neurotransmitters, and Behavior*, vol. 8, Plenum, New York, 1977.

[74]White et al., op. cit.

[75]James Q. Wilson and Richard J. Herrnstein, *Crime and Human Nature*, New York: Simon & Schuster, 1985. See especially ch. 7.

[76]Farrington, "Introduction," op. cit., pp. xix–xx.

through their child-rearing practices. While criminal behavior may be directly learned through modeling by parents, peers, or the media, most crime is assumed to be the result of the failure to learn internal inhibitions against it.

Within the context of these general assumptions, Wilson and Herrnstein propose that the key individual-level factor associated with criminality is the tendency to think in terms of short-term rather than long-term consequences. The rewards from not committing crime almost always are in the future, while the rewards from committing it almost always are in the present. The tendency to think in terms of short-term consequences is associated with a variety of factors, including impulsivity and low intelligence. Wilson and Herrnstein also argue that the tendency to engage in criminal actions is associated with five other types of factors: (1) certain features of family life, such as poor child-rearing techniques, can produce weak internalized inhibitions; (2) membership in subcultures such as street gangs can increase the value placed on crime; (3) the mass media can directly affect aggressiveness through modeling and can indirectly affect it by convincing people they are being treated unfairly; (4) the economic system can influence the ability to achieve rewards through legitimate activity; and (5) schools can influence whether children believe they can achieve rewards through legitimate activity. Wilson and Herrnstein reviewed a massive amount of data to support their theory, but the extent to which this data support the theory has been questioned by several reviewers.[77]

Glenn Walters also proposed a theory with a strong focus on impulsivity as an enduring personality characteristic.[78] Walters defines "lifestyle criminals" as those who are characterized by "a global sense of irresponsibility, self-indulgent interests, an intrusive approach to interpersonal relationships, and chronic violation of societal rules, laws, and mores." He argues that these criminals have eight specific thinking patterns that allow them to perpetuate this pattern of actions. With *mollification*, these criminals point out the inequities and unfairnesses of life, and

---

[77]See book reviews by Lawrence E. Cohen, (*Contemporary Sociology* 16: 202–5 [March 1987]); Jack P. Gibbs (*Criminology* 23 [2]: 381–88 [May 1985]); Philip Jenkins (*Contemporary Crises* 10: 329–35 [1986]); and Joseph Gusfield (*Science* 231: 413–14 [January 1986]). In addition, Michael R. Gottfredson and Travis Hirschi (*A General Theory of Crime*, Stanford University Press, Stanford, CA, 1990) have criticized the theory as being theoretically contradictory.

[78]Glenn D. Walters, *The Criminal Lifestyle: Patterns of Serious Criminal Conduct*, Sage, Newbury Park, Calif., 1990. Walters's work is based in part on the earlier description of fifty-two "thinking errors" by Samuel Yochelson and Stanton E. Samenow, *The Criminal Personality*, Jason Aronson, New York, vol. I, 1976; vol. II, 1977. For a description of Yochelson and Samenow's theory, see George B. Vold, *Theoretical Criminology*, 2nd ed. prepared by Thomas J. Bernard, Oxford University Press, New York, 1979, pp. 153–56.

blame others for their own choices. The *cutoff* is some visual image or verbal cue (e.g., "f____ it") which has the effect of terminating all thought in the moment and simply allows the criminals to act without worrying about the consequences. A sense of *entitlement* means that any actions are considered justifiable to achieve what is desired. *Power orientation* means that these criminals believe it is a dog-eat-dog world, and those who are strong can do whatever they can get away with. *Sentimentality* is the tendency for these criminals to look back at all the good things they have done in their lives, and to claim that they therefore should not be held responsible for the bad things. *Superoptimism* is the tendency to believe that nothing bad will ever happen to them, including being punished for the crimes they commit. *Cognitive indolence* means that they just don't pay attention to the details in life. *Discontinuity* means they fail to follow through on commitments, carry out intentions, and remain focused on goals over time.

A third theory with a strong focus on impulsivity is Moffitt's theory of "life-course-persistent" offenders.[79] Moffitt describes these as a small group of people who engage "in antisocial behavior of one sort or another at every stage of life." Examples of such behavior would be biting and hitting at age 4, shoplifting and truancy at age 10, drug dealing and car theft at age 16, robbery and rape at age 22, and fraud and child abuse at age 30.[80] Moffitt argues that these behaviors begin with early neuropsychological problems that are caused by factors such as drug use or poor nutrition by the mother while she is pregnant, complications at birth resulting in minor brain damage, or deprivation of affection or child abuse and neglect after birth. These neuropsychological problems then tend to generate a cycle that results in an impulsive personality style. Parents dealing with children who have these problems often have psychological deficiencies themselves, and their attempts to discipline and socialize their children tend to intensify the children's problem behaviors.[81] As the children age, these problems can directly cause problems by interfering with their ability to control their behavior and to think of the future consequences of their actions. In addition, these problems can disrupt the children's success in school, which can reduce their ability to acquire rewards in legitimate activities and increase the likelihood they will turn to illegitimate, antisocial actions for rewards. Although this the-

---

[79]Terrie E. Moffitt, "Life-Course-Persistent and Adolescent-Limited Antisocial Behavior," *Psychological Review* 100:674–701 (1993).

[80]Ibid., p. 679.

[81]Ibid., p. 682.

ory is quite recent, a number of studies have produced supportive results.[82]

More recently, Caspi, Moffitt and their colleagues examined personality traits in two very different groups: about 1,000 youths born in Dunedin, New Zealand, in 1972–73, and about 500 ethnically diverse 12- and 13-year-old boys from Pittsburgh.[83] They found that crime-proneness was associated with a combination of impulsivity and "negative emotionality," which they described as "a tendency to experience aversive affective states such as anger, anxiety, and irritability." Youths with "negative emotionality," they suggested, perceive more threats and dangers than other people in the normal affairs of daily life. When these youths also have "great difficulty in modulating impulses," they tend to quickly turn those negative emotions into actions. Using an analogy from the Wild West, they describe these youths as "quick on the draw."

POLICY IMPLICATIONS OF PERSONALITY RESEARCH

At the present time, it seems best to ignore the results from personality inventories, along with psychiatric diagnoses of antisocial personality disorder and psychiatric predictions about which individuals are likely to become violent in the future. These seem to consist mostly of fancy labels that psychologists and psychiatrists apply to criminals, but they do not seem to add anything to our knowledge about the causes of crime or to our ability to reduce it.

On the other hand, there may actually be some personality characteristics associated with an increased risk of crime and delinquency. At present, the best candidate is impulsivity, which recent research consistently links to antisocial, delinquent, or criminal behavior. To say that impulsivity causes crime and delinquency, however, is not very useful unless we also have some ability to deal with impulsivity. This is a prob-

---

[82]Moffitt contrasted the "life-course-persistent" offenders with what she called "adolescent-limited" offenders who desist from delinquency as they mature to adults. Daniel Nagan and Kenneth Land ("Age, Criminal Careers, and Population Heterogeneity," *Criminology* 31[3]: 327–62 [1993]) identified separate groups of "life-course-persistent" and "adolescent-limited" offenders. They also found that the "life-course-persistent" group can be separated into low- and high-level chronic offenders. Nagan, Land, and Moffitt ("Life-Course Trajectories of Different Types of Offenders," *Criminology* 33[1]: 111–39 [1995]) then explored the nature of these groups of offenders further. They found that adolescent-limited offenders do not completely desist from antisocial behavior after adolescence, but still engage in behaviors such as heavy drinking, drug use, fighting, and minor criminal acts. Finally, Moffit, Donald Lynam, and Phil Silva ("Neuropsychological Tests Predicting Persistent Male Delinquency," *Criminology* 32[2]: 277–300 [1994]) found that poor neuropsychological status predicts delinquency which begins in early childhood but not that which begins in adolescence.

[83]Avshalom Caspi, Terrie E. Moffitt, Phil A. Silva, Magda Stouthamer-Loeber, Robert F. Krueger, and Pamela S. Schmutte, "Are Some People Crime-Prone?" *Criminology* 32(2): 163–95 (1994).

lem with theories like Wilson and Herrnstein's, which describe impulsivity as a stable personality characteristic but have few indications for how to change it.

Walters's theory, in contrast, connects impulsivity to eight thinking patterns. The policy implications therefore focus on changing those thinking patterns through cognitive restructuring techniques. The question for this theory is the extent to which these techniques can successfully change the thinking patterns and therefore reduce future crime and delinquency. If these techniques produce real results, then Walters's theory will gain credibility.[84] But if they cannot, then the theory probably will fade into obscurity.

Moffitt's theory is the most promising from a policy point of view because it explains the causes of the impulsivity itself—the early neuropsychological problems, the cyclical interactions with parents that tend to intensify the children's problem behaviors, and the later problems in school that are caused by impulsivity and then result in crime and delinquency. If we can fully understand the origins of impulsivity, then we may be able to intervene early in children's lives in ways that reduce crime and delinquency when they become teenagers and adults.

Much as with impulsivity studies, psychologists have concluded that a variety of factors in early childhood are useful for predicting later criminal and delinquent behavior. These include problem behaviors in very young children, early school failure, and poor child-management techniques by parents. Early interventions with high-risk children can address these problems. For example, special classes can teach parenting skills to parents of high-risk children, and the high-risk children themselves can get extra help in school that can reduce the risk of school failure. In fact, such polices seem to produce significant reductions in later crime and delinquency in high-risk children. In addition, they cost much less than locking up the offenders after their crimes have already been committed.[85] Thus, these policies appear to have great potential for reducing future crime and delinquency by intervening early in the lives of young and troubled children.

CONCLUSIONS

There is a widespread perception that people with low intelligence and/or certain personality characteristics are more likely to commit

---

[84]For some preliminary results, see Glenn D. Walters, "Short-term Outcome of Inmates Participating in the Lifestyle Change Program," *Criminal Justice and Behavior* 26(3): 322–37 (1999).

[85]See, for example, Peter W. Greenwood, Karyn E. Model, C. Peter Rydell, and James Chiesa, *Diverting Children from a Life of Crime*, Rand Corporation, Santa Monica, CA, 1996.

crime and delinquency. There may be truth to this perception, but the research to date is insufficient to support any strong conclusions.

At present, it seems best to conclude that low intelligence has no direct causal impact on crime and delinquency. The differences in IQ scores between delinquents and nondelinquents probably result from environmental rather than genetic factors. In particular, these differences probably reflect the underachievement of delinquents in schools rather than any genetic inferiority. In addition, if there is any causal link at all between low intelligence and crime, it is probably mediated by some other factor, such as school failure. To the extent that this is the case, then policies to reduce crime and delinquency should deal with the actual cause (e.g., the school failure) rather than with the low intelligence.

The research linking personality to crime has been beset with a whole host of methodological problems.[86] These problems have led many criminologists, even those who are largely favorable to this approach, to discard much of the research as meaningless. For example, Wilson and Herrnstein assert that delinquents score higher than nondelinquents on fourteen separate personality dimensions.[87] Gottfredson and Hirschi comment that this evidence is "at best, unimpressive" since most of it "is produced by attaching personality labels to differences in rates of offending between offenders and nonoffenders."[88] They conclude that "all these 'personality' traits can be explained without abandoning the conclusion that offenders differ from nonoffenders only in their tendency to offend."

Recent research, such as that focused on impulsivity, seems to be addressing these methodological problems, so that researchers may be closing in on personality characteristics that are actually associated with crime. On the other hand, the relation between impulsivity and crime has been the subject of a great deal of research in the past without producing the consistent results suggested by these recent studies.[89] For example, Scale 9 on the MMPI, previously described as the "hypomania" scale, is largely a measure of impulsivity, but this scale never consis-

---

[86]These are reviewed in Robert F. Kruger et al., "Personality Traits Are Linked to Crime among Men and Women: Evidence from a Birth Cohort," *Journal of Abnormal Psychology* 103(2): 328–38 (1995). See also Moffitt, op. cit., 1993. For a brief defense of trait-based personality theories, see Caspi et al., op. cit., pp. 164–65.

[87]Wilson and Herrnstein, op. cit., ch. 7.

[88]Gottfredson and Hirschi, op. cit., p. 209. Their own theory of crime is quite close to a personality theory, and is presented in Chapter 10.

[89]Blackburn, op. cit., pp. 191–96.

tently distinguished between offenders and nonoffenders. How these earlier findings can be reconciled with the more recent research on impulsivity is unclear at present.

Thus, it is not yet clear how large a role either personality or intelligence plays in explaining crime in general. Some individuals may be more likely to commit crime regardless of the situation they are in. But it is also true that some situations are more likely to be associated with crime, regardless of the people who are in them. To understand the behavior of most criminals and delinquents, it may be more profitable to start by analyzing the situations people find themselves in rather than their psychological characteristics.

CHAPTER FIVE

Crime and Economic Conditions

In sharp contrast to the explanations of criminal behavior that focus on the characteristics of the individual are those theories that minimize or ignore entirely the significance of the individual's biological or psychological makeup. Perhaps the oldest and most elaborately documented of the theories with a nonindividual orientation are those that explain criminal behavior in terms of economic differences or influence. Discussions of the sad state of the poor, with arguments about the undesirable consequences of poverty such as sickness, crime, and despair, go far back into antiquity.[1] These discussions have generated a great many empirical studies concerning the relationship between poverty and crime.

Some of these studies focus on variations in economic conditions to see if they correspond to variations in crime rates. If crime is caused by poverty, so the reasoning goes, then there should be more crime in places and at times where there are more poor people. Thus these studies have compared times of economic depression with times of economic prosperity, and wealthy areas of a country with poor areas, to see if there are any systematic differences in their crime rates. Later studies looked at whether there is any systematic relationship between crime rates and unemployment rates, and whether crime is associated with economic inequality, that is, with poverty that exists next to wealth.

From the very beginning, however, there has been disagreement about the findings and debate about whether the conclusions being drawn were justified. This chapter examines some of the studies to

---

[1] For a brief history of these arguments as they relate to crime, see Lynn McDonald, *The Sociology of Law and Order*, Faber and Faber, London, 1976.

demonstrate those disagreements and to draw conclusions about the relationship between crime and poverty.

RESEARCH ON CRIME AND ECONOMIC CONDITIONS: CONTRADICTIONS AND DISAGREEMENTS

There is an enormous amount of research on the relationship between crime and economic conditions. Many of the results of this research are inconsistent with each other and result in contradictory conclusions about the relationship between these two phenomena. The following is a brief review of a few of these studies to give a sense of the general situation.

As discussed in Chapter 2, as soon as national crime statistics were available in France in the early 1800s, attempts were made by Guerry and Quetelet to demonstrate the relationship between crime and poverty. Both compared wealthy areas of France with poor areas, expecting to find more crime in the poor areas because there were more poor people there. Neither found what he had expected. Guerry found that the wealthiest regions of France had more property crime but less violent crime. He concluded that the higher levels of property crime were caused by opportunity. There were more things to steal in the wealthy provinces. Quetelet found a similar pattern, and also suggested that opportunity might be a factor. But he also pointed to the great inequality between poverty and wealth in the wealthy provinces. This, he suggested, might generate resentment among the poor. In contrast, poor provinces tended to have less inequality because everyone was poor although people generally had enough to survive.

Since that time, hundreds of studies have been published on this subject in Europe and in the United States. These studies, extending back over a period of almost 200 years, often have given complicated and apparently contradictory results. For example, numerous studies have been done on the relationship between crime and the business cycle.[2] The thinking is that there should be more crime during times of economic downturns, such as recessions and depressions, because there are more

---

[2]European and American studies up to 1935 are reviewed in Thorsten Sellin, *Research Memorandum on Crime in the Depression*, Social Science Research Council Bulletin No. 27, New York, 1937; reprinted by Arno Press, New York, 1972. A number of older studies also are reviewed in the first and second editions of the present text. See George B. Vold, *Theoretical Criminology*, 2nd ed., prepared by Thomas J. Bernard, Oxford University Press, New York, 1979, pp. 168–71. For a discussion of the many problems interpreting the relation between crime and the business cycle in two recent studies, see Chris Hale, "Crime and the Business Cycle in Post-War Britain Revisited," *British Journal of Criminology* 38(4): 681–98 (1998).

poor people during those times. Similarly, there should be less crime during times of economic prosperity because there are fewer poor people.

Many of these studies, however, find that the general crime rate does not increase during economic downturns.[3] Some studies even find that crime actually decreases during depressions and recessions.[4] In addition, economic prosperity is not necessarily associated with decreases in crime. For example, in the United States the 1960s and early 1970s were years of great economic expansion, but crime and delinquency increased greatly at that time.[5] In the early 1990s, the United States again entered a long period of economic expansion, but crime and delinquency began dropping about the same time, and by the beginning of the 2000s the levels were at their lowest in over thirty years.[6] Thus, economic expansion apparently was associated with increases in crime in the 1960s but with decreases in crime in the 1990s.

Back in the early 1800s, Quetelet had pointed out that even wealthy areas may have many poor people in them. Similarly, it may be that there are more poor people even in times of economic expansion, and this would account for the increases in crime rates. A more direct measure of poverty therefore would be to count the number of poor people in a particular time or place, to see if times or places with more poor people have greater amounts of crime. Results of such studies, however, have also proved inconsistent and even contradictory.

For example, using 1970 statistics, Cho found that the percentage of people below the poverty line in the forty-nine largest cities of the United States was not associated with any of the seven index crimes reported by the FBI.[7] Jacobs reached a similar conclusion with respect to the crimes of burglary, robbery, and grand larceny.[8] In contrast, Ehrlich

---

[3]Sharon K. Long and Ann D. Witte, "Current Economic Trends: Implications for Crime and Criminal Justice," pp. 69–143 in Kevin Wright, ed., *Crime and Criminal Justice in a Declining Economy,* Oelgeschlager, Gunn and Hain, Cambridge, MA, 1981. For example, Henry and Short (*Suicide and Homicide,* The Free Press, New York, 1954) found that crimes of violence in American cities from the late 1920s to the late 1940s declined during times of economic downturn and increased during periods of economic expansion.

[4]See Ralph C. Allen, "Socioeconomic Conditions and Property Crime: A Comprehensive Review and Test of the Professional Literature," *American Journal of Economics and Sociology* 55(3): 293–308 (1996).

[5]Gary LaFree, *Losing Legitimacy,* Westview, Boulder, CO, 1998, pp. 122–26.

[6]E.g., see Alfred Blumstein and Joel Wallman, eds., *The Crime Drop in America,* Cambridge University Press, New York, 2000; and a special issue of *Journal of Criminal Law and Criminology* 88(4), 1998, addressing the question of "Why is Crime Decreasing?"

[7]Y. H. Cho, *Public Policy and Urban Crime,* Ballinger, Cambridge, MA., 1974.

[8]D. Jacobs, "Inequality and Economic Crime," *Sociology and Social Research* 66:12–28 (Oct. 1981).

found that there was a positive relationship between state property crime rates for 1940, 1950, and 1960 and the percentage of households receiving less than half the median income.[9] An even stronger result was found by Loftin and Hill, who created an index of "structural poverty" including measures of infant mortality, low education, and one-parent families, as well as income.[10] They found very strong correlation between this measure and state homicide rates. Similar results using the same index of structural poverty were found in two additional studies, one of which concluded that it was strongly correlated with homicides involving families and friends but not homicides involving strangers.[11] To make matters even more confusing, some studies have found that there are different poverty-crime relationships in different regions of the country.[12] More recently, researchers have looked at the effects of concentrated poverty, theorizing that poverty causes crime when poor people all live in the same place, as opposed to being dispersed among middle-class people. Using 1990 data on 121 U.S. central cities, Lee found that concentrated poverty in a city was much more important than overall poverty in explaining homicide by both African Americans and European Americans.[13] But Parker and Pruitt, using similar data, found that both overall poverty and concentrated poverty affected homicide rates for European Americans, but that only overall poverty affected homicide rates for African Americans.[14] Thus, they found that the extent to which poor African Americans all live in the same place did not seem to affect their homicide rates.

---

[9]Isaac Ehrlich, "Participation in Illegal Activities," in Gary S. Becker and W. M. Landes, eds., *Essays in the Economics of Crime and Punishment*, Columbia University Press, New York, 1974.

[10]Colin Loftin and R. H. Hill, "Regional Subculture and Homicide," *American Sociological Review* 39: 714–24 (1974).

[11]Steven F. Messner, "Regional and Racial Effects on the Urban Homicide Rate: The Subculture of Violence Revisited," *American Journal of Sociology* 88: 997–1007 (1983); M. Dwayne Smith and Robert Nash Parker, "Type of Homicide and Variation in Regional Rates," *Social Forces* 59(1): 136–47 (Sept. 1980). Smith and Parker argue that structural poverty is related to homicides between families and friends, but not between strangers.

[12]Steven F. Messner, "Regional Differences in the Economic Correlates of the Urban Homicide Rate," *Criminology* 21(4): 477–88 (Nov. 1983); John D. McCarthy, Omer Galle, and William Zimmern, "Population Density, Social Structure, and Interpersonal Violence," *American Behavioral Scientist* 18(6): 771–89 (July–Aug. 1975); and Alan Booth, David R. Johnson, and Harvey Choldin, "Correlates of City Crime Rates: Victimization Surveys Versus Official Statistics," *Social Problems* 25: 187–97 (1977).

[13]Matthew R. Lee, "Concentrated Poverty, Race, and Homicide," *Sociological Quarterly* 41(2): 189–206 (2000).

[14]Karen F. Parker and Matthew V. Pruitt, "Poverty, Poverty Concentration, and Homicide," *Social Science Quarterly* 8(2): 555–70 (2000).

CRIME AND UNEMPLOYMENT: A DETAILED LOOK
AT RESEARCH

Many people believe that unemployment causes crime, and so they believe that crime should increase when unemployment is high and decrease when unemployment is low. This popular view is presumably
based on the assumption that unemployment causes poverty, and poverty causes crime. The popular assumption that crime is related to the
business cycle is probably also based on the assumption that crime goes
up with unemployment. A detailed look at research on unemployment
and crime is presented here both to explore this specific issue and to
give a general sense of the problems that arise with research that attempts to relate crime to economic conditions.

Consider first the studies that focus on the relationship between unemployment and juvenile delinquency. A study by Glaser and Rice
found that delinquency is inversely related to unemployment (i.e.,
delinquency is high when unemployment is low).[15] Glaser and Rice suggest that this might be because unemployed parents are more available
to their children. Among the youths themselves, a number of studies
find that employment while in school increases delinquency in high-risk
males.[16] Other studies, however, conclude that delinquency is directly
related to juvenile unemployment—i.e., delinquency is high when unemployment is high.[17] In contrast, Danser and Laub found no relationship between delinquency and juvenile unemployment rates, even within specific age, sex, and racial groups.[18] Specifically, Ehrlich found that

---

[15]Daniel Glaser and Kent Rice, "Crime, Age, and Employment," *American Sociological Review* 24:
679–86 (Oct. 1959). Additional support for this study can be found in Jack P. Gibbs, "Crime, Unemployment and Status Integration," *British Journal of Criminology* 6(1): 49–58 (Jan. 1966). The
study was criticized as a statistical artifact in Marcia Guttentag, "The Relationship of Unemployment to Crime and Delinquency," *Journal of Social Issues* 24(1): 105–14 (Jan. 1968).

[16]E.g., John Paul Wright, Francis T. Cullen, and Nicolas Williams, "Working While in School and
Delinquent Involvement," *Crime and Delinquency* 43(2): 203–21 (1997), see also a review of this
issue in Williams, Cullen, and Wright, "Labor Market Participation and Youth Crime," *Social
Pathology* 2(3): 195–217 (1996). See also Matthew Ploeger, "Youth Employment and Delinquency:
Reconsidering a Problematic Relationship," *Criminology* 35(4): 659–75 (1997).

[17]Larry D. Singell, "An Examination of the Empirical Relationship Between Unemployment and
Juvenile Delinquency." *The American Journal of Economics and Sociology* 26(4): 377–86; and Bel-
ton M. Fleischer, "The Effect of Unemployment on Juvenile Delinquency," *Journal of Political
Economy* 71: 543–55 (Dec. 1963). Related works by Fleischer are "The Effect of Income on Delin-
quency," *The American Economic Review*, March 1966, pp. 118–37, and *The Economics of Delin-
quency*, Quadrangle Books, Chicago, 1966. This position is supported in Harold L. Votey, Jr., and
Llad Phillips, "The Control of Criminal Activity: An Economic Analysis," in Daniel Glaser, ed.,
Handbook of Criminology, Rand McNally, Chicago, 1974, pp. 1065–69.

[18]Kenneth R. Danser and John H. Laub, *Juvenile Criminal Behavior and Its Relation to Economic
Conditions*, Criminal Justice Research Center, Albany, N.Y., 1981. See also Isaac Ehrlich, "Participation in Illegitimate Activities: A Theoretical and Empirical Investigation," *Journal of Political*

unemployment had no effect on the criminality of urban males in the age group 14 to 24.[19] But Calvin argued that there is a close and direct relationship between unemployment and crime for African American youths, and that those who argue otherwise are using incorrect data or faulty interpretations.[20]

There also have been contradictory findings on the question of the relationship between unemployment and adult crime. A number of researchers concluded that there is either no relationship between unemployment and crime or that the relationship (sometimes found to be positive and sometimes negative) is insignificant.[21] In contrast, Berk and his colleagues studied programs that provide unemployment benefits to released prisoners, and concluded: "For ex-offenders at least, unemployment and poverty do cause crime."[22] Still other researchers have found that increased hourly wage, higher quality jobs, and jobs that last for longer periods of time are associated with decreased property crime.[23]

Such inconsistent and contradictory results continue to be generated by research. By the early 1980s, several reviews of this research had concluded that higher unemployment rates are associated with higher crime rates, but that the relationship is weak and generally insignificant.[24] In 1987, however, Chiricos reviewed sixty-three studies of crime

---

Economy, May–June 1973, pp. 521–64; Ehrlich found that unemployment had no effect on the criminality of urban males in the age group 14 to 24.

[19] Isaac Ehrlich, "Participation in Illegitimate Activities: A Theoretical and Empirical Investigation," *Journal of Political Economy*, May–June 1973, pp. 521–64

[20] Allen D. Calvin, "Unemployment Among Black Youths, Demographics, and Crime," *Crime and Delinquency* 27(2): 234–44 (1981).

[21] See, for example, Long and Witte, op. cit.; D. Jacobs, "Inequality and Economic Crime," *Sociology and Social Research* 66: 12–28 (Oct. 1981); Booth, Johnson, and Choldin, op. cit.; and Paul E. Spector, "Population Density and Unemployment," *Criminology* 12(4): 399–401 (1975).

[22] Richard A. Berk, Kenneth J. Lenihan, and Peter H. Rossi, "Crime and Poverty: Some Experimental Evidence from Ex-Offenders," *American Sociological Review* 45: 766–86 (Oct. 1980). See also their *Money, Work, and Crime: Experimental Evidence*, Academic Press, New York, 1980.

[23] On the hourly wage, see Jeff Grogger, *Market Wages and Youth Crime*, National Bureau of Economic Research, Cambridge, MA, 1997; on higher quality jobs, see Christopher Uggen, "Ex-Offenders and the Conformist Alternative: A Job Quality Model of Work and Crime," *Social Problems* 46(1): 127–51 (1999); and on longer lasting jobs, see Robert D. Cruthfield and Susan R. Pitchford, "Work and Crime: The Effects of Labor Stratification," *Social Forces* 76(1): 93–118 (1997).

[24] Richard B. Freeman, "Crime and Unemployment," Ch. 6 in James Q. Wilson, ed., *Crime and Public Policy*, ICS Press, San Francisco, 1983; Long and Witte, op. cit.; and R. W. Gillespie, "Economic Factors in Crime and Delinquency: A Critical Review of the Empirical Evidence," pp. 601–26 in House of Representatives, *Unemployment and Crime: Hearings Before the Subcommittee on Crime of the Committee on the Judiciary*, U.S. Government Printing Office, Washington, DC., 1978. See also Thomas Orsagh, "Unemployment and Crime," *Journal of Criminal Law and Criminology* 71(2): 181–83 (summer 1980).

and unemployment.[25] He concluded that the relationship between unemployment and crime is positive and frequently significant, especially for property crime, and that this effect was especially strong after 1970.[26] Chiricos also argued that the positive relation between crime and unemployment is more likely to be found when smaller units are examined (e.g., neighborhoods) rather than larger units (e.g., nations), because these smaller units "are more likely to be homogeneous."[27] In contrast, economic conditions in larger units often have little impact on the extent of poverty and deprivation in particular areas.[28]

But after Chiricos's review, Land and his colleagues found consistently negative relationships between homicide and unemployment after controlling for other variables related to economic deprivation,[29] negative relationships more often than positive ones for robbery, and positive but nonsignificant effects for rape and assault.[30] Commenting on Chiricos's conclusion, Land, Cantor, and Russell suggest that all the evidence, taken together, supports the inference of a weak negative relationship between crime and unemployment from 1960 to 1980.[31] That is, in their view, crime goes down when unemployment goes up, but not very much. However, they agreed with Chiricos that positive relationships between crime and unemployment (crime goes up when unemployment goes up) are more likely to be found with smaller units of analysis and for property crimes.[32]

In addition to these attempts to reach general conclusions about the relationship between crime and unemployment rates, some efforts have been made to focus on particular aspects of unemployment. For example, using data from 1970 to 1990, White examined the effects of the decline in manufacturing jobs in the 100 largest American cities.[33] He

[25]Theodore G. Chiricos, "Rates of Crime and Unemployment: An Analysis of Aggregate Research Evidence," *Social Problems* 34(2): 187–211 (April 1987).

[26]Ibid., p. 203.

[27]Ibid., p. 195.

[28]See Kenneth C. Land, Patricia L. McCall, and Lawrence E. Cohen, "Structural Covariates of Homicide Rates: Are There Any Invariances Across Time and Space," *American Journal of Sociology* 95: 922–63 (1990).

[29]Ibid.

[30]Patricia L. McCall, Kenneth C. Land, and Lawrence E. Cohen, "Violent Criminal Behavior: Is There a General and Continuing Influence of the South?" *Social Science Research* 21(3): 286–310 (1992).

[31]Kenneth C. Land, David Cantor, and Stephen T. Russell, "Unemployment and Crime Rate Fluctuations in the Post-World War II United States," ch. 3 in John Hagan and Ruth D. Peterson, eds., *Crime and Inequality,* Stanford University Press, Stanford, CA 1995, fn. 2 (p. 309).

[32]Ibid., pp. 56–57.

[33]Garland White, "Crime and the Decline of Manufacturing, 1970–1990," *Justice Quarterly* 16(1): 81–97 (1999).

found that reductions in manufacturing jobs led to increased poverty and unemployment, which then led to increased robberies, burglaries, and drug-related offenses. However, he found no effect on violent crimes such as murder and aggravated assault. In contrast, Shihadeh and Ousey also used data from 1970–1990 and found that declines in access to low-skill jobs in central cities resulted in increased poverty, which then resulted in increased violence among both African Americans and European Americans.[34]

PROBLEMS INTERPRETING RESEARCH ON CRIME AND ECONOMIC CONDITIONS

There are six major problems with interpreting this research, and they lead to all the inconsistent and contradictory conclusions reviewed above. The first problem is that *poverty is always in part a subjective condition,* relative to what others have, rather than the simple presence or absence of a certain amount of property or other measure of wealth. What one person considers poverty another may view as a level of satisfactory comfort, if not of abundance. Because of the lack of any clear definition of poverty, it has been measured in at least twenty different ways in different studies.[35] These different ways of measuring poverty can lead to the inconsistent and contradictory results reviewed above. Unemployment, too, is an unclear concept. Official unemployment rates only count people who are "able and available" for work. This often is defined in terms of having actually applied for more than one job in the previous week. People who do not actively seek work therefore are not counted as unemployed in official unemployment statistics.[36] In addition, many people are "underemployed" in low wage, dead-end jobs with terrible working conditions. Regardless of how they feel about

---

[34]Edward S. Shihadeh and Graham C. Ousey, "Industrial Restructuring and Violence," *Social Forces* 77: 185–206 (1998).

[35]Robert J. Sampson and Janet L. Lauritsen, "Violent Victimization and Offending," in Albert J. Reiss, Jr., and Jeffrey A. Roth, eds., *Understanding and Preventing Violence—Social Influences,* vol. 3, National Academy Press, Washington, DC, 1994, p. 5.

[36]Elliott Curry, *Confronting Crime,* Pantheon, New York, 1985, ch. 4, argues that "labor market participation" is more likely to be related to crime than "unemployment." "Labor market participation" measures the number of people who are in the labor market, which includes those who are employed and those who are unemployed but "able and available" to work. This contrasts with those who have dropped out of the labor market altogether. These are the people who are not counted in unemployment statistics, and they are more likely to be involved in crime than "unemployed" people who are actively seeking work. Robert D. Crutchfield, Ann Glusker, and George S. Bridges ("A Tale of Three Cities: Labor Markets and Homicide," *Sociological Focus* 32(1): 65–83 [1999]) found that the rate of labor market participation was related to homicide in three American cities.

those jobs, these people are counted as employed.[37] Thus, despite the fact that poverty and unemployment are genuine kinds of human experience, they nevertheless do not lend themselves readily to the accurate and consistent gathering of information.

The second problem is that *there are two contradictory theoretical assumptions* about the relationship between economic conditions and crime. The first assumption is that the relationship is inverse or negative; that is, when economic conditions are good, the amount of crime should be low, while when economic conditions are bad, crime should be high. That assumption is found throughout history and is still fairly commonly believed by the public.

But as described above, many studies have found the opposite of that assumption. As a result, a second theoretical assumption has arisen about the relation between crime and economic conditions—that the relationship is direct or positive. This second assumption looks at criminality as an extension of normal economic activity (a criminal fringe, as it were), and therefore assumes that it increases and decreases in the same manner as other economic activity. If the second assumption is correct, the amount of crime should increase and be at its highest point when economic conditions are good, and it should decrease when economic conditions are bad.

In 1931, Morris Ploscowe used the second assumption in an attempt to explain the generally accepted belief that crime had increased throughout much of the Western world during the previous 150 years, despite an obvious increase in the economic well-being of nearly everyone.[38] Ploscowe argued that the unparalleled economic and social progress had given ordinary workers a much better economic position than they had ever enjoyed in the past, but this progress also brought new pressures and demands that often resulted in criminality. Ploscowe concluded: "Where increased incentives and increased occasions for illegitimate activities result from an increased amount of legitimate activity, there is apt to be an increase in crime."[39]

But Ploscowe's assumption that crime has been rising for 150 years was later contradicted in a study by Gurr and his colleagues, which found that the crime rates of London, Stockholm, and Sydney had actu-

---

[37]For some of the problems of counting unemployed persons, see Gwynn Nettler, *Explaining Crime*, 3rd ed., McGraw-Hill, New York, 1984, pp. 127–29.

[38]Morris Ploscowe, "Some Causative Factors in Criminality," *Report on the Causes of Crime*, vol. 1, part 1, no. 13, Report of the National Commission on Law Observance and Law Enforcement, Washington, DC, June 26, 1931, pp. 115–16.

[39]Ibid., p. 114.

ally decreased from the 1840s to the 1930s (Ploscowe wrote his report in 1931) and at that time were only about one-eighth of their earlier levels.[40] Gurr also found that from the 1930s to the 1970s crime had increased by approximately the same amount as the previous decrease. He speculated that some of the recent increases in crime rates may be due to more complete police reporting of crimes, but argued that, in general, these statistics reflected basic trends in the incidence of criminal behavior.

Gurr considered the relationship between crime and economic conditions, and found support for both assumptions:[41]

The evidence of the city studies is that poverty *and* wealth are correlated with the incidence of common crime, not only theft but crimes against the person as well. In nineteenth century London, Stockholm, and New South Wales both theft and assault increased during periods of economic slump and declined when economic conditions improved again. Economic distress had very little effect on crime rates in either direction in the twentieth century, but as total productivity (wealth) increased, so did common crime. Evidently two separate causal processes were at work at different times.

Gurr's notion that separate causal processes may be at work at different times raises the possibility that both of these interpretations may be correct. This gives rise to the third problem, which lies in *specifying the amount of time* before economic changes are said to have an effect on criminality. Should one assume that changes in crime rates will occur at the same time as changes in economic conditions, or should one assume that there will be some period of delay, or "lag," before the crime rates are affected? Some studies find very different relationships between economic conditions and criminality when different time lags are considered.[42] The same study can then be cited as support for both contra-

---

[40]Ted Robert Gurr, *Rogues, Rebels, and Reformers,* Sage, Beverly Hills, Calif., 1976. This study also considers crime rates of Calcutta, a non-Western city that had a different pattern of crime rates. For the complete study, see Ted Robert Gurr, Peter N. Grabosky, and Richard C. Hula, *The Politics of Crime and Conflict: A Comparative History of Four Cities,* Sage, Beverly Hills, CA, 1977. A shorter version is found in Gurr's article "Contemporary Crime in Historical Perspective: A Comparative Study of London, Stockholm, and Sydney," *Annals of the American Academy of Political and Social Science* 434: 114–36 (Nov. 1977).

[41]Gurr, op. cit., p. 179.

[42]See, for example, Dorothy Swaine Thomas, *Social Aspects of the Business Cycle,* Routledge & Kegan Paul, London, 1925, p. 143. This point is argued more extensively and with supporting data in earlier editions of the present text. See George B. Vold, *Theoretical Criminology,* Oxford University Press, New York, 1958, pp. 177–81; see also the 2nd ed., prepared by Thomas J. Bernard, 1979, pp. 176–78.

dictory theoretical assumptions simply by selecting the data at different time lags.

Cantor and Land argue that these two theoretical assumptions are correct but that they operate at different times.[43] On the one hand, they agree with the general and widely held view that unemployment increases the motivation to commit crime. Thus, higher unemployment rates should be associated with higher crime rates. But this "motivation" effect, they argue, should be "lagged" by some period of time. People only experience the full effects of unemployment after some period of time because of their own savings, support from their families and friends, and government programs such as unemployment compensation.

On the other hand, they agree with Ploscowe's argument that economic activity is associated with increased opportunities to commit crime. When unemployment rates are higher, overall economic activity tends to be lower and there should be lower crime rates because there are fewer opportunities to commit it. But, they argue, this "opportunity" effect should occur immediately. As economic activities decline, the opportunities to commit crime decline simultaneously with them. Thus, there should be no "lag" in the effect of decreased opportunities on crime rates.

Using national data on unemployment rates and index crimes in the United States from 1946–1982,[44] these researchers found the predicted positive-negative effect for the property-related crimes of robbery, burglary, and larceny-theft. That is, in each case, they found both an immediate "opportunity" effect and a lagged "motivation" effect. Thus, when unemployment went up, robbery, burglary, and larceny-theft decreased immediately but then increased the next year. The overall impact of these two contradictory trends was negative—i.e., when unemployment increased, these crimes declined overall but not by much. Homicide and auto theft showed only the immediate negative "opportunity" effect— that is, they declined when unemployment went up but did not increase the next year. Finally, rape and assault did not seem to be associated with unemployment at all.

---

[43]David Cantor and Kenneth C. Land, "Unemployment and Crime Rates in the post-World War II United States: A Theoretical and Empirical Analysis," *American Sociological Review* 50: 317–23 (1985).

[44]Cantor and Land, op. cit. This analysis was replicated and extended, using data to 1990, in Land, Cantor, and Russell, op. cit. See also the interchange between Chris Hale and Dima Sabbagh ("Unemployment and Crime") and Cantor and Land ("Exploring Possible Temporal Relationships of Unemployment and Crime: A Comment on Hale and Sabbagh") in *Journal of Research in Crime and Delinquency* 28(4): 400–425 (1991).

The fourth problem with interpreting this research relates to Chiricos's conclusion that the positive relation between crime and unemployment was more likely to be found in smaller units, such as neighborhoods and communities, rather than in larger units such as metropolitan areas and nations. The problem is *determining the size of the unit* that economic factors affect. Thus, economic conditions in a neighborhood might strongly affect crime in that neighborhood, but economic conditions in a nation might have little impact on national crime rates.

The conclusion that unemployment is associated with crime at the community level is consistent with research on the experience of people who live in areas with high unemployment. Individuals in those areas may mix crime and employment in a variety of ways, and participation in illegal work may depend considerably on the nature of the legal work market.[45] Especially since the 1980s, the legitimate work traditionally available to "unskilled" young males in inner-city areas has declined significantly, while the illegal work available to them, particularly that associated with illegal drug markets, has expanded rapidly.[46] The illegal work pays better and provides better working conditions than legal work, so these youths have an incentive to become involved in crime. Early involvement in crime and incarceration as an adolescent then further limits their access to legal jobs as an adult. In contrast, youths who have early successful legitimate work experiences tend to have limited access to illegal work later in life.

Fagan argued that these experiences shape the cultural and social context of inner-city adolescents:[47]

With limited access to legal work, and in segregated neighborhoods with high concentrations of joblessness, alienated views of legal work and diminished expectations for conventional success spread through social contagion and become normative. Tastes and preferences are driven by definitions of status dominated by material consumption. Violence substitutes for social control as a

---

[45]Jeffrey Fagan, "Legal and Illegal Work: Crime, Work and Unemployment," in Burton Weisbrod and James Worthy, eds., *Dealing with Urban Crisis: Linking Research to Action*, Northwestern University Press, Evanston, IL, 1996. For relatively similar conclusions, see Richard B. Freeman, "The Labor Market," ch. 8 in James Q. Wilson and Joan Petersilia, eds., *Crime*, ICS Press, San Francisco, 1995.

[46]Jeffrey Fagan and Richard B. Freeman, "Crime and Work" pp. 225–90 in Michael Tonry, ed., *Crime and Justice: A Review of Research*, vol. 25, University of Chicago Press, Chicago, 1999.

[47]Fagan, op. cit., pp. 37–38. See also John Hagan, "The Social Embeddedness of Crime and Unemployment," *Criminology* 31(4): 465–91 (1993). Hagan argues that there are different directions of causality between crime and unemployment at different levels of analysis. Macro-level theory and research tends to view unemployment as a cause of crime, but micro-level theory and research tends to view crime as a cause of unemployment. What is missing in this literature is "an understanding of the proximate causes of joblessness in the lives of individuals."

means to resolve disputes and attain status, increasing the likelihood either of mortality or incarceration. Legal work at low pay is defined poorly and carries a negative social stigma. With intergenerational job networks disrupted, the ability of young people to access increasingly complex labor markets with limited human capital or personal contacts foretells poor work outcomes.

The fifth problem with interpreting research on economic conditions and crime is illustrated by this description. High crime communities usually have a whole host of factors that might cause crime—poverty, unemployment, high rates of divorce and single-parent households, high population density, dilapidated housing, poor schools and other social services, frequent residential mobility and population turnover, and concentrations of racial and ethnic minorities. Any or all of these factors might cause crime, but all of them tend to be found in the same places at the same times. The problem, then, is *determining which factors actually cause crime* and which ones just happen to be there but have no actual effect. This problem is called "multicollinearity"—i.e., a number of possible causal factors are all highly intercorrelated with each other.[48] In this situation, relatively small changes in statistical techniques can result in different conclusions about which factors have a causal impact and which do not. Thus, the changes can give rise to the type of inconsistent and contradictory results that are reviewed above.

To address this problem, Land and his colleagues incorporated all the variables used in twenty-one studies of homicide at city, metropolitan area, and state levels into one "baseline regression model."[49] They then "clustered" these variables to see what would "hang together" over time and place. The most important clustering of variables was around what they called "resource deprivation/affluence," which included measures of poverty and income inequality, as well as percent of African American population and percent of children not living with both parents. While these factors are conceptually separate, the statistical techniques could not separate them from each other in the effects they had on homicide. This cluster of variables had a significant positive effect on city, metropolitan area, and state levels of homicide in 1960, 1970, and 1980, with some tendency for this effect to increase over time.

The sixth problem with interpreting research on crime and economic conditions has to do with adequately *distinguishing between concepts of poverty and economic inequality.*[50] The "resource deprivation/afflu-

---

[48]Sampson and Lauritsen, op. cit., p. 66; Land et al., 1990.

[49]Land, McCall, and Cohen, op. cit., 1990.

[50]Many studies of inequality use the Gini coefficient, which is a statistic that measures the extent to which incomes are dispersed in a society relative to the average income in that society. The coeffi-

ence" cluster described above includes both poverty and economic inequality. These are quite different concepts. Poverty refers to the lack of some fixed level of material goods necessary for survival and minimum well-being. In contrast, economic inequality refers to a comparison between the material level of those who have the least in a society and the material level of other groups in that society. Countries in which everyone has an adequate material level have little or no poverty, but they may still have a great deal of economic inequality if there is a very large gap between those who have the least and those who have the most. On the other hand, countries in which everyone is poor have a great deal of poverty but little or no economic inequality.

One of the most consistent findings in the criminology literature is a connection between economic inequality and homicide.[51] For example, one recent study examined data from 50 different countries around the year 1990 and found a strong connection between economic inequality and homicide rates.[52] Research has also found a connection between inequality and other violent crime. For example, another recent study looked at firearm robbery and assault rates in the 50 U.S. states in the early 1990s.[53] This study found that firearm violence was strongly correlated with economic inequality, even when controlled for poverty and access to firearms.

More recently, attention has turned to the specific effects of racial inequality in the United States. The issue is whether the specific inequality between African Americans and European Americans, rather than general inequality in the entire society, has a specific effect on African American crime rates. For example, Messner and Golden examined the effect of inequality between African Americans and European Americans in the 154 largest U.S. cities.[54] First, they performed analyses similar to the one done by Land and his colleagues, as described above, and found similar results about the "resource deprivation/affluence" cluster. But then they went on to construct a measure of racial inequality, which

---

cient ranges from "0," where everyone has equal shares of the total income, to "1," where one person has all the income and everyone else has none. See S. Yitzhaki, "Relative Deprivation and the Gini Coefficient," *Quarterly Journal of Economics* 93: 321–24 (May 1974); and M. Bronfenbrenner, *Distribution Theory*, Aldine-Atherton, New York, 1971.

[51]Gary LaFree, "A Summary and Review of Cross-National Comparative Studies of Homicide," pp. 125–45 in M. Dwayne Smith and Margaret A. Zahn, *Homicide: A Sourcebook of Social Research*, Sage, Thousand Oaks, CA, 1999.

[52]Matthew R. Lee and William B. Bankston, "Political Structure, Economic Inequality, and Homicide," *Deviant Behavior* 20(1): 27–55 (1999).

[53]Bruce P. Kennedy, Ichiro Kawachi, Deborah Prothrow-Stith, et al., "Social Capital, Income Inequality, and Firearm Violent Crime," *Social Science Medicine* 47(1): 7–17 (1998).

[54]Steven F. Messner and Reid M. Golden, "Racial Inequality and Racially Disaggregated Homicide Rates: An Assessment of Alternative Theoretical Explanations," *Criminology* 30(3): 421–45 (1992).

included the gap between African Americans and European Americans in income, education, and unemployment levels, and the extent of residential segregation. They found that increased levels of inequality between the races were associated with higher African American, European American, and total homicide rates, separate from the effects of the "resource deprivation/affluence" cluster. They concluded that "Racial inequality evidently affects the social order in some generalized way that increases criminogenic pressures on the entire population." Other results on this subject, however, have been very mixed.[55]

IMPLICATIONS AND CONCLUSIONS

At the present time, a reasonably strong case can be made that the economic inequality in a society—i.e., the gap between the richest and the poorest—has a causal impact on the level of violence in that society. That is, poor people may tend to commit more violent crime when there are many wealthy people around them. This finding would suggest that policies to reduce economic inequality, particularly between the races, should result in lower rates of violence in the society as a whole.

This conclusion would be consistent with the recent experience in the United States. During the 1980s, there was a vast expansion of wealth in American society, but there was also the largest increase in economic inequality in the country's history.[56] Despite the growth in wealth, violent crime increased significantly during this period. It may be that, embedded in the heart of this increasing wealth, an increasing concentration of extreme poverty in inner-city areas lead to the development of a relatively isolated segment of the population sometimes described as "the underclass." It is within this group that the relationship between crime and economic conditions seems to have the most direct effect.[57] In con-

---

[55]E.g., Tomislav V. Kovandzic, Lynne M. Vieraitis, and Mark R. Yeisley, "The Structural Covariates of Urban Homicide: Reassessing the Impact of Income Inequality and Poverty in the Post-Reagan Era," *Criminology* 36(3): 569–99 (1998); Karen F. Parker and Patricia L. McCall, "Adding Another Piece to the Inequality-Homicide Puzzle," *Homicide Studies* 1(1): 35–60 (1997); Edward S. Shihadeh and Darrell J. Steffensmeier, "Economic Inequality, Family Disruption, and Urban Black Violence," *Social Forces* 73(22): 729–51 (1994); Gary LaFree, Kriss A. Drass, and Patrick O'Day, "Race and Crime in Postwar America: Determinants of African-American and White Rates, 1957–1988," *Criminology* 30(2): 157–85 (1992); Miles D. Harer and Darrell J. Steffensmeier, "The Different Effects of Economic Inequality on Black and White Rates of Violence," *Social Forces* 70: 1035–54 (1992).

[56]Kovandzic, Vieraitis, and Yeisley, op. cit.

[57]In general, see John Hagan and Ruth D. Peterson, "Criminal Inequality in America," and Robert J. Sampson and William Julius Wilson, "Toward a Theory of Race, Crime, and Urban Inequality," chs. 1 and 2 in Hagan and Peterson, eds., *Inequality and Crime,* Stanford University Press, Stanford, CA, 1994. See also John Hagan, *Crime and Disrepute,* Pine Forge Press, Thousand Oaks, CA, 1994.

trast, in the 1990s, wealth continued to expand in the United States, but economic inequality declined and crime declined with it.[58]

At the neighborhood level, it appears that unemployment, but not poverty, has a causal impact on crime and delinquency. For example, after reviewing numerous studies about local areas, Sampson and Lauritsen concluded that "Almost without exception, studies of violence find a positive and usually large correlation between some measure of area poverty and violence—especially homicide."[59] But in the end, they conclude that poverty itself does not directly cause crime because crime rates do not consistently increase and decrease as the number of poor people increases and decreases.

Consistent with this conclusion, Sampson and Lauritsen suggest that, despite the overwhelming association between violence and poverty, the data suggest that the direct effect of poverty on crime is weak and probably is conditional on other community factors. They particularly point to a variety of factors, including unemployment, involved in the processes of rapid community change at the neighborhood level. These factors will be further discussed in the next chapter, which looks at the rapid social changes associated with economic modernization.

---

[58]E.g., see Alfred Blumstein and Richard Rosenfeld, "Explaining Recent Trends in U.S. Homicide Rates," *Journal of Criminal Law & Criminology* 88(4): 1175–1216, 1998.

[59]Sampson and Lauritsen, op. cit., p. 63.

CHAPTER SIX

Durkheim, Anomie, and Modernization

The preceding chapter concluded that economic inequality may be associated with crime. In contrast Emile Durkheim viewed inequality as a natural and inevitable human condition that is not associated with social maladies such as crime unless there is also a breakdown of social norms or rules. Durkheim called such a breakdown *anomie* and argued that it had occurred in his own society as a result of the rapid social changes accompanying the modernization process. Like Lombroso's theories, written approximately twenty years earlier, Durkheim's theories were in part a reaction to the classical assumptions that humans were free and rational in a contractual society. But where Lombroso had focused on the determinants of human behavior within the individual, Durkheim focused on society and its organization and development.

Durkheim's theories are complex, but his influence on criminology has been great. The present chapter examines his theories and discusses them in the context of later research on the relationship between crime and modernization. But Durkheim's ideas also appear in several later chapters. In the 1920s a group of Chicago sociologists used his theories, among others, as the basis for an extensive research project linking juvenile delinquency to rapid social changes in urban areas. These *ecological* studies are presented in Chapter 7. In 1938 Robert K. Merton revised Durkheim's conception of anomie and applied it directly to American society. This and other similar theories are now known as *strain* theories of crime and delinquency and are presented in Chapter 8. In 1969 Travis Hirschi returned to Durkheim's original conception of anomie and used it as the basis for his *control* theory of delinquency. Control theories are discussed in Chapter 10. Finally, Durkheim's view of "crime as normal" is the basis for *social reaction* views of the law-enactment process, which are discussed in Chapter 12.

EMILE DURKHEIM

Emile Durkheim (1858–1917) has been called "one of the best known and one of the least understood major social thinkers."[1] Presenting his thought is no easy task, since "the controversies which surround this thought bear upon essential points, not details."[2] For this reason it is best to approach his work by first considering the political and intellectual climate in which it evolved.

The nineteenth century in France was an age of great turmoil generated by the wake of the French Revolution of 1789 and by the rapid industrialization of French society. Speaking of these two "revolutions," Nisbet has pointed out that "In terms of immediacy and massiveness of impact on human thought and values, it is impossible to find revolutions of comparable magnitude anywhere in human history."[3] The writings of the day were filled with a "burning sense of society's sudden, convulsive turn from a path it had followed for millennia" and a "profound intuition of the disappearance of historic values—and with them, age-old securities, as well as age-old tyrannies and inequalities—and the coming of new powers, new insecurities, and new tyrannies that would be worse than anything previously known unless drastic measures were taken. . . ."[4]

Sociology had been developed by Auguste Comte in the first half of the century largely in response to the effects of these two revolutions; it was part of a more general effort to construct a rational society out of the ruins of the traditional one.[5] Sociologists saw themselves providing a rational, scientific analysis of the monumental social changes that were occurring, in order to "mastermind the political course of 'social regeneration.'"[6] This regeneration would consist primarily of the reestablishment of social solidarity, which appeared to have substantially disintegrated in French society.

---

[1]Dominick LaCapra, *Emile Durkheim, Sociologist and Philosopher,* Cornell University Press, Ithaca, N.Y., 1972, p. 5.

[2]Ibid., p. 5.

[3]Robert A. Nisbet, *Emile Durkheim,* Prentice Hall, Englewood Cliffs, NJ 1965, p. 20.

[4]Ibid., p. 20.

[5]LaCapra, op. cit., p. 41.

[6]Julius Gould, "Auguste Comte," in T. Raison, ed., *The Founding Fathers of Social Science,* Penguin, Harmondsworth, U.K., 1969, p. 40.

Emile Durkheim was born in a small French town on the German border, one year after the death of Comte. After completing his studies in Paris he spent several years teaching philosophy at various secondary schools in the French provinces near Paris. He then spent a year in Germany, where he studied social science and its relation to ethics under the famed experimental psychologist Wilhelm Wundt. Durkheim's publication of two articles as a result of these studies led to the creation of a special position for him at the University of Bordeaux, where in 1887 he taught the first French university course in sociology. In 1892 Durkheim received the first doctor's degree in sociology awarded by the University of Paris, and ten years later he returned to a position at the university, where he dominated sociology until his death in 1917.

Durkheim's analysis of the processes of social change involved in industrialization is presented in his first major work, *De la division du travail social (The Division of Labor in Society)*,[7] written as his doctoral thesis and published in 1893. In it he describes these processes as part of the development from the more primitive "mechanical" form of society into the more advanced "organic" form. In the mechanical form each social group in society is relatively isolated from all other social groups, and is basically self-sufficient.[8] Within these social groups individuals live largely under identical circumstances, do identical work, and hold identical values. There is little division of labor, with only a few persons in the clan or village having specialized functions. Thus there is little need for individual talents, and the solidarity of the society is based on the uniformity of its members.

Contrasted with this is the organic society, in which the different segments of society depend on each other in a highly organized division of labor. Social solidarity is no longer based on the uniformity of the individuals, but on the diversity of the functions of the parts of the society. Durkheim saw all societies as being in some stage of progression between the mechanical and the organic structures, with no society being totally one or the other. Even the most primitive societies could be seen to have some forms of division of labor, and even the most advanced societies would require some degree of uniformity of its members.[9]

Law plays an essential role in maintaining the social solidarity of each of these two types of societies, but in very different ways. In the me-

---

[7]Emile Durkheim, *The Division of Labor in Society*, translated by George Simpson, The Free Press, New York, 1965.

[8]Raymond Aron, *Main Currents in Sociological Thought*, vol. II, translated by Richard Howard and Helen Weaver, Basic Books, New York, 1967, p. 12.

[9]Ibid., pp. 12–13.

chanical society law functions to enforce the uniformity of the members of the social group, and thus is oriented toward repressing any deviation from the norms of the time. In the organic society, on the other hand, law functions to regulate the interactions of the various parts of society and provides restitution in cases of wrongful transactions. Because law plays such different roles in the two types of societies, crime appears in very different forms. Durkheim argued that to the extent a society remains mechanical, crime is "normal" in the sense that a society without crime would be pathologically overcontrolled. As the society develops toward the organic form, it is possible for a pathological state, which he called anomie, to occur, and such a state would produce a variety of social maladies, including crime. Durkheim developed his concept of "crime as normal" in his second major work, *The Rules of the Sociological Method,*[10] published in 1895, only two years after *The Division of Labor;* he went on to develop anomie in his most famous work, *Suicide,*[11] published in 1897. These concepts will be explored in the following sections.

CRIME AS NORMAL IN MECHANICAL SOCIETIES

Mechanical societies are characterized by the uniformity of the lives, work, and beliefs of their members. All the uniformity that exists in a society, that is, the "totality of social likenesses," Durkheim called the *collective conscience.*[12] Since all societies demand at least some degree of uniformity from their members (in that none are totally organic), the collective conscience may be found in every culture. In every society, however, there will always be a degree of diversity in that there will be many individual differences among its members. As Durkheim said, "There cannot be a society in which the individuals do not differ more or less from the collective type."[13]

To the extent that a particular society is mechanical, its solidarity will come from the pressure for uniformity exerted against this diversity. Such pressure is exerted in varying degrees and in varying forms. In its strongest form it will consist of criminal sanctions. In weaker forms,

---

[10]Emile Durkheim, *The Rules of the Sociological Method,* translated by Sarah A. Solovay and John H. Mueller, edited by George E. G. Catlin, The Free Press, New York, 1965.

[11]Durkheim, *Suicide,* translated by John A. Spaulding and George Simpson, edited by George Simpson, The Free Press, New York, 1951.

[12]Durkheim, *Division of Labor,* p. 80, n. 10. In French, the term *conscience* has overtones of both "conscience" and "consciousness," but the term is usually translated as "collective conscience."

[13]Durkheim, *Rules,* p. 70.

however, the pressure may consist of designating certain behaviors or beliefs as morally reprehensible or merely in bad taste.

If I do not submit to the conventions of society, if in my dress I do not conform to the customs observed in my country and my class, the ridicule I provoke, the social isolation in which I am kept, produce, although in attenuated form, the same effects as a punishment in the strict sense of the word. The constraint is nonetheless efficacious for being indirect.[14]

Durkheim argued that "society cannot be formed without our being required to make perpetual and costly sacrifices."[15] These sacrifices, embodied in the demands of the collective conscience, are the price of membership in society, and fulfilling the demands gives the individual members a sense of collective identity, which is an important source of social solidarity. But, more important, these demands are constructed so that it is inevitable that a certain number of people will not fulfill them. The number must be large enough to constitute an identifiable group, but not so large as to include a substantial portion of the society. This enables the large mass of the people, all of whom fulfill the demands of the collective conscience, to feel a sense of moral superiority, identifying themselves as good and righteous, and opposing themselves to the morally inferior transgressors who fail to fulfill these demands. It is this sense of superiority, of goodness and righteousness, which Durkheim saw as the primary source of the social solidarity. Thus criminals play an important role in the maintenance of the social solidarity, since they are among the group of those identified by society as inferior, which allows the rest of society to feel superior.

The punishment of criminals also plays a role in the maintenance of the social solidarity. When the dictates of the collective conscience are violated, society responds with repressive sanctions not so much for retribution or deterrence, but because without them those who are making the "perpetual and costly sacrifices" would become severely demoralized.[16] For example, when a person who has committed a serious crime is released with only a slap on the wrist, the average, law-abiding citizens may become terribly upset. They may feel they are playing the game by the rules, and so everyone else should too. The punishment of the crim-

---

[14]Ibid., pp. 2–3.

[15]Kurt Wolff, ed., *Emile Durkheim et al., Writings on Sociology and Philosophy*, Harper & Row, New York, 1960, p. 338.

[16]Nisbet, op. cit., p. 225. See also Jackson Toby, "Is Punishment Necessary?" *Journal of Criminal Law, Criminology and Police Science* 55: 332–37 (1964).

inal is necessary to maintain the allegiance of average citizens to the social structure. Without it average citizens may lose their overall commitment to the society and their willingness to make the sacrifices necessary for it. But beyond this, the punishment of criminals also acts as a visible, societal expression of the inferiority and blameworthiness of the criminal group. This reinforces the sense of superiority and righteousness found in the mass of the people, and thus strengthens the solidarity of the society.

Crime itself is normal in society because there is no clearly marked dividing line between behaviors considered criminal and those considered morally reprehensible or merely in bad taste. If there is a decrease in behaviors designated as criminal, then there may be a tendency to move behaviors previously designated as morally reprehensible into the criminal category. For example, not every type of unfair transfer of property is considered stealing. But if there is a decrease in the traditional forms of burglary and robbery, there then may be an associated increase in the tendency to define various forms of white-collar deception as crime. These behaviors may always have been considered morally reprehensible, and in that sense they violated the collective conscience. They were not, however, considered crimes. Society moves them into the crime category because criminal sanctions are the strongest tool available to maintain social solidarity.

Since the institution of punishment serves an essential function, it will be necessary in any society.

Imagine a society of saints, a perfect cloister of exemplary individuals. Crimes, properly so called, will there be unknown; but faults which appear venial to the layman will create there the same scandal that the ordinary offense does in ordinary consciousnesses. If, then, this society has the power to judge and punish, it will define these acts as criminal and will treat them as such. For the same reason, the perfect and upright man judges his smallest failings with a severity that the majority reserve for acts more truly in the nature of an offense.[17]

Thus a society without crime is impossible. If all the behaviors that are presently defined as criminal no longer occurred, new behaviors would be placed in the crime category.[18] Crime, then, is inevitable because there is an inevitable diversity of behavior in society. The solidarity of the society is generated by exerting pressure for conformity against

---

[17]Durkheim, *Rules*, pp 68–69.
[18]Ibid., p. 67.

this diversity, and some of this pressure will inevitably take the form of criminal sanctions.[19]

Let us make no mistake. To classify crime among the phenomena of normal sociology is not merely to say that it is an inevitable, although regrettable, phenomenon, due to the incorrigible wickedness of men; it is to affirm that it is a factor in public health, an integral part of all societies.

The abnormal or pathological state of society would be one in which there was no crime. A society that had no crime would be one in which the constraints of the collective conscience were so rigid that no one could oppose them. In this type of situation crime would be eliminated, but so would the possibility of progressive social change. Social change is usually introduced by opposing the constraints of the collective conscience, and those who do so are frequently declared to be criminals. Thus Socrates and Jesus were declared criminals, as were Mahatma Gandhi and George Washington. The leaders of the union movement in the 1920s and 1930s were criminalized, as were the leaders of the civil rights movement of the 1960s. If the demands of the collective conscience had been so rigidly enforced that no crime could exist, then these movements would have been impossible also.

Thus crime is the price society pays for the possibility of progress. As Durkheim wrote,[20]

To make progress, individual originality must be able to express itself. In order that the originality of the idealist whose dreams transcend his century may find expression, it is necessary that the originality of the criminal, who is below the level of his time, shall also be possible. One does not occur without the other.

In a similar way individual growth cannot occur in a child unless it is possible for that child to misbehave. The child is punished for misbehavior, and no one wants the child to misbehave. But a child who never did anything wrong would be pathologically overcontrolled. Eliminating the misbehavior would also eliminate the possibility of independent growth. In this sense the child's misbehavior is the price that must be paid for the possibility of personal development. Durkheim concluded:[21]

---

[19]Ibid., p. 67.

[20]Ibid., p. 71.

[21]Ibid., p. 72.

From this point of view, the fundamental facts of criminality present themselves to us in an entirely new light. Contrary to current ideas, the criminal no longer seems a totally unsociable being, a sort of parasitic element, a strange and unassimilable body, introduced into the midst of society. On the contrary, he plays a definite role in social life. Crime, for its part, must no longer be conceived as an evil that cannot be too much suppressed. There is no occasion for self-congratulation when the crime rate drops noticeably below the average level, for we may be certain that this apparent progress is associated with some social disorder.

ANOMIE AS A PATHOLOGICAL STATE IN ORGANIC SOCIETIES

To the extent that a society is mechanical, it derives its solidarity from pressure for conformity against the diversity of its members. The criminalizing of some behaviors is a normal and necessary part of this pressure. But to the extent that a society is organic, the function of law is to regulate the interactions of the various parts of the whole. If this regulation is inadequate, there can result a variety of social maladies, including crime. Durkheim called the state of inadequate regulation anomie.

Durkheim first introduced this concept in *The Division of Labor in Society,* where he argued that the industrialization of French society, with its resulting division of labor, had destroyed the traditional solidarity based on uniformity. But this industrialization had been so rapid that the society had not yet been able to evolve sufficient mechanisms to regulate its transactions. Periodic cycles of overproduction followed by economic slowdown indicated that the relations between producers and consumers were ineffectively regulated. Strikes and labor violence indicated that the relations between workers and employers were unresolved. The alienation of the individual worker and the sense that the division of labor was turning people into mere "cogs in the wheel" indicated that the relation of the individual to work was inadequately defined.[22]

Durkheim expanded and generalized his notion of anomie four years later with the publication of his most famous work, *Le Suicide.* In it he statistically analyzed data that showed that the suicide rate tends to increase sharply both in periods of economic decline and economic growth. Whereas suicide in a time of economic decline might be easily understood, the key question is why suicide would increase in a time of prosperity. Durkheim proposed that society functions to regulate not only the economic interactions of its various components, but also how

---

[22]Durkheim, *Division of Labor,* pp. 370–73.

the individual perceives his own needs. Durkheim's theory of anomie has been used as the basis for later explanations of crime and a variety of other deviant behaviors.[23]

The theory began with a comparison of animal and human nature.[24] In animals, Durkheim argued, the physical body naturally limits appetites. Thus, animals with full stomachs and safe warm places to sleep will feel quite satisfied. But humans have active imaginations that allow them to feel dissatisfied even when their physical needs are met. In humans, satisfying some wants and needs tends to awaken new wants and needs, so that "the more one has, the more one wants." Thus, where an animal's physicality puts natural limits on its appetites, human appetites are naturally unlimited.

The only mechanism that can limit human appetites, according to Durkheim, is human society. Societies create moral rules about what people in various social positions can reasonably expect to acquire:

As a matter of fact, at every moment of history there is a dim perception, in the moral consciousness of societies, of the respective value of different social services, the relative reward due each, and the consequent degree of comfort appropriate on the average to workers in each occupation. . . . Under this pressure, each in his sphere vaguely realizes the extreme limit set to his ambitions and aspires to nothing beyond. . . . Thus, an end and goal are set to the passions. . . .

There are various situations in which these societal rules may weaken or even break down, but Durkheim focused on situations of rapid social change, including those in which the society goes into an economic recession or depression:

In the case of economic disasters, indeed, something like a declassification occurs which suddenly casts certain individuals into a lower state than their previous one. Then they must reduce their requirements, restrain their needs, learn greater self-control. . . . So they are not adjusted to the condition forced on them, and its very prospect is intolerable. . . .

Durkheim used this experience to explain the high rates of suicide during times of economic downturns. More importantly, he argued that something similar happened in times of rapid economic expansion:

---

[23]Marshall B. Clinard, ed., *Anomie and Deviant Behavior,* The Free Press, New York, 1964.

[24]The theory of anomie is presented in Emile Durkheim, *Suicide,* Macmillan, New York, 1952, pp. 246–53, and the following quotations are from those pages. For an extensive series of quotations summarizing the theory, see George B. Vold, Thomas J. Bernard, and Jeffrey B. Snipes, *Theoretical Criminology,* 4th ed., Oxford University Press, New York, 1998, pp. 130–32.

It is the same if the source of the crisis is an abrupt growth of power and wealth. Then, truly, as the conditions of life are changed, the standard according to which needs were regulated can no longer remain the same. . . . The scale is upset; but a new scale cannot be immediately improvised. Time is required for the public conscience to reclassify men and things. So long as the social forces thus freed have not regained equilibrium, their respective values are unknown and so all regulation is lacking for a time. . . .

He then made the surprising argument that anomie (or the deregulation of appetites) would be worse in times of prosperity than in times of depression, since prosperity stimulates the appetites just at the time when the restraints on those appetites have broken down:

With increased prosperity desires increase. At the very moment when traditional rules have lost their authority, the richer prize offered these appetites stimulates them and makes them more exigent and impatient of control. The state of de-regulation or anomy is thus further heightened by passions being less disciplined, precisely when they need more disciplining.

Durkheim went on to argue that French society, over the previous 100 years, had deliberately destroyed the traditional sources of regulation for human appetites.[25] Religion had almost completely lost its influence over both workers and employers. Traditional occupational groups, such as the guilds, had been destroyed. Government adhered to a policy of laissez-faire, or noninterference, in business activities. As a result human appetites were no longer curbed. This freedom of appetites was the driving force behind the French industrial revolution, but it also created a chronic state of anomie, with its attendant high rate of suicide.

ASSESSING DURKHEIM'S THEORY OF CRIME

Durkheim presented his theory of crime in the context of an overall theory of modernization—the progression of societies from the mechanical to the organic form. One of the problems with assessing his theory is that he predicted that different things would happen at different times. Specifically he argued that: (1) the punishment of crime would remain fairly stable in mechanical societies, independent of changes in the extent of criminal behavior; (2) as those societies made the transition to organic societies in the process of modernization, a greater variety of behaviors would be tolerated, punishments would become less violent as their purpose changed from repression to restitution, and there would be a vast expansion of "functional" law to regulate the interactions of the

---

[25]Ibid., pp. 254–58.

emerging organic society; and (3) in organic societies, the extent of criminal behavior would increase during periods of rapid social change. Each of these ideas has generated additional theories and research in more recent times.

Erikson reformulated Durkheim's theory about the stability of punishment in mechanical societies, based on a study of the Puritan colony in seventeenth-century Massachusetts.[26] This society had a relatively constant level of punishment throughout the century despite three "crime waves" attributed to Antinomians, Quakers, and witches. Erikson concluded:[27] "When a community calibrates its control machinery to handle a certain volume of deviant behavior it tends to adjust its . . . legal . . . definitions of the problem in such a way that this volume is realized."

Blumstein and his colleagues attempted to demonstrate a similar process in modern societies.[28] They examined imprisonment rates in the United States from 1924 to 1974, in Canada from 1880 to 1959, and in Norway from 1880 to 1964, arguing that these rates remained stable over the time periods and that the stability was maintained by adjusting the types of behaviors that resulted in imprisonment. Later studies either failed to find a similar effect or have criticized the research methods of studies that do find an effect.[29] More recently, the explosion of incarceration in the United States associated with the "get tough" era has clearly demonstrated that punishment in the United States is no longer "stable," if it ever was. For example, before 1970, the imprisonment rate in the United States had generally remained somewhere around 100 prisoners for every 100,000 people in the population, whether crime

---

[26]Kai T. Erikson, *Wayward Puritans*, John Wiley, New York, 1966.

[27]Ibid., p. 26.

[28]Alfred Blumstein and Jacqueline Cohen, "A Theory of the Stability of Punishment," *Journal of Criminal Law and Criminology* 64: 198–207 (June 1973); Alfred Blumstein, Jacqueline Cohen, and Daniel Nagin, "The Dynamics of a Homeostatic Punishment Process," *Journal of Criminal Law and Criminology* 67: 317–34 (Sept. 1977); and Alfred Blumstein and Soumyo Moitra, "An Analysis of the Time Series of the Imprisonment Rate in the States of the United States: A Further Test of the Stability of Punishment Hypothesis," *Journal of Criminal Law and Criminology* 70: 376–90 (Sept. 1979). See also Nils Christie, "Changes in Penal Values," in Christie, ed., *Scandinavian Studies in Criminology*, vol. 2, Scandinavian University Books, Oslo, 1968, pp. 161–72. For a review of these studies, see Allen E. Liska, "Introduction," in Liska, ed., *Social Threat and Social Control*, State University of New York Press, Albany, NY, 1992, pp. 13–16.

[29]M. Calahan, "Trends in Incarceration in the United States," *Crime and Delinquency* 25: 9–41 (1979); David F. Greenberg, "Penal Sanctions in Poland," *Social Problems* 28: 194–204 (1980); David Rauma, "Crime and Punishment Reconsidered: Some Comments on Blumstein's Stability of Punishment Hypothesis," *Journal of Criminal Law and Criminology* 72: 1772–98 (1981); Richard A. Berk, David Rauma, Sheldon L. Messinger, and T. F. Cooley, "A Test of the Stability of Punishment Hypothesis," *American Sociological Review* 46: 805–29 (1981); and Richard A. Berk, David Rauma, and Sheldon L. Messinger, "A Further Test of the Stability of Punishment Hypothesis," in John Hagan, ed., *Quantitative Criminology*, Sage, Beverly Hills, CA, 1982, pp. 39–64.

rates were high or low. Since then, however, the imprisonment rate has been steadily rising and by 2000 it was 478 prisoners for every 100,000 people in the population.

Durkheim's theory, however, does not predict that punishment levels in modern industrialized societies will remain constant, since those cannot be considered mechanical societies. The Puritan colony in Massachusetts can reasonably be considered such a society, so that Erikson's study supports Durkheim's theory while the others neither support nor challenge it. On the other hand, Erikson's interpretation has been challenged by Chambliss, who suggests that "his conclusion is hardly supported by the data he presents."[30] Erikson, following Durkheim, had described the three crime waves as being generated by the need to establish the moral boundaries of the community. Chambliss pointed out that each of these crime waves occurred when the power and authority of the ruling groups were threatened. He concluded:

Deviance was indeed created for the consequences it had. But the consequences were not "to establish moral boundaries"; rather, they aided those in power to maintain their position. . . . Erikson gives no evidence that any of these crime waves actually increased social solidarity except through the elimination of alternative centers of authority or power.

Durkheim made three arguments about crime during the process of transition from mechanical to organic societies: A greater variety of behaviors would be tolerated, punishments would become less violent as their purpose changed from repression to restitution, and there would be a vast expansion of "functional" law to regulate the interactions of the emerging organic society. Wolfgang has stated that contemporary American society illustrates Durkheim's first argument about the increasing tolerance for diversity in more advanced societies: "My major point is that we are currently experiencing in American culture, and perhaps in Western society in general, an expansion of acceptability of deviance and a corresponding contraction of what we define as crime."[31] A similar argument has been made more recently by conservative commentators who argue that Western societies are losing all their morals.

With respect to Durkheim's second argument, Spitzer found that more developed societies were characterized by severe punishments, while simple societies were characterized by lenient punishments,

---

[30]William J. Chambliss, "Functional and Conflict Theories of Crime," in Chambliss and Milton Mankoff, eds., *Whose Law? What Order?*, John Wiley, New York, 1976, pp. 11–16.

[31]Marvin E. Wolfgang, "Real and Perceived Changes in Crime," in Simha F. Landau and Leslie Sebba, *Criminology in Perspective*, D. C. Heath, Lexington, MA, 1977, pp. 27–38.

which is the opposite of what Durkheim predicted.[32] Spitzer's findings
are consistent with several studies which have found that rural areas in
Western societies before modernization were characterized by fairly
high levels of violence, and also by a considerable degree of tolerance
for it.[33] It was only after modernization, with the concentration of populations in anonymous cities, that societies began to punish violence consistently and severely. Durkheim may have derived his idea from the
fact that punishments in European societies were becoming much less
severe at the time, due to the reforms introduced by Beccaria and other
classical theorists. But the extremely harsh punishments that had been
imposed prior to those reforms were not associated with simple, undeveloped societies, but rather with absolute monarchies. Those types of
punishments were not found in earlier, simpler societies.[34]

Third, Durkheim predicted a great expansion in functional law as
modern societies attempt to regulate all their new functions. In his case
study of four cities from 1800 to the present, Gurr found "a veritable explosion of laws and administrative codes designed to regulate day-to-day
interactions, in domains as dissimilar as trade, public demeanor, and
traffic."[35] While some of this was generated by "the functional necessity
of regulating the increased traffic and commercial activities of growing
cities," as Durkheim had argued, Gurr also found that a great deal of
other legislation was passed defining and proscribing new kinds of offenses against morality and against "collective behavior" such as riots
and protests.[36] Gurr argued that the new offenses against morality arose
primarily from the effort to apply middle-class values to all social
groups, while the offenses against collective behavior arose from efforts
of the elite groups to maintain their power.[37]

Finally, Durkheim argued that the source of high crime rates in organic societies lay in normlessness or anomie generated by the rapid social changes associated with modernization. Durkheim's theory of
anomie led to the later ecological, strain, and control theories of crime,
so that the assessment of this argument must, to a certain extent, await

---

[32]Steven Spitzer, "Punishment and Social Organization," *Law and Society Review* 9: 613–37 (1975).

[33]See, for example, Howard Zehr, *Crime and Development of Modern Society*, Rowman & Littlefield, Totowa, NJ, 1976.

[34]Michel Foucault, *Discipline and Punish*, Pantheon, New York, 1977, pp. 3–69. See also Philippe
Ariès, *Centuries of Childhood*, Knopf, New York, 1962, ch. 1, for a discussion of the tendency to
idealize the past as harmonious and peaceful.

[35]Ted Robert Gurr, *Rogues, Rebels, and Reformers*, Sage, Beverly Hills, CA, 1976, p. 180.

[36]Ibid., p. 177.

[37]Ibid., pp. 93–115.

the presentation of those theories in Chapters 7, 8, and 10. But those theories do not directly link the breakdown of social norms to the processes of modernization, as did Durkheim's theory. Durkheim's theory of anomie is therefore assessed here in the context of his theory of modernization.

Durkheim attributed the high rates of crime and other forms of deviance in his own society to the normlessness generated by the French and Industrial revolutions. One very basic criticism of this argument is that crime in France was not rising at the time. Lodhi and Tilly conclude that between 1831 and 1931 the incidence of theft and robbery declined in France, citing a massive decline in the statistics for serious property crime during that period.[38] The statistics for violent crime remained approximately stable over the same period, with some tendency toward a decline. Durkheim had formulated his theory of anomie in the context of a study of suicide rates, not crime rates. Having done so, he simply presumed that crime was also increasing, although he nowhere presented data to support his conclusion. McDonald argues that the statistics showing decreases in crime rates were available to Durkheim, as well as to other prominent criminologists of the time who also presumed that crime rates were increasing, but that none of them took any notice:[39] "Marxists of that time were no more willing to admit that social and economic conditions were improving than Durkheimians that industrialization and urbanization did not inevitably lead to higher crime."

Recent research has led to a generally accepted conclusion that economic development is associated with increases in property crime but with decreases in violent crime.[40] For example, Neuman and Berger reviewed seventeen cross-national crime studies and concluded that urbanism and industrialization are both associated with increased property crime, but neither was associated with increases in violent crime.[41] In

---

[38]A. Q. Lodhi and Charles Tilly, "Urbanization, Crime and Collective Violence in Nineteenth-Century France," *American Journal of Sociology* 79: 297–318 (1973). See also A. V. Gatrell and T. B. Hadden, "Criminal Statistics and Their Interpretations," in E. A. Wrigley, ed., *Nineteenth-Century Society,* Cambridge University Press, Cambridge, U.K., 1972, pp. 336–96.

[39]Lynn McDonald, "Theory and Evidence of Rising Crime in the Nineteenth Century," *British Journal of Sociology* 33: 404–20 (Sept. 1982), p. 417.

[40]For a review, see Gary D. LaFree and Edward L. Kick, "Cross-National Effects of Development, Distributional and Demographic Variables on Crime: A Review and Analysis," *International Annals of Criminology* 24: 213–36 (1986). A single recent study found that, with proper controls for the age structure of populations and for region, both homicide and theft rates rise with modernization. See Suzanne T. Ortega et al., "Modernization, Age Structure, and Regional Context: A Cross-National Study of Crime," *Sociological Spectrum* 12: 257–77 (1992).

[41]W. Lawrence Neuman and Ronald J. Berger, "Competing perspectives on Cross-National Crime: An Evaluation of Theory and Evidence," *Sociological Quarterly* 29(2) :281–313 (1988).

addition, they found no support for the argument that the increases in property crime were caused by the change from traditional to modern values. All of this is inconsistent with Durkheim's basic argument.

Neuman and Berger therefore question the continued dominance of Durkheim's theory in explaining the link between modernization and crime. They suggest that much more attention be paid to the role of economic inequality in this process, as opposed to Durkheim's emphasis on the breakdown of traditional values. They point out that the relationship between economic inequality and homicide is "the most consistent finding in the literature,"[42] and suggest that criminologists examine the large literature on the relation between inequality and economic development.[43] The basic finding of this literature is that in developing nations, foreign investment by multinational corporations and dependency on exports of raw material slow long-term economic growth and increase economic inequality. The economic inequality, then, increases both criminal behavior and the criminalization of that behavior by criminal justice agencies. This is particularly true in moderately repressive, as opposed to highly repressive or democratic, regimes. The authors conclude that "future studies should examine the relationship that exists between multinational penetration, inequality, and type of regime."

A study by Bennett also challenged Durkheim's theory as the explanation of the linkage between crime and modernization.[44] Durkheim had argued that crime is caused by rapid social change. If that is true, Bennett reasoned, then: (1) the rate of increase in crime would be directly proportional to the rate of growth in the society; (2) both theft and homicide should increase during periods of rapid growth; and (3) the level of development itself (i.e., whether the country is underdeveloped or advanced) should not affect crime rates as long as the country is not rapidly changing. Using data from fifty-two nations from 1960 to 1984, Bennett then showed that the rate of growth does not significantly affect either homicide or theft, and that the level of development itself, independent of the rate of growth, significantly affects theft offenses but not homicides. Bennett concludes: "These findings refute the Durkheimian hypotheses."[45]

---

[42]Ibid., p. 296.

[43]Ibid., pp. 298–99. A still different causal path was suggested by Sethard Fisher ("Economic Development and Crime," *American Journal of Economics and Sociology* 46[1]: 17–34 [1987]) who argued that crime is associated with the unplanned drift of rural populations into urban areas and with changes in elite groups as the society attempts to modernize and achieve economic growth.

[44]Richard R. Bennett, "Development and Crime," *Sociological Quarterly* 32(3): 343–63 (1991).

[45]Ibid., p. 356.

CONCLUSION

Durkheim's influence has been extremely broad in criminology and sociology. His primary impact is that he focused attention on the role that social forces play in determining human conduct at a time when the dominant thinking held either that people were free in choosing courses of action or that behavior was determined by inner forces of biology and psychology. Although the focus on social forces is now the dominant view used to explain crime, it was considered quite radical at the time.[46]

There is now considerable evidence that the basic patterns of crime found in the modern world can only be explained by a theory that focuses on modernization as a fundamental factor. Shelley reviewed studies of crime and modernization and found that the same changes in crime patterns that occurred first in Western Europe have reoccurred in Eastern European socialist nations and in the emerging nations of Asia, Africa, and Latin America as they have undergone modernization.[47] She concluded: "The evidence . . . suggests that only the changes accompanying the developmental process are great enough to explain the enormous changes that have occurred in international crime patterns in the last two centuries."

Many of the changes that have accompanied the modernization process, however, are not those predicted by Durkheim's theory. Premodern societies were characterized by high levels of violent crime, in contrast to Durkheim's arguments about their stability. There appears to have been a long-term decline in violent crime over the last several hundred years as the process of modernization has occurred, something that Durkheim's theory does not predict.[48] Short-term increases in that long-term decline occurred in the early stages of urbanization and industrialization, but those short-term increases seem to have been associated with the retention, not the breakdown, of rural culture. Gurr argues that other sources of short-term increases in violent crime rates include wars and growths in the size of the youth population.[49]

Modernization does appear to be associated with higher property

---

[46]See the chapter on Durkheim in Ian Taylor, Paul Walton, and Jock Young, *The New Criminology*, Harper, New York, 1973, pp. 67–90.

[47]Louise I. Shelley, *Crime and Modernization*, Southern Illinois University Press, Carbondale, Ill., 1981, pp. 141–42.

[48]See Steven F. Messner, "Societal Development, Social Equality, and Homicide," *Social Forces* 61: 225–40 (1982).

[49]Ted Robert Gurr, "Historical Forces in Violent Crime," in Michael Tonry and Norval Morris, eds., *Crime and Justice*, vol. 3, University of Chicago Press, Chicago, 1981, pp. 340–46. See also Gurr, "On the History of Violent Crime in Europe and America," in Hugh David Graham and Ted Robert Gurr, eds., *Violence in America*, 2nd ed., Sage, Beverly Hills, CA, 1979.

crime rates, but the increased property crime does not appear to be caused by the breakdown of moral values associated with rapid social change. Rather, it probably involves societal changes that result in more opportunities to commit property crime. For example, when people own more property that is both valuable and portable, and when they frequently are away from their property and cannot personally guard it, then property crime is likely to increase. This argument will be further explored in Chapter 11.

On the other hand, Durkheim's basic argument was that modernization is linked to crime through the breakdown of social norms and rules—that is, he associated crime with the absence of social controls. It may be that Durkheim's argument itself is correct but that Durkheim was wrong in assuming that pre-modern societies had strong social control and little crime. It now seems likely that they had little social control and a great deal of violent crime. The long-term decline in violent crime may then be explained by the continuously increasing level of social controls associated with increasing modernization.[50] The relationship between crime and social controls will be further explored in Chapter 10.

---

[50]This basically is Gurr's interpretation. See the sources in footnote 49.

CHAPTER SEVEN

Neighborhoods and Crime

One of Durkheim's arguments was that rapid social change was associated with increases in crime due to the breakdown of social controls. This idea was one of several used by members of the Department of Sociology at the University of Chicago in the 1920s in their attempt to pinpoint the environmental factors associated with crime and to determine the relationship among those factors. However, instead of focusing on rapid change in entire societies, they focused on rapid change in neighborhoods.

Their procedure involved correlating the characteristics of each neighborhood with the crime rates of that neighborhood. This first large-scale study of crime in America produced a mass of data and a large number of observations about crime that led directly to much of the later work in American criminology. Since this research was based on an image of human communities taken from plant ecology, it became known as the Chicago School of Human Ecology.

THE THEORY OF HUMAN ECOLOGY

The term *ecology*, as it is used today, is often linked to the idea of protecting the natural environment. In its original meaning, however, it is a branch of biology in which plants and animals are studied in their relationships to each other and to their natural habitat. Plant life and animal life are seen as an intricately complicated whole, a web of life in which each part depends on almost every other part for some aspect of its existence. Organisms in their natural habitat exist in an ongoing balance of nature, a dynamic equilibrium in which each individual must struggle to survive. Ecologists study this web of interrelationships and interdependencies in an attempt to discover the forces that define the activities of each part.

Human communities, particularly those organized around a free-market economy and a laissez-faire government, could be seen to resemble this biotic state in nature. Each individual struggles for his or her survival in an interrelated, mutually dependent community. The Darwinian law of survival of the fittest applies here as well.

Robert Park proposed a parallel between the distribution of plant life in nature and the organization of human life in societies.[1] He had been a Chicago newspaper reporter for twenty-five years and had spent much of that time investigating social conditions in the city. Chicago at that time had a population of over 2 million; between 1860 and 1910 its population had doubled every ten years, with wave after wave of immigrants. Park was appointed to the Sociology Department at the University of Chicago in 1914. From the study of plant and animal ecology he derived two key concepts that formed the basis of what he called the "theory of human ecology."

The first concept came from the observations of the Danish ecologist Warming, who noted that a group of plants in a given area might have many characteristics that, in combination, were similar to those of an individual organism.[2] Warming called such groups "plant communities." Other ecologists argued that the plant and animal life in a given habitat tended to develop a "natural economy" in which different species are each able to live more prosperously together than separately. This is called "symbiosis," or the living together of different species to the mutual benefit of each. Since each plant and animal community was said to resemble an organism, the balance of nature in the habitat was said to resemble a super-organism.

Park's work as a newspaperman had led him to view the city in a similar way—not merely as a geographic phenomenon, but as a kind of "super-organism" that had "organic unity" derived from the symbiotic interrelations of the people who lived within it.[3] Within this superorganism Park found many "natural areas" where different types of people

---

[1]Park's background and a review of the theory of human ecology are presented in Terence Morris, *The Criminal Area,* Humanities Press, New York, 1966, pp. 1–18. See also Winifred Raushenbush, *Robert E. Park: Biography of a Sociologist,* Duke University Press, Durham, 1979; and Amos H. Hawley, "Human Ecology," *International Encyclopedia of the Social Sciences,* vol. 4, Macmillan and The Free Press, New York, 1968, pp. 328–37.

[2]Eugenius Warming, "Plant Communities," in Robert E. Park and Ernest W. Burgess, *Introduction to the Science of Sociology,* University of Chicago Press, Chicago, 1969, pp. 175–82.

[3]Robert E. Park, *Human Communities,* The Free Press, Glencoe, IL, 1952, p. 118.

lived. These natural areas, like the natural areas of plants, had an organic unity of their own. Some of them were racial or ethnic communities, such as "Chinatown," "Little Italy," or the "Black Belt." Other natural areas included individuals in certain income or occupational groups, or they were industrial or business areas. Still other areas were physically cut off from the rest of the city by railroad tracks, rivers, major highways, or unused space. Symbiotic relationships existed not only among the people within a natural area (where the butcher needed the baker for bread and the baker needed the butcher for meat), but also among the natural areas within the city. Each natural area was seen as playing a part in the life of the city as a whole.

The second basic concept Park took from plant ecology involved the process by which the balance of nature in a given area may change. A new species may invade the area, come to dominate it, and drive out other life forms. For example, a cleared field in one of the southern states will first be covered with tall weeds. Later this field will be invaded and dominated by broomsedge and, even later, by pine trees. Finally the field will stabilize as an oak-hickory forest. Ecologists call this process "invasion, dominance, and succession."

This process can also be seen in human societies. The history of America is a process of invasion, dominance, and succession by Europeans into the territory of Native Americans. And in cities one cultural or ethnic group may take over an entire neighborhood from another group, beginning with the shift of only one or two residents. Similarly, business or industry may move into and ultimately take over a previously residential neighborhood.

The processes of invasion, dominance, and succession were further explored by Park's associate, Ernest Burgess, who pointed out that cities do not merely grow at their edges. Rather, they have a tendency to expand radially from their center in patterns of concentric circles, each moving gradually outward. Burgess described these concentric circles as "zones."

Zone I is the central business district, while Zone II is the area immediately around it. Zone II generally is the oldest section of the city, and it is continually involved in a process of invasion, dominance, and succession by the businesses and industry that are expanding from Zone I. Houses in this zone are already deteriorating, and will be allowed to deteriorate further because they will be torn down in the foreseeable future to make way for incoming business and industry. Since this is the least desirable residential section of the city, it is usually occupied by the poorest people, including the most recent immigrants to the city. Zone III is the zone of relatively modest homes and apartments, occupied by workers and their families who have escaped the deteriorating conditions in Zone II. The final zone within the city itself is Zone IV, the residential districts of single-family houses and more expensive apartments. Beyond the city limits are the suburban areas and the satellite cities, which constitute Zone V, the commuter zone. Each of these five zones is growing and thus is gradually moving outward into the territory occupied by the next zone, in a process of invasion, dominance, and succession.

Natural areas occur within each zone, and often are linked to natural areas in other zones. For example, Burgess noted the location in Chicago's Zone II where Jewish immigrants initially settled. Zone III was an area of Jewish workers' homes that was constantly receiving new residents from Zone II and at the same time was constantly losing residents to more desirable Jewish neighborhoods in Zones IV and V.[4]

Within the framework of these ideas Park and his colleagues studied the city of Chicago and its problems. They attempted to discover "the processes by which the biotic balance and the social equilibrium are maintained once they are achieved, and the processes by which, when the biotic balance and the social equilibrium are disturbed, the transition is made from one relatively stable order to another."[5]

RESEARCH IN THE "DELINQUENCY AREAS" OF CHICAGO

Park's theories were used as the basis for a broadly ranging study of the problem of juvenile delinquency in Chicago by Clifford R. Shaw. The problem of crime and delinquency had become of increasing concern to social scientists in the 1920s because the country was gripped in a crime wave generated by resistance to Prohibition, a problem that was particularly severe in Chicago.

Shaw worked as a probation and parole officer during this period and became convinced that the problem of juvenile delinquency had its origin in the juvenile's "detachment from conventional groups" rather than in any biological or psychological abnormalities.[6] Following his appointment to the Institute for Juvenile Research in Chicago, Shaw devised a

---

[4]Ernest W. Burgess, "The Growth of the City," in Park, Burgess, and Roderick D. McKenzie, Jr., *The City*, University of Chicago Press, Chicago, 1928, p. 62.

[5]Robert E. Park, "Human Ecology," *American Journal of Sociology* 42: 158 (1936).

[6]James F. Short, Jr., "Introduction to the Revised Edition," in Clifford R. Shaw and Henry D. McKay, *Juvenile Delinquency and Urban Areas*, University of Chicago Press, Chicago, 1969, p. xlvii. Additional background material on Shaw and his colleague Henry McKay can be found in Jon Snodgrass, "Clifford R. Shaw and Henry D. McKay: Chicago Criminologists," *British Journal of Criminology* 16: 1–19 (Jan. 1976). A detailed assessment of their impact on criminology can be found in Harold Finestone, "The Delinquent and Society: The Shaw and McKay Tradition," in James F. Short, ed., *Delinquency, Crime and Society*, University of Chicago Press, Chicago, 1976,

strategy, based on the theory of human ecology, to study the process by which this "detachment from conventional groups" occurred.

Because he saw delinquents as essentially normal human beings, he believed that their illegal activities were somehow bound up with their environment. Therefore the first stage of his strategy involved analyzing the characteristics of the neighborhoods that, according to police and court records, had the most delinquents. But even in the worst of these neighborhoods only about 20 percent of the youth were actually involved with the court. Shaw therefore compiled extensive "life histories" from individual delinquents to find out exactly how they had related to their environment.

Shaw first published his neighborhood studies in 1929 in a volume entitled *Delinquency Areas,* and he subsequently published more of his research in two studies coauthored with Henry D. McKay, *Social Factors in Juvenile Delinquency* (1931) and *Juvenile Delinquency and Urban Areas* (1942). Shaw and McKay reached the following conclusions as a result of studying neighborhoods:

1. *Physical Status:* The neighborhoods with the highest delinquency rates were found to be located within or immediately adjacent to areas of heavy industry or commerce. These neighborhoods also had the greatest number of condemned buildings, and their population was decreasing. The population change was assumed to be related to an industrial invasion of the area, which resulted in fewer buildings being available for residential occupation.[7]

2. *Economic Status:* The highest rates of delinquency were found in the areas of lowest economic status as determined by a number of specific factors, including the percentage of families on welfare, the median rental, and the percentage of families owning homes.[8] These areas also had the highest rates of infant deaths, active cases of tuberculosis, and insanity. But Shaw and McKay concluded that economic conditions did not in themselves *cause* these problems. This conclusion was based on the fact that the rates of delinquency, of adult criminality, of infant deaths, and of tuberculosis for the city as a whole remained relatively stable between 1929 and 1934, when the Great Depression hit, and there was a tenfold increase in the number of families on public or private assistance. Median rentals, welfare rates, and other economic measures continued to show that the areas with the highest concentrations of these problems were in the lowest economic status relative to other areas of the city. These problems appeared to be associated with the

---

pp. 23–49; and Finestone, *Victims of Change: Juvenile Delinquency in American Society,* Greenwood, Westport, CT, 1977, pp. 77–150.

[7]Clifford R. Shaw and Henry D. McKay, *Juvenile Delinquency and Urban Areas,* University of Chicago Press, Chicago, 1969, p. 145.

[8]Ibid., pp. 147–52.

least privileged groups in society, regardless of the actual economic conditions of that society as a whole.

3. *Population Composition:* Areas of highest delinquency were consistently associated with higher concentrations of foreign-born and African American heads of families.[9] To determine the precise role of racial and ethnic factors in the causation of delinquency, Shaw and McKay further analyzed these data. They found that certain inner-city areas in Zone II remained among those with the highest delinquency rates in the city despite shifts of almost all the population of these areas. In 1884 approximately 90 percent of the population in these areas was German, Irish, English, Scottish, or Scandinavian. By 1930 approximately 85 percent of the population was Czech, Italian, Polish, Slavic, or other. In spite of this dramatic shift in ethnic populations, these eight areas continued to have some of the highest delinquency rates in the city. At the same time there was no increase in delinquency rates in the areas into which the older immigrant communities moved.

Shaw and McKay also found that, within similar areas, each group, whether foreign-born or native, recent immigrant or older immigrant, African American or European American, had a delinquency rate that was proportional to the rate of the overall area. No racial, national, or nativity group exhibited a uniform characteristic rate of delinquency in all parts of the city. Each group produced delinquency rates that ranged from the lowest to the highest in the city, depending on the type of area surveyed. Although some variation associated with the group could be seen, it was apparent that the overall delinquency rate of a particular group depended primarily on how many individuals of that group resided in "delinquency areas." Shaw and McKay concluded:[10]

In the face of these facts it is difficult to sustain the contention that, by themselves, the factors of race, nativity, and nationality are vitally related to the problem of juvenile delinquency. It seems necessary to conclude, rather, that the significantly higher rates of delinquents found among the children of Negroes, the foreign born, and more recent immigrants are closely related to existing differences in their respective patterns of geographical distribution within the city. If these groups were found in the same proportion in all local areas, existing differences in the relative number of boys brought into court from the various groups might be expected to be greatly reduced or to disappear entirely.

In addition to this research, Shaw compiled and published a series of "life histories" of individual delinquents, including *The Jackroller*

---

[9]Ibid., p. 155.

[10]Ibid., pp. 162–63.

(1930), *The Natural History of a Delinquent Career* (1931), and *Brothers in Crime* (1938). The basic findings of these histories are summed up in the following points.

1. Delinquents, by and large, "are not different from large numbers of persons in conventional society with respect to intelligence, physical condition, and personality traits."[11]

2. In delinquency areas "the conventional traditions, neighborhood institutions, public opinion, through which neighborhoods usually effect a control over the behavior of the child, were largely disintegrated."[12] In addition, parents and neighbors frequently approved of delinquent behavior, so that the child grew up "in a social world in which [delinquency] was an accepted and appropriate form of conduct."[13]

3. The neighborhoods included many opportunities for delinquent activities, including "junk dealers, professional fences, and residents who purchased their stolen goods" and "dilapidated buildings which served as an incentive for junking." There was also a "lack of preparation, training, opportunity, and proper encouragement for successful employment in private industry."[14]

4. Delinquent activities in these areas began at an early age as a part of play activities of the street.[15]

5. In these play activities, there is a continuity of tradition in a given neighborhood from older boys to younger boys.[16] This tradition includes the transmission of such different criminal techniques as jackrolling, shoplifting, stealing from junkmen, or stealing automobiles, so that different neighborhoods were characterized by the same types of offenses over long periods of time.[17]

6. The normal methods of official social control could not stop this process.[18]

7. It was only later in a delinquent career that the individual began "to identify himself with the criminal world, and to embody in his own philosophy of life the moral values which prevailed in the criminal groups with which he had

---

[11]Clifford R. Shaw, *Brothers in Crime,* University of Chicago Press, Chicago, 1938, p. 350. See also Shaw's *The Jackroller,* University of Chicago Press, Chicago, 1930, p. 164; and *The Natural History of a Delinquent Career,* University of Chicago Press, Chicago, 1931, p. 226.

[12]Shaw, *Natural History,* p. 229. See also *The Jackroller,* p. 165, and *Brothers in Crime,* p. 358.

[13]Shaw, *Brothers in Crime,* p. 356. See also Shaw and McKay, op. cit., p. 172; *The Jackroller,* p. 165; and *Natural History,* p. 229.

[14]Shaw, *Brothers in Crime,* p. 356.

[15]Shaw, *Brothers in Crime,* pp. 354, 355; *Natural History,* p. 227; *The Jackroller,* p. 164. See also Short, op. cit., p. xli.

[16]Shaw and McKay, op. cit., pp. 174–75.

[17]Ibid., p. 174.

[18]Shaw, *Natural History,* p. 233; *Brothers in Crime,* p. 260; Shaw and McKay, op. cit., p. 4.

contact."[19] This was due both to the continuous contact the delinquent had with juvenile and adult criminals on the street and in correctional institutions, and to rejection and stigmatization by the community.

Shaw concluded that delinquency and other social problems are closely related to the process of invasion, dominance, and succession that determines the concentric growth patterns of the city. When a particular location in the city is "invaded" by new residents, the established symbiotic relationships that bind that location to a natural area are destroyed. Ultimately this location will be incorporated as an organic part of a new natural area, and the social equilibrium will be restored. Meanwhile the natural organization of the location will be severely impaired.

These "interstitial areas" (so called because they are *in between* the organized natural areas) become afflicted with a variety of social problems that are directly traceable to the rapid shift in populations. The formal social organizations that existed in the neighborhood tend to disintegrate as the original population retreats. Because the neighborhood is in transition, the residents no longer identify with it, and thus they do not care as much about its appearance or reputation. There is a marked decrease in "neighborliness" and in the ability of the people of the neighborhood to control their youth. For example, in an established neighborhood, a resident who is aware that a child is getting into trouble may call that child's parents or may report that child to the local authorities. But because new people are continuously moving into the interstitial area, residents no longer know their own neighbors or their neighbors' children. Thus children who are out of their parents' sight may be under almost no control, even in their own neighborhood. The high mobility of the residents also means that there is a high turnover of children in the local schools. This turnover is disruptive both to learning and to discipline. Finally, the area tends to become a battleground between the invading and retreating cultures. This change can generate a great deal of conflict in the community, which tends to be manifested in individual and gang conflicts between the youth of the two cultures.

Although other areas only periodically undergo this process, areas in Zone II are continually being invaded both by the central business district and by successive waves of new immigrants coming into the city from foreign countries and from rural areas.[20] These new immigrants al-

---

[19]Shaw, *Natural History*, p. 228. See also *The Jackroller*, pp. 119, 165; *Brothers in Crime*, p. 350.

[20]For a recent review of research on the subject, see Matthew G. Yeager, "Immigrants and Criminality," *Criminal Justice Abstracts* 29(1): 143–71 (1997).

ready have many problems associated with their adjustment to the new culture. In addition, the neighborhood into which an immigrant moves is in a chronic state of "social disorganization." This state presents the immigrant with many additional problems, and there is almost no help available to solve any of them. Thus recent immigrants tend to have a wide range of social problems, including delinquency, among their youth. These problems are resolved as recent immigrants acquire some of the resources necessary both to solve their own problems and to move into the better-established neighborhoods of Zone III, with its natural processes of social control.

POLICY IMPLICATIONS

Because Shaw believed that juvenile delinquency was generated by social disorganization in interstitial areas, he did not believe that treatment of individual delinquents would have much effect in reducing overall delinquency rates. Rather, he thought that the answer had to be found in "the development of programs which seek to effect changes in the conditions of life in specific local communities and in whole sections of the city."[21] In Shaw's view these programs could only come from organizations of neighborhood residents, so that the natural forces of social control could take effect. Thus, in 1932, he launched the Chicago Area Project, which established twenty-two neighborhood centers in six areas of Chicago.[22] Control of these centers rested with committees of local residents rather than with the central staff of the project, and local residents were employed as staff.

These centers had two primary functions. First, they were to coordinate such community resources as churches, schools, labor unions, industries, clubs, and other groups in addressing and resolving community problems. Second, they were to sponsor a variety of activity programs including recreation, summer camping and scouting activities, handicraft workshops, discussion groups, and community projects.[23] Through these activities the project sought "to develop a positive interest by the inhabitants in their own welfare, to establish democratic bodies of local

---

[21]Shaw and McKay, op. cit., p. 4.

[22]See Solomon Kobrin, "The Chicago Area Project—A 25-Year Assessment," *Annals of the American Society of Political and Social Science,* March 1959, pp. 19–29; or Anthony Sorrentino, "The Chicago Area Project After 25 Years," *Federal Probation,* June 1959, pp. 40–45. A review of this and other similar programs is found in Richard Lundman, *Prevention and Control of Juvenile Delinquency,* 2nd ed., Oxford, New York, 1993, ch. 3.

[23]Shaw and McKay, op. cit., p. 324.

citizens who would enable the whole community to become aware of its problems and attempt their solution by common action."[24]

The Chicago Area Project operated continuously for twenty-five years, until Shaw's death in 1957, but its effect on delinquency in these areas was never precisely evaluated,[25] A similar project in Boston was carefully evaluated by Walter B. Miller over a three-year period.[26] Here it was found that the project was effective in achieving many admirable goals. It established close relationships with local gangs and organized their members into clubs, it increased their involvement in recreational activities, it provided them with access to occupational and educational opportunities, it formed citizens' organizations, and it increased inter-agency cooperation in addressing community problems.

The goal of all these activities, however, was to reduce the incidence of delinquent behavior. To assess the impact of the project on the behavior of the youth, Miller analyzed the daily field reports of the outreach workers, which included a description of the activities of each youth. The behaviors were then classified as "moral" or "immoral" (where "immoral" meant disapproval by the community, but not necessarily a violation of the law) and as "legal" or "illegal." It was found that the ratio of moral to immoral behaviors remained relatively constant throughout the project, and that, although the total number of illegal acts decreased slightly during the project, the number of major offenses by boys increased. In addition, data were compiled on the number of court appearances made by each youth before, during, and after contact with the project, and these data were compared with the number of court appearances by a control group. There was almost no difference in these statistics. Miller concluded that the project had had a "negligible impact" on delinquency.[27] The failure of this and other similar projects led Lundman to conclude that it was likely that "the Chicago Area Project also failed to prevent juvenile delinquency."[28]

RESIDENTIAL SUCCESSION, SOCIAL DISORGANIZATION, AND CRIME

After the failure to show that the Chicago Area Projects prevented delinquency, Shaw and McKay's theory went into a period of decline. In

---

[24]Morris, *The Criminal Area*, p. 83.

[25]Short, op. cit., p. xlvi.

[26]Walter B. Miller, "The Impact of a 'Total-Community' Delinquency Control Project," *Social Problems* 10: 168–91 (fall 1962).

[27]Ibid., p. 187.

[28]Lundman, op. cit., p. 81.

1978, however, the theory was revitalized by the publication of an influential book by Kornhauser.[29] She argued that Shaw and McKay's theory actually contains two separate arguments: a "social disorganization" argument that delinquency emerges in neighborhoods where the neighborhood relationships and institutions have broken down and can no longer maintain effective social controls, and a "subcultural" argument that, over time, these delinquent behaviors come to be supported by the shared values and norms of neighborhood residents.[30] After considerable deliberation, Shaw and McKay had concluded that the second argument was more important than the first, and that delinquent subcultures accounted for most slum delinquency. Kornhauser, however, argued that this conclusion was illogical. Shaw and McKay's theory describes the delinquency as emerging first, because of the social disorganization, and then the delinquent subculture arises later on, in order to provide social supports for the delinquency. Thus, Kornhauser argued that disorganized neighborhoods would have delinquency whether or not they had delinquent subcultures, but the delinquent subculture would not exist without the delinquency caused by the social disorganization. Thus, at the theoretical level, the social disorganization is the primary cause of delinquency.

Kornhauser therefore extracted a "community control" model from Shaw and McKay's theory that summarized their arguments about social disorganization. The basic argument is that people who are poor, who live in racially and ethnically diverse neighborhoods, and who move frequently from one place to another, will have trouble establishing and maintaining the normal social relationships and institutions by which neighborhood residents normally achieve their common aspirations and goals. Thus, neighborhoods with high poverty, high racial and ethnic heterogeneity, and high residential mobility should also have high rates of crime and delinquency. Kornhauser then reviewed a very large number of empirical studies to demonstrate support for that model.[31]

In 1982, Bursik and Webb similarly concluded that neighborhood social disorganization is the primary explanation of neighborhood delinquency rates.[32] They focused on Shaw and McKay's concept of residential succession, the fact that neighborhoods often retain their high crime and delinquency rates despite total turnovers in population. Using data

---

[29]Ruth Rosner Kornhauser, *Social Sources of Delinquency,* University of Chicago Press, Chicago, 1978.

[30]Ibid., pp. 61–69.

[31]Ibid., pp. 69–138 The model is summarized in a table on p. 73 of *Social Sources of Delinquency*

[32]Robert J. Bursik, Jr., and Jim Webb, "Community Change and Patterns of Delinquency," *American Journal of Sociology* 88(1): 24–42 (1982).

on Chicago neighborhoods directly comparable to that used by Shaw and McKay, Bursik and Webb found that the residential succession argument was supported by data from 1940 to 1950. That is, neighborhood crime rates tended to remain the same despite total turnovers in population. However, after 1950 all neighborhoods undergoing race-based turnovers in their population were characterized by high delinquency rates, regardless of their delinquency rates before the change.

Bursik and Webb interpreted this finding in terms of community stability. At the time Shaw and McKay wrote, the zones of transition were found exclusively in the inner-city areas, and the process of dispersion to outlying residential areas was gradual. This "natural" process was disrupted in more recent times as African Americans attempted to follow in the footsteps of other ethnic groups. Strong European American resistance to any African Americans moving into the neighborhood would be followed by total "white flight" and total racial turnover in a very short time. Neighborhood social institutions would disappear entirely or persevere but resist including the new residents. This process resulted in near total neighborhood social disorganization, which then caused the high delinquency rates.

Bursik and Webb also found that, after the neighborhood populations had stabilized, the neighorhoods "had delinquency rates not much different than would have been expected from their previous patterns."[33] Thus, after things settled down, the residential succession phenomenon seemed to reappear. This finding was consistent with several other studies that found delinquency rates were increasing in African American neighborhoods that had recently undergone residential changes but were decreasing in African American neighborhoods that had been stable for some time.[34]

In an attempt to further explain the findings about residential succession, Stark asked what it is about neighborhoods themselves that is associated with high crime rates, independent of the people who live there. As an answer to this question, he presented a formal theory in thirty integrated propositions.[35] These thirty propositions focused on five structural aspects of urban neighborhoods: density (many people in a small area), poverty (people have little money), mixed land use (residences, industries, and stores are all in the same place), residential mobility

---

[33]Ibid., p. 39.

[34]Robert E. Kapsis, "Residential Succession and Delinquency," *Criminology* 15(4): 459–86 (Feb. 1978). See also findings by McKay reported in the 1969 edition of Shaw and McKay, op. cit., p. 345, and interesting comments by Snodgrass, op. cit., pp. 5–6.

[35]Rodney Stark, "Deviant Places: A Theory of the Ecology of Crime," *Criminology* 25(4): 893–909 (November, 1987).

(people frequently move into, out of, and around the neighborhood), and delapidation (the buildings themselves are falling apart). Stark argues that, in a variety of ways, these five structural characteristics increase moral cynicism among community residents, provide more opportunities to commit crime, increase motivations to commit crime, and decrease the informal surveillance by which crime in a community is held in check. As a consequence, crime-prone people are attracted to the neighborhood, while law-abiding people get out if they can. This pattern results in high crime rates that tend to persist even when there are complete turnovers in the people who live there.

SAMPSON'S THEORY OF COLLECTIVE EFFICACY

Similarly, Sampson reviewed recent research on the relation between neighborhoods and crime in an attempt to determine how community structures and cultures create different crime rates.[36] Sampson found that, although poverty itself is not associated with crime, poverty combined with residential mobility (i.e., frequent moves by residents) is associated with higher levels of violent crime. Neighborhood rates of family disruption (divorce rates and rates of female-headed households) are strongly and consistently related to rates of violence. Neighborhoods with high percentages of African Americans have higher crime rates, but race itself tends to drop out when family disruption and poverty are taken into account. Finally, neighborhoods with high population density, many apartments, and high concentrations of individuals who do not live within a family situation tend to have higher rates of crime and violence.

Sampson explained this pattern of findings with Shaw's concept of social disorganization, which he defined as the inability of the community to realize its common values. An example would be when community residents oppose drug use but cannot get rid of the drug dealers who have taken over a nearby corner or house for a drug market. There may be a variety of reasons why some communities cannot realize their common values, but one reason is the lack of what Coleman calls "social capital"—i.e., networks of relationships among people that facilitate common actions and make possible the achievement of common goals.[37] Sampson argued that, when there are many social relationships among

---

[36]Robert J. Sampson, "The Community," pp. 193–216 in James Q. Wilson and Joan Petersilia, eds., *Crime,* ICS Press, San Francisco, 1995. See also Sampson and Janet Lauritsen, "Violent Victimization and Offending: Individual, Situational, and Community-Level Risk Factors," Chapter 1 in Albert J. Reiss and Jeffrey A. Roth, eds., *Understanding and Preventing Violence,* vol. 3, National Academy Press, Washington, DC, 1994.

[37]James Coleman, "Social Capital in the Creation of Human Capital," *American Journal of Sociology* 94(Supplement): 95–120 (1988).

community residents (i.e., a lot of social capital), there is less crime. Even criminals do not want crime in their own neighborhoods, and social relationships allow people to achieve their common goal of driving the crime out.

Sampson then proposed a causal sequence that ties all this research together in a way that resembles Shaw's earlier work.[38] Poverty, family disruption, and high residential mobility are community characteristics that result in anonymity, the lack of social relationships among neighborhood residents, and low participation in community organizations and in local activities. Because of this low social capital, neighbors are not able to exert effective control over public or common areas, such as streets and parks, and so these areas are free to be taken over by criminals. In addition, local teenagers have considerable freedom because the anonymity of the neighborhood means that they and their friends are unknown to adults even though the teenagers may be only a short distance from their homes. This anonymity results in increased crime and violence in the neighborhood, independent of the people who live there. The high crime and violence then promotes further disintegration of the community, as law-abiding residents withdraw from community life and try to move out of the neighborhood.

The concentration of crime among African Americans, according to Sampson, is caused primarily by differences in the neighborhoods in which they live. About 38 percent of poor African Americans live in extremely poor neighborhoods, compared to about 7 percent of poor European Americans. About 70 percent of poor European Americans live in neighborhoods that are not poor, while only 16 percent of poor African Americans live in non-poor neighborhoods. Thus, poor European Americans are much more dispersed in the population, while poor African Americans are much more concentrated in locations where everyone else is also poor. In addition, the "worst" urban neighborhoods in which European Americans live are considerably better, in terms of poverty and family disruption, than the average urban neighborhoods in which poor African Americans live.[39] To the extent that neighborhoods themselves cause crime, these statistics would produce marked differences in the crime rates of these two groups.

Additional research has supported the argument that high African American rates of crime and delinquency are largely explained by their

---

[38]Sampson, "The Community," op. cit., pp. 200–201.

[39]Ibid., pp. 201–02. See also Robert Sampson and William Julius Wilson, "Toward a Theory of Race, Crime and Urban Inequality," in John Hagan and Ruth Peterson, eds., *Crime and Inequality*, Stanford University Press, Stanford, CA, 1995.

concentration in extremely poor neighborhoods,[40] particularly when those neighborhoods are isolated from the rest of the city.[41] Attention therefore has turned to the precise mechanisms by which neighborhoods control (or fail to control) crime and delinquency. Sampson had argued that this mechanism involved the social relationships among community residents, including participation in community organizations and local activities, especially as such participation relates to the informal processes by which residents control activities in the public spaces in the neighborhoods (e.g., streets and parks). A series of studies have attempted to test this basic argument.

Using data from England, Sampson and Groves found that the presence of unsupervised adolescent peer groups on the streets of a community had the largest overall effect on street crimes in that community, as well as the largest overall effect on the personal rates of violent behavior among the adolescents themselves.[42] The presence of these groups on the street suggested the absence of neighborhood social control of adolescents. In a more direct attempt to measure informal social control of adolescents in public areas, Sampson asked people from 80 Chicago neighborhoods how likely it was that neighbors would do something if neighborhood children were skipping school, spray-painting graffiti on a local building, or showing disrespect to an adult?[43] How these three measures of neighborhood social control were fulfilled in turn explained half of the relation between crime and residential mobility in the neighborhood.

Sampson and his coauthors then introduced the term "collective efficacy," which is defined in terms of the neighborhood's ability to maintain

---

[40]See, for example, Lauren J. Krivo and Ruth D. Peterson, "Extremely Disadvantaged Neighborhoods and Urban Crime," *Social Forces* 75(2): 619–48 (1996); Edem F. Avakame, "Urban Homicide," *Homicide Studies*, 1(4): 338–58 (1997). For a review, see Robert J. Sampson and Janet L. Lauritsen, "Racial and Ethnic Disparities in Crime and Criminal Justice in the United States," pp. 311–74 in Michael Tonry, ed., *Ethnicity, Crime, and Immigration: Comparative and Cross National Perspectives (Crime and Justice: A Review of Research*, vol. 21), University of Chicago Press, Chicago, 1997.

[41]Edward S. Shihadeh and Nicole Flynn, "Segregation and Crime," *Social Forces* 74(4): 1325–52 (1996).

[42]Robert J. Sampson and W. Byron Groves, "Community Structure and Crime," *American Journal of Sociology* 94: 774–802 (1989). Mixed support for these conclusions is found in a later elaboration by Bonita M. Veysey and Steven F. Messner, "Further Testing of Social Disorganization Theory," *Journal of Research in Crime and Delinquency* 36(2): 156–74 (1999).

[43]Robert J. Sampson, "Collective Regulation of Adolescent Misbehavior," *Journal of Adolescent Research* 12(2): 227–44 (1997). See also Delbert Elliott et al., "The Effects of Neighborhood Disadvantage on Adolescent Development," *Journal of Research in Crime and Delinquency* 33: 389–426 (1996), which asked neighbors in Denver how likely it was that a person would take action if someone were breaking into a neighbor's house in plain sight.

order in public spaces such as streets, sidewalks, and parks.[44] Collective efficacy is implemented when neighborhood residents take overt actions to maintain public order, such as by complaining to the authorities or by organizing neighborhood watch programs. The authors argued that residents take such actions only when "cohesion and mutual trust" in the neighborhood is linked to "shared expectations for intervening in support of neighborhood social control."[45] If either the mutual trust or the shared expectations are absent, then residents will be unlikely to act when disorder invades public space.

In order to test this theory of collective efficacy, both sides of the street in about 12,000 blocks in 196 Chicago neighborhoods were videotaped during daylight hours from a slowly moving car.[46] The videotapes then were analyzed and coded for the presence of *physical* disorder in public spaces (e.g., abandoned buildings or cars, graffiti, litter in the streets, syringes on the sidewalks). Over 3,800 adults in these neighborhoods were then interviewed about *social* disorder in public spaces (e.g., drug selling, solicitation by prostitutes, public drinking or fighting).[47] To measure the "shared expectations for intervening in support of neighborhood social control," the residents were asked whether it was likely that their neighbors would take action in response to five specific situations involving public disorder. Finally, to measure "cohesion and mutual trust," they were asked five questions about whether it was a "close-knit neighborhood" and whether "people in this neighborhood share the same values." The videotape and interview data then were joined with official police reports on crime, and with 1990 census data on concentrated poverty, concentrated immigration, residential stability, land use, and density in the neighborhoods.

After analyzing all of this data, Sampson and Raudenbush found that both physical and social disorder were very strongly related to concentrated poverty and mixed land use. Within the context of that relationship, however, there was less crime in neighborhoods with more social cohesion and more shared expectations for intervening in support of

---

[44]Robert J. Sampson, Stephen W. Raudenbush, and Felton Earls, "Neighborhoods and Violent Crime: A Multilevel Study of Collective Efficacy," *Science* 277: 918–24 (1997); Robert J. Sampson and Stephen W. Raudenbush, "Systematic Social Observation of Public Spaces," *American Journal of Sociology* 105(3): 603–51 (1999). "Collective efficacy" is more or less the opposite of "social disorganization"—the first term refers to the ability and the second term to the inability to achieve common goals. "Collective efficacy," however, is narrowly defined in terms of the goal of controlling public space.

[45]Sampson and Raudenbush, ibid., pp. 611–12.

[46]Ibid., pp. 617–19.

[47]Ibid., p. 620. Social disorder was also coded from the videotapes, but this was rarely captured.

neighborhood social control. Thus, they concluded that "the active in-gredients in crime seem to be structural disadvantage and attenuated collective efficacy . . ."[48]

IMPLICATIONS AND CONCLUSIONS

The Chicago School of Human Ecology can be described as a gold mine that continues to enrich criminology today. Shaw's individual case stud-ies remain classic portrayals of delinquents and their social worlds, his urban research methods have led to a wide variety of empirical studies, and the social disorganization theory forms the basis for several other theories in contemporary criminology.

Despite the richness of this historic legacy, the ecological approach to crime was somewhat stagnant for many years. Since about 1980, howev-er, there has been a veritable explosion of new theory and research that has ecological theory as its foundation. The basic point of this new theo-ry and research is that crime cannot be understood without also under-standing its immediate context: the neighborhoods. Ultimately, this con-clusion relies on Shaw and McKay's finding about residential succession: that crime rates in neighborhoods tend to remain the same despite total turnovers in the population of those neighborhoods.

Residential succession suggests that policy recommendation to re-duce crime can be directed at high-crime neighborhoods themselves, rather than at the people who live in the high-crime neighborhoods. While the initial attempts of the Chicago Area Projects seemed to have little impact on crime, Sampson has proposed a variety of new policies that focus on "changing places, not people." These include targeting "hot spots" in the community where there is frequent criminal activity; stopping the "spiral of decay" by cleaning up trash, graffiti, and so on; in-creasing the social relationships between adults and teenagers through organized youth activities; reducing residential mobility by enabling res-idents to buy their homes or take over management of their apartments;

---

[48]Ibid., p. 638. See also Sampson, Raudenbush and Earls, op. cit., who found that social cohesion among neighbors, combined with the willingness of neighbors to intervene on behalf of the com-mon good, is associated with reduced violence in the neighborhood. They also found that concen-trated poverty and residential mobility undermine this willingness, which in turn increases crime and public disorder. In contrast, using data from Seattle, Barbara D. Warner and Pamela Wilcox Rountree ("Local Social Ties in a Community and Crime Model," *Social Problems* 44[4]: 520–36 [1997] found that neighborhood social ties reduced assaults in European-American neighborhoods but they had no effect in African-American or racially mixed neighborhoods. In addition, Paul Bel-lair ("Social Interaction and Community Crime," Criminology 35[4]: 677–703 [1997] found that the frequency of social interactions among neighborhood residents had no effect on crime. However, neither of these studies directly measured the shared expectations or mutual cohesion that make up collective efficacy.

scattering public housing in a broad range of neighborhoods rather than concentrating it in poor neighborhoods; maintaining and increasing urban services, such as police, fire, and public health services, especially those aimed at reducing child abuse and teen pregnancy; and generally increasing community power by promoting community organizations. Sampson concedes that such programs have had limited success in the past, but argues that small successes can produce cumulative changes that will result in a more stable community in the long run. In fact, several researchers have argued that the recent major reductions in crime in inner-city areas can be explained by the increasingly effective organization of residents to fight crime in their own neighborhoods.[49] Thus, these approaches may be a major component of crime policies in the future.

---

[49]Richard Curtis, "The Improbable Transformation of Inner-City Neighborhoods," pp. 1233–76, and Warren Friedman, "Volunteerism and the Decline of Violent Crime," pp. 1453–74, both in *Journal of Criminal Law & Criminology* 88(4), 1998.

CHAPTER EIGHT

Strain Theories

In adapting Durkheim's theory to American society, Shaw and McKay retained Durkheim's argument about rapid social change but shifted the focus from societies to neighborhoods. Robert K. Merton also adapted Durkheim's theory to American society, but he shifted the focus away from rapid social change. Instead, he argued that there were certain relatively stable social conditions that were associated with the higher overall crime rates in American society, as well as with the higher rates of crime in the lower social classes. Merton used the term "social structural strain" to describe those social conditions, so that the theories that followed Merton's lead have come to be known as "strain theories."

ROBERT K. MERTON AND ANOMIE IN AMERICAN SOCIETY

Durkheim had analyzed anomie as a breakdown in the ability of society to regulate the natural appetites of individuals. Merton, in an article first published in 1938,[1] argued out that many of the appetites of individuals are not "natural," but rather originate in the "culture" of American society. At the same time, the "social structure" of American society limits the ability of certain groups to satisfy those appetites. The result is "a

---

[1] Robert K. Merton, *Social Theory and Social Structure*, The Free Press, Glencoe, Ill., 1968, p. 186. The most recent presentation and discussion of this theory is found in Merton, "Opportunity Structure: The Emergence, Diffusion, and Differentiation as Sociological Concept, 1930s–1950s," in Freda Adler and William Laufer, eds., *Advances in Criminological Theory: The Legacy of Anomie Theory*, vol. 6, Transaction Press, New Brunswick, NJ, 1995, pp. 3–78. For a discussion of the relationship between Durkheim's and Merton's theories, see Thomas J. Bernard, "Merton vs. Hirschi: Who Is Faithful to Durkheim's Heritage?" in Adler and Laufer, op. cit., pp. 81–90.

definite pressure on certain persons in the society to engage in noncon-
formist rather than conformist conduct."[2]

Merton began by pointing out that the culture of any society defines
certain goals it deems "worth striving for."[3] There are many such goals in
every society, and they vary from culture to culture. Perhaps the most
prominent culture goal in American society, however, is to acquire
wealth. This might be regarded merely as a "natural aspiration," as
Durkheim maintained. But American culture encourages this goal far
beyond any intrinsic rewards the goal itself might have. Accumulated
wealth is generally equated with personal value and worth and is associated with a high degree of prestige and social status. Those without
money may be degraded even if they have personal characteristics that
other cultures may value, such as age or spiritual discipline.

In addition, whereas Durkheim said that culture functioned to limit
these aspirations in individuals (although at certain times it did not do
this well), Merton argued that American culture specifically encourages
all individuals to seek the greatest amount of wealth. American culture
is based on an egalitarian ideology that asserts that all people have an
equal chance to achieve wealth. Although all individuals are not expected to achieve this goal, all are expected to try. Those who do not may be
unfavorably characterized as "lazy" or "unambitious."[4]

Cultures also specify the approved norms, or institutionalized means,
all individuals are expected to follow in pursuing the culture goals. These
means are based on values in the culture, and generally will rule out many
of the technically most efficient methods of achieving the goal. For example, in American culture the institutionalized means that should be
used to achieve wealth can generally be identified as "middle-class values" or "the Protestant work ethic." They include hard work, honesty, education, and deferred gratification. The use of force and fraud, which
may be more efficient methods of gaining wealth, is forbidden.[5]

Merton argued that because all persons cannot be expected to
achieve the goals of the culture, it is very important that the culture
place a strong emphasis on the institutionalized means and the necessity
of following them for their own value.[6] These means must provide some
intrinsic satisfactions for all persons who participate in the culture. This

---

[2]For definitions of structure and culture in Merton's theory, see Merton, "Opportunity Structure,"
op. cit., pp. 6–7.

[3]Merton, *Social Theory and Social Structure*, op. cit., p. 187.

[4]Ibid., p. 193.

[5]Ibid., p. 187.

[6]Ibid., p. 188.

is similar to the situation in athletics, in which the sport itself must provide enjoyment, even if the person does not win. The phrase "It's not whether you win, it's how you play the game" expresses the notion that the primary satisfaction comes from following the institutionalized means (rules) rather than achieving the goal (winning).

In athletics, however, the goal of winning may be unduly emphasized, so that there is a corresponding deemphasis on the rewards provided by the sport itself. In this situation ("It's not how you play the game, it's whether you win") the institutionalized means are placed under a severe strain. Merton argues that this is the situation in American culture regarding the goal of achieving wealth.[7] The goal has been emphasized to the point that the institutionalized means are little reward in themselves. The person who adheres to these methods—that is, hard work, education, honesty, deferred gratification—receives little social reward for it unless he or she also achieves at least a moderate degree of wealth as a result. But the person who achieves wealth, even if it is not by the approved means, still receives the social rewards of prestige and social status. This situation places a severe strain on the institutionalized means, particularly for those persons who cannot achieve wealth through their use.

This strain falls on a wide variety of people in the society, but it tends to be more concentrated among persons in the lower class. In that group the ability to achieve wealth is limited not only by the talents and efforts of the individual, but by the social structure itself. Only the most talented and the most hard-working individuals from this class can ever expect to achieve wealth through the use of the institutionalized means. For the majority of persons this possibility is simply not realistic, and therefore the strain can be most severe. By the same token, the strain is least apparent among those in the upper classes, in which, using the same institutionalized means, a person of moderate talents can achieve a degree of wealth with only moderate efforts.

For certain groups, then, a severe strain on the cultural values arises because (1) the culture places a disproportionate emphasis on the achievement of the goal of accumulated wealth and maintains that this goal is applicable to all persons, and (2) the social structure effectively limits the possibilities of individuals within these groups to achieve this goal through the use of institutionalized means. This contradiction between the culture and the social structure of society is what Merton defines as anomie.[8]

---

[7]Ibid., p. 190.
[8]Ibid., p. 216.

Merton therefore used a *cultural argument* to explain the high rate of crime in American society as a whole, and a *structural argument* to explain the concentration of crime in the lower classes.[9] The high level of crime in American society was explained in terms of "cultural imbalance"—the imbalance between the strong cultural forces that valued the goal of monetary success and the much weaker cultural forces that valued the institutional means of hard work, honesty, and education. However, Merton described American culture as relatively uniform throughout the class structure, so that everyone is similarly pressured to achieve wealth and everyone has a relatively weak allegiance to the institutionalized means. Thus "cultural imbalance" does not explain why the lower classes in America have higher crime rates than the upper classes. Merton therefore used social structure, not culture, to explain why lower-class people in America have higher crime rates than upper-class people. That explanation focused on the distribution of legitimate opportunities in the social structure—that is the ability to achieve wealth through institutionalized means. Merton argued that those opportunities were relatively concentrated in the higher classes and relatively absent in the lower classes. The distribution of criminal behavior is said to be a sort of mirror image of the distribution of legitimate opportunities, being relatively concentrated in the lower classes and relatively absent in the upper classes.

There are various ways in which an individual can respond to this problem of anomie, depending on his attitude toward the culture goals and the institutionalized means. Merton describes these options as conformity, innovation, ritualism, retreatism, and rebellion.

To the extent that a society is stable, most persons in it will choose conformity, which entails acceptance of both the culture goals and the institutionalized means. These persons strive to achieve wealth through the approved methods of middle-class values and will continue to do so whether or not they succeed.

Most crime that exists in society, however, will probably take the form of innovation. Persons who innovate retain their allegiance to the culture goal of acquiring wealth (since this is so heavily emphasized), but they find that they cannot succeed at this through the institutionalized means. Therefore they figure out new methods by which wealth can be acquired. Businessmen may devise different forms of white-collar crime entailing fraud and misrepresentation, or they may cheat on their in-

---

[9]These cultural and structural arguments are presented in propositional form in Thomas J. Bernard, "Testing Structural Strain Theories," *Journal of Research in Crime and Delinquency* 24(4): 264–70 (1987).

come tax. Workers may systematically steal from their place of employment. Poor people may develop illegal operations, such as gambling, prostitution, or drug dealing, or they may burglarize and rob. In each of these cases the individual has retained his commitment to the culture goal, but is pursuing it through unapproved means.

This situation is very similar to that described by the classical thinkers, who maintained that since humans were hedonistic, they would always choose the most technically efficient methods of achieving their goals, unless limited by punishments, imposed by society.[10] Although the classical thinkers thought this was the normal condition of people, Merton argued that it was the condition only when the cultural goals were overemphasized to the point that the norms broke down.

A third possible adaptation involves rejecting the possibility of ever achieving wealth, but retaining allegiance to the norms of hard work, honesty, etc. This is the adaptation of those persons who wish to "play it safe." They will not be disappointed by failure to achieve their goals, since they have abandoned them. At the same time they will never find themselves in any trouble since they abide by all the cultural norms. This is the perspective of "the frightened employee, the zealously conformist bureaucrat in the teller's cage"[11] and tends to be found most frequently among persons in the lower middle class. These persons have achieved a minimum level of success through the institutionalized means, but have no real hope of achieving anything more. The fear of losing even this minimum level locks them into their adaptation.

The fourth adaptation—retreatism—involves simply dropping out of the whole game. Dropouts neither pursue the cultural goals nor act according to the institutionalized means. Those who choose this adaptation include "psychotics, autists, pariahs, outcasts, vagrants, vagabonds, tramps, chronic drunkards and drug addicts."[12] Merton points out that this adaptation does not necessarily arise from a lack of commitment to the culture. It can also occur when there is a strong commitment to both the goals and the means, but no real possibility of achieving success.

There results a twofold conflict: the interiorized moral obligation for adopting institutional means conflicts with pressures to resort to illicit means (which may attain the goal) and the individual is shut off from means which are both legitimate and effective. The competitive order is maintained, but the frustrated and handicapped individual who cannot cope with this order drops out.

---

[10]Merton, op. cit., p. 211.

[11]Ibid., p. 204.

[12]Ibid., p. 207.

Rebellion is the last of the possible adaptations to the problem of anomie. Here the person responds to his frustrations by replacing the values of the society with new ones. These new values may be political, in which the goals are, for example, the achievement of a socialist society, and the approved means might involve violent revolution. On the other hand these values might be spiritual, in which the goals entail the achievement of certain states of consciousness, and the means involve fasting and meditation. Or the values might be in one of any number of other areas. The basic point is that this person ceases to function as a member of the existing society and begins to live within an alternate culture.

These adaptations do not describe personality types. Rather they describe an individual's choice of behaviors in response to the strain of anomie. Some individuals may consistently choose one adaptation, such as low-level bureaucrats who respond to their situation through ritualism. But the same bureaucrats may occasionally innovate by stealing small amounts from their employers, or they may occasionally retreat through the use of alcohol. Other persons develop patterns of behavior involving the use of several adaptations simultaneously. For example, a professional criminal (innovation) may also consistently use narcotics (retreatism) while at the same time promoting a militant, revolutionary philosophy (rebellion). These behaviors might not be seen as consistent with each other unless it is understood they are all responses to the anomic situation the individual faces.

These same adaptations may be seen in other situations in which there is a discrepancy between the emphasis placed on the goals and the means to achieve them. In athletics, if the goal of winning is overemphasized, those who cannot win within the institutionalized means (rules) may be strongly motivated to cheat (innovate), they may merely continue playing without hope of winning (ritualism), they may quit playing altogether (retreatism), or they may attempt to get a different game going (rebellion). Students are often faced with a strong overemphasis of the goal of achieving high grades, and may resort to similar adaptations. Deviant behavior among scientists has been analyzed in terms of an overemphasis on the goal of originality in scientific research.[13] Those who cannot achieve this goal may resort to various adaptive behaviors such as "reporting only the data which support an hypoth-

---

[13]Robert K. Merton, "Priorities in Scientific Discovery: A Chapter in the Sociology of Science," *American Sociological Review* 22: 635–59 (Dec. 1957). See also Harriet Zuckerman, "Deviant Behavior and Social Control in Science," in Edward Sagarin, ed., *Deviance and Social Change*, Sage, Beverly Hills, CA, 1977, pp. 87–138.

esis, making false charges of plagiarism, making self-assertive claims, being secretive lest one be forestalled, occasionally stealing ideas, and in rare cases, even fabricating data."[14]

Finally, Merton makes the point that "the foregoing theory of anomie is designed to account for some, not all, forms of deviant behavior customarily described as criminal or delinquent."[15] The intention of the theory is to focus attention on one specific problem, "the acute pressure created by the discrepancy between culturally induced goals and socially structured opportunities," and does not attempt to explain all the diverse behaviors that at one time or another are prohibited by the criminal law.

A number of theorists have attempted to extend and refine Merton's theories. The most significant of these attempts was by Richard Cloward, writing in 1959.[16] Whereas Merton focuses on the fact that lower-class people had limited access to legal means of achieving success goals, Cloward pointed out that these same people often had very broad access to illegal means that existed in their neighborhoods. The local pawn shop, which would fence stolen goods, the junkyard, which would take that hot car off their hands, the numbers racket, and the drug and prostitution rings all provided illegal opportunities to achieve the success goals of society. Cloward also pointed out that the mere presence of an opportunity is not enough unless one has been introduced to the ways of taking advantage of it.[17] This "learning structure" had been described by Shaw and McKay in their studies of delinquency areas and by Sutherland in his theory that crime is normal, learned behavior; and Cloward regarded his formulation as a consolidation of these three approaches. Merton agreed with Cloward's theory, regarding it as a substantial extension of his own theory.[18]

STRAIN AS THE EXPLANATION OF GANG DELINQUENCY

Merton's reformulation of anomie theory focused on the special strains under which certain segments of the population are placed, and used those strains to explain criminality. This type of argument has also been

---

[14]Marshall B. Clinard, "The Theoretical Implications of Anomie and Deviant Behavior," in Clinard, ed., *Anomie and Deviant Behavior,* The Free Press, New York, 1964, p. 23.

[15]Merton, *Social Theory and Social Structure,* p. 195.

[16]Richard A. Cloward, "Illegitimate Means, Anomie, and Deviant Behavior," *American Sociological Review* 24: 164–76 (April 1959).

[17]Ibid., p. 168.

[18]Robert K. Merton, "Social Conformity, Deviation and Opportunity Structures: A Comment on the Contributions of Dubin and Cloward," *American Sociological Review* 24: 188 (April 1959).

used in two major theories to explain urban, lower-class, male gang delinquency, one by Albert Cohen and the other by Richard Cloward and Lloyd Ohlin.

In his work with juveniles, Cohen found that most delinquent behavior occurred in gangs rather than individually, and that most of it was "non-utilitarian, malicious, and negativistic."[19] This type of delinquency, in contrast to most adult crime, seemed to serve no useful purpose. Juvenile gangs stole things they did not want or need, vandalized and maliciously destroyed property, and participated in gang wars and unprovoked assaults. Purposeless crimes could not be explained by Merton's theory, which argued that crimes had the purpose of acquiring money, although by illegitimate means. Cohen believed that these actions were methods of gaining status among the delinquent's peers, but then he had to ask why these behaviors were "a claim to status in one group and a degrading blot in another."[20] He concluded that gangs have a separate culture from the dominant culture, with a different set of values for measuring status. The question that Cohen then addressed was why and how this separate culture had evolved.

Merton described people as seeking the cultural goal of success. In a similar way Cohen saw youths as seeking the goal of status among their peers. He utilized the classic distinction between achieved status, which is earned in competition with one's own age and sex group, and ascribed status, which is acquired by virtue of one's family, such as when one's father is an important person. Competition for achieved status normally takes place within the school. Cohen saw the school as a solidly middle-class institution, permeated by the values of its middle-class teachers and administrators. Status in school was judged on the basis of such values as ambition, responsibility, achievement (especially in the areas of academic work and athletics), deferred gratification, rationality, courtesy, ability to control physical aggression, constructive use of time, and respect for property.[21]

Youths who have no ascribed status by virtue of their families, and who typically lose in the competition for achieved status, are placed under a severe strain. They can continue to conform to middle-class values, but they must then be content with a low-status position among their peers. Or they can rebel against middle-class values and set up a new value

---

[19]Albert K. Cohen, *Delinquent Boys: The Culture of the Gang*, The Free Press, New York, 1955. For an analysis of the theory and a statement of its major arguments in propositional form, see Bernard, "Testing Structural Strain Theories," op. cit. Merton discusses and analyzes the theory in "Opportunity Structure," op. cit., pp. 33–44.

[20]Ibid., p. 27.

[21]Ibid., pp. 88–91.

structure according to which they can increase their status and self-worth. Youths who rebel in such a way tend to come together to form a group in order to validate their choices and reinforce their new values. The delinquent gang is such a group. It is a spontaneous development in which a number of youths, each of whom faces a similar problem (low status), together create a common solution to that problem.

Lack of status may affect youths in different social classes, but, like Merton's anomie, it disproportionately affects youths from the lower class. These youths generally have no ascribed status from their families, since their parents normally have low-status occupations. At the same time they are at a disadvantage in competing for achieved status in schools. Lower-class children often have internalized values different from those of middle-class children prior to entering the school. When measured against these values, they perform poorly and must either adjust to these new values or reject them. Thus members of delinquent gangs will generally be lower-class children. And because the gang is primarily rebelling against middle-class values, it takes on the "negativistic" character noticed by Cohen.

Merton's and Cohen's theories differ in several respects. Merton emphasized the utilitarian nature of crime, focusing on innovation as a response to the social structural pressures, whereas Cohen sought to explain the nonutilitarian character of much delinquency. Cohen's theory is similar to the "rebellion" adaptation proposed by Merton, but it differs in that the particular form the rebellion takes is determined by a reaction against middle-class values. In Merton's theory rebellion may take any one of a number of different forms. Finally, Cohen saw the choice of rebellion as linked to the choices of other members of the group, whereas Merton portrayed the choice of an adaptation as an individual response.

Cloward and Ohlin's theory of gang delinquency returned to Merton's emphasis on the utilitarian nature of crime.[22] Cloward and Ohlin agreed with Cohen that some gang delinquency is motivated by the pursuit of status and by a reaction against middle-class values. But they argued that these youths tend to be the less serious delinquents. The more serious delinquents, according to Cloward and Ohlin, are simply looking for money, not status. In particular, serious delinquents are oriented toward conspicuous consumption, "fast cars, fancy clothes, and swell dames," goals that are phrased solely in economic terms and have no relationship

---

[22]Richard A. Cloward and Lloyd E. Ohlin, *Delinquency and Opportunity: A Theory of Delinquent Gangs*, The Free Press, New York, 1960. For an analysis of the theory and a statement of its major arguments in prepositional form, see Bernard, "Testing Structural Strain Theories," op. cit. Merton discusses and analyzes the theory in "Opportunity Structure," op. cit., pp. 44–71.

to middle-class values. These youths experience the greatest conflict with middle-class values, since they "are looked down upon both for what they do *not* want (i.e., the middle-class style of life) and for what they *do* want (i.e., 'crass materialism')."[23] These are the youths, Cloward and Ohlin claim, who have been repeatedly described in the literature of juvenile delinquency.

Cloward and Ohlin then refer to the earlier extension of Merton's theory by Cloward to explain the particular form of delinquency that these youths will commit. It is assumed that there are no legitimate opportunities for these youths to improve their economic position. If illegitimate opportunities are presented, as described by Cloward, then these youths will tend to form "criminal" gangs, in which the emphasis is on production of income. If, however, neither legitimate nor illegitimate opportunities are available, then the youths' frustration and discontent will be heightened. In addition, lack of opportunities is often a symptom of a lack of social organization (whether legitimate or illegitimate) in the community, which means there will be fewer controls on the youths' behavior. In this circumstance the youths will tend to form a violent, or "conflict," gang to express their anger. This is the source of the "non-utilitarian, malicious, and negativistic" activity described by Cohen. Finally, Cloward and Ohlin describe a "retreatist subculture" similar to Merton's "retreatist" adaptation and similarly populated with "double failures." Youths in this subculture are unable to achieve the economic improvement they seek, whether because of lack of opportunity or because of internal prohibitions against the use of illegitimate means. They also fail in the resort to conflict and violence. This group turns to alcohol or to drugs, and drops out.

POLICY IMPLICATIONS

During the 1960s, strain theories came to dominate criminology, and eventually had a great impact on federal policy toward crime and delinquency.[24] After Robert Kennedy, who was then attorney general of the

---

[23]Cloward and Ohlin, op. cit, p. 97.

[24]For a brief review of the attempt to implement Cloward and Ohlin's ideas in federal policy, see LaMar T. Empey, *American Delinquency*, rev. ed., Dorsey, Homewood, IL, 1982, pp. 240–45. For more extended accounts, see Peter Maris and Martin Rein, *Dilemmas of Social Reform*, 2nd ed., Aldine, Chicago, 1973; James F. Short, Jr., "The Natural History of an Applied Theory: Differential Opportunity and Mobilization for Youth," in N. J. Demerath, ed., *Social Policy and Sociology*, Academic Press, New York, 1975, pp. 193–210; Joseph J. Helfgot, *Professional Reforming: Mobilization for Youth and the Failure of Social Science*, Health, Lexington, MA, 1981; and Stephen M. Rose, *The Betrayal of the Poor: The Transformation of Community Action*, Schenkmann, Cambridge, MA, 1972.

United States, read Cloward and Ohlin's book, he asked Lloyd Ohlin to help develop a new federal policy on juvenile delinquency. The result was the passage of the Juvenile Delinquency Prevention and Control Act of 1961, which was based on a comprehensive action program developed by Cloward and Ohlin in connection with their book. The program included improving education, creating work opportunities, organizing lower-class communities, and providing services to individuals, gangs, and families. The program was later expanded to include all lower-class people and became the basis of Lyndon Johnson's War on Poverty. Although billions of dollars were spent on these programs, the only clear result seems to have been the massive political resistance that was generated against this attempt to extend opportunities to people without them. The programs, having failed to achieve their goals, were eventually dismantled by Richard Nixon.

Since no genuine extension of opportunities ever took place, this failure might be attributed to the opposition the programs encountered. Rose has offered an alternative interpretation of the failure of these programs.[25] The War on Poverty was based on strain theories, which argue that crime and poverty have their origins in social structural arrangements. Therefore, these theories imply that the solution to the problems of crime and poverty require social structural change. As originally conceived, the War on Poverty was designed to change social structural arrangements, not to change individual people. However, most of these programs were taken over by the bureaucracies of poverty-serving agencies, who immediately acted to protect and enhance their own bureaucratic interests. As a consequence, when the poverty programs were actually implemented, virtually all of them were designed to change poor people, and very few were designed to change social structural arrangements. Rose maintains that the War on Poverty failed because its original purpose was subverted as it was transformed to serve the interests of the established poverty-serving bureaucracies. Thus, he entitles his book *The Betrayal of the Poor.*

THE DECLINE AND RESURGENCE OF STRAIN THEORIES

After the failure of strain-based federal policies of the 1960s, strain theories were subjected to a great deal of scrutiny and to a very large number of criticisms. Some of the criticisms were theoretical, focusing on the adequacy of their terms and concepts, while other criticisms were empirical, focusing on whether the theories are supported by research.

---

[25]Rose, op. cit.

The most extensive criticisms were made by Kornhauser in an influential book published in 1978.[26] She described the central element of "strain" theories as the assertion that stress or frustration causes crime and delinquency. The source of this stress or frustration was said to be the "gap" between what criminals and delinquents want (aspirations) and what they expect to get (expectations). She then reviewed empirical research on the aspirations and expectations of delinquents and argued that the research showed that delinquency is associated with both low expectations and low aspirations.[27] She maintained that such youths would not be "strained" since there is no gap between what they want and what they expect to get. These and other criticisms were widely accepted in criminology, resulting is a general decline of interest in strain theories.

In 1984, Bernard attacked the validity of Kornhauser's criticisms of strain theories.[28] For example, research showing that delinquents did not have a gap between their aspirations and their expectations, Bernard pointed out, asked youths about aspirations and expectations related to obtaining more education and high status jobs. But Cloward and Ohlin had specifically argued that delinquents do not have such aspirations and instead wanted "fast cars, fancy clothes, and swell dames." Later research by Farnsworth and Leiber found that, when measured in strictly monetary terms, the gap between aspirations and expectations was associated with delinquency.[29]

Also in 1984, Cullen published a theoretical book that reinterpreted the major strain theories of Merton, Cohen, and Cloward and Ohlin.[30] Cullen argued that Merton actually proposed two different theories—one at the individual level and the other at the societal level. At the individual level, Cullen agreed with Kornhauser that, according to Merton's theory, people in situations of social structural strain would feel frustrated and those feelings would motivate them to act in deviant ways.[31] But at the aggregate level, Cullen argued that Merton proposed a separate

---

[26]Ruth Rosner Kornhauser, *Social Sources of Delinquency*, University of Chicago Press, Chicago, 1978, pp. 139–80.

[27]Kornhauser, op. cit., pp. 167–80.

[28]Thomas J. Bernard, "Control Criticisms of Strain Theories: An Assessment of Theoretical and Empirical Adequacy," *Journal of Research in Crime and Delinquency* 21(4): 353–72 (Nov. 1984). See also the discussion of Kornhauser on pp. 199–201 of the third edition of the present text.

[29]Margaret Farnsworth and Michael J. Lieber, "Strain Theory Revisited: Economic Goals, Educational Means, and Delinquency," *American Sociological Review* 54: 263–74 (April 1989).

[30]Francis T. Cullen, *Rethinking Crime and Deviance Theory: The Emergence of a Structuring Tradition*, Rowman and Allanheld, Totowa, NJ, 1983. See also Francis T. Cullen, "Were Cloward and Ohlin Strain Theorists?" *Journal of Research in Crime and Delinquency* 25(3): 214–41 (1988).

[31]Ibid., pp. 36–37.

theory in which criminals are not described as stressed or frustrated at all.[32]

Merton did not maintain that an unregulated individual has to experience any special stress or pressure to become deviant. . . In the place of (the "strained" deviant), Merton substituted a thoroughly classical view of the deviant, arguing that the deregulated or anomic actor is free to choose any course of conduct. The only guide to the person's activity is the rational calculation of the costs and benefits of the various means available. Deviant behavior now occurs when illegitimate means are the 'technically most effective procedure' that can be employed to secure a desired end. As Merton has noted, this attenuation of institutional controls creates a "situation erroneously held by the utilitarian philosophers to be typical of society, a situation in which the calculations of personal advantage and fear of punishment are the only regulating agencies."

This "anomie theory" operates at the societal level, linking social structural characteristics to rates and distributions of deviant behavior.

STRAIN IN INDIVIDUALS AND IN SOCIETIES: NEGATIVE EMOTIONS AND INSTITUTIONAL ANOMIE

Cullen's interpretation makes it clear that the term "strain" can be used in two completely different ways. First, it can refer to characteristics of a society: a situation in which the social structure fails to provide legitimate means to achieve what the culture values. Second, it can refer to feelings and emotions that an individual experiences: feelings of stress or frustration or anxiety or depression or anger. The line of argument connecting these two meanings is that people in situations of "social structural strain" (i.e., people who cannot achieve culturally valued goals through legitimate means provided by the social structure) may feel "strained" (i.e., may feel stressed, frustrated, anxious, depressed, and angry), and feelings then are the actual cause of the higher crime rates associated with those people. There is disagreement about whether the original strain theories of Merton, Cohen, and Cloward and Ohlin included this line of argument or not.[33] But regardless of whether they

---

[32]Ibid., pp. 80–82.

[33]See the interchange between Bernard and Agnew in *Journal of Research in Crime and Delinquency* 24(4): 262–90 (Nov. 1987). Agnew argued that each of the traditional strain theories necessarily contained this individual-level argument. In contrast, Bernard argued that these theories did not make any individual-level argument in which frustration in individuals causes those individuals to commit crime. Related to this disagreement, Merton's most recent statement ("Opportunity Structures, op. cit., p. 9) includes a statement that "the basic point" of theories in the anomie tradition "centers on *rates* of structurally generated and constrained behavior, not on the behavior of this or that individual." See also Merton, p. 27.

did, new "strain" theories using both types of characteristics—social and individual—have appeared recently.

At the individual level, Agnew has proposed a "general strain theory" that focuses on negative relationships with others.[34] He argues that these negative relationships generate negative emotions in the person, and the negative emotions then cause crime. This is a general theory of crime, but Agnew uses it specifically to explain why adolescents engage in delinquency and drug use.

Negative relationships include relationships in which other people prevent a person from achieving a valued goal, take away something valued that the person already has, or impose on the person something that is "noxious" and unwanted. According to Agnew, previous strain theories have focused on relationships in which people were prevented from reaching their valued goals, such as monetary success and status. Agnew, however, focuses on relationships in which the person is presented with a "noxious" situation and is unable to escape from it—i.e., "relationships in which others do not treat the individual as he or she would like to be treated . . ." These can include a wide variety of relationships, but for adolescents they often are associated with living at home and being in school. Unlike adults, adolescents cannot legally leave these relationships if they experience them as "noxious"—if they do leave, they can be arrested for truancy or running away. These relationships then generate a variety of negative emotions, such as disappointment, depression, fear, and anger. It is these negative emotions that Agnew defines as "strain."

Delinquency and drug use are both ways of coping with and managing the "strain" of these negative emotions. Delinquency may be a way that the adolescents have of achieving their valued goals, of retrieving what is being taken away from them, or of removing themselves from the negative relationship. Alternately, delinquency may be a means for retaliating against those who are the source of the negative relationships. Finally, drug use may be a means of managing the negative emotions directly, rather than addressing the negative relationships themselves. Thus, Agnew explains delinquency and drug use as coping responses to interpersonal problems.

A fairly large number of studies find support for Agnew's basic argument that negative relationships and stressful life events are associated

---

[34]Robert Agnew, "Foundation for a General Strain Theory of Crime and Delinquency," *Criminology* 30: 47–87 (1992).

with increases in a variety of delinquent behaviors.[35] An additional study has found that delinquent behavior is more successful than nondelinquent behavior as a technique for managing the negative emotions caused by strain.[36] That is, given the same level of strain, youths who engage in delinquency experience "modest relief" from negative emotions as compared to youths who obey the law. Other studies have found that strain has similar effects for both males and females.[37] Still other studies have found that anger as a response to strain tends to be associated with violent crime,[38] including one study of court-adjudicated youths.[39]

At the societal level, Messner and Rosenfeld have presented an "institutional anomie" theory that is similar to Merton's.[40] They explain the high levels of crime in American society by pointing to "the American dream," which they describe as "a broad cultural ethos that entails a commitment to the goal of material success, to be pursued by everyone

---

[35]Robert Agnew and Helene Raskin White, "An Empirical Test of General Strain Theory," *Criminology* 30: 475–99 (1992); Raymond Paternoster and Paul Mazerolle, "General Strain Theory and Delinquency: A Replication and Extension," *Journal of Research in Crime and Delinquency* 31: 235–63 (1994); John P. Hoffman and Alan S. Miller, "A Latent Variable Analysis of General Strain Theory," *Journal of Quantitative Criminology* 14(1): 83–110 (1998); Timothy Brezina, "Teenage Violence Toward Parents as an Adaptation to Family Strain," *Youth & Society* 30(4): 416–44 (1999); John P. Hoffman and Felicia Gray Cerbone, "Stressful Life Events and Delinquency Escalation in Early Adolescence," *Criminology* 37(2): 343–73 (1999); and Paul Mazerolle and Jeff Maahs, "General Strain and Delinquency," *Justice Quarterly* 17(4): 753–78 (2000). See also two earlier articles by Agnew, "A Revised Strain Theory of Delinquency," *Social Forces* 64: 151–67 (1985) and "A Longitudinal Test of the Revised Strain Theory," *Journal of Quantitative Criminology* 5: 373–87 (1989).

[36]Timothy Brezina, "Adapting to Strain: An Examination of Delinquent Coping Responses," *Criminology* 34(1): 39–60 (1996).

[37]Robert Agnew and Timothy Brezina, "Relational Problems with Peers, Gender, and Delinquency," *Youth and* Society 29: 84–111 (1997); Paul Mazerolle, "Gender, General Strain, and Delinquency," *Justice Quarterly* 15(1): 65–91 (1998); John P. Hoffman and S. Susan Su, "The Conditional Effects of Stress on Delinquency and Drug Use: A Strain Theory Assessment of Sex Differences," *Journal of Research in Crime and Delinquency* 34: 46–78 (1997). On the other hand, Lisa Broidy and Robert Agnew ("Gender and Crime," *Journal of Research in Crime and Delinquency* 34: 275–306 [1997]) have found that females evaluate certain strains more negatively than males. See also a comment on these studies by Agnew in "An Overview of General Strain Theory," pp. 161–74 in Raymond Paternoster and Ronet Bachman, eds., *Explaining Criminals and Crime,* Roxbury, Los Angeles, 2001.

[38]Paul Mazerolle, Velmer S. Burton, Jr., Francis T. Cullen, et al., "Strain, Anger, and Delinquent Adaptations," *Journal of Criminal Justice* 28(2): 89–101 (2000); Paul Mazerolle and Alex Piquero, "Linking Exposure to Strain with Anger," *Journal of Criminal Justice* 26: 195–211 (1998).

[39]Nicole Leeper Piquero and Miriam D. Sealock, "Generalizing General Strain Theory," *Justice Quarterly* 17(3): 449–84 (2000).

[40]Steven F. Messner and Richard Rosenfeld, *Crime and the American Dream* 3rd ed., Wadsworth, Belmont, Calif., 2001. The term "institutional anomie" is taken from Mitchell B. Chamlin and John K. Cochran, "Assessing Messner and Rosenfeld's Institutional Anomie Theory," *Criminology* 33(3): 411–29 (Aug. 1995), which found partial support for the theory. See also the comment by Gary Jensen and reply by Chamlin and Cochran in *Criminology* 34(1): 129–34 (Feb. 1996).

in society, under conditions of open, individual competition."[41] Like Merton, they argue that this cultural ethos generates intense cultural pressures for monetary success. At the same time, the American Dream does not strongly prohibit people from using more efficient illegal means to achieve monetary success.

Messner and Rosenfeld diverge from and extend Merton's theory in two ways. First, they argue that redistributing legitimate opportunities may actually increase, rather than decrease, the pressures toward criminal behavior unless the culture, with its emphasis on the goal of monetary success at the expense of following the institutional means, also changes. Expanding opportunities may change who wins and who loses in the competition for monetary success, but there will still be losers. People who lose this competition have no one to blame but themselves and their own inadequacies. This situation may put even more pressure on them to commit crime (i.e., achieve monetary success through illegitimate means) than if they could blame an unfair "system."

A second divergence from Merton's theory involves Messner and Rosenfeld's explanation of the overemphasis on monetary success in American culture. They point to the overwhelming influence of economic institutions in American society, and argue that other institutions, such as families, schools, and even politics, tend to be subservient to the economy:[42]

Prosocial cultural messages tend to be overwhelmed by the anomic tendencies of the American Dream . . . because of the dominance of the economy in the institutional balance of power. A primary task for noneconomic institutions such as the family and schools is to inculcate beliefs, values, and commitments other than those of the marketplace. But as these noneconomic institutions are relatively devalued and forced to accommodate to economic considerations, and as they are penetrated by economic standards, they are less able to fulfill their distinctive socialization functions successfully.

Messner and Rosenfeld therefore propose a number of policies to strengthen these institutions in their relations to the economy, and to weaken the impact of the economy on them.[43] First, they argue that families in American society are heavily driven by economic concerns, to the extent that the family as a social institution is relatively unable to influence the behavior of its members. Families can be strengthened in

---

[41]Messner and Rosenfeld, op. cit., p. 85.

[42]Ibid., p. 78.

[43]Ibid., pp. 101–10.

their relation to the economy by implementing policies such as family leave, job sharing for husbands and wives, flexible work schedules, and employer-provided child care. These policies provide parents with some freedom from the demands of the economy, and parents then are able to spend more time and energy on family concerns. Schools have become subservient to the economy. Good jobs usually require high school or college degrees, so many students stay in school because they want a good job in the future, and not because they want an education. As teachers respond to this demand from students, the entire educational enterprise tends to become driven by the job market. If job success were less tied to number of years in school, then students who were not really interested in acquiring an education could drop out of school and go to work, and schools then could actually focus on education as a goal. Political institutions also have tended to be subservient to the economy, and Messner and Rosenfeld recommend that other elements of political life be emphasized. For example, the creation of a national service corps would engage young people in the life of the community in ways that emphasize collective goals other than material success. The economy itself could also be modified to reduce somewhat its control of individuals. Messner and Rosenfeld point to the mixed economies of Western Europe and Japan, which ensure that a level of material well-being is not totally dependent on economic performance. Finally, at the cultural level, goals other than material success must be given greater prominence in our society, especially activities such as parenting, teaching, and serving the community. In general, Messner and Rosenfeld suggest an increased emphasis on mutual support and collective obligations in American society, and a decreased emphasis on individual rights, interests, and privileges.

In an initial test of Messner and Rosenfeld's theory, Chamblin and Cochran looked at rates of church membership, divorce, and voting in the various states of the United States.[44] These rates were taken to indicate the strength of three non-economic institutions: church, family, and state. As the theory predicted, Chamblin and Cochran found lower property crime in states with higher church memberships, lower divorce, and greater voter turnout. They then tested a more subtle prediction of Messner and Rosenfeld's theory: The strength of non-economic institutions should moderate the effects of economic hardship on crime. That is, there should be less association between poverty and crime in

---

[44]Chamblin and Cochran, op. cit.

states with stronger non-economic institutions. Chamblin and Cochran therefore looked at the relationship between crime and a variety of measures of economic deprivation, and found the predicted pattern. This was taken as strong support for the theory.

In another test, Messner and Rosenfeld focused on "social safety net" policies (such as welfare, health care and parental leave) by which nations protect their citizens from the hazards of the marketplace.[45] These policies are an indicator of the strength of the state as a non-economic institution—i.e., the extent to which the state does not solely serve the needs of the economy. In a sample of about forty nations, Messner and Rosenfeld found that nations in which citizens are better protected from the marketplace have lower rates of homicide.

A third test looked at these same "social safety net" policies.[46] This study hypothesized that economic inequality would be more strongly linked to homicide in nations where there were weak "safety nets," and less strongly linked in nations with strong "safety nets." The results strongly supported the theory. In fact, at higher levels of welfare spending, economic inequality was no longer associated with homicide at all. This was quite surprising, since one of the most consistent findings in the criminology literature is the link between economic inequality and homicide.[47]

CONCLUSION

The failure of the War on Poverty illustrates that the policy implications of strain theories may be difficult to achieve in the real world. The problem is that patterns of self-interest always develop around existing social structural arrangements.[48] People who benefit from those arrangements protect their self-interests by resisting social change. Messner and Rosenfeld's policy recommendations may be more politically appealing than the policies associated with the War on Poverty because they em-

---

[45]Steven F. Messner and Richard Rosenfeld, "Political Restraint of the Market and Levels of Criminal Homicide," *Social Forces* 75(4): 1393–1416 (1997). This finding is consistent with a number of other studies that have found that better welfare policies are associated with lower levels of crime. See Junsen Zhang, "The Effect of Welfare Programs on Criminal Behavior," *Economic Inquiry* 35(1): 120–37, (1997); Lance Hannon and James DeFronzo, "Welfare and Property Crime," *Justice Quarterly* 15(2): 273–88 (1998); Hannon and DeFronzo, "The Truly Disadvantaged, Public Assistance, and Crime," *Social Problems* 45(3): 383–92 (1998); and DeFronzo and Hannon, "Welfare Assistance Levels and Homicide Rates," *Homicide Studies* 2(1): 31–45 (1998).

[46]Jukka Savolainen, "Inequality, Welfare State, and Homicide: Further Support for Institutional Anomie Theory," *Criminology* 38(4): 1021–42 (2000).

[47]See the discussion of inequality and homicide above in Chapter 5.

[48]Talcott Parsons, *Politics and Social Structure*, The Free Press, New York, 1969, p. 95.

phasize strengthening families and schools. To some extent, these policies may appeal to both liberals and conservatives.[49] On the other hand, the thrust of their recommendations is to reduce the overwhelming influence of the economy in American society. The rhetoric in recent elections suggests that economic concerns almost totally dominate the political process, and that government policies are overwhelmingly directed toward promoting economic growth. It does not seem likely that, in the near future, the American people would be willing to compromise economic growth in order to promote "the general welfare."

There is no question that the problems described by strain theories are complex. It is not merely a matter of talented individuals confronted with inferior schools and discriminatory hiring practices. Rather, a good deal of research indicates that many delinquents and criminals are untalented individuals who cannot compete effectively in complex industrial societies.[50] When viewed in the light of that research, strain theories can be interpreted as suggesting that untalented people want many of the same things as talented people but find they cannot obtain these things through legitimate means. Some of them therefore attempt to obtain those things through criminal activity. From this perspective, strain theories would seem to pose some disturbing questions for public policy. Do untalented people have the same rights as talented people to want material goods, the respect of their peers, and power and control over their own lives? Would society be well-advised to provide untalented as well as talented people with legitimate opportunities to obtain these things? Or is the economy so dominant in American society that we cannot even consider such questions?

---

[49]Messner and Rosenfeld, op. cit., pp. 101–2.

[50]See, for example, Richard J. Herrnstein and Charles Murray, *The Bell Curve*, The Free Press, New York, 1994, for a general argument that America is spinning toward a society radically divided between the talented and the untalented, with the talented totally in control of the economy and the untalented having very high rates of crime. Like Messner and Rosenfeld, Herrnstein and Murray recommend that the dominance of the economy in American society be reduced to prevent a social catastrophe.

CHAPTER NINE

Learning Theories

This chapter focuses on the role of normal learning in the generation of criminal behavior. It includes theories about ideas and behaviors that can be learned and that support and encourage law violation. It also includes theories about the processes by which the learning of these ideas and behaviors takes place. Finally, it includes theories about cultures and subcultures that contain ideas supportive of criminal behavior within in particular groups.[1]

Learning and cultures played important roles in the strain theories described in the last chapter. Merton, and later Messner and Rosenfeld, linked crime to ideas in the dominant American culture. Cohen described how a separate negativistic subculture arose among gang youths who deliberately inverted the values of the dominant American culture. Cloward pointed out that the mere presence of an opportunity, whether legitimate or illegitimate, was meaningless unless the person also had

---

[1]In the past, these theories were described as "cultural deviance" theories. This term was based on the argument that the cultures themselves could be deviant, and that individuals who conform to such deviant cultures will therefore commit crimes. This term and the interpretation associated with it originated in Ruth Rosner Kornhauser ("Theoretical Issues in the Sociological Study of Juvenile Delinquency," unpublished manuscript, Center for the Study of Law and Society, Berkeley, CA, 1963; *Social Sources of Delinquency,* University of Chicago Press, Chicago, 1978). The use of this term and the interpretation of the theories associated with it have been extensively criticized. See Ross L. Matsueda, "The Current State of Differential Association Theory," *Crime & Delinquency* 34(3): 277–306 (July 1988); and Thomas J. Bernard and Jeffrey B. Snipes, "Theoretical Integration in Criminology," in Michael Tonry, ed., *Crime and Justice: A Review of Research,* University of Chicago Press, Chicago, 1996, pp. 327–30. For a recent discussion of this issue, see Ronald L. Akers, "Is Differential Association/Social Learning Cultural Deviance Theory," and the response by Travis Hirschi, "Theory Without Ideas: Reply to Akers," in *Criminology* 34(2): 229–56 (May 1996).

learned how to take advantage of it. These strain theories, however, focus on the social structural conditions, such as the distribution of legitimate and illegitimate opportunities or the institutional imbalance of power, that give rise to the learning of these ideas and behaviors in the first place.[2]

In contrast, the learning theories described in this chapter focus on the content of what is learned and the processes by which that learning takes place. Some of these learning theories briefly point to the structural conditions that give rise to the learning in the first place, while others describe those structural conditions more extensively. But in each case, the theories focus on the learning itself rather than on the underlying structural conditions. In that sense, "strain" and "learning" theories are complementary with each other, but they have different emphases.[3]

BASIC PSYCHOLOGICAL APPROACHES TO LEARNING

Learning refers to habits and knowledge that develop as a result of the experiences of the individual in entering and adjusting to the environment.[4] These are to be distinguished from unlearned or instinctual behavior, which in some sense is present in the individual at birth and determined by biology.

One of the oldest formulations about the nature of learning is that we learn by association.[5] Aristotle (384–322 B.C.) argued that all knowledge is acquired through experience and that none is inborn or instinctive.

---

[2]Bernard and Snipes, op. cit., pp. 332–35.

[3]See the description of structure and process in Ronald Akers, *Deviant Behavior: A Social Learning Approach*, Wadsworth, Belmont, Calif., 1985, p. 66. For an extended discussion, see Akers, *Social Learning and Social Structure*, Northeastern University Press, Boston, 1998.

[4]Basic information about learning theories may be found in Gordon H. Bower and Ernest R. Hilgard, *Theories of Learning*, Prentice Hall, Englewood Cliffs, NJ, 1981; Stewart H. Hulse, Howard Egeth, and James Deese, *The Psychology of Learning*, 5th ed., McGraw-Hill, New York, 1980; Robert C. Bolles, *Learning Theory*, 2nd ed., Holt, Rinehart, and Winston, New York, 1979; Winifred F. Hill, *Learning: A Survey of Psychological Interpretations*, 3rd ed., Crowell, New York, 1977. These theories are briefly reviewed in Gwynn Nettler, *Explaining Crime*, 3rd ed., McGraw-Hill, New York, 1984, pp. 296–300.

[5]For a detailed account of the development of associationism, see J. R. Anderson and Gordon H. Bower, *Human Associative Memory*, Winston and Sons, Washington, D.C., 1973. Concise accounts can be found in Hulse, Egeth, and Deese, op. cit., pp. 2–4, and Bower and Hilgard, op. cit., pp. 2–4. The major alternative to associationism began with Plato (427?–347 B.C.), who emphasized the rational aspects of human learning. See Bower and Hilgard, op. cit., pp. 4–8; and Hulse, Egeth, and Deese, op. cit., pp. 4–8. Where Aristotle broke complex learning down to its simplest components, Plato argued that the whole was greater than the sum of its parts. He emphasized the inborn capacity of the human mind to organize raw sense data, and his ideas appear in modern times in the form of Gestalt psychology. This school has gained support recently from research on "species-specific" behaviors. See Keller Breeland and Marian Breeland, "The Misbehavior of Organisms," *American Psychologist* 16: 681–84 (1961); M. E. P. Seligman, "On the Generality of the Laws of

Basic sensory experiences become associated with each other in the mind because they occur in certain relationships to each other as we interact with the object. Aristotle formulated four laws of association that described those relationships: the law of similarity; the law of contrast; the law of succession in time; and the law of coexistence in space. The most complex ideas, according to Aristotle, are all built out of these simple associations between sensory experiences.

Associationism has been the dominant learning theory through the centuries to the present time. It was elaborated by such philosophers as Hobbes, Locke, and Hume, and was the basis for the first experiments on human memory, carried out by Ebbinhaus,[6] as well as for the first experiments on animal learning, carried out by Thorndike.[7] The *behaviorist* revolution substituted observable stimuli and responses for the mental images and ideas of earlier times, but retained the basic idea that learning is accomplished through association. At the present time a major controversy among learning theorists is between such behavioral theorists and the *cognitive* theorists, who retain the original Aristotelian notion that learning takes place because of the association of ideas and factual knowledge.[8] Where behaviorists argue that we acquire habits through the association of stimuli with responses, cognitive theorists argue that we acquire factual knowledge through the association of memories, ideas, or expectations. Behaviorists argue that learning occurs primarily through trial and error, while cognitive theorists describe learning as taking place through insight into problem solving. Despite these and other controversies between behavioral and cognitive learning theories, both can be traced back to Aristotle's original ideas about association as the basis of learning.

There are three basic ways that individuals learn through association. The simplest way is *classical* conditioning, as originally described by Pavlov. Some stimuli will reliably produce a given response without any prior training of the organism. For example, a dog will consistently salivate when presented with meat. Pavlov consistently presented meat to dogs along with some other stimulus that did not by itself produce the salivation—for example, the sound of a bell. He found that after a few

---

Learning," *Psychological Review* 77: 406–18 (1970); and J. Garcia and R. Koelling, "Relation of Cue to Consequence in Avoidance Learning," *Psychonomic Science* 4: 123–24 (1996). However, this view has not been applied to crime, so it is not presented here.

[6]H. Ebinghaus, *Memory,* Teachers College, New York, 1913; reprinted by Dover, New York, 1964.

[7]E. L. Thorndike, "Animal Intelligence," *Psychological Review Monograph Supplement* 2(8): (1898).

[8]Bower and Hilgard, op. cit., pp. 15–17.

pairings the sound of the bell itself was sufficient to produce salivation in the dog. What Pavlov demonstrated was that behaviors could be learned by association: If the sound of a bell is associated consistently with the presentation of the meat, then the dog learns to salivate at the sound of the bell alone.

In classical conditioning the organism is passive and learns what to expect from the environment. In *operant* conditioning the organism is active and learns how to get what it wants from the environment. Operant conditioning is associated with B. F. Skinner and is now probably the dominant learning theory in psychology. Operant conditioning uses rewards and punishments to reinforce certain behaviors. For example, rats may be taught to press a lever by rewarding that behavior with a food pellet or by punishing with an electric shock its failure to push the lever. The rat learns to operate on its environment by associating rewards and punishments with its own behaviors. Thus operant conditioning is another way of learning by association.

While both classical and operant conditioning are associated with the behaviorist school of learning theory, a third theory describing how people learn by association attempts to combine both operant conditioning and elements from cognitive psychology. Called *social learning* theory, it emphasizes the point that behavior may be reinforced not only through actual rewards and punishments, but also through expectations that are learned by watching what happens to other people. Bandura, for example, argues that "virtually all learning phenomena resulting from direct experiences can occur on a vicarious basis through observation of other persons' behavior and its consequences for them."[9] While classical and operant conditioning are both tested extensively with animal experiments, social learning theory is more focused on human learning, since it directs attention to higher mental processes.

TARDE'S LAWS OF IMITATION

An early criminologist who presented a theory of crime as normal learned behavior was Gabriel Tarde (1843–1904).[10] Tarde rejected Lombroso's theory that crime was caused by biological abnormality, ar-

---

[9]Albert Bandura, *Principles of Behavior Modification,* Holt, Rinehart, and Winston, New York, 1969, p. 118.

[10]The following account is taken from Margaret S. Wilson Vine, "Gabriel Tarde," in Hermann Mannheim, ed., *Pioneers in Criminology,* 2nd ed., Patterson Smith, Montclair, NJ, 1972, pp. 292–304. See also Don Martindale, *The Nature and Types of Sociological Theory,* Houghton Mifflin, Boston, 1960, pp. 305–9; and Jack H. Curtis, "Gabriel Tarde," in Clement S. Mihanovich, ed., *Social Theorists,* Bruce, Milwaukee, 1953, pp. 142–57.

guing that criminals were primarily normal people who, by accident of birth, were brought up in an atmosphere in which they learned crime as a way of life. He phrased his theory in terms of "laws of imitation," which were similar to Aristotle's laws of learning except that they focused on associations among individuals rather than associations among sensations within one individual. Like Aristotle's original theory, Tarde's theory was essentially a cognitive theory in which the individual was said to learn ideas through the association with other ideas, and behavior was said to follow from those ideas.

Tarde's first law was that people imitate one another in proportion to how much close contact they have with one another. Thus imitation is most frequent, and changes most rapidly, in cities. Tarde described this as "fashion." In rural areas, in contrast, imitation is less frequent and changes only slowly. Tarde defined that as "custom." Tarde argued that crime begins as a fashion and later becomes a custom, much like any other social phenomenon.

The second law of imitation was that the inferior usually imitates the superior. Tarde traced the history of crimes such as vagabondage, drunkenness, and murder, and found that they began as crimes committed by royalty, and later were imitated by all social classes. Similarly, he argued that many crimes originated in large cities, and were then imitated by those in rural areas.

The third law of imitation was that the newer fashions displace the older ones. Tarde argued, for example, that murder by knifing had decreased while murder by shooting increased.

Tarde's theory was important at the time for its role in opposing Lombroso's theories. It retains some importance for us at the present time, since it was the first attempt to describe criminal behavior in terms of normal learning rather than in terms of biological or psychological defects. From this point of view, the major problem with the theory is that it was based on such a simplistic model of learning. This was the state of learning theory at the time that Tarde wrote. A later theory with some elements of the same basic idea—criminal behavior is the result of normal learning—was presented by Sutherland. Although the model of learning on which the theory was based is also relatively simple, Sutherland's theory continues to have a profound impact on criminology.

SUTHERLAND'S DIFFERENTIAL ASSOCIATION THEORY

Edwin H. Sutherland (1883–1950) was born in a small town in Nebraska and received his bachelors degree from Grand Island College there.[11] He taught for several years at a small Baptist college in South Dakota before leaving to obtain his PhD from the University of Chicago. Sutherland's interests were primarily focused on problems of unemployment, and that was the subject of his dissertation. Following his graduation he taught for six years at a small college in Missouri, and then went to the University of Illinois, where his department chair suggested that he write a book on criminology. The result was the first edition of *Criminology*, published in 1924.

Sutherland's theory of criminal behavior emerged gradually in several editions of this book, as he formulated his thinking on the subject and systematized his presentation of that thinking.[12] He was influenced in this endeavor by a report on criminology written by Jerome Michael and Mortimer J. Adler, which appeared in 1933 and severely criticized the state of criminological theory and research.[13] Sutherland was extremely annoyed by the report, and responded to it by attempting to create a general theory that could organize the many diverse facts known about criminal behavior into some logical arrangement. The first brief statement of that general theory appeared in the second edition of *Criminology*, published in 1934. In the third edition of the book, published in 1939, Sutherland made a more systematic and formal presentation of his theory, and further expanded and clarified it in the fourth edition, appearing in 1947. The theory has remained unchanged since that edition, and consists of the following nine points:[14]

1. Criminal behavior is learned. . . .
2. Criminal behavior is learned in interaction with other persons in a process of communication. . . .
3. The principal part of the learning of criminal behavior occurs within intimate personal groups. . . .
4. When criminal behavior is learned, the learning includes: (a) techniques of committing the crime, which are sometimes very complicated, sometimes

---

[11]See Mark Warr, "The Social Origins of Crime: Edwin Sutherland and the Theory of Differential Association," pp. 182–91 in Raymond Paternoster and Ronet Bachman, eds., *Explaining Criminals and Crime*, Roxbury, Los Angeles, 2001.

[12]For an account of the development of the theory, see Ross L. Matsueda, op. cit., pp. 278–84.

[13]Jerome Michael and Mortimer J. Adler, *Crime, Law, and Social Science*, Harcourt, Brace, New York, 1933. Sutherland's reaction to this report is discussed in the "Introduction" (by Gilbert Geis) to a reprint edition published by Patterson Smith, Montclair, NJ, 1971. See also Donald R. Cressey, "Fifty Years of Criminology," *Pacific Sociological Review* 22: 457–80 (1979).

[14]Edwin H. Sutherland *Criminology*, 4th ed., Lippincott, Philadelphia, 1947, pp. 6–7. The most recent edition is Edwin H. Sutherland, Donald R. Cressey, and David F. Luckenbill, *Principles of Criminology*, 11th ed., General Hall, Dix Hills, NY, 1992, where the theory appears on pp. 88–90.

very simple; (b) the specific direction of the motives, drives, rationalizations, and attitudes. . . .

5. The specific directions of the motives and drives is learned from definitions of the legal codes as favorable or unfavorable. In some societies an individual is surrounded by persons who invariably define the legal codes as rules to be observed, while in others he is surrounded by persons whose definitions are favorable to the violation of the legal codes. . . .

6. A person becomes delinquent because of an excess of definitions favorable to violation of law over definitions unfavorable to violation of law. This is the principle of differential association. . . .

7. Differential associations may vary in frequency, duration, priority, and intensity. This means that associations with criminal behavior and also associations with anticriminal behavior vary in those respects. . . .

8. The process of learning criminal behavior by association with criminal and anticriminal patterns involves all of the mechanisms that are involved in any other learning. . . .

9. While criminal behavior is an expression of general needs and values, it is not explained by those general needs and values, since noncriminal behavior is an expression of the same needs and values. Thieves generally steal in order to secure money, but likewise honest laborers work in order to secure money. The attempts by many scholars to explain criminal behavior by general drives and values, such as the happiness principle, striving for social status, the money motive, or frustration, have been, and must continue to be, futile, since they explain lawful behavior as completely as they explain criminal behavior. They are similar to respiration, which is necessary for any behavior, but which does not differentiate criminal from noncriminal behavior.

Sutherland's theory has two basic elements. The *content* of what is learned includes specific techniques for committing crimes; appropriate motives, drives, rationalizations, and attitudes; and more general "definitions favorable to law violation." All these are cognitive elements; that is, they are all ideas rather than behaviors. In addition, the *process* by which the learning takes place involves associations with other people in intimate personal groups. Both elements of Sutherland's theory are derived from "symbolic interactionism," a theory developed by George Herbert Mead (1863–1931), who was on the faculty at the University of Chicago while Sutherland was getting his doctorate there.[15]

Sutherland's description of the content of what is learned was derived from Mead's argument that "human beings act toward things on the ba-

---

[15]For a review of Mead's thought, see Herbert Blumer, *Symbolic Interactionism,* Prentice Hall, Englewood Cliffs, NJ, 1969. The theory is briefly reviewed in George B. Vold, *Theoretical Criminology,* 2nd ed., prepared by Thomas J. Bernard, Oxford University Press, New York, 1979, pp. 255–58.

sis of the meanings that the things have for them."[16] In Mead's theory a cognitive factor—"meanings"—determines behavior. Mead then argued that people construct relatively permanent "definitions" of their situation out of the meanings they derive from particular experiences.[17] That is, they generalize the meanings they have derived from particular situations, and form a relatively set way of looking at things. It is because of these different "definitions" that different people in similar situations may act in very different ways. To cite an old example, two brothers may grow up in identical terrible situations but one may become a criminal while the other becomes a priest. Drawing on this theory, Sutherland argued that the key factor determining whether people violate the law is the meaning they give to the social conditions they experience, rather than the conditions themselves. Ultimately, whether persons obey or violate the law depends on how they *define* their situation.

Sutherland's description of the process by which definitions are learned was also derived from Mead's theory. Mead had argued that "the meaning of such things is derived from, or arises out of, the social interaction one has with one's fellows."[18] Following Mead's theory, Sutherland argued that the meaning of criminal acts, whether murder or shoplifting, marijuana smoking or income tax evasion, prostitution or embezzlement, arises primarily from the meanings given those acts by other people with whom the individual associates in intimate personal groups. In an attempt to explain why some associations were more important than others for the learning of these definitions, Sutherland also argued that those associations vary in "frequency, duration, priority, and intensity."

Sutherland also discussed the general social conditions underlying the differential association process. In the 1939 version of his theory Sutherland described those general social conditions in terms of *culture conflict*, where that term meant that different groups in a society have different ideas about appropriate ways to behave.[19] *Social disorganization* was then introduced to describe the presence of culture conflict in a society, the term taken from general sociological theories, including the Chicago School of Human Ecology.[20]

In the 1949 and final version of his theory Sutherland rejected the term *social disorganization* and replaced it with the term *differential so-*

---

[16]Blumer, op. cit., pp. 2–3.

[17]Cf. W. I. Thomas, *The Unadjusted Girl,* Little, Brown, Boston, 1923, pp. 41–53. For a more recent discussion, see Peter McHugh, *Defining the Situation,* Bobbs-Merrill, Indianapolis, 1968.

[18]Blumer, op. cit.

[19]Sutherland, *Criminology,* 1939 ed., p. 7.

[20]Ibid., p. 8.

cial organization. Social disorganization implies that there is an absence of organization. In contrast with that implication, Sutherland argued that there are numerous divergent associations organized around different interests and for different purposes. Under this condition of divergent, differential social organizations, it is inevitable that some of these groups will subscribe to and support criminal patterns of behavior, others will be essentially neutral, and still others will be definitely anticriminal and self-consciously law-abiding.[21]

Because of some confusion about the term *culture conflict,* Sutherland's coauthor, Donald R. Cressey, substituted the term *normative conflict* after Sutherland's death. Norms are socially accepted rules about how people are supposed to act in specific situations and circumstances.[22] Normative conflict, then, refers to the situation in which different social groups (i.e., differential social organization) hold different views about appropriate ways to behave in specific situations and circumstances. In making this substitution, Cressey stated that he was clarifying, not changing, the meaning of Sutherland's argument.

Sutherland's theory, then, states that in a situation of differential social organization and normative conflict, differences in behavior, including criminal behaviors, arise because of differential associations. That is really only another way of saying that a person who associates with Methodists is likely to become a Methodist, a person who associates with Republicans is likely to become a Republican, and a person who associates with criminals is likely to become a criminal.

RESEARCH TESTING SUTHERLAND'S THEORY

In Sutherland's theory, crime and delinquency are caused by associating with other people who transmit "definitions" that favor violations of the law. Research testing this theory has tended to focus on the explanation of juvenile delinquency rather than on the explanation of adult criminality. In general, this is because delinquency is largely a group phenomenon in that juveniles are likely to commit crime and delinquency in the company of other juveniles.[23]

While this fact is consistent with Sutherland's theory, it does not in itself demonstrate that delinquency is *caused by* the transmission of "def-

---

[21]Ibid.

[22]Donald R. Cressey, "Culture Conflict, Differential Association, and Normative Conflict," in Marvin E. Wolfgang, ed., *Crime and Culture,* John Wiley, New York, 1968, pp. 43–54.

[23]In general, see Albert J. Reiss, Jr., "Co-offender Influences on Criminal Careers," in Alfred Blumstein, Jacqueline Cohen, Jeffrey Roth, and Christy Visher, eds., *Criminal Careers and "Career Criminals,"* vol. 2, National Academy Press, Washington, DC, 1986, pp. 145–52.

initions" through associating with other delinquents. It may be, as Sheldon and Eleanor Glueck said, that "birds of a feather flock together"[24]—that is, delinquents may select as friends other youths whose values and behaviors are similar to their own. If that is the case, then delinquency "causes" delinquent friends, but delinquent friends do not cause delinquency. Related to this is the obvious fact that not everyone who associates with criminals and delinquents adopts or follows the criminal pattern. What, then, is the difference in the quality of the associations that in one instance lead to acceptance of "definitions favorable to law violation" but in another leads only to an acquaintance with but not acceptance of them? Sutherland suggested that the "frequency, duration, priority, and intensity" of associations determined how much impact they had on a person, and he supported this argument with case histories and with self-appraisal statements by various individuals who had followed a criminal pattern.[25] Finally, Sheldon Glueck also questioned whether Sutherland's theory was inherently untestable, asking, "Has anyone actually counted the number of definitions favourable to violation of law and definitions unfavourable to violation of law, and demonstrated that in the predelinquency experience of the vast majority of delinquents and criminals, the former exceed the latter?"[26] In 1960, Sutherland's coauthor Donald Cressey agreed that, at the broadest level, differential association theory is untestable.[27]

In 1988, however, Matsueda asserted that differential association theory can be tested and that a considerable amount of research supports it.[28] First, he argued that a variety of studies have found that juveniles who report having more delinquent friends also report committing more delinquent acts, and that these studies provide general support for the theory. Second, Matsueda stated that a number of studies have focused on the content of definitions favorable to law violation and showed that these definitions are associated with increased tendencies to engage in criminal and delinquent behavior. Matsueda says that these definitions are not "oppositional values that repudiate the legitimacy of

---

[24]Sheldon Glueck and Eleanor T. Glueck, *Unraveling Juvenile Delinquency,* Commonwealth Fund, New York, 1950, p. 164.

[25]See, for example, Edwin H. Sutherland, *White Collar Crime,* Dryden, New York, 1949, pp. 222–56.

[26]Sheldon Glueck, "Theory and Fact in Criminology: A Criticism of Differential Association," *British Journal of Delinquency* 7: 92–109 (Oct. 1956).

[27]Donald Cressey, "Epidemiology and Individual Conduct," *Pacific Sociological Review* 3: 47–58, (1960).

[28]Matsueda, "The Current State of Differential Association Theory," op. cit., pp. 284–87. See also James D. Orcutt, "Differential Association and Marijuana Use," *Criminology* 25(2): 341–58 (May 1987).

the law and make crimes morally correct."[29] Rather, they are disagreements with the larger culture about the specific situations in which the
laws should apply. For example, Matsueda describes the legal defenses
to crime, such as self-defense and insanity, as "prototypical definitions
favorable to crime," but states that these are included in the law rather
than excluded from it.[30] Third, Matsueda argues that recent advances in
statistical techniques have found support for the complex causal structure in Sutherland's theory, especially involving the ratio of definitions
favorable and unfavorable to violating the law.[31]

A great deal of modern theory and research in criminology can be
traced to Sutherland's original formulation. Cultural and subcultural
theories are based on Sutherland's arguments about normative conflict
and focus on the *content* of what is learned. These theories retain the
cognitive orientation of Sutherland's original theory and examine the
role of ideas in causing criminal behaviors. Other theories, however, focus on the learning *process* that Sutherland described rather than on the
content of the ideas that were said to be learned. These theories tend to
be associated with the more modern theories of learning, although at
least some of them retain Sutherland's emphasis on differential association. These two branches of modern theory and research are presented
in the next two sections.

THE CONTENT OF LEARNING: CULTURAL AND
SUBCULTURAL THEORIES

In Sutherland's theory the actual causes of criminal behavior are *ideas*—
the definitions favorable to law violation. Cultural and subcultural theo-

---

[29]Matsueda, op. cit., p. 296.

[30]Ibid., p. 301, fn. 11; see also fn. 6.

[31]The studies he cites here are Orcutt, op. cit.; Matsueda, "Testing Control Theory and Differential
Association," *American Sociological Review* 47: 489–504 (1982); Matsueda and Karen Heimer,
"Race, Family Structure, and Delinquency," *American Sociological Review* 52: 826–40 (1988); Elton
F. Jackson, Charles R. Tittle, and Mary Jean Burke, "Offense-Specific Models of the Differential Association Process," *Social Problems* 33: 335–56 (1986); and Charles R. Tittle, Mary Jean Burke, and
Elton F. Jackson, "Modeling Sutherland's Theory of Differential Association," *Social Forces* 65:
405–32 (1986). More recently, Mark Warr ("Age, Peers, and Delinquency," *Criminology* 31[1]:
17–40 [Feb. 1993]) argued that differential associations can explain the relation between age and
crime. In particular, he found support for Sutherland's concept of duration, but argued that it was the
recency rather than the priority of delinquent friends that had an impact on delinquent behavior. In
addition, Daniel P. Mears, Matthew Ploeger, and Mark Warr ("Explaining the Gender Gap in Delinquency," *Journal of Research in Crime and Delinquency* 35[3]: 251–66, [1998]) argued that Sutherland's theory is useful in explaining the gender distribution of delinquency. They found that the number of delinquent friends was the strongest predictor of delinquency, and that males were
significantly more likely to have delinquent friends than females. However, females' stronger moral
evaluations also appeared to protect them from delinquency when they did have delinquent friends.
This suggests that, in order to explain the gender gap, Sutherland's theory may have to be modified.

ries also focus on the role of ideas in causing criminal behaviors. These theories, like Sutherland's, may explore the sources of those ideas in general social conditions, but they are characterized by the argument that it is the ideas themselves, rather than the social conditions, that directly cause criminal behavior.[32]

Walter B. Miller presented one such cultural theory, focusing on the explanation of gang delinquency.[33] He argued that the lower class has a separate, identifiable culture distinct from the culture of the middle class, and that this culture has a tradition at least as old as that of the middle class. Where the middle class has "values" such as achievement, the lower class has "focal concerns" that include *trouble* (getting into and staying out of trouble are dominant concerns of lower-class people); *toughness* (masculinity, endurance, strength, etc., are all highly valued); *smartness* (skill at outsmarting the other guy; "street sense" rather than high IQ); *excitement* (the constant search for thrills, as opposed to just "hanging around"); *fate* (the view that most things that happen to people are beyond their control, and nothing can be done about them); and *autonomy* (resentment of authority and rules). Miller described this lower-class culture as a "generating milieu" for gang delinquency because it interacts with several social conditions typically found in poor areas. Lower-class families are frequently headed by females, so that male children do not have a masculine role model in the family. These boys may then acquire an exaggerated sense of masculinity. In addition, crowded conditions in lower-class homes means that the boys tend to hang out on the street, where they form gangs. The delinquent nature of much gang activity is then a rather obvious consequence of the way the boys think, that is, of the lower-class culture and its focal concerns.

A general theory of criminal violence was presented by Wolfgang and Ferracuti, called the "subculture of violence."[34] This theory relied to some extent on Wolfgang's earlier study of homicide in Philadelphia.[35] Wolfgang had found that a significant number of the homicides that occurred among lower-class people seemed to result from very trivial

---

[32]In contrast, the strain theories of Cohen and of Cloward and Ohlin both use the term *subculture*, but both locate the primary causes of criminal behavior directly in social conditions. There are common thinking patterns that arise among delinquents, but the thinking patterns are not the cause of the criminal behavior. In strain theories, both the thinking patterns and the criminal behaviors are caused by the same social structural forces. See Chapter 8.

[33]Walter B. Miller, "Lower Class Culture as a Generating Milieu of Gang Delinquency," *Journal of Social Issues* 14(3): 5–19 (1958).

[34]Marvin E. Wolfgang and Franco Ferracuti, *The Subculture of Violence*, Sage, Beverly Hills, CA, 1981.

[35]Marvin E. Wolfgang, *Patterns in Criminal Homicide*, University of Pennsylvania Press, Philadelphia, 1958.

events that took on great importance because of mutually held expectations about how people would behave. Wolfgang interpreted these events in theoretical terms taken from Sutherland's theory:[36]

The significance of a jostle, a slightly derogatory remark, or the appearance of a weapon in the hands of an adversary are stimuli differentially perceived and interpreted by Negroes and whites, males and females. Social expectations of response in particular types of social interaction result in differential "definitions of the situation." A male is usually expected to defend the name or honor of his mother, the virtue of womanhood . . . and to accept no derogation about his race (even from a member of his own race), his age, or his masculinity. Quick resort to physical combat as a measure of daring, courage, or defense of status appears to be a cultural expression, especially for lower socio-economic class males of both races. When such a culture norm response is elicited from an individual engaged in social interplay with others who harbor the same response mechanism, physical assaults, altercations, and violent domestic quarrels that result in homicide are likely to be common.

Wolfgang and Ferracuti generalized the findings of this and a number of other studies on criminal violence into an overall theory that was designed to explain one type of homicide, the passion crimes that were neither planned intentional killings nor manifestations of extreme mental illness.[37] They described underlying conflicts of values between the dominant culture and this subculture of violence. For example, people in the subculture of violence tend to value honor more highly than people in the dominant culture. On the other hand they tend to value human life less highly. There are also normative conflicts between the subculture of violence and the dominant culture. Those refer to "rules" about what behaviors are expected in response to the trivial jostles or remarks that were the cause of so many homicides. Those norms are backed up with social rewards and punishments: People who do not follow the norms are criticized or ridiculed by other people in the subculture, and those who follow them are admired and respected. These

---

[36]Ibid., pp. 188–89. For discussions of male violence as honor defense, see Kenneth Polk, "Males and Honor Contest Violence," *Homicide Studies* 3(1): 30–46, (1999); and Nancy V. Baker, Peter R. Gregware, and Margery A. Cassidy, "Family Killing Fields: Honor Rationales in the Murder of Women," *Violence Against Women* 5(2): 164–84 (1999).

[37]Wolfgang and Ferracuti, op. cit., p. 141. The theory itself is presented in seven points on pp. 158–61, and is summarized on pp. 314–16. A similar theoretical approach, focusing on cultural differences in disputatiousness (the tendency to define negative interactions as grievances and to demand reparations for them) and aggressiveness (the tendency to pursue a grievance and to use force to settle the dispute), is presented in David F. Luckenbill and Daniel P. Doyle, "Structural Position and Violence: Developing a Cultural Explanation," *Criminology* 27(3): 419–36 (Aug. 1989).

norms take on a certain life of their own, independent of whether they are approved by the individuals who follow them, since the failure to follow the norms may result in the person becoming a victim of the violence. Thus each individual may respond to a situation violently because he or she expects the other individual to respond violently, even if neither person approves of the violence. In this sense the subculture of violence is similar to a wartime situation in which "it is either him or me."[38]

Wolfgang and Ferracuti, like Sutherland, argued that the immediate causes of these passion homicides are ideas—values, norms, and expectations of behavior. Like Sutherland, they agreed that these ideas had originated in general social conditions, and suggested that theories such as those by Cohen, Cloward and Ohlin, or Miller might explain the origin of the subculture. They themselves, however, refused to speculate on how the subculture of violence had arisen.[39] That question was not vital to their theory, since the cause of the violent behaviors was said to be the ideas themselves rather than the social conditions that had generated those ideas in the past. Essentially they argued that the subculture had arisen in the past for specific historical reasons, but that it was transmitted from generation to generation as a set of ideas after those original social conditions had disappeared. Thus their policy recommendations did not require dealing with general social conditions, but only required doing something to break up the patterns of ideas that constituted the subculture of violence. For example, one of their major policy recommendations was to disperse the subculture by scattering low-income housing projects throughout the city rather than concentrating them in inner-city areas.[40] Once the subculture was dispersed, individuals would gradually be assimilated into the dominant culture and the violent behaviors would diminish.

The subculture of violence thesis has generated a large amount of additional theory and research, especially with respect to explaining higher levels of violent crime in the American South and among African Americans. A number of theorists have argued that there is a Southern subculture of violence that has its historical roots in the exaggerated sense of "honor" among Southern gentlemen, the institutionalized violence associated with maintaining a part of the population in slavery, the defeat at the hands of Northerners in the Civil War, the subsequent eco-

---

[38]Ibid., p. 156.

[39]Ibid., p. 163.

[40]Ibid., p. 299.

nomic exploitation of Southern states by the North, and so on.[41] As with Wolfgang and Ferracuti's theory, these studies argue that the subculture of violence arose in the South for a variety of historical reasons, but that it continues now because the ideas are passed from generation to generation, although the conditions that originally gave rise to the ideas no longer exist.[42]

Elijah Anderson presented a subcultural theory of violence among African Americans, based on the "code of the street" that is found in America's inner cities.[43] According to Anderson, people in these areas face a situation in which there is a high concentration of very poor people, a declining number of legitimate jobs, an increasing number of illegitimate jobs, widespread drug and gun availability, high crime and violence, declining welfare payments, and little hope for the future. In these circumstances, everyone feels isolated and alienated from the rest of America. But residents themselves distinguish "decent" people from "street" people based on the degree of isolation and alienation.

Decent people in the inner city live according to a "civil code" that includes many of the middle-class values of the larger society. But this civil code has no value on the street, where the "code of the street" demands that you always communicate, in both subtle and overt ways, that "I can take care of myself." The code of the street is a product of the total despair felt by many inner-city residents, and particularly their pro-

---

[41]See, for example, S. Hackney, "Southern Violence," in Hugh D. Graham and Ted Robert Gurr, eds., *The History of Violence in America*, Bantam, New York, 1969, pp. 505–27; and R. D. Gastil, "Homicide and a Regional Subculture of Violence," *American Sociological Review* 36: 412–27 (June 1971.)

[42]Recent research on race, region, and homicide rates has focused this argument considerably. Overall homicide rates are higher in the South than in other regions of the country, but the West has the highest homicide rates for both whites and blacks. See Patrick W. O'Carroll and James A. Mercy, "Regional Variation in Homicide Rates: Why Is the West So Violent," *Violence and Victims* 4: 17–25 (1989); and Gregory S. Kowalski and Thomas A. Petee, "Sunbelt Effects on Homicide Rates," *Sociology and Social Research* 75: 73–79 (1991). This is because blacks have higher homicide rates than whites, and the South has a higher proportion of blacks in the population. But Southern blacks themselves are not more violent than blacks elsewhere in the country. In fact, black homicide rates are lower in the South than in any other region of the country. Thus, there is no "southern subculture of violence" among the black population there. On the other hand, there may be such a subculture among the whites there. Whites in Western states have higher homicide rates than whites in the South, but this is largely due to the high homicide rates for Hispanic whites. Homicide rates for non-Hispanic whites are highest in the South. Thus, if there is a southern subculture of violence, it affects non-Hispanic whites only. See Candice Nelsen, Jay Corzine, and Lin Huff-Corzine, "The Violent West Re-Examined," *Criminology* 32(1): 149–61 (Feb. 1994); and Rebekah Chu, Craig Rivera, and Colin Loftin, "Herding and Homicide," *Social Forces* 78(3): 971–87, 2000.

[43]Elijah Anderson, *Code of the Street*, W. W. Norton, Philadelphia, 1999. See also Anderson, "The Social Ecology of Youth Violence," pp. 65–104 in Michael Tonry and Mark H. Moore, eds., *Youth Violence* (vol. 24 of *Crime and Justice: A Review of Research*), University of Chicago Press, Chicago, 1998. For an earlier such theory, see Lynn A. Curtis, *Violence, Race and Culture*, Heath, Lexington, MA, 1975.

found lack of faith in the criminal justice system. It is also a cultural adaptation to the actual situation of inner-city residents, a realistic set of behavioral rules for living in those circumstances. Even "decent" people, especially juveniles from "decent" families, can switch from the civil code to the code of the street at a moment's notice when the situation demands.

At the heart of the code of the street is the issue of respect—being treated "right" or being granted one's "props" (proper due). Inner-city residents are able to control little in their own lives, and so being in physical control of their immediate environment is extremely important. In addition, being "dissed" (disrespected) is considered an indication of the other person's intentions, a warning of a possible physical attack, and so it is likely to call forth a preemptive first strike in return. Even decent parents socialize their children to respond in this way ("If someone disses you, you got to straighten them out").

Children from "street" families (as opposed to "decent" families) grow up largely without adult supervision. Even when they are eight or nine years old, they may hang out on the street until late at night, where they socialize primarily with other children. In these peer groups, children pool their knowledge and hone their skills for surviving on the streets. In particular, they learn how to fight, and they learn the significance that fighting has in the street world.

When they are very young, children from decent families are kept out of the street world by their parents, but by age ten or so, decent and street children are mingling in the neighborhoods and are trying to create identities for themselves in the neighborhood context. Decent children observe the behaviors of other children their own age, notice how older children negotiate and resolve disputes, and watch decent and street adults live their lives in the context of the inner-city environment. In addition, decent children hear many verbal messages about the constant dangerousness of the environment and the constant need to be physically tough and to show nerve. Showing nerve is more important than the actual fighting, since it can prevent the need to fight. In the code of the street, the point is to subtly communicate a predisposition to violence, a willingness and an ability to create total chaos and mayhem, in order to deter potential aggression. This is done through words, behavioral gestures and bodily postures, as well as through clothing, jewelry, and personal grooming. Jackets, sneakers, gold chains, and even expensive firearms are not just fashion. They all are part of a look that is designed to prevent problems before they happen.

By the time they are teenagers, even decent children must be skilled at negotiating and fitting into this world. This process affects both boys and girls, but is more important to boys because of the association between "nerve" and "manhood." In the code of the street, manhood involves the ability to be physically ruthless in relations with other people. It is the ability to gain respect through size and strength and physical prowess. Nerve, in contrast, communicates a lack of fear of death, a sense that death is preferable to being dissed. Even small and weak boys can have nerve—in many ways, nerve is more important to them because they have little else to deter attacks. In the coming of age process in the inner city, manhood requires that smaller boys find ways to use their size and strength to gain respect from larger boys. Having nerve is essential to this effort.

A major differences between street and decent boys, however, is that decent boys can put on street behavior when it is useful and necessary, but they can then switch back to the decent code. They understand that some people and situations demand street behavior but that other people use the "decent" code and expect it in return. Street boys, in contrast, live in a world in which everyone lives according to the code of the street. Thus, street boys interpret all other behaviors according to the code of the street, even the behaviors of middle-class people who have no knowledge of that code.

Anderson argues that outsiders tend to blame the individuals who live in the inner cities, to believe they are people with no moral values. But he argues passionately that the focus should be on the socioeconomic structure, particularly the absence of jobs, job training, and job networks (contacts that can help a person get a job).[44] In addition, Anderson blames the historical legacy of slavery and segregation, arguing that "the attitudes of the wider society are deeply implicated in the code of the street." At least some children, especially the most alienated and vulnerable ones, internalize a sense of rejection and contempt from mainstream society. This "may strongly encourage them to express contempt for the more conventional society in turn." Some will even "consciously invest themselves and their considerable mental resources in what amounts to an oppositional culture to preserve themselves and their self-respect." Anderson concludes:[45]

A vicious cycle has been formed. The hopelessness and alienation many young inner-city black men and women feel, largely a result of endemic joblessness and persistent racism, fuels the violence they engage in. This violence serves to confirm the negative feelings many whites and some middle-class blacks harbor

---

[44]Anderson, "The Social Ecology," p. 102.
[45]Ibid., p. 103.

toward the ghetto poor, further legitimating the oppositional culture and the code of the street in the eyes of many poor blacks. Unless this cycle is broken, attitudes on both sides will become increasingly entrenched, and the violence, which claims victims black and white, poor and affluent will only escalate.

   Unlike Wolfgang and Ferracuti in their theory, Anderson ties the subcultural views found in the code of the street directly to the social conditions that generate it. Thus, Anderson's theory is partly a cultural theory like Wolfgang and Ferracuti's, describing the direct causal impact of ideas on behaviors, and is partly a structural theory like the strain theories presented in the last chapter, ones that describe the direct causal impact of general social conditions on behaviors. Anderson's policy recommendations reflect this double causation. Unlike Wolfgang and Ferracuti, Anderson argues that the general social conditions that are responsible for producing the code of the streets must be addressed.

   Matsueda and his colleagues argue that all subcultural theories should include an account of the structural conditions that give rise to them:[46]

The salience of values, whether subcultural or cultural, is an important link between social structure and individual behavior. . . Any theory of subcultures that ignores social structure is incomplete and will fail to predict when individuals who have been exposed to the values of the subculture will act on those values. . . Subcultures, then, are intimately tied to structural opportunities. Because structural opportunities affect crime partly through affecting subcultures, any structural explanation of crime that ignores subcultures is incomplete.

THE LEARNING PROCESS: SOCIAL LEARNING THEORY

While cultural and subcultural theories are derived from Sutherland's arguments about the content of what is learned, other theory and research has focused on his description of the learning process. Several authors have maintained Sutherland's view that criminal behavior is normally learned behavior, but have updated the conception of what is in-

---

[46]Ross L. Matsueda, Rosemary Gartner, Irving Piliavin, and Michael Polakowski, "The Prestige of Criminal and Conventional Occupations," *American Sociological Review* 57 752–70, 1992, pp. 767–68. See also Thomas J. Bernard, "Angry Aggression Among the Truly Disadvantaged," *Criminology* 28(1): 73–96, 1990; Bernard focuses more directly on the structural conditions underlying cultural beliefs. For other examples of the relationship between structure and subculture, see Karen Heimer, "Socioeconomic Status, Subcultural Definitions, and Violent Delinquency," *Social Forces* 75(3): 799–834, 1997; and John Hagan, "Deviance and Despair: Subcultural and Structural Linkages Between Delinquency and Despair in the Life Course," *Social Forces* 76(1): 119–34, 1997.

volved in "normal learning" to include arguments found in more modern learning theories.[47] In particular, these more recent theories drop Sutherland's argument that the principal part of normal learning takes place in intimate personal groups, although they may retain that as one important source of learning. These theories argue that learning can also take place through direct interactions with the environment, independent of associations with other people, through the principles of operant conditioning. In addition to changing the description of the learning process, the more recent theories also change the description of the content of what is learned. Specifically, these theories switch from Sutherland's original cognitive orientation that only ideas are learned, and adopt the more recent theoretical orientation that behaviors themselves can be directly learned through both operant conditioning and social learning.

The most important such reformulation is by Ronald Akers, in what he describes as "differential reinforcement" or "social learning" theory. In an original article with Burgess, Akers rewrote the principles of differential association into the language of operant conditioning.[48] This reformulation held that "criminal behavior is learned both in nonsocial situations that are reinforcing or discriminative and through that social interaction in which the behavior of other persons is reinforcing or discriminative for criminal behavior."[49] The addition of "nonsocial situations" constitutes a recognition that the environment itself can reinforce criminality, aside from the person's "social interactions" with other individuals. But Burgess and Akers maintain, with Sutherland, that "the principal part of the learning of criminal behavior occurs in those groups which comprise the individual's major source of reinforcement."[50]

Akers later revised and updated this theory, and expanded the principles of operant conditioning to include modeling, or social learning, theory,[51] which argues that a great deal of learning among humans takes place by observing the consequences that behaviors have for other people. Akers's formulation of social learning theory focused on four major

---

[47]See Daniel Glaser, "Criminality Theories and Behavioral Images," *American Journal of Sociology* 61: 433–44 (March 1956); and C. R. Jeffery, "Criminal Behavior and Learning Theory," *Journal of Criminal Law, Criminology and Police Science* 56: 294–300 (Sept. 1965).

[48]Robert L. Burgess and Ronald L. Akers, "A Differential Association—Reinforcement Theory of Criminal Behavior," *Social Problems* 14: 128–47 (fall 1968).

[49]Ibid., p. 146.

[50]Ibid., p. 140.

[51]Ronald L. Akers, *Deviant Behavior: A Social Learning Approach*, pp. 39–70.

concepts.[52] The most important source of social learning, according to Akers, is *differential association*. This refers to the patterns of interactions with others who are the source of definitions that either favorable or unfavorable to violating the law. Akers retains Sutherland's argument that differential associations vary according to priority, duration, frequency, and intensity, but argues that they include both the direct transmission of the definitions through interpersonal communication, and the indirect transmission through identification with more distant reference groups. The *definitions* themselves, according to Akers, reflect the meanings one attaches to one's own behavior. "General" definitions reflect overall religious, moral, or ethical beliefs, while "specific" definitions reflect the meanings that one applies to a particular behavior (e.g., smoking marijuana, burglarizing a house, killing the witnesses to an armed robbery). *Differential reinforcement* refers to the actual or anticipated consequences of a given behavior. People do things that they think will result in rewards or will avoid punishments in the future and they don't do things that they think will result in punishments. These rewards and punishments can be social (approval or disapproval by other people) or nonsocial (e.g., getting high or getting sick on drugs). Finally, *imitation* involves observing what others do. Whether or not a behavior will be imitated depends on the characteristics of the person being observed, the behavior the person engages in, and the observed consequences of that behavior.

Akers also proposed a specific sequence of events by which the learning of criminal behavior is said to take place.[53] The sequence originates with the differential association of the individual with other individuals who have favorable definitions of criminal behavior, who model criminal behaviors for the person to imitate, and who provide social reinforcements for those behaviors. Thus, the initial participation of the individual in criminal behavior is explained primarily by differential association, definitions, imitation, and social reinforcements. After the person has begun to commit criminal behaviors, differential reinforcements determine whether the behaviors are continued or not. These include both social and nonsocial reinforcements in the form of the rewards and pun-

---

[52]Ronald L. Akers, *Criminological Theories,* Roxbury, Los Angeles, 1994, pp. 94–107. See also Akers, "Social Learning Theory," pp. 192–210 in Raymond Paternoster and Ronet Bachman, eds., *Explaining Criminals and Crime,* Roxbury, Los Angeles, 2001. For an extended discussion of the theory, see Akers, *Social Learning and Social Structure,* op. cit.

[53]Ronald L. Akers, Marvin D. Krohn, Lonn Lanza-Kaduce, and Marcia Radosevich, "Social Learning and Deviant Behavior," *American Sociological Review* 44: 636–55 (1979).

ishments directly experienced by the individual as a consequence of participating in the criminal behavior, and also the rewards and punishments the person experiences vicariously, by observing the consequences that criminal behavior has for others.

Akers maintains that the social learning process explains the link between social structural conditions and individual behaviors.[54] For example, economic inequality, the modernization process, social disorganization, and social structural strain have all been linked to criminal
behavior in Chapters 5, 6, 7, and 8 above. Akers argues that structural
conditions such as these affect crime by affecting a person's differential
associations, definitions, models, and reinforcements.

Finally, Akers reviews a large volume of research to argue that "almost all research on social learning theory has found strong relationships in the theoretically expected direction. . . . When social learning
theory is tested against other theories using the same data collected
from the same samples, it is usually found to account for more variance
in the dependent variables than the theories with which it is being compared."[55] In particular, he argues that research supports the "typical" sequence in which social learning operates, in which criminal behaviors
are acquired through differential associations, definitions, imitation, and
social reinforcements, and then are maintained through social and
nonsocial reinforcements.

IMPLICATIONS

Sutherland's theory has had a massive impact on criminology. At the
time it was written criminology was dominated by physicians and psychiatrists who searched for the causes of criminal behavior in biological
and psychological abnormalities. Sutherland's theory, more than any
other, was responsible for the decline of that view and the rise of the
view that crime is the result of environmental influences acting on biologically and psychologically normal individuals.

To assess this school of thought it is necessary to distinguish between
Sutherland's theory itself and the more modern learning theories that
have followed it. To a considerable extent Sutherland's theory was based
on an outdated theory of learning. His argument that learning consists
entirely in ideas ("definitions") and that the principal part of learning occurs in differential associations in intimate personal groups must be as-

---

[54]Ronald L. Akers, "Linking Sociology and Its Specialties," *Social Forces* 71: 1–16 (1992); Akers, *Criminological Theories*, op. cit., pp. 101–2.

[55]Akers, *Criminological Theories*, ibid., pp. 102–7.

sessed in terms of general research on the nature of human learning. The field of learning theory has its own controversies, and to some extent Sutherland's theory, as a cognitive theory, must do its own battle with other cognitive theories and with the more popular behavioral theories. There is no reason to think that Sutherland's theory will emerge triumphant from that battle. Quite to the contrary, there are many reasons to believe that, as a learning theory, Sutherland's theory has virtually no importance whatsoever. Sutherland, after all, was not a learning theorist and was not particularly familiar with the major theory and research on human learning that was going on at the time.

Sutherland's legacy to criminology is not his specific learning theory but his argument that criminal behavior is normal learned behavior. The task Sutherland focused on, and the task still facing criminologists today, is to explore the implications of that argument for criminology. In the first edition of this book Vold argued that the logical implication of Sutherland's theory is that crime must be viewed in the context of political and social conflict.[56]

If criminal behavior, by and large, is the normal behavior of normally responding individuals in situations defined as undesirable, illegal, and therefore criminal, then the basic problem is one of social and political organization and the established values or definitions of what may, and what may not, be permitted. Crime, in this sense, is political behavior and the criminal becomes a member of a "minority group" without sufficient public support to dominate and control the police power of the state.

Sutherland seemed to draw a similar implication from his theory. After making the first systematic presentation of the theory in 1939, he turned his attention to white-collar crime and retained that focus until his death.[57] Sutherland argued that white-collar crimes are normal learned behaviors and that there are no essential differences between those behaviors and the behaviors of lower-class criminals when viewed from the perspective of causation. The differences in official crime rates between the upper and lower classes arise because upper-class people have sufficient political power to control the enactment and enforcement of criminal laws. When their normal learned behaviors are socially

---

[56]George B. Vold, *Theoretical Criminology*, Oxford University Press, New York, 1958, p. 202; see also the 2nd ed. prepared by Thomas J. Bernard, 1979, pp. 247–48. For a similar argument, see Matsueda, op. cit., pp. 298–99.

[57]Edwin H. Sutherland, "White Collar Criminality," *American Sociological Review* 5: 1–12 (Feb. 1940); "Is 'White Collar Crime' Crime?" *American Sociological Review* 10: 132–39 (April 1945); and *White Collar Crime*, op. cit.

harmful, these behaviors either are not defined as wrongs at all or are defined as civil wrongs. But when the normal learned behaviors of lower-class people are socially harmful, these behaviors are defined and processed as crimes. Thus, lower-class people end up with high official crime rates, while upper-class people end up with low official crime rates. Further discussion of this implication will be presented in Chapter 13 on conflict criminology.

CONCLUSIONS

Sutherland described criminal behavior as normal learned behavior and went on to make specific assertions about the nature of normal learning. He asserted that normal learning primarily involves the learning of ideas and beliefs in the process of associating with other people. Behaviors, including criminal behaviors, follow from and are a product of those ideas and beliefs.

The adequacy of Sutherland's assertions can only be assessed in the context of general theories and research about human learning. In general, it seems reasonable to conclude that ideas and beliefs learned in association with other people do have a direct causal impact on criminal behaviors. However, criminal behaviors may also be associated with other types of normal learning. More recent learning theories of criminal behavior, such as Akers's social learning theory, retain Sutherland's view that criminal behavior is normal learned behavior but more adequately incorporate modern learning principles in the description of the normal learning process.

To assert that criminal behavior is directly caused by beliefs does not deny that there are structural sources for beliefs—that is one of the most fundamental propositions in sociology. The question is whether those beliefs attain some life of their own as causes of behavior in general and as causes of criminal behavior in particular. The most reasonable position at the present time seems to be that adopted by Matsueda and his colleagues: that culture functions as a crucial intervening variable between social structure and individual behavior.[58] That is, ideas and beliefs—including "definitions" of behavior, expectations about how to behave in particular situations, social approval or valuation of certain behaviors, and social responses that back up those expected and approved behaviors with rewards and punishments—have a direct causal impact on behavior, independent of their social structural sources.

---

[58]Matsueda, Gartner, Piliavin, and Polakowski, op. cit., pp. 767–68. For the argument that beliefs have no direct causal impact on criminal behavior, see Kornhauser, *Social Sources of Delinquency,* op. cit., pp. 207–10.

CHAPTER TEN

Control Theories

Many theories of criminal behavior assume that people naturally obey the law if left to their own devices, and argue that there are special forces—either biological, psychological, or social—that drive people to commit crime. Control theories take the opposite approach. They assume that all people naturally would commit crimes if left to their own devices. The key question, then, is why most people do *not* commit crimes. Control theories answer that question by focusing on special "controlling" forces that restrain the person from committing crimes. These forces break down in certain situations, resulting in crime and other "uncontrolled" behaviors. Thus individuals are said to commit crime because of the weakness of forces restraining them from doing so, not because of the strength of forces driving them to do so.

This chapter examines a number of recent sociological theories that take the control perspective and are described as control theories. These theories are especially important as explanations of delinquency, since most of the research supporting them has been done with juvenile populations. Control theories, however, may also be used to explain adult criminality.

EARLY CONTROL THEORIES: REISS TO NYE

In 1951 Albert J. Reiss published an article in which he examined a number of factors related to the control perspective to see if they might be used to predict probation revocation among juvenile offenders.[1] Reiss reviewed the official court records of 1,110 white male juvenile probationers between the ages of 11 and 17. He found that probation revocation was more likely when the juvenile was psychiatrically diagnosed as having weak ego or superego controls and when the psychiatrist recommended either intensive psychotherapy in the community or treatment in a closed institution. Reiss argued that such diagnoses and recommendations were based on an assessment of the juvenile's "personal controls"—that is, the ability to refrain from meeting needs in ways that conflicted with the norms and rules of the community. In addition, he found that probation revocation was more likely when juveniles did not regularly attend school, and when they were described as behavior problems by school authorities. Reiss argued that these were a measure of the acceptance or submission of the juvenile to "social controls"—i.e., the control of socially approved institutions.[2]

Reiss's theory influenced later control theories, but his findings in support of that theory were quite weak. A variety of factors related to family and community controls over the juvenile did not predict probation revocation. The strongest associations were found between probation revocation and the diagnoses and recommendations of the psychiatrists. Reiss argued that the failure of personal controls explained both phenomena, thus accepting at face value the theoretical framework of the psychiatrists. But such an explanation is tautological unless it is supported by some additional evidence about the strength or weakness of personal controls.[3] The association of probation revocation with truancy and school problems was much weaker and can be explained from other perspectives besides control theory.

In 1957 Jackson Toby introduced the concept of "stakes in conformity"—i.e., how much a person has to lose when he or she breaks the law.[4] He argued that all youths are tempted to break the law, but some youth risk much more than others when they give in to those temptations. Youths who do well in school not only risk being punished for breaking the law, but they also jeopardize their future careers. Thus they have

---

[1] Albert J. Reiss, "Delinquency as the Failure of Personal and Social Controls," *American Sociological Review* 16: 196–207 (April 1951).

[2] Ibid., p. 206.

[3] Cf. Travis Hirschi, *Causes of Delinquency*, University of California Press, Berkeley, 1969, pp. 11 and 198, n. 4.

[4] Jackson Toby, "Social Disorganization and Stake in Conformity: Complementary Factors in the Predatory Behavior of Hoodlums," *Journal of Criminal Law, Criminology and Police Science* 48: 12–17 (May–June 1957). A similar concept was presented in a later article by Scott Briar and Irving Piliavin, "Delinquency, Situational Inducements, and Commitment to Conformity," *Social Problems*, summer 1965, pp. 35–45.

high "stakes in conformity." In contrast, youths who do poorly in school risk only being punished for their offense, since their future prospects are already dim. Thus they have less to lose when they break the law—i.e., lower stakes in conformity. Toby also argued that peer support for deviance can develop in communities that have a large number of youths with low stakes in conformity, so that the community develops even higher crime rates than would be expected by considering the stakes in conformity of the individual youths. Conversely, youths in suburbs who have low stakes in conformity normally obtain no support from their peers for delinquency. Thus these youths may be unhappy, but usually do not become delinquent.

Toby focused on how well the youth did in school, but he stated: "In all fairness, it should be remembered that the basis for school adjustment is laid in the home and the community."[5] The following year, F. Ivan Nye published a study that focused on the family as the single most important source of social control for adolescents.[6] He argued that most delinquent behavior was the result of insufficient social control, and that delinquent behavior "caused" by positive factors was relatively rare.[7] *Social control* was used as a broad term that included direct controls imposed by means of restrictions and punishments, internal control exercised through conscience, indirect control related to affectional identification with parents and other noncriminal persons, and the availability of legitimate means to satisfy needs.[8] With respect to the final type of social control, Nye argued that "if all the needs of the individual could be met adequately and without delay, without violating laws, there would be no point in such violation, and a minimum of internal, indirect, and direct control would suffice to secure conformity."

Nye surveyed 780 boys and girls in grades 9 through 12 in three towns in the state of Washington to test the theory. Included in the survey were a wide variety of questions on family life, as well as seven items intended to measure delinquency. Those seven items were: skipped school without a legitimate excuse; defied parents' authority to their face; took things worth less than $2; bought or drank beer, wine, or liquor (including at home); purposely damaged or destroyed public or private property; and had sexual relations with a person of the opposite

---

[5]Ibid., p. 14.

[6]F. Ivan Nye, *Family Relationships and Delinquent Behavior*, John Wiley, New York, 1958.

[7]Ibid., p. 4.

[8]Ibid., p. 5–8.

sex.[9] On the basis of how often they said they had committed these acts since the beginning of grade school, about one fourth of the youths were placed in a "most delinquent" group, and the remainder in a "least delinquent" group.[10]

Nye found that youths in the "most delinquent" group were more likely to be given either complete freedom or no freedom at all, to have larger sums of money available, to be rejecting of their parents and to disapprove of their parents' appearance, to describe their parents as being seldom cheerful and often moody, nervous, irritable, difficult to please, dishonest, and who "took things out" on the youth when things went wrong. Youths whose mothers worked outside the home and who were rejected by their parents were slightly more likely to fall in the "most delinquent" group. In contrast, youths in the "least delinquent" group were significantly more likely to come from families that attended church regularly, did not move often, and were from rural areas. They were likely to be the oldest or only child, from a small family, to have a favorable attitude toward their parents' disciplinary techniques and toward recreation with their parents, to agree with their parents on the importance of a variety of values, to be satisfied with the allocation of money by their parents, and to get information and advice concerning dating and religion from their parents. In all, Nye tested 313 relationships between youths and their parents. He found that 139 of those were consistent with his control theory, 167 were not significant, and only seven were inconsistent with it.[11]

Nye's contribution to the development of control theory was quite significant because of the theory he proposed and because he undertook a broad empirical test of the theory. His findings in support of the theory are impressive, but one can question the extent to which they apply to groups that are normally referred to as delinquents. Nye's sample did not include any youths from large cities, and included only negligible numbers of non–European American youths or youth with foreign-born parents. Toby pointed out that "the group which Professor Nye calls 'most delinquent' would be considered nondelinquents by many criminologists."[12] Also, because the questionnaire was administered in high schools, the sample would not include any youths age 15 or younger who

---

[9]Ibid., pp. 13–14.

[10]See ibid., pp. 15–19, and Nye and James F. Short, Jr., "Scaling Delinquent Behavior," *American Sociological Review* 22: 26–31 (June 1957).

[11]Nye, *Family Relationships*, p. 155.

[12]Jackson Toby, "Review of *Family Relationships and Delinquent Behavior* by F. Ivan Nye," *American Sociological Review* 24: 282–83 (Feb. 1959).

were more than one year behind in school (they would still be in grade school), or any youths age 16 or over who had legally dropped out of school. Only two behaviors on the questionnaire constituted criminal offenses: taking things worth less than $2 and purposely damaging or destroying public or private property. Thus the results of Nye's study might be interpreted as describing the effect of family relationships on minor delinquent activities among basically nondelinquent youths.

Toby also pointed out that Nye's research apparently assumes that the same causal processes would be involved with more serious delinquents, but that other researchers might very well disagree with the assumption. Finally, Toby noted that a response bias among the youths answering the questionnaire could account for many of Nye's findings. Youths who were more willing to report their delinquent activities may also have been more willing to describe the less desirable aspects of their family life. Other youths may have both underreported their delinquent activities and described their family life in more positive terms. Thus the study would show that better family relationships are associated with fewer delinquent activities. Toby concluded that Nye's results should be interpreted with great caution.

MATZA'S *DELINQUENCY AND DRIFT*

While the early control theories presented above have been soundly criticized, they provided the basic concepts and framework for the modern control theories of David Matza and Travis Hirschi. Those control theories present a strong challenge to the more common view that juvenile delinquency is caused by special biological, psychological, or social factors.

In *Delinquency and Drift* Matza stated that traditional theories of delinquency emphasize constraint and differentiation: Delinquents are said to be different from nondelinquents in some fundamental way, and that difference constrains them to commit their delinquencies.[13] In some theories the differences are said to be biological or psychological, and the constraint takes the form of compulsion. In other theories the differences are said to be social, and the constraint takes the form of commitment to delinquent values. Matza maintained that these theories predicted and explained too much delinquency. Most of the time delinquents are engaged in routine, law-abiding behaviors just like everyone else, but if you believe the picture painted in these theories, delinquents

---

[13]David Matza, *Delinquency and Drift*, John Wiley, New York, 1964, pp. 1–27.

should be committing delinquencies all the time. In addition, these theories cannot account for the fact that most delinquents "age out" of delinquency and settle down to law-abiding lives when they reach late adolescence or early adulthood. The factors that supposedly explained the delinquency are still present (for example, lack of legitimate opportunities), but the delinquency itself disappears.[14]

Matza proposed an alternate image for delinquents that emphasizes freedom and similarity rather than constraint and differentiation. That image is *drift*[15] Drift is said to occur in areas of the social structure in which control has been loosened, freeing the delinquent to respond to whatever conventional or criminal forces happen to come along. The positive causes of delinquency, then, "may be accidental or unpredictable from the point of view of any theoretical frame of reference, and deflection from the delinquent path may be similarly accidental or unpredictable."[16] Within the context of such an image a theory of delinquency would not attempt to describe its positive causes, but rather would describe "the conditions that make delinquent drift possible and probable," that is, the conditions under which social control is loosened. Matza did not deny that there were "committed" and "compulsive" delinquents, as described by the traditional theories. However, he argued that the vast majority of delinquents were "drifters" who were neither.

Matza's criticism of traditional theories of delinquency focused on the sociological argument that their behaviors are generated by commitment to delinquent values. Matza argued that delinquents portray themselves this way because they are unwilling to appear "chicken."[17] But private interviews reveal that delinquents do not value delinquent behavior itself. Rather, they describe the behavior as morally wrong but argue that there are extenuating circumstances, so that their own delinquent actions are "guiltless."[18] The delinquent's portrayal of these circumstances is similar to, but much broader than, the extenuating circumstances defined in the law relating to intent, accident, self-defense, and insanity. Thus delinquents do not reject conventional moral values, but "neutralize" them in a wide variety of circumstances so that they are able to commit delinquent actions and still consider themselves guilt-

---

[14]For a discussion of age and crime, see Chapter 16.

[15]Matza, op. cit., pp. 27–30.

[16]Ibid., p. 29.

[17]Ibid., pp. 33–59.

[18]Ibid., pp. 59–98.

less. This *sense of irresponsibility* is reinforced by the ideology of the juvenile court, which declares that juveniles are not responsible for their actions.

The sense of irresponsibility is the immediate condition that makes delinquent drift possible, but the delinquent is prepared to accept the sense of irresponsibility by a pervasive *sense of injustice*.[19] Just as the sense of irresponsibility is derived from a broad interpretation of conventional legal standards for extenuating circumstances, so the sense of injustice is derived from a broad interpretation of conventional legal standards for justice. For example, by conventional legal standards of justice it is necessary to prove beyond a reasonable doubt that a given individual has committed a given criminal act. Delinquents use excessively legalistic standards to argue that "they didn't prove it." Thus they may passionately argue that they were unjustly treated even though they admit that they committed the act.

Once the moral bind of the law has been loosened by the sense of irresponsibility and the sense of injustice, the juvenile is in a state of drift and is then free to choose among a variety of actions, some delinquent, some lawful. At this point Matza suggests that there are some "positive" causes of delinquency in the sense that there are reasons why the juvenile chooses delinquent, as opposed to lawful, behaviors.[20] The juvenile feels that he exercises no control over the circumstances of his life and the destiny awaiting him. In such a mood he moves to make something happen, to experience himself as a cause of events. This mood of desperation provides the motivation to commit new acts of delinquency. Once those actions have been committed, he is motivated to continue committing them because he has learned the moral rationalizations necessary to consider himself guiltless, and because he has learned the technical means to carry out the offenses.

HIRSCHI'S SOCIAL CONTROL THEORY

The theorist who is most closely identified with control theory is Travis Hirschi. In his 1969 book entitled *Causes of Delinquency*, Hirschi argued that it is not necessary to explain the motivation for delinquency, since "we are all animals and thus all naturally capable of committing criminal acts."[21] He then proposed a comprehensive control theory that

---

[19]Ibid., pp. 101–77. See also Marvin Krohn and John Stratton, "A Sense of Injustice?" *Criminology* 17(4): 495–504 (Feb. 1980).

[20]Matza, op. cit., pp. 181–91. Compare with Hirschi, *Causes of Delinquency*, pp. 33–34.

[21]Hirschi, op. cit., p. 31.

individuals who were tightly bonded to social groups such as the family, the school, and peers would be less likely to commit delinquent acts.[22] The most important element of the social bond is *attachment*—i.e., affection for and sensitivity to others. Attachment is said to be the basic element necessary for the internalization of values and norms, and thus is related to Reiss's conception of personal controls and Nye's conceptions of internal and indirect controls. A second element is *commitment,* the rational investment one has in conventional society and the risk one takes when engaging in deviant behavior. Commitment is similar to what Toby described as a "stake in conformity." The third element is *involvement* in conventional activities. This variable is based on the common sense observation that "idle hands are the devil's workshop," and that being busy restricts opportunities for delinquent activities. The final element of the social bond is *belief.* Matza had argued that delinquents had conventional moral beliefs, but neutralized them with excuses so that they could commit delinquent acts without feeling guilty. Hirschi, in contrast, argued that "there is variation in the extent to which people believe they should obey the rules of society, and, furthermore, that the less a person believes he should obey the rules, the more likely he is to violate them."[23] Thus Matza's theory had emphasized that delinquents are tied to the conventional moral order and must free themselves from it to commit delinquent acts, while Hirschi's theory assumes that they are free from the conventional order to begin with.

Like Nye, Hirschi tested his theory with a self-report survey. The sample consisted of about 4,000 junior and senior high school youths from a county in the San Francisco Bay area. The questionnaire contained a variety of items related to family, school, and peer relations, as well as six items that served as an index of delinquency.[24] Three of those six items referred to stealing (things worth less than $2, things worth between $2 and $50, and things worth more than $50), while the other three asked whether the youth had ever "taken a car for a ride without the owner's permission," "banged up something that did not belong to you on purpose," and "beaten up on anyone or hurt anyone on purpose" (not counting fights with a brother or sister). Youths were given one point for each of the six offenses they reported committing in the last year, regardless of how often they reported committing it.[25] Hirschi also used school records and official police records as data for the study.

---

[22]Ibid., pp. 16–34.

[23]Ibid., p. 26.

[24]Ibid., p. 54.

[25]Ibid., p. 62. This was defined as the "recency" index, and was used throughout the study.

Hirschi was particularly concerned with testing the adequacy of his theory against theories that argued the motivation for delinquency was to be found in social strain (such as Merton's, Cohen's, or Cloward and Ohlin's) and theories that explained delinquency in terms of cultural or group influence (such as Sutherland's or Miller's).[26] Each of these three types of theories explains many well-known facts about delinquency such as that delinquents do poorly in school, but each proposes a different chain of causation. Much of Hirschi's book is devoted to testing the different chains of causation found in the three types of theories.

Hirschi reported that, in general, there was no relationship between reported delinquent acts and social class, except that children from the poorest families were slightly more likely to be delinquent.[27] In addition, he found only minimal racial differences in self-reported delinquency, although their official arrest rates were substantially different.[28] Hirschi concluded that these findings were most difficult to reconcile with strain theories, since those were explicitly class-based theories.[29]

Hirschi then analyzed the effects of attachment to parents, schools, and peers on reported delinquent acts. He found that, regardless of race or class, and regardless of the delinquency of their friends, boys who were more closely attached to their parents were less likely to report committing delinquent acts than those who were less closely attached.[30] That finding is consistent with control theory but inconsistent with cultural theories, where attachment to deviant friends or deviant parents would theoretically be associated with increased reporting of delinquency. Hirschi also found that youths who reported more delinquent acts were more likely to have poor verbal scores on the Differential Aptitude Test, to get poor grades in school, to care little about teachers' opinions, to dislike school, and to reject school authority. He argued that these findings are consistent with control theory, since such boys would be free from the controlling forces of schools. However, he argued that they were inconsistent with strain theories such as Cohen's, since the most "strained" youths would be those who did poorly but who continued to care about success in the school. Youths who did poorly and did

---

[26]Strain theories are reviewed in Chapter 8 of this book, while what Hirschi called "cultural deviance" theories are reviewed in Chapter 9. One of the arguments made in Chapter 9 is that the description of these theories as cultural deviance theories is inaccurate. This argument implies that Hirschi's test is invalid.

[27]Hirschi, op. cit., pp. 66–75.

[28]Ibid., pp. 75–81.

[29]Ibid., pp. 226–27.

[30]Ibid., pp. 97, 99.

not care about school success would not be "strained."[31] He also found that boys who reported more delinquent acts were less attached to their peers than were boys who reported fewer delinquent acts. Again Hirschi argued that this finding is consistent with control theory, since attachment to peers would be conducive to delinquency only if those peers valued delinquent behavior. However, it is inconsistent with cultural theories, where the assumption is made that the motivation for delinquency is passed through intimate, personal relationships. Hirschi found that association with delinquent companions could increase delinquent behavior, but only when social controls had been weakened. Youths with large stakes in conformity are unlikely to have delinquent friends, and when they do have such friends, they are unlikely to commit delinquent acts themselves. For youths with low stakes in conformity, however, the greater the exposure to "criminal influences," the more delinquent activities the youth reported.[32]

Having examined the effect of attachment on reported delinquent acts, Hirschi examined the effects of the other three elements of his theory. He found that the educational and occupational aspirations of delinquents are lower than nondelinquents, as are the educational and occupational expectations. This finding is consistent with control theory, since youths with low aspirations and low expectations have little commitment to conformity—that is, they risk little by committing delinquent acts. In contrast, the findings are inconsistent with strain theories since, according to those theories, youths with high aspirations but low expectations should be the most strained and therefore the most delinquent. Hirschi found that "the higher the aspiration, the lower the rate of delinquency, regardless of the student's expectations."[33] Hirschi also found that youths who worked, dated, spent time watching TV, reading books, or playing games were more likely to report delinquencies.[34] That finding was the opposite of what was expected from his theory, since these behaviors represent involvement in conventional activities. Hirschi did find, however, that boys who spent less time on homework, reported being bored, spent more time talking to friends, and riding around in cars were more likely to report delinquent acts. These can be considered measures of the lack of involvement in conventional activi-

---

[31]Hirschi admits that his formulation may not adequately test strain because of Cohen's idea of reaction formation: Boys may care about school success, but if they are unable to succeed, they may then deny that they care at all. However, Hirschi argues that such an argument is virtually impossible to falsify; ibid., pp. 124–26.

[32]Ibid., pp. 159–61.

[33]Ibid., p. 183.

[34]Ibid., p. 190.

ties. Finally, Hirschi found a strong correlation between reported delinquent activities and agreement with the statement "It is alright to get
around the law if you can get away with it."[35] He took this to be a measure of the extent to which boys believe they should obey the law. He
also found support for the neutralizing beliefs that Matza had described
as freeing the delinquent from the moral bind of the law, although he argued that "the assumption that delinquent acts come before the justify-
ing beliefs is the more plausible causal ordering with respect to many of
the techniques of neutralization."[36] Finally, Hirschi found no support
for a separate lower-class culture as described by Miller. Hirschi found
instead that these beliefs are held by academically incompetent youths,
whether lower or middle class, and that academically competent youths,
whether lower or middle class, held what are often called "middle-class
values." Thus he concluded that lower-class values are not cultural in
that they are not transmitted as a valued heritage. Rather, they "are
available to all members of American society more or less equally; they
are accepted or rejected to the extent they are consistent or inconsistent
with one's realistic position in that society."[37] Thus Hirschi believes that
"the class of the father may be unimportant, but the class of the child
most decidedly is not.[38]

ASSESSING SOCIAL CONTROL THEORY

A large number of empirical studies have attempted to test social control theory. Most of these studies conclude that social control theory is
supported by the data, and they most frequently find support for two of
Hirschi's four variables: attachment and commitment.[39] Some support
for beliefs is also found, but whether this finding represents weak conventional beliefs (as proposed by Hirschi) or strong deviant beliefs (as
proposed by learning theorists) is less clear. The statement in Hirschi's
own study, "It is alright to get around the law if you can get away with it"
illustrates the problem. Hirschi argues that the statement represents a
weak conventional belief, but learning theorists argue that it represents
a strong deviant belief.

Neither Hirschi's study nor later studies have found much support for
Hirschi's fourth variable, involvement in conventional activities. Instead,

---

[35]Ibid., pp. 202–3.

[36]Ibid., p. 208.

[37]Ibid., p. 230.

[38]Ibid., p. 82.

[39]Barbara J. Costello and Paul R. Vowell, "Testing Control Theory and Differential Association,"
Criminology 37(4): 815–42 (1999).

studies generally have found that youths with more conventional involvement (e.g., participating in organized sports, holding a job) commit
more delinquency than those with less conventional involvement.
Hirschi found this in his own study, and he made the following comment
on his surprising finding.[40]

The difficulty, it seems, is that the definition of delinquency used here is not the
definition that makes the involvement hypothesis virtually tautological. When
Cohen, for example, says the delinquent gang "makes enormous demands upon
the boy's time," he is of course not saying that delinquency as here defined takes
an enormous amount of the boy's time. In fact, as defined, delinquency requires
very little time: the most delinquent boys in the sample may not have devoted
more than a few hours in the course of a year to the acts that define them as
delinquent.

Hirschi's comment raises a question about the adequacy of his theory: It
may explain delinquency in boys who spend only a few hours per year
engaged in it, but does it explain delinquency among the boys that Cohen described? Hirschi admitted that there were few serious delinquents in his sample. In fact, he stated that other criminologists might
hold that "delinquents are so obviously underrepresented among those
completing the questionnaires that the results need not be taken seriously."[41] He then argued that, if more serious delinquents had been included in the sample, his results would have been even stronger. But
Hirschi's argument is valid only if the same causal processes are at work
for seriously delinquent youths as for minor delinquents. In contrast,
Matza had described different causal processes: minor delinquents were
described as "drifters" (i.e., freed from controls) while serious delinquents were described as committed or compulsive. If Matza is correct,
then the inclusion of more serious delinquents in Hirschi's sample
would have weakened Hirschi's results.[42]

This problem is related to the control theory assumption that criminality and delinquency consist in "naturally motivated" behaviors that do
not need any other explanation. It is relatively easy to think of the minor
offenses in Hirschi's study as being naturally motivated, requiring no
other explanation than that they are "fun."[43] But explaining delinquency

---

[40]Hirschi, op. cit., p. 190.

[41]Hirschi, op. cit., p. 41. Jackson Toby ("Review of *Family Relationships and Delinquent Behavior*
by F. Ivan Nye," *American Sociological Review* 24 282–83 [1959]) raised the same issue about Nye's
original self-report study testing a control theory.

[42]Toby (op. cit.) made this same argument about Nye's results.

[43]The absence of serious delinquents in Hirschi's sample requires that Hirschi's definition of delinquency (op. cit. p. 46) focus on non-serious offenses. If Hirschi had defined delinquency in terms of

as "fun" is not as appealing when one considers serious violent crime or the gang activities that make "enormous demands on the boys' time," as described by Cohen.

In 1993, Kempf reviewed 71 studies on control theory.[44] She reports that most of these studies found correlations between delinquent behavior and one or another of Hirschi's variables. However, the variables themselves were operationalized in many different ways. In addition, when one looks at each of the four variables individually, the results are mixed and inconsistent. For example, attachment is the most frequently tested variable and the most frequently found to be correlated with delinquent behavior. However, the different tests have different objects of attachment (e.g., parents, mother, peers, schools) and the results range from no relation at all to a strong relation. Kempf concludes that these were "essentially separate studies which have little relation to each other and fail to build on experience. Thus, the research reveals little about the viability of social control as a scientific theory."[45] The research conducted since Kempf's 1993 review has tended to support her conclusion.[46] Hirschi himself has now abandoned his social control theory and, with Michael Gottfredson, has presented a new theory that focuses on what he calls "self-control."

GOTTFREDSON AND HIRSCHI'S *A GENERAL THEORY OF CRIME*

In 1990, Michael Gottfredson and Travis Hirschi presented a theory that claimed to explain all types of crime and delinquency. The main concept in the theory is low self-control.[47] Self-control theory is a single concept, in contrast to the multiple social controls (attachments, involvements, commitments, and beliefs) in Hirschi's 1969 theory. In ad-

---

serious offenses, then his sample would have had so few delinquents that he would have been unable to reach any conclusions. Toby (op. cit.) made a similar comment about Nye's definition of delinquency.

[44]Kimberly L. Kempf, "The Empirical Status of Hirschi's Control Theory," in Freda Adler and William S. Laufer, eds., *New Directions in Criminological Theory: Advances in Criminological Theory*, vol. 4, Transaction, New Brunswick, NJ, 1993.

[45]Kempf, op. cit., p. 173. See also Thomas J. Bernard, "Twenty Years of Testing Theories: What Have We Learned and Why?" *Journal of Research in Crime and Delinquency* 27(4): 325–47 (1990).

[46]For example, David F. Greenberg ("The Weak Strength of Social Control Theory," *Crime & Delinquency* 45[1]: 66–81 [1999] reanalyzed Hirschi's original data and found little support for control theory itself. Greenberg found greater support for strain theories, although the support for either theory was fairly weak. In addition, in two different studies, Robert Agnew ("Delinquency: A Longitudinal Test," *Criminology* 23[1]: 47–59 [1985] and "A Longitudinal Test of Social Control Theory and Delinquency," *Journal of Research in Crime and Delinquency* 28[2]: 126–156 [1991] found that the effects of control variables may have been overestimated in cross-sectional studies such as Hirschi's.

[47]Michael Gottfredson and Travis Hirschi, *A General Theory of Crime,* Stanford University Press, Stanford, CA, 1990.

dition, self-control is said to be internal to the individual, whereas social controls largely reside in the external social environment. Finally, self-control theory focuses attention on events in early childhood, long before crime and delinquency manifest themselves. In contrast, Hirschi's social control theory focuses on events and processes that transpire at the same time as the delinquency. In the new theory, "social controls" are relevant to explaining criminal behavior only to the extent that they influence self-control, which is instilled in individuals by around age 8 and remains relatively constant after that.

Gottfredson and Hirschi first make some assertions about "the characteristics of ordinary crimes": They are said to be acts that involve simple and immediate gratification of desires but few long-term benefits, are exciting and risky but require little skill or planning, and generally produce few benefits for the offender while causing pain and suffering for the victim.[48] Second, they describe the characteristics of people who would commit these kinds of actions: They "will tend to be impulsive, insensitive, physical (as opposed to mental), risk-taking, short-sighted, and nonverbal."[49] These characteristics not only lead them to engage in a variety of "ordinary crimes," but also result in other similarities in behavior—e.g., these people will tend to smoke and drink heavily and to be involved in many accidents.[50] Third, Gottfredson and Hirschi argue:[51] "Since these traits can be identified prior to the age of responsibility for crime, since there is considerable tendency for these traits to come together in the same people, and since the traits tend to persist through life, it seems reasonable to consider them as comprising a stable construct useful in the explanation of crime." They call this stable construct "low self-control." Fourth, Gottfredson and Hirschi argue that ineffective child rearing is the most important contributor to low self-control.[52] Adequate child rearing, which results in high self-control in the child, occurs when the child's behavior is monitored and any deviant behavior is immediately recognized and punished. Essentially, external controls on the child's behavior eventually are internalized by the child in a process described as "socialization." An additional source of socialization, especially important for those who do not receive adequate socialization through their families, is the school.

---

[48]Ibid., pp. 15–44; 89–91.

[49]Ibid., pp. 90–91.

[50]Ibid., p. 94.

[51]Ibid.

[52]Ibid., p. 97.

Gottfredson and Hirschi go on to argue that low self-control explains many of the known relationships between delinquency and other factors. For example, they argue that the relationship between delinquent peers and delinquency is explained by the fact that low self-control juveniles are likely to seek out others with low-self control as a peer group.[53] On the relationship between delinquency and poor school performance, they argue that individuals who lack self-control do not perform well in school and therefore tend to leave or avoid it.[54] Finally, those with low self-control have difficulties keeping jobs, which explain any relationship between unemployment and criminal behavior.[55]

Gottfredson and Hirschi argue that self-control is relatively constant in the individual after the age of about 8, but they recognize that there may be a great deal of change in the rates at which individuals commit crime.[56] These variations cannot, within their theory, be explained by changes in the person's self-control, since self-control stays constant throughout the person's life. So Gottfredson and Hirschi argue that variations in crime are explained by variation in opportunities for different types of criminal and noncriminal behaviors. For example, in a community with few opportunities for property crime, low self-control people will engage in little property crime but will engage in other sorts of low self-control behavior.

ASSESSING GOTTFREDSON AND HIRSCHI'S GENERAL THEORY

A General Theory of Crime has generated some heated discussion among criminologists, along with quite a large number of empirical studies.[57] The studies have used different ways of measuring low self-control, but most consider it as attitudes related to impulsivity, risk seeking, physical activities, self-centeredness, temper, and simple tasks.[58] The behaviors

---

[53]Ibid., pp. 157–58.

[54]Ibid., pp. 162–63.

[55]Ibid., p. 165.

[56]The major variation found in individuals is the age-crime curve. For a discussion of Gottfredson and Hirschi's position on this issue, see Chapter 16.

[57]Travis C. Pratt and Francis T. Cullen ("The Empirical Status of Gottfredson and Hirschi's General Theory of Crime: A Meta-Analysis," *Criminology* 38[3]: 931–64 [2000] lists 21 different empirical studies.

[58]These six attitudes are taken from a 24-item scale first presented in Harold G. Grasmick, Charles R. Tittle, Robert J. Bursik Jr., and Bruce K. Arneklev, "Testing the Core Empirical Implications of Gottfredson and Hirschi's General Theory of Crime," *Journal of Research in Crime and Delinquency* 30(1): 5–29 (1993). Note that this list is not identical to the six characteristics identified by Gottfredson and Hirschi as the characteristics of low self-control: impulsive, insensitive, physical, risk-taking, short-sighted, and non-verbal. Grasmick et al. suggest that these six attitudes form a latent

explained by low self-control have included various forms of delinquency and adult criminal behavior, as well as what Gottfredson and Hirschi describe as "analogous behaviors": cutting classes, drinking, smoking, gambling, drunk driving, and being prone to accidents. All the studies have found at least some support for Gottfredson and Hirschi's theory, and some have found fairly strong support. However, there have been few attempts to control for alternate explanations from other theories.

Perhaps the theory's most controversial argument is that self-control is essentially stable by the age of 8 or so, having been determined by parental child-rearing practices in early childhood. Research to date has not tested this particular assertion, and until it is tested, a general assessment of the theory cannot be made. One study did find that self-control in childhood has positive relationships with both criminal behavior and analogous behaviors in adolescence (e.g., road-accident involvement, loitering, gambling, drinking).[59] However, the authors of this study concluded that the relationship between criminal and analogous behaviors could not be entirely explained by low self-control, and that other factors must also be involved.[60]

Gottfredson and Hirschi's theory also has been extensively criticized on theoretical grounds.[61] Perhaps the most frequent criticism, as well as the most potentially damaging, is that the theory is tautological.[62] According to Akers, the only way to determine whether people have low self-control is to see whether they engage in low self-control behaviors. But once they do, then their behaviors are explained by the low self-control.[63] Akers argued that, until low self-control can be measured in

---

trait, so that this is a unidimensional scale. Using a sample of 233 college students, Alex R. Piquero, Randall MacIntosh, and Matthew Hickman ("Does Self-Control Affect Survey Response?" *Criminology* 38[3]: 897–930 [2000] concluded that it is unidimensional.

[59]Raymond Paternoster and Robert Brame, "The Structural Similarity of Processes Generating Criminal and Analogous Behaviors," *Criminology* 36: 633–69 (1998).

[60]See the criticism of this conclusion in Chester L. Britt, "Comment on Paternoster and Brame," pp. 965–70, and the response from Paternoster and Brame, "On the Association Among Self-Control, Crime, and Analogous Behaviors," pp. 971–82, both in *Criminology* 38(3), 2000.

[61]For the most sweeping criticisms of the theory, including an argument about tautology, see Gilbert Geis, "On the Absence of Self-control as the Basis for a General Theory of Crime: A Critique," *Theoretical Criminology* 4(1): 35–53 (2000). A response by Hirchi and Gottfredson ("In Defense of Self-Control," pp. 55–69) follows.

[62]E.g., Ronald Akers, "Self-Control as a General Theory of Crime," *Journal of Quantitative Criminology* 7(2): 201–211 (1991).

[63]This argument is tautological because other concepts besides low self-control can be inserted into the argument and the argument itself remains the same. For example, the tendency to engage in impulsive, risky, self-centered, physical activities could be explained by socialization into a "criminal subculture." Evidence for the subculture would be found in the behaviors of the people who were supposedly socialized into it, and then the behaviors themselves would be explained by the subculture. Control theorists have criticized subcultural theories as being tautological in exactly this way.

some other way, the theory will remain tautological. Hirschi and Gott-fredson, however, strongly reject this criticism:[64]

In our view, the charge of tautology is in fact a compliment; an assertion that we followed the path of logic in producing an internally consistent result... We started with a conception of crime, and from it attempted to *derive* a conception of the offender... What makes our theory *peculiarly* vulnerable to complaints about tautology is that we explicitly show the logical connections between our conception of the actor and the act, whereas many theorists leave this task to those interpreting or testing their theory ... In a comparative framework, the charge of tautology suggests that a theory that is nontautological is preferable. But what would such a theory look like? It would advance definitions of crime and of criminals that are independent of one another ..."

They go on to say that Akers misunderstands the concept of low self-control: "... we see self-control as the barrier that stands between the actor and the obvious momentary benefits crime provides."

Other criticisms challenge the generality of Gottfredson and Hirschi's theory, arguing that certain types of criminals, such as white-collar or organized criminals, do not have low self-control.[65] Gottfredson and Hirschi therefore devote considerable effort to debunking these arguments. For example, they argue that "organized crime" is not really organized, and any apparent organization is short-lived and consists of unstable temporary alliances.[66] Furthermore, they claim that the reason for the failure of many cooperative attempts at criminality is that the individuals involved lack self-control. They discount the importance of organized drug dealing by arguing that for every successful organized effort, there are hundreds of failed efforts.

Other criminologists question how differential-opportunity structures may interact with low self-control to produce variations in crime rates. Barlow notes that the opportunity part of Gottfredson and Hirschi's theory is insufficiently developed and does not answer such questions.[67] Longshore and Turner find a relation between low self-control and opportunity for crimes of fraud, but not for crimes of force.[68] Using a

---

[64]Hirschi and Gottfredson, "Commentary: Testing the General Theory of Crime," *Journal of Research in Crime and Delinquency* 30(1): 52–53 (1993).

[65]E.g., see Gary E. Reed and Peter Cleary Yeager, "Organizational Offending and Neoclassical Criminology: Challenging the Reach of a General Theory of Crime," *Criminology* 34(3): 357–82 (1996).

[66]Gottfredson and Hirschi, *A General Theory of Crime*, p. 213.

[67]Hugh Barlow, "Explaining Crimes and Analogous Acts, or the Unrestrained Will Grab at Pleasure Whenever They Can," *Journal of Criminal Law and Criminology*," 82(1): 229–242 (1991).

[68]Douglas Longshore and Susan Turner, "Self-Control and Criminal Opportunity," *Criminal Justice and Behavior* 25(1): 81–98, 1998.

somewhat larger version of the same data set, Longshore finds that both low self-control and criminal opportunity have an effect on criminal behavior, but both effects are very small (4% of the variance).[69]

The primary advantage of Gottfredson and Hirschi's theory is also its chief point of vulnerability: its simplicity. The idea that a single simple concept can explain the entire range of criminal behavior is quite appealing, and many criminologists are enthused about this possibility. But other criminologists argue that criminal behavior is far too complex to be explained by a single theory, particularly a simple one.

IMPLICATIONS AND CONCLUSIONS

Control theories have more or less dominated criminology since Hirschi published his social control theory in 1969. That theory focused on restraints on behavior grounded in the external environment (attachment to others, involvement in legitimate activities, commitment to a future career, and belief in the moral validity of law). More recently, Gottfredson and Hirschi proposed a self-control theory that focuses on internal restraints. That theory holds that early childhood parenting practices result in the formation in the child of a stable level of self-control by the age of 8 or so. Those low in self-control will tend to take advantage of the momentary benefits that crime and delinquency frequently offer them throughout their lives, while those high in self-control will resist those opportunities.

Both social and self-control theories have many policy implications. Hirschi's social control theory argues that juveniles are less likely to engage in delinquent behavior when they are more attached to others, more involved in conventional activities, have more to lose from committing crime, and have stronger beliefs in the moral validity of the law. All these arguments could be linked to policies to reduce delinquency. Curfew laws require juveniles to be at home after a certain hour, which should increase attachment to and supervision by parents. After-school activities and midnight basketball programs in school gyms increase involvement in legitimate activity in the hopes that idle hands won't become the devil's workshop. Programs to provide jobs to inner-city youth increase their commitment to the economic system and give them more to lose if they get arrested. And moral education programs can strengthen beliefs in the legitimacy of law by teaching that all people benefit from an orderly society in which everyone obeys the rules.

---

[69]Douglas Longshore, "Self-Control and Criminal Opportunity," *Social Problems* 45(1): 102–113, 1998.

In self-control theory, the policies likely to have the greatest impact on crime will be those that enhance self-control in children 8 and younger.[70] Hirschi and Gottfredson therefore recommend "policies that promote and facilitate two-parent families and that increase the number of caregivers relative to the number of children," In particular, programs to prevent pregnancy among unmarried adolescent girls should be given high priority. They also recommend "programs designed to provide early education and effective child care." This recommendation includes "programs that target dysfunctional families and seek to remedy lack of supervision" of pre-adolescent children. Finally, they recommend programs to "restrict the unsupervised activities of teenagers." Curfews, truancy prevention programs, school uniforms, and license restrictions all limit the opportunities that teenagers have to commit crime. On the other hand, they argue that programs to deter, rehabilitate, or incapacitate adult offenders should be abandoned, as should aggressive police tactics (such as drug stings) that essentially create opportunities for offenders to commit crimes.

---

[70]The following recommendations are taken from Travis Hirschi and Michael R. Gottfredson, "Self-Control Theory," pp. 81–96 in Raymond Paternoster and Ronet Bachman, eds., *Explaining Criminals and Crime,* Roxbury, Los Angeles, 2001.

CHAPTER ELEVEN

Contemporary Classicism: Deterrence, Routine Activities, and Rational Choice

In 1764, Beccaria proposed a simple model of human choice based on the rational calculation of costs and benefits. Based on this model, he argued that punishments should be proportional to the seriousness of offenses so that the cost of crime always exceeds its reward. Potential offenders then would be deterred—i.e., rational calculation would lead them to avoid committing crime. This approach, now called classical criminology, became the basis for all modern criminal justice systems, but the expected reductions in crime did not occur. Beginning in the 1870s, criminologists abandoned classicism (although criminal justice systems did not) and embarked on the positivist search for the causes of crime. After another one hundred years, positivism too had failed to reduce crime and the classical point of view reemerged in criminology.

Beginning in 1968, this contemporary classical approach focused on theory and research about the deterrent effect of criminal justice policies. Then in 1978, Cohen and Felson proposed the "routine activities" approach, which argued that rationally-calculating potential offenders respond to opportunities to commit crimes, and that these opportunities are systematically related to the "routine activities" by which people live their lives. This concept led to policy recommendations to limit criminal opportunities rather than increase the deterrent effect of criminal justice policies. Gottfredson and Hirschi, as discussed in the last chapter, incorporated the "routine activities" approach into their general theory of crime by arguing that all crime could be explained by the combination of low self-control and opportunities. Finally, in 1985, Clarke and Cornish proposed the "rational choice" approach, which developed a more complex view of how offenders in particular situations calculate their costs and benefits. This approach led to policy recommendations that focused on changing situations in order to influence a potential offender's calculations.

EARLY DETERRENCE THEORY AND RESEARCH

After a century of neglecting deterrence, a resurgence of interest among criminologists began in 1968 when Gibbs published the first study that actually attempted to test the deterrence hypothesis.[1] Gibbs defined the *certainty* of punishment as the ratio between the number of admissions to state prisons for a given crime and the number of those crimes known to the police in the prior year. *Severity* was defined as the mean number of months served by all persons convicted of a given crime who were in prison in that year. Gibbs found that greater certainty and severity of imprisonments was associated with fewer homicides in the fifty states for the year 1960 (the effect of certainty was about twice as great as the effect of severity). Gibbs concluded that homicide might be deterred by both certainty and severity of imprisonment.

The following year, Tittle computed similar statistics on certainty and severity for all seven "index offenses" in the FBI Uniform Crime Reports.[2] His results indicated that more certainty was associated with less crime for all seven offenses. However, with the exception of homicide, more severity (i.e., more time in prison) was associated with more crime, not less. Tittle concluded that the certainty of imprisonment deters crime, but that severity only deters crime when certainty is quite high.

In 1970, Chiricos and Waldo challenged Tittle's results on certainty by arguing that they could be explained by variations in police record keeping.[3] If police in a particular jurisdiction handle many offenses informally without making an official record, then that jurisdiction will have lower official crime rates (because fewer criminal events are officially recorded) and greater certainty of imprisonment (because the more serious offenses are recorded, and those offenses are more likely to result

---

[1]Jack P. Gibbs, "Crime, Punishment and Deterrence," *Southwestern Social Science Quarterly* 48: 515–30 (1968). In that same year, the economist Gary S. Becker ("Crime and Punishment: An Economic Approach," *Journal of Political Economy* 76: 169–217 [1968]) published a largely theoretical argument that both crime and criminal justice could be explained as choices resulting from cost-benefit analyses.

[2]Charles R. Tittle, "Crime Rates and Legal Sanctions," *Social Problems* 16: 409–23, 1969.

[3]Theodore G. Chiricos and Gordon P. Waldo, "Punishment and Crime: An Examination of Some Empirical Evidence," *Social Problems* 18(2): 200–17 (1970). Chiricos and Waldo, in turn, were challenged by Charles H. Logan, "General Deterrent Effects of Imprisonment," *Social Forces* 51: 64–73 (1972).

in imprisonment). But if police meticulously make official records for every single criminal event, then that jurisdiction will have higher official crime rates (because more criminal events are officially recorded) but less certainty (because many of these criminal events will not be serious and therefore will not result in imprisonment).

Similarly, in 1974, Glaser and Zeigler challenged both Gibbs's and Tittle's conclusions that increased imprisonment deters homicide.[4] They pointed out that death penalty states have substantially higher murder rates than non-death penalty states, but murderers in death penalty states who are not executed serve shorter prison sentences than murderers in non-death penalty states. This is the pattern that both Gibbs and Tittle had found: shorter prison sentences and higher murder rates (in death penalty states), and longer prison sentences and lower murder rates (in non-death penalty states). Glaser and Zeigler argued that it is unlikely that longer prison sentences deter homicide while the death penalty does not deter it. Instead, they attributed all three of these statistics (higher murder rates, use of the death penalty, and shorter prison sentences for murderers who are not executed) to a lower valuation of human life in states that use the death penalty.

This brief review of a few early studies gives a sense of the complexity of the issues involved in what otherwise would seem like a simple assertion about the effectiveness of criminal punishments. In 1975, this complexity was more fully revealed in a book by Gibbs, who presented a lengthy and sophisticated theoretical analysis of the issue along with an extensive review of relevant empirical research.[5] This was followed in 1978 by a report from the National Academy of Sciences that focused directly on the research and reached the very cautious conclusion that the evidence favoring a deterrent effect was greater than the evidence against it.[6]

---

[4]Daniel Glaser and Max S. Zeigler, "Use of the Death Penalty v. Outrage at Murder," *Crime and Delinquency* 20: 333–38 (1974). See also Glaser, "A Response to Bailey," *Crime and Delinquency* 22: 40–43 (1976).

[5]Jack P. Gibbs, *Crime, Punishment and Deterrence*, Elsevier, New York, 1975. Two other largely theoretical analyses were published just prior to Gibbs's work: Franklin E. Zimring and Gordon J. Hawkins, *Deterrence—The Legal Threat in Crime Control*, University of Chicago Press, Chicago, 1973; and Johannes Andenaes, *Punishment and Deterrence*, University of Michigan Press, Ann Arbor, 1974. However, Gibbs was the first author to extensively review empirical research on the matter.

[6]Alfred Blumstein, Jacqueline Cohen, and Daniel Nagin, eds., *Deterrence and Incapacitation: Estimating the Effects of Criminal Sanctions on Crime Rates*, National Academy of Sciences, Washington, DC 1978, p. 7. See also Philip Cook, "Research in Criminal Deterrence: Laying the Groundwork for the Second Decade," pp. 211–68 in Norval Morris and Michael Tonry, ed., *Crime and Justice: A Review of Research*, vol. 2, University of Chicago Press, Chicago, 1980. Cook's article also focused on the research but reached the more optimistic conclusion that "the criminal

THREE TYPES OF DETERRENCE RESEARCH

Since this 1978 review, a great many studies have examined the deterrent effectiveness of criminal justice policies on crime. In 1998 Nagin reviewed these studies and concluded that "the evidence for a substantial deterrent effect is much firmer than it was two decades ago."[7] He also argued that deterrence research has evolved into "three distinctive and largely disconnected literatures."[8]

The first type of deterrence research that Nagin described looks at the effects of specific criminal justice policies that target specific types of crimes, such as police crackdowns on drug markets, drunk driving, disorderly conduct, or illegal gun usage.[9] Research shows that these policies generally achieve an initial deterrent effect but that this effect tends to deteriorate rather quickly, even while the crackdown is still in operation. At the same time, a small deterrent effect often persists after the crackdown has ended. Sherman uses the terms "initial deterrence decay" and "residual deterrence" to describe these two effects.[10] He suggests that the initial deterrence decay probably occurs because "potential offenders learn through trial and error that they had overestimated the certainty of getting caught at the beginning of the crackdown." On the other hand, he suggests that residual deterrence persists even after the crackdown has ended because it takes a while for offenders to conclude that "it is once again 'safe' to offend."[11]

Sherman's conclusion suggests a distinction between objective risks and the perception of those risks by potential offenders, and the second type of deterrence research identified by Nagin looks at this issue.[12] Most of these "perceptual deterrence" studies involve survey research in which people are asked about their perceptions of the risks of being

---

justice system, ineffective as it may seem in many areas, has an overall crime deterrent effect of great magnitude" (p. 213).

[7]Daniel S. Nagin, "Criminal Deterrence Research at the Outset of the Twenty-First Century," pp. 1–42 in Michael Tonry, ed., *Crime and Justice: A Review of Research,* University of Chicago Press, Chicago, 1998, p. 1. The following discussion of deterrence research relies heavily on Nagin's review and analysis.

[8]Ibid., p. 2.

[9]Ibid., pp. 8–12.

[10]Lawrence W. Sherman, "Police Crackdowns: Initial and Residual Deterrence," pp. 1–48 in Michael Tonry and Norval Morris, eds, *Crime and Justice: A Review of Research,* vol. 12, University of Chicago Press, Chicago, 1990, p. 10.

[11]Sherman (ibid.) offers a second possible explanation for these effects: Even if the policy does not change the actual risks of punishment, it may increase uncertainty about those risks and thereby reduce offending behavior.

[12]Nagin, op. cit., pp. 12–23.

punished for specific offenses and about whether they have actually have committed or intend to commit those offenses. This research finds fairly consistent associations between offending and the perceptions of the certainty of punishments, but less consistent associations between offending and the perceptions of severity.

One problem with this research is that the direction of causation is unclear.[13] It is possible, as the deterrence hypothesis suggests, that increased perception of risk leads to reduced criminal behavior, but it is also possible that engaging in criminal behavior leads to a more realistic (i.e., decreased) perception of risk. In an attempt to resolve this issue, researchers conducted panel studies in which the same people were asked the same questions every year for a number of years in a row. This research generally finds little or no relation between the perception of risk that the person reports at the beginning of a year and the extent of offending during the year that the person reports at the end of the year.[14] This finding suggests there is little or no deterrent effect.

Other researchers argued that this panel research is flawed because risk perceptions must be measured close in time to offending decisions and because perceptions of risk are highly situation-specific. That is, general questions about risk cannot predict very much about what people will actually do when they find themselves in very specific situations that offer them opportunities to commit crime.[15] As a result, researchers began using a scenario: What would you do if you found yourself in this situation? Scenerio research has consistently produced deterrence-like associations between perceptions of risk and the reported likelihood of offending. After reviewing all of this research, Nagin states: "I believe that a consensus has emerged among perceptual deterrence researchers that the negative association between sanction risk perceptions and offending behavior or intentions is measuring deterrence."[16] He therefore turns to the question of whether perceptions of risk can be influenced by criminal justice policy. The evidence here is extremely weak, particularly in terms of the knowledge that potential offenders have about ob-

---

[13]David F. Greenberg, "Methodological Issues in Survey Research on the Inhibition of Crime," *Journal of Criminal Law and Criminology* 72: 1094–1101 (1981).

[14]For a review, see Raymond Paternoster, "The Deterrent Effect of the Perceived Certainty and Severity of Punishment: A Review of the Evidence and Issues," *Justice Quarterly* 4: 173–217 (1987).

[15]E.g., Irving Piliavin, Rosemary Gartner, Craig Thornton, and Ross L. Matsueda, "Crime, Deterrence, and Rational Choice," *American Sociological Review* 51: 101–19 (1986).

[16]Nagin, op. cit., p. 15.

jective risks and the extent to which that knowledge can be influenced by public policy. At this point, it seems impossible to reach a conclusion on the matter.

The third type of deterrence research identified by Nagin looks at criminal justice policies in different jurisdictions and at the crime rates associated with those policies to see if there is a deterrent effect.[17] For example, the deterrence hypothesis would suggest that jurisdictions that have more police officers, imprison more people, and utilize the death penalty should have less crime. A very large volume of research has been done on this type of question, but for the most part the results are unsatisfying.

For example, the deterrence hypothesis suggests that jurisdictions with more police officers should have less crime. A very large number of studies have been done on this issue but they find the opposite situation: Jurisdictions with more police officers have more crime. For example, one of the first such studies, published in 1971, found that "The correlations between the number of police per capita and crime rates were positive and significant . . . This is most probably explained by the hypothesis that in an area with high crime rates, more police are employed."[18] The problem, as this article points out, is that there are two directions of causation here. The fact is that more crime "causes" more police. This makes it very difficult to determine whether more police "causes" less crime.[19] At present, the issue is probably best considered unresolved.[20]

A similar situation exists with the death penalty. The deterrence hypothesis suggests that states with the death penalty should have lower homicide rates than states without the death penalty. But as mentioned above in the discussion of Gibbs's and Tittle's early research, the opposite situation is very clearly the case: States with the death penalty have

---

[17]Ibid., pp. 23–33.

[18]Israel Pressman and Arthur Carol, "Crime as a Diseconomy of Scale," *Review of Social Economy* 29: 227–36 (1971).

[19]Nagin, op. cit., p. 29, refers to this as the "endogeneity" problem.

[20]Nagin (op. cit., p. 33) reaches a different conclusion, that "the treatment effect of police presence . . . is contingent on the way the force is mobilized." In support of this conclusion, he extensively discusses a study by Robert J. Sampson and Jacqueline Cohen ("Deterrent Effects of Police on Crime," *Law and Society Review* 22: 163–89 [1988]) that found that proactive policing directed against public disorder offenses (e.g., public drunkness) has a deterrent effect on serious crime. However, in research published since Nagin wrote, his 1998 article, Sampson and Stephen W. Raudenbush ("Systematic Social Observation of Public Spaces," *American Journal of Sociology* 105[3]: 603–51 [1999]) found no support for the "broken windows" theory behind these enforcement policies, which suggests that the policies themselves would not have such an effect.

substantially higher murder rates than states without it.[21] The reason, most likely, is that the death penalty is implemented in jurisdictions that have high murder rates. As with deterrence research on the police, the problem is that there are two directions of causation: Since higher murder rates "cause" the death penalty, it is therefore difficult to determine whether the death penalty in turn "causes" lower murder rates.

Despite this problem, the deterrent effectiveness of the death penalty is probably the single most researched issue in the field of criminology. On the whole, there is little or no empirical support that the death penalty achieves deterrence beyond the effect that is achieved by extended incarceration.[22] As a consequence, most criminologists have concluded that the death penalty does not reduce violent crime, nor does it have the potential to do so.[23] Beyond that, several researchers have presented complex statistical analyses that conclude that the death penalty actually increases homicides.[24] This finding would suggest that the higher levels of homicide in death-penalty jurisdictions are partly generated by the death penalty itself. The explanation of this rather surprising finding resembles the explanation that Glaser and Zeigler offered in their criticism of Gibbs's and Tittle's early findings: The death penalty has a "brutalization" effect that tends to devalue human life and thereby increases homicide.

Considerable attention has also focused on the deterrent effectiveness of imprisonment. In general, the deterrence hypothesis predicts that more imprisonment will be associated with less crime, but the opposite situation is usually found, presumably because more crime "causes" more imprisonment.[25] However, the steep rise in imprisonment in the United States beginning about 1970 was followed by a precipitous drop in crime that began in the early 1990s. This pattern raises the question of whether drop in crime in the 1990s represents the deterrent effect of high imprisonment rates. The problem is that there is a clear al-

---

[21]For example, Raymond Bonner and Ford Fessenden ("States With No Death Penalty Share Lower Homicide Rates," and Ford Fessenden, "Deadly Statistics: A Survey of Crime and Punishment," both in the *New York Times,* September 22, 2000) report that "during the last 20 years, the homicide rate in states with the death penalty has been 48 percent to 101 percent higher than in states without the death penalty."

[22]This is called "marginal," as opposed to "absolute" deterrence. See Nagin, op. cit., pp. 3–4.

[23]Michael Radelet and Ronald L. Akers, "Deterrence and the Death Penalty: The Views of the Experts," *Journal of Criminal Law and Criminology* 87(1): 1–16 (1996).

[24]See, for example, William C. Bailey, "Deterrence, Brutalization and the Death Penalty," *Criminology* 36(4): 711–33 (1998), which examined homicide in Oklahoma following its return to capital punishment in 1990. The study found consistent support for a brutalization effect for a variety of killings involving both strangers and non-strangers.

[25]Nagin, op. cit., pp. 24–25.

ternate explanation for the 1990s crime drop: Beginning in the early 1990s, the United States entered the longest sustained period of economic expansion in its history, with unemployment and welfare rates reaching historic low levels as the benefits of the prosperity reached the most deprived sectors of the society. Sorting out the causal impacts of these different factors is complex. In general, researchers conclude that large increases in imprisonment had at least some causal impact on the declining crime rates, although most conclude that it was not the most important cause.[26]

Other measures of the deterrent effectiveness of imprisonment have looked at the new "three strikes" laws that provide extended sentences for a third felony. A study of the California law found that it did not impact preexisting crime trends.[27] In addition, a cost-benefit analysis by the Rand Corporation concluded that the law is extremely expensive to implement, that it achieves only modest crime reductions, and that if the money were redirected to other programs, much greater crime reductions would be achieved.[28]

RATIONAL CHOICE AND OFFENDING

The classical model of human choice assumes that offenders rationally calculate the costs and benefits of committing a crime. Several recent theories examine the situations and circumstances in which potential offenders engage in such rational calculations and find that they have the opportunity to commit a crime.[29] These theories do not explain the motivation to commit crime—rather, they assume that there are always people around who will commit a crime if given a chance.

For example, looting often accompanies large-scale disasters such as floods, earthquakes, violent storms, wars, and riots. Homeowners and

---

[26]William Spelman ("The Limited Importance of Prison Expansion," pp. 97–129 in Alfred Blumstein and Joel Wallman, eds., *The Crime Drop in America*, Cambridge University Press, Cambridge, 2000) estimates that "the crime drop would have been 27% smaller without the prison buildup" (p. 122). Richard Rosenfeld, "Patterns in Adult Homicide 1980–1995," pp. 130–63 in Blumstein and Wallman, op. cit., estimates that "At most, incarceration explains 15 to 20 percent of that decline" in adult homicide (p. 152). See also Rosenfeld, "Explaining Recent Trends in U.S. Homicide Rates," pp. 1175–1216, and Gary LaFree, "Social Institutions and the Crime 'Bust' of the 1990s," pp. 1325–68, both in *Journal of Criminal Law & Criminology* 88(4), 1998; and Gary LaFree, *Losing Legitimacy*, Westview, Boulder, CO, 1998.

[27]Lisa Stolzenberg and Stewart J. D'Alessio, "Three Strikes and You're Out: The Impact of California's New Mandatory Sentencing Law on Serious Crime Rates," *Crime and Delinquency* 43(4): 457–69 (1997).

[28]Peter W. Greenwood, Karyn E. Model, C. Peter Rydell, and James Chiesa, "Diverting Children from a Life of Crime," Rand Corporation, Santa Monica, CA, 1996.

[29]For a review, see Christopher Birkbeck and Gary LaFree, "The Situational Analysis of Crime and Deviance," *Annual Review of Sociology* 19: 113–37 (1993).

storeowners flee the disaster, leaving their property unprotected. The police often are busy with more pressing matters, such as saving human lives. People who normally would not commit crime may take advantage of the opportunities in the disaster situation and steal whatever they think they can get away with. Because these theories focus on situations that offer opportunities for rational-calculating potential offenders to commit crime, they are sometimes called "opportunity theories."

The above example of looting involves "situational selection," which describes the types of situations that motivated offenders select to commit their crimes.[30] In general, motivated offenders consider ease of access to the target, the likelihood of being observed or caught, and the expected reward. This perspective assumes that offenders are largely rational in their decision-making processes, so the process is associated with "rational choice" theories of crime.[31]

Rational choice theories develop, at much greater length, Beccaria's original simple model of human choice, as described in Chapter 2. Their goal, however, is to consider how potential offenders might weigh the costs and benefits in particular situations, and then to determine how those situations might be changed so that potential offenders will decide not to commit crime. Thus, rational choice theories are associated with "situational crime prevention,"[32] rather than with the deterrent effects of certainty and severity of punishments.

These theories assume that all crime is purposeful, committed with the intention to benefit the offender. The "cardinal rule" of rational choice theories is to never dismiss a criminal act as wanton or senseless or irrational, but rather to seek to understand the purposes of the offender.[33] Such theories also assume that the rationality of criminals is always limited—i.e., that "in seeking to benefit themselves, offenders do not always succeed in making the best decisions because of the risks and uncertainty involved."[34] Finally, the theories assume that offender decision-making is quite different for different types of crimes. For example, the same offenders may commit both robbery and rape, but these offenses are committed against different victims, in different settings, with different weapons and with different purposes. Thus, situa-

---

[30]Ibid., pp. 124–26.

[31]Derek B. Cornish and Ronald V. Clarke, eds., *The Reasoning Criminal*, Springer-Verlag, New York, 1986.

[32]See Graeme Newman, Ronald V. Clarke, and S. Giora Shoham, eds., *Rational Choice and Situational Crime Prevention: Theoretical Foundations*, Ashgate, Dartmouth, U.K., 1997.

[33]Ronald V. Clarke and Derek B. Cornish, "Rational Choice," pp. 23–42 in Raymond Paternoster and Ronet Bachman, eds., *Explaining Criminals and Crime*, Roxbury, Los Angeles, 2001, p. 25.

[34]Ibid., p. 24.

tional crime prevention must have a crime-specific focus. Based on these principles, rational choice theories recommend that situations be changed to increase the perceived effort to commit a crime, to increase the perceived risks, and to reduce the perceived benefits.[35] This approach has been applied in quite a few different situations; two examples are airport baggage screening (which has virtually eliminated airplane hijackings) and exact fare systems in city buses (which has virtually eliminated robberies of bus drivers).

ROUTINE ACTIVITIES AND VICTIMIZATION

An approach similar to rational choice theories of crime has been used to explain differences in the rates at which groups are victimized.[36] Hindelang and his colleagues have argued that the differences in risks of victimization are associated with differences in lifestyles, which they describe in terms of "routine daily activities, both vocational activities (work, school, keeping house, etc.) and leisure activities."[37] In general, they argue that people who are younger, male, unmarried, poor, and African American have higher risks of victimization than people who are older, female, married, wealthy, and European American because the former group has an increased tendency to be away from home, especially at night, to engage in public activities while away from home, and to associate with people who are likely to be offenders.[38] These habits lead to increased risk of property and personal victimization.

Cohen and Felson argue that certain changes in the modern world have provided motivated offenders with a greatly increased range of opportunities to commit crime.[39] They point out that most violent and property crimes involve direct contact between the offender and the

---

[35]See Ronald V. Clarke, ed., *Situational Crime Prevention: Successful Case Studies*, 2nd ed., Harrow and Heston, Albany, NY, 1997.

[36]Michael J. Hindelang, Michael R. Gottfredson, and James Garofalo, *Victims of Personal Crime*, Ballinger, Cambridge, MA, 1978. James Garofalo, "Reassessing the Lifestyle Model of Criminal Victimization," in Michael Gottfredson and Travis Hirschi, eds., *Positive Criminology: Essays in Honor of Michael J. Hindelang*, Sage, Beverly Hills, CA, 1987, updates the theory and argues that there is no substantive difference between the "lifestyle" and the "routine activities" approaches. See also Michael G. Maxfield, "Lifestyle and Routine Activity Theories of Crime," *Journal of Quantitative Criminology*, 3(4): 275–82 (1987).

[37]Hindelang et al., p. 241.

[38]For a good summary, see Robert F. Meier and Terance D. Miethe, "Understanding Theories of Criminal Victimization," in Michael Tonry, ed., *Crime and Justice: An Annual Review of Research*, 17: 459–99 (1993). See also Birkbeck and LaFree, op. cit.

[39]Lawrence E. Cohen and Marcus Felson "Social Change and Crime Rate Trends: A Routine Activity Approach," *American Sociological Review* 44: 588–608 (1979). Where Cohen and Felson focuse on crime-rate trends of predatory crimes, Felson himself has extended this approach to a

"target"—i.e., the person or property of the victim.[40] These crimes therefore require the convergence in time and space of a motivated offender, a suitable target, and the absence of a capable guardian (police) to prevent the crime. Most criminology theories assume that changes in crime rates reflect changes in the number of motivated offenders or changes in the strength of their motivation. But Cohen and Felson argue that changes in crime rates may instead be explained in terms of changes in the availability of targets and the absence of capable guardians. This is exactly what happens when looting follows a disaster—there is no increase in criminal motivation, but suddenly there are many available targets and few capable guardians.

Cohen and Felson argue that there have been a great increase in the availability of targets and in the absence of capable guardians in the modern world as a result of changes in "routine activities"—i.e., how normal people live their lives in terms of work, home life, child rearing, education, and leisure. When people are home, they function as guardians for their own property. But the routine activities of modern life have led to the "dispersion of activities away from family and household." This means that many households no longer have capable guardians for extended and fairly predictable periods of time. In addition, there has been a large increase in goods which are portable and therefore suitable as targets for thieves. For example, Cohen and Felson calculate that, in 1975, $26.44 in motor vehicles and parts was stolen for each $100 of these goods consumed. In comparison, $6.82 worth of electronic appliances, and twelve cents worth of furniture and nonelectronic household durables, were stolen for every $100 consumed. The vast differences in the worth of goods stolen are due to the suitability of the goods as targets for theft. Cohen and Felson then demonstrate that changes in crime rates in the United States from 1947 to 1974 can be explained largely by these trends. In 1947 people were home more of the time and more of what they owned was similar to furniture; by 1974 people were away from home more of the time and more of what they owned was similar to cars and electronic appliances. So despite large in-

---

broader range of crimes and examines the implications of routine activities for individual offending. See Marcus Felson, "Linking Criminal Choices, Routine Activities, Informal Control, and Criminal Outcomes," pp. 119–28 in Cornish and Clarke, op. cit.; Marcus Felson, *Crime and Everyday Life*, Pine Forge Press, Thousand Oaks, CA, 1994; and Felson and Michael R. Gottfredson, "Social Indicators of Adolescent Activities Near Peers and Parents," *Journal of Marriage and the Family* 46: 709–14 (1984).

[40]Some crimes do not involve direct contact—e.g., many white-collar crimes. Cohen and Felson do not analyze these types of crime, but the organization of the modern world obviously has made crimes without direct contact much more available to motivated offenders.

creases in crime over that time period, there may be no changes whatsoever in the number of motivated offenders or in the reasons for offender motivations.

ROUTINE ACTIVITIES AND MODERNIZATION

The routine activities approach offers an alternative to Durkheim's theory of modernization as an explanation for changes in crime rates as nations undergo modernization, as discussed in Chapter 6. Durkheim explained these changes primarily in terms of the breakdown of traditional
values and beliefs. Neuman and Berger reviewed 17 studies that compared Durkheim's theory with the routine activities theory, and found
only weak support for either one.[41] Bennett also compared the two, using data from 52 nations from 1960 to 1984.[42] In general, he found that
neither approach could account for changes in homicide rates, since
homicide was not affected either by developmental level or the rate of
growth. But the changes in theft rates were consistent with the routine
activities approach—i.e., more development was associated with more
theft, independent of the rate at which the development was occurring.
He also found a "threshold" point at a very high level of development, at
which further economic development did not seem to be associated
with more theft. Bennett suggested that this was probably due to a variety of adaptive social mechanisms that became effective at that point,
such as "theft target hardening" (e.g., better locks, higher fences, bur-
glar alarms), development of community watches, increased surveillance over goods, and more effective police strategies and tactics (e.g.,
community-oriented policing)."[43]

CONCLUSIONS

The present chapter reviews criminological theory and research on deterrence, routine activities, and rational choice. All three approaches are
based on the relatively simple classical model of human choice, as originally proposed by Beccaria. None, however, directly attempts to test
that model. Rather, each approach develops policies that should reduce
crime if its model is correct. Research then tests the effectiveness of

---

[41]W. Lawrence Neuman and Ronald J. Berger, "Competing Perspectives on Cross-National
Crime," *The Sociological Quarterly* 29(2): 281–313 (1988).

[42]Richard R. Bennett, "Development and Crime," *The Sociological Quarterly* 32(3): 343–63 (1991).

[43]Ibid., p. 356.

those policies, and the results are taken as evidence about the validity of the underlying classical model of human choice.

In general, support for the deterrence hypothesis is much greater today than it was twenty years ago. Nevertheless, the research seems to indicate that current policies place too much emphasis on the severity of punishments and not enough on their certainty. The most severe punishments, such as the death penalty and "three strikes" laws, do not seem to provide any greater deterrent effect than less severe punishments. In addition, the massive explosion in imprisonment in the United States since 1970 appears to have had some impact on crime, but not as much impact as other factors unrelated to deterrence. The overall conclusion at this point, while tentative, seems to be that further increases in the severity of punishments probably will have no impact on crime reduction and, for various reasons, may actually increase crime. Increases in the certainty of apprehension, conviction, and punishment, on the other hand, probably will result in further reductions in crime.

More potential for crime reduction is probably found in the rational choice and routine activities approaches, which base their policy recommendations on altering the situations and circumstances in which potential offenders rationally calculate the costs and benefits of crime. These approaches are relatively new and thus far have achieved only limited successes. Nevertheless, they seem to have considerable long-range potential for achieving significant crime reduction in the future.

CHAPTER TWELVE

The Meaning of Crime

The "cardinal rule" of rational choice theories, as discussed in the last chapter, is never to dismiss a criminal act as wanton or senseless or irrational, but to seek to understand the *purposes* of the offender in committing the offense. Consistent with classical criminology's relatively simple model of human choice, these purposes are conceptualized in terms of the offender's self-interest: People's behaviors reflect a rational pursuit of self-interest based on an analysis of costs and benefits.

A much broader view of human purposes is presented in symbolic interactionism, which was briefly discussed in Chapter 9 as the theoretical foundation for Sutherland's differential association theory. Symbolic interactionism argues that human actions are best understood in terms of the *meanings* that those actions have for actors.[1] In symbolic interactionism, people first define the meanings of the situations they find themselves in, and then they act toward those situations in ways that make sense within the context of those meanings. The meanings themselves are to some extent created by the individual, but mostly they are derived from personal communications and interactions with other people. Symbolic interactionism provides a theoretical framework within which human purposes and meanings can be probed more deeply than within the relatively simple classical framework. Using a general focus

---

[1] Symbolic interactionism is very briefly described in Chapter 9, and is more extensively summarized in the second edition of the present book. See George B. Vold, *Theoretical Criminology*, 2nd ed. prepared by Thomas J. Bernard, Oxford University Press, New York, 1979, pp. 255–58. See also a brief discussion of the theory in Ross L. Matsueda, "Labeling Theory: Historical Roots, Implications, and Recent Developments," pp. 223–41 in Raymond Paternoster and Ronet Bachman, eds., *Explaining Criminals and Crime*, Roxbury, Los Angeles, 2001.

on human purposes and meaning as the key to understanding the phenomenon of crime, criminologists have made theoretical arguments in four general areas.

Beginning in the 1930s, so-called labeling theory focused on how and why society applies the label of "criminal" to certain people and behaviors, and the effect that label has on the future behavior of the person who is so labeled. This approach looks at the meaning of the label "criminal" in relation to the criminal's self-image. A second approach within the general framework of symbolic interactionism probes much more deeply into the meaning of crime to criminals on an experiential basis. This approach goes well beyond the simple pursuit of self-interest, as described in classical criminology, and the meaning of the label of "criminal," as described in labeling theory. Instead, it describes the meanings of crimes in terms of moral and sensuous projects undertaken by the criminal. The third approach looks at the meaning of crime to the larger society. In particular, it looks at the processes by which general categories of behavior are defined as crimes in the criminal law and specific people and events are defined as criminal by criminal justice agencies. Most recently, in the fourth approach, theorists have examined the meaning of crime within the context of state power, focusing on the meaning of the project undertaken by the state when it defines people and behaviors as criminal.

In each case, the focus of theory and research is on the meanings and purposes that people have in relation to crime and criminals. Their actions therefore are understood as a product of those meanings and purposes.

THE MEANING OF CRIME TO THE SELF: LABELING THEORY

One of the most important meanings within symbolic interaction theory is the meaning that people give to themselves—i.e., their self-image. People may define themselves as handsome, cowardly, kind, faithful, smart, worthless, or all of the above. They then act toward themselves according to the meanings they have for themselves. Symbolic interactionism argues that each person's self-image is constructed primarily through social interactions with other people—what Mead called "the self as a social construct"[2] and what Cooley called "the looking-glass self."[3]

---

[2]See Bernard N. Meltzer, "Mead Social Psychology," in Jerome G. Manis and Bernard N. Meltzer, eds., *Symbolic Interaction,* Allyn and Bacon, Boston, 1967, pp. 9–13.

[3]Charles H. Cooley, *Human Nature and the Social Order,* Charles Scribner's Sons, New York, 1902, pp. 183–85, 196–99, reprinted in Manis and Meltzer, op. cit., pp. 217–19.

In 1938, Frank Tannenbaum used these ideas as the basis for a "labeling theory" of crime that arises from the conflicts between youths and adults in urban neighborhoods.[4] He argued that the youths see themselves as participating in playgroups on the streets, as they have been doing since they were small children. This is their "definition of the situation," to use the term from symbolic interactionism. But as the youths become teenagers, the playgroups increasingly engage in exciting and adventurous and dangerous and threatening activities that provoke the hostility of the adults in the neighborhood. Adults initially "define the situation" as "good kids" doing "bad actions." But as the conflict between adolescents and adults persists, adults eventually define the youths themselves as bad. The youths then begin to identify with these definitions, to view themselves as bad, and they begin to act the part. Tannenbaum concludes: "The person becomes the thing he is described as being."[5]

In 1951, Lemert presented a general theory of deviance that incorporated this basic labeling process.[6] He argued that criminal and deviant behaviors originate in any number of biological, psychological, or social factors in the person's life. Thus, for example, Tannenbaum had described delinquency as originating in juvenile playgroups in urban neighborhoods. Lemert calls people who engage in such criminal or deviant behavior "primary deviants."[7] This deviant behavior then generates a negative reaction from other people, and that reaction tends to transform from a negative definition of the act into a negative definition of the person. People who are unwilling or unable to stop the offending behavior (i.e., the behavior that generates the negative social reaction) will at some point tend to reorganize their self-images to incorporate the new negative definitions of themselves. This is the process described by Tannenbaum, as adults transform the definition of the youths' actions as bad into a definition of the youths themselves as bad, whereupon the youths tend to reorganize their self-images to incorporate these negative definitions of themselves. This transformation of the self-image is a self-protective move, since those who already define themselves as criminals or delinquents are less threatened when other people define them that way. Lemert calls a person who has taken on a deviant self-image a "sec-

---

[4]Frank Tannenbaum, *Crime and the Community,* Ginn, Boston, 1938.

[5]Ibid., p. 20.

[6]Edwin M. Lemert, *Social Pathology,* McGraw-Hill, New York, 1951; see also Lemert, *Human Deviance, Social Problems, and Social Control,* Prentice-Hall, Englewood Cliffs, NJ, 1967.

[7]Lemert, *Human Deviance,* ibid., pp. 17, 40.

ondary deviant."[8] The redefinition of self opens the door to full participation in the deviant life and allows the person to make a commitment to a deviant career. At this point, Lemert argues, the criminal and deviant behavior is no longer generated by the various biological, psychological, and social factors in the person's life, but is generated directly by the person's self-image.

Despite Lemert's arguments, many people who commit criminal behaviors do not think of themselves as criminals—that is, have a criminal self-image. Yochelson and Samenow found that even the most hardened, consistent offenders were unwilling to admit that they were criminals, although they could easily recognize criminality in others.[9] Cameron pointed out that nonprofessional shoplifters often deny that their actions constitute theft, and tend to rationalize their behavior as "merely naughty or bad" or as "reprehensible but not really criminal."[10] Cressey's analysis of embezzlement is quite similar.[11] Embezzlers are people who hold positions of trust and normally conceive of themselves as upstanding citizens. Therefore they must define their actions as "only borrowing the money" before they can proceed. Sykes and Matza argue that most juvenile delinquents do not have an overt commitment to delinquent values and do not conceive of themselves as criminals.[12] Their own delinquent behavior contradicts their self-image, and therefore they often justify the behavior by arguing that it is "not really criminal." Five "techniques of neutralization" may be used in this way: denial of responsibility ("It wasn't my fault"); denial of injury ("They can afford it"); denial of victims ("They had it coming"); condemnation of condemners ("Everyone is crooked anyway"); and appeal to higher loyalties ("I did it for the gang"). Police who use illegal violence justify it in terms of the need to accomplish their jobs.[13] Illegal activities by government agencies may be justified in terms of "national security." Antiwar activists who committed illegal acts stated that the "real criminals" were the ones running the war. And, in general, Chambliss and Seidman state: "It is a truism that every person arrested for crime perceives him-

---

[8]Lemert, *Social Pathology*, pp. 75–76; Lemert, *Human Deviance.*, pp. 40–64.

[9]Samuel Yochelson and Stanton E. Samenow, *The Criminal Personality*, vol. I, Jason Aronson, New York, 1976, p. 19.

[10]Mary Cameron Owen, *The Booster and the Snitch*, The Free Press, New York, 1964, pp. 159, 161, 168.

[11]Donald R. Cressey, *Other People's Money: A Study of the Social Psychology of Embezzlement*, The Free Press, Glencoe, IL, 1953.

[12]Gresham M. Sykes and David Matza, "Techniques of Neutralization: A Theory of Delinquency," *American Sociological Review* 22: 667–70 (Dec. 1957).

[13]William A. Westley, "Violence and the Police," *American Journal of Sociology* 59: 34–41 (July 1953).

self as innocent, for there are always circumstances which to him seem to place his action outside the appropriate definition of the crime."[14]

These examples illustrate the fact that criminal behaviors are frequently committed by persons who do not conceive of themselves as criminals. To maintain a noncriminal self-image, these persons "define the situation" so that they can maintain that their actions are not really crimes. They are then free to continue committing criminal behaviors without changing their self-image.

The maintenance of a noncriminal self-image is very important to most people. Pressure to accept a criminal self-image depends in part on the number of others who define the person as a criminal, and the process of informing others that a person is a criminal is frequently used as a technique of social control. For example, consider the case of a person who has a non-criminal self-image, but who is caught shoplifting and is brought to the store office. Store officials communicate to the person that "you *are* a shoplifter." This is threatening to the person precisely because the self is constructed in the process of interacting with others, including the store officials. The officials can increase the power of the threat by increasing the number of persons who know about the new identity. The ultimate threat to the identity, however, involves the process of arrest and conviction in which the person is officially declared to be a criminal in the view of the society at large. From this point of view a criminal trial can be interpreted as a "status degradation ceremony" in which the public identity of the person is lowered on the social scale. Garfinkel maintains that literally every society maintains such ceremonies as a method of social control, and that the structure of these ceremonies is essentially similar although the societies differ dramatically.[15]

Once applied, Becker has argued, the criminal label overrides other labels, so that other people think of the person primarily as a criminal.[16] Such a person may then be forced into criminal roles because of public stereotypes about criminals.[17] For example, on release from prison a person may be unable to obtain legitimate employment due to the crim-

---

[14]William J. Chambliss and Robert B. Seidman, *Law, Order and Power,* Addison-Wesley, Reading, MA, 1971, p. 71.

[15]Harold Garfinkel, "Conditions of Successful Degradation Ceremonies," *American Journal of Sociology* 61(5): 420–24 (March 1965).

[16]Howard S. Becker, *Outsiders—Studies in the Sociology of Deviance,* Free Press of Glencoe, New York, 1963, pp. 32–33. See also Kai T. Erikson, "Notes on the Sociology of Deviance," *Social Problems* 9: 311 (spring 1962). An example would be Ray's argument that a cured heroin addict relapses in part because other people continue to treat him as an addict. See Marsh B. Ray, "The Cycle of Abstinence and Relapse among Heroin Addicts," *Social Problems* 9: 132–40 (fall 1961).

[17]Becker, op. cit., pp. 34–35.

inal conviction and may then return to crime to survive. Finally, those who have been labeled criminal may associate primarily with other people who have been similarly labeled, either because they are all institutionalized together or because other people refuse to associate with them.[18] Membership in an exclusively criminal group can increase the likelihood that individuals will resort to a criminal self-image rather than attempt to retain a noncriminal self-image.

This discussion represents one of the basic arguments of the so-called labeling approach to crime: that the formal and informal processes of social control can have the effect of increasing criminal behavior because the labeling process increases the likelihood that the person will develop a criminal self-image. Several criticisms of the labeling approach should be mentioned. First, labeling theorists sometimes have overemphasized the importance that the official labeling process can have. As Akers has remarked:[19]

One sometimes gets the impression from reading this literature that people go about minding their own business, and then—"wham"—bad society comes along and slaps them with a stigmatized label. Forced into the role of deviant the individual has little choice but to be deviant.

Second, labeling theory generally portrays the deviant as resisting the deviant label, and accepting it only when it can no longer be avoided. Although this may be true in some cases, in others it would appear that the deviant identity is actively sought and that the person may form a deviant identity without ever having been officially or unofficially labeled. For example, youths who join a delinquent gang may form a deviant identity centered on their gang activities. Although official labeling may make it harder to change that identity in the future, it did not push the youth into the identity in the first place, and there is no particular reason to believe that failure to label the youth would lead him to seek a law-abiding identity instead.

Third, it is generally recognized that for the typical, law-abiding member of society who has a noncriminal self-image, the labeling or stigmatizing function of the criminal court is the primary technique of social control and is much more important than the actual imposition of punishments.[20] The average citizen is deterred from committing most

---

[18]Ibid., pp. 37–39.

[19]Ronald L. Akers, "Problems in the Sociology of Deviance: Social Definitions and Behavior," *Social Forces* 46: 455–65 (1967).

[20]Franklin E. Zimring and Gordon J. Hawkins, *Deterrence,* University of Chicago Press, Chicago, 1973, pp. 190–94.

crimes because he or she fears the conviction itself rather than the punishment associated with it. This is why courts are frequently able to suspend sentence or impose such minor punishments as small fines or unsupervised probation with no loss of effectiveness. Only in cases in which conviction does not hold a stigma—for example, traffic offense cases—do the courts rely heavily on the actual imposition of punishments in the social control of the average citizen. Reducing the stigmatizing or labeling effects of the criminal court could possibly lead to an increase in the incidence of criminal behaviors and to an increase in the imposition of other, harsher punishments for those behaviors. Thus the basic question is not whether the labeling function creates crime, but whether it creates more crime than it eliminates. Although this is a very complicated question to analyze, it seems probable that labeling does not create more crime than it eliminates.[21]

More recently, Matsueda and his colleagues offered a labeling theory of delinquency that focused on the labels applied to juveniles by their parents, rather than by criminal justice agents.[22] He found that delinquency is significantly affected by juveniles' perception that other people think of them as "rule-violators," and that this perception itself is significantly affected by the actual label that parents place on the youth. In a later study, Heimer and Matsueda found that delinquency results largely from the juvenile assuming the role of delinquent, rather than from being labeled a rule-violator by parents.[23] One of the most important factors in taking on this role is the youth's perception that others see him or her as a rule violator, and other factors associated with delinquency tend to operate through the role-taking:[24]

Youths who are from older, nonblack, urban residents, and from nonintact homes commit more initial delinquent acts than others, which increases the chances that their parents will see them as rule-violators. In turn, labeling by

---

[21]Charles R. Tittle, "Labelling and Crime: An Empirical Evaluation," in Walter R. Gove, ed., *The Labelling of Deviance—Evaluating a Perspective,* John Wiley, New York, 1975, pp. 181–203.

[22]Ross L. Matsueda, "Reflected Appraisals, Parental Labeling, and Delinquency: Specifying a Symbolic Interactionist Theory," *American Journal of Sociology* 97: 1577–1611, 1992; Karen Heimer and Ross L. Matsueda, "Role-Taking, Role Commitment, and Delinquency: A Theory of Differential Social Control," *American Sociological Review* 59: 365–90, June, 1994; Heimer, "Gender, Interaction, and Delinquency," *Social Psychology Quarterly* 59: 39–61, 1996; Dawn Jeglum Bartusch and Ross L. Matsueda, "Gender, Reflected Appraisals, and Labeling," *Social Forces* 75: 45–77, 1996; and Ross L. Matsueda and Kaven Heimer, "A Symbolic Interactionist Theory of Role Transitions, Role Commitments, and Delinquency," pp. 163–214 in Terence P. Thornberry, ed., *Developmental Theories in Crime and Delinquency,* vol. 7 in *Advances in Criminological Theory,* Transaction, New Brunswick, NJ, 1996. See also the summary of the theory in Matsueda, "Labeling Theory," op. cit., p. 235.

[23]Heimer and Matsueda, op. cit.

[24]Ibid., pp. 381–82.

parents increases the likelihood that these youths will affiliate with delinquent peers and see themselves as rule-violators from the standpoint of others, which ultimately increases the likelihood of future delinquent behavior.

Heimer and Matsueda also found that African American youths commit fewer initial delinquent acts than non-African American youth but that, controlling for prior delinquency, African American youths are more likely to be labeled as "rule violators" by their parents. This then leads to increased views of the self as a rule-violator and increased associations with delinquent peers, both of which increase the likelihood of delinquency in the future. Thus, with African American youths, Heimer and Matsueda found some support for the traditional labeling argument that criminal labels are applied to youths who are not especially delinquent, and then those labels generate higher levels of delinquency in the future.

THE MEANING OF CRIME TO THE CRIMINAL: KATZ'S *SEDUCTIONS OF CRIME*

A very different theory based on symbolic interactionism is by Jack Katz in his book *Seductions of Crime.*[25] Katz argues that criminologists have traditionally explained crime in terms of "background" variables such as race, class, gender, urban location, and so on. But he argues that it is far more important to understand the "foreground" variable of what it feels like to commit a crime when you are committing it. Over and over, Katz asks: What are people trying to do when they commit a crime?[26] That is, he focuses on the meaning that crime has for the criminal.

Katz looks at a wide variety of sources, including biographies and autobiographies of criminals, journalistic accounts, and participant observation studies, and tries to read into these accounts the real explanation that the criminal has for the criminal behavior. He then applies this technique to five types of crimes: passion murders, adolescent property crime, gang violence, persistent robbery, and cold-blooded murder. In each case, he finds that the criminal is engaged in a "project"—i.e., is trying to accomplish something by committing the crime. That project is primarily moral—i.e., involves right and wrong, justice and injustice. It therefore involves emotions that have strong moral components: humil-

---

[25]Jack Katz, *Seductions of Crime: Moral and Sensual Attractions in Doing Evil*, Basic, New York, 1988.
[26]Ibid., p. 9.

iation, righteousness, arrogance, ridicule, cynicism, defilement, and vengeance. In each case, the criminal action itself is fundamentally an attempt to transcend a moral challenge faced by the criminal in the immediate situation.

The moral challenge faced by the passion killer, Katz finds, is "to escape a situation that is otherwise inexorably humiliating."[27] Rather than accept this humiliation, the killer engages in "righteous slaughter," which the killer interprets as participating in some higher form of good. Adolescents who engage in shoplifting and petty vandalism engage in a melodrama in which "getting away with it" demonstrates personal competence in the face of persistent feelings of incompetence. Adolescents who engage in urban gang violence generally come from poor families who have recently arrived from rural areas, and who therefore are humbled by the rational environment of the city and are deferential to the people who inhabit it. In response to this moral challenge, these adolescents are deliberately irrational in their own actions and arrogantly dominating in relation to other people. They thereby create a "territory" for themselves in the city, both in geographic and in moral terms. Those who persistently engage in robbery must become "hardmen" who take total control of the immediate situation by being willing to back their intentions violently and remorsely.[28] Robbery therefore transcends the total lack of control these robbers experience in the rest of their lives— i.e., they experience their lives as completely out of control or as controlled by the "system." Finally, cold-blooded killers have a pervasive sense of having been defiled by conventional members of society, who for years have treated them as pariahs and outcasts. In their minds, these killers finally exact vengeance for this defilement by "senselessly" killing some of those conventional members of society.

In each case, then, engaging in crime involves transcending a moral challenge and achieving a moral dominance. This moral transcendence produces a "thrill" that is experienced during the actual commission of the crime as sensual, seductive, magic, creative, even compelling. Beyond these "moral and sensual attractions in doing evil," Katz argues that there really are no general explanations for crime and deviance. But Tittle suggests that there may be some further similarities among the different types of crime described by Katz: "All appear to involve efforts to escape control exercised by others or dictated by circumstances, and they all seem to express efforts to impose control back over proximate

---

[27]Ibid.

[28]Ibid., p. 218.

people and circumstances."[29] According to Tittle, then, Katz's descriptions also suggest that a fundamental meaning of crime for the criminal is to escape the control of others and to impose control on others.

Research on the meaning of crime to criminals is not new. In the 1930s, Clifford Shaw published a series of life histories of juvenile delinquents, as described in Chapter 7.[30] These attempted to portray the social worlds in which these juveniles lived, including the meanings that delinquency had for them in the context of their worlds. At about the same time, Sutherland published an extensive portrayal of a professional thief as part of differential association theory, which is described in Chapter 9.[31] In the 1950s, Sutherland's coauthor Cressey wrote about the world of embezzlers in connection with the same theory.[32] In the 1960s, Becker provided a vivid portrayal of marijuana smoking among jazz musicians,[33] and Polsky described the worlds of hustlers and gangsters.[34] More recently there has been a considerable expansion of this type of work.[35] Adler has examined the worlds of upper-level drug dealers,[36] while Tunnell has described the worlds of ordinary adult property offenders.[37] Wright and Decker have described the worlds of active burglars and of active armed robbers.[38] Jacobs describes the worlds of active crack dealers[39] and of those who rob drug dealers.[40] Ferrell argues that such research raises a host of legal and ethical issues, including the risk of the researcher being labeled as criminal by the criminal justice

---

[29]Charles R. Tittle, *Control Balance: Toward a General Theory of Deviance*, Westview, Boulder, Col., 1995, p. 279.

[30]Clifford Shaw, *The Jackroller* (1930), *The Natural History of a Delinquent Career* (1931), and *Brothers in Crime* (1938), all University of Chicago Press, Chicago.

[31]Edwin H. Sutherland, *The Professional Thief*, University of Chicago Press, Chicago, 1937.

[32]Donald R. Cressey, *Other People's Money: A Study in the Social Psychology of Embezzlement*, Patterson Smith, Montclair, NJ, 1973. This is a reprint edition with new introduction by the author.

[33]Becker, op. cit.

[34]Ned Polsky, *Hustlers, Beats, and Others*, rev. ed., Lyons Press, New York, 1998.

[35]See Jeff Ferrell, Mark S. Hamm, Patricia A. Adler and Peter Adler, eds., *Ethnography at the Edge: Crime, Deviance and Field Research*, Northeastern University Press, Boston, 1998.

[36]Patricia A. Adler, *Wheeling and Dealing: An Ethnography of Upper-Level Drug Dealing and Smuggling Community*, 2nd ed., Columbia University Press, New York, 1993.

[37]Kenneth Tunnell, *Choosing Crime*, Nelson-Hall, Chicago, 1992.

[38]Richard T. Wright and Scott H. Decker, *Burglars on the Job: Street Life and Residential Break-Ins*, 1994, and *Armed Robbers in Action: Stick-ups and Street Culture*, 1997, both Northeastern University Press, Boston.

[39]Bruce A. Jacobs, *Dealing Crack: The Social World of Streetcorner Selling*, Northeastern University Press, Boston, 1999.

[40]Jacobs, *Robbing Drug Dealers: Violence Beyond the Law*, Hawthorne Aldine de Gruyter, 2000.

system.[41] Nevertheless, he argues that criminological research should focus more on the "lived meanings" of crime and criminal justice, and presents theoretical and methodological frameworks to support this argument.

THE MEANING OF CRIME TO THE LARGER SOCIETY: DEVIANCE AND SOCIAL REACTION

Legally speaking, societies "create" crime by passing laws.[42] For example, if criminal laws are passed concerning political contributions or truth in advertising or pollution control, then whole classes of crimes exist where none existed before. If laws against marijuana smoking or homosexuality or public drunkenness are repealed, then whole classes of crimes simply disappear. In every society there are people who kill their spouses if they find them having an affair. Some societies define this as murder, others find it regrettable but understandable, and still others consider it honorable behavior. Thus, whether a particular act is defined and processed as criminal depends on the meaning that act is given by agents of the larger society.

Social reaction theorists view the process of defining actions as crimes as part of the more general process in society of defining and suppressing deviance. Societies define deviance by declaring (either formally or informally) certain human behaviors to be "bad," and then by attempting to minimize or eliminate these behaviors. Because the specific behaviors chosen for this process vary from time to time and from place to place, social reaction theorists maintain that the process of defining and suppressing deviance is itself important to social solidarity, independent of the particular behaviors involved.[43] The process works by simplifying

---

[41]Jeff Ferrell, "Criminological *Verstehen:* Inside the Immediacy of Crime," *Justice Quarterly* 14(1): 1–23, 1997. On pp. 4–7, he describes his participant observation of non-gang graffiti artists, which culminated in his arrest and appearance in court. Wright and Decker (op. cit., 1994, p. 28), in contrast, obtained a prior agreement from the police not to interfere with their work.

[42]See Clayton A. Hartjen, *Crime and Criminalization,* Praeger, New York, 1974, pp. 1–39 for a discussion of this view. See also the brief discussion of "reactive" definitions, as compared to other conceptualizations of defiance, in Charles R. Tittle and Raymond Paternoster, *Social Deviance and Crime,* Roxbury, Los Angeles, 2000, ch. 1.

[43]Durkheim originally made this point in his discussion of "crime as normal." See ch. 6 above. For excellent development of this view in the context of specific crimes, see the various works of Philip Jenkins, including *Intimate Enemies: Moral Panics in Contemporary Great Britain,* Hawthorne Aldine de Gruyter, 1992; *Using Murder: The Social Construction of Serial Homicide,* Hawthrone, Aldine de Gruyter, 1994; and *Synthetic Panics: The Symbolic Politics of Designer Drugs,* New York University Press, New York, 1999.

the problems of good and evil for the average member of society.[44] Defining the deviants as evil and inferior implies that the remaining members of society are good and superior, thus strengthening their commitment to each other. Combating the evil of deviance consolidates individuals into a tightly knit group and makes it possible for them to use the most ignoble methods to control deviance without questioning these methods. Thus the average member of society is not faced with difficult moral choices, which might undermine a commitment to the path society has taken.

The behavior of the individual is the normal criterion used to select those who will be defined as deviants in a society, but the process works in exactly the same way when other criteria are used. "Heretical" beliefs have been used as a criterion for selecting deviants in a number of societies, including the early Puritan colonies on Massachusetts Bay.[45] Hitler defined deviance on the basis of race and attempted a "final solution" by exterminating the Jews. Sometimes deviant behaviors are imagined and attributed to particular individuals. For example, in Renaissance Europe approximately one-half million persons were executed as witches,[46] and in the great purge under Stalin, millions of loyal Soviet citizens were declared traitors or saboteurs and were executed or shipped to Siberia.[47] Szasz argues that these all represent various manifestations of a deep-seated need for people to ritually expel evil from their communities, and that in primitive communities this took the form of the ritual destruction of a scapegoat.[48]

Campaigns to define and suppress deviance are always launched in the name of benefiting the whole society, but they are often promoted and supported primarily by those who benefit directly. For example, Chambliss's analysis of the law of vagrancy indicates that it was originally created in England shortly after the Black Death had wiped out approximately 50 percent of the population.[49] The result was a serious la-

---

[44]This description is taken from the description of the benefits of anti-Semitism in J.-P. Sartre, *Anti-Semite and Jew*, Schocken, New York, 1965, as described by Thomas S. Szasz, *The Manufacture of Madness*, Harper & Row, New York, 1970, pp. 270–27.

[45]Kai Erikson, "On the Sociology of Deviance," in *Wayward Puritans*, John Wiley, New York, 1966, pp. 3–19.

[46]Elliott P. Currie, "Crimes Without Criminals: Witchcraft and Its Control in Renaissance Europe," *Law and Society Review* 3(1): 7–32 (Aug. 1968).

[47]Walter D. Connor, "The Manufacture of Deviance: The Case of the Soviet Purge, 1936–1938," *American Sociological Review* 37: 403–13 (Aug. 1972).

[48]Szasz, *The Manufacture of Madness*, op. cit., pp. 260–75.

[49]William J. Chambliss, "A Sociological Analysis of the Law of Vagrancy," *Social Problems* 12(1): 66–77 (fall 1964).

bor shortage and a great increase in wages. The vagrancy statute made it a crime to give alms to any person who was unemployed while being of sound mind and body, and required that any such person serve any landowner who needed him at the wage level paid before the Black Death. Up to this time beggars had been common and tolerated in England, and there is little doubt that they were defined as criminals to provide a source of cheap labor for landowners.

Sometimes the benefits of a campaign against deviance are primarily the acquisition of political or bureaucratic power. An example can be found in the campaign to define narcotics users as criminals.[50] In the nineteenth century narcotics were widely available in the form of patent medicines, and addiction was viewed more or less as alcoholism is today—addicts were tolerated and pitied, but not considered criminals. In an attempt to control narcotics distribution, Congress passed the Harrison Narcotics Act in 1914, which required that official records be kept on all sales and distribution of narcotics, and that a nominal tax of one cent per ounce be paid. There is no indication in the law of any legislative intent to restrict or deny addicts access to legal drugs, and the law was passed with little publicity. A narcotics bureau was set up in the Internal Revenue Division of the Treasury Department to enforce the registration procedures and collect the tax. From this tiny beginning the narcotics control bureaucracy promoted its own growth and expansion by launching an extensive public relations campaign against narcotics use and by sponsoring a series of court cases that resulted in the reinterpretation of the Harrison Act so that all narcotics use was declared illegal. As a result of these efforts "The Narcotics Division succeeded in creating a very large criminal class for itself to police . . . instead of the very small one Congress . . . intended."[51]

Sometimes the benefits of a campaign against deviance are not so much economic as symbolic. Gusfield has analyzed the temperance movement and the resulting enactment of Prohibition as a "symbolic crusade" to reassert the traditional values of rural, middle-class Protestants over the increasing influence of urban, lower-class Catholics in national life.[52] This law created a huge class of criminals by forbidding the

---

[50]Donald T. Dickson, "Bureaucracy and Mortality: An Organizational Perspective on a Moral Crusade," *Social Problems* 16(2): 143–56 (fall 1968). For other examples, see Isadore Silver, ed., *The Crime Control Establishment*, Prentice Hall, Englewood Cliffs, NJ, 1974.

[51]Rufus King, "The Narcotics Bureau and the Harrison Act: Jailing the Healers and the Sick," *Yale Law Journal* 62: 736–49 (1953), p. 738, quoted in Dickson, op. cit., p. 151.

[52]Joseph Gusfield, *Symbolic Crusade*, University of Illinois Press, Urbana, 1963. For a somewhat comparable analysis of the recent movement to enact hate crimes legislation, see James B. Jacobs and Kimberly Potter, *Hate Crimes: Criminal Law and Identity Politics*, Oxford, New York, 1998.

manufacture, sale, or transportation of alcoholic beverages, and resulted in the establishment of organized crime syndicates to meet the demand for illegal alcohol. The volume of crime created by this act was so great that it ultimately had to be repealed.

Since campaigns against deviance usually result in the redistribution of benefits from some groups (the deviants) to others (the promoters and supporters of the campaigns), it seems likely that the social coalescence produced depends at least partially on the coalescence of power relationships between groups in the society. One group will succeed in defining the other as deviant only if it is able to generate sufficient power to overcome the support the other group has. This group then obtains the support of the official social control agencies, which normally has the effect of solidifying their power base and institutionalizing their dominance over the other group.

Liazos points out that deviance theorists frequently state that those who define others as deviants must be more powerful than the deviants themselves.[53]

But this insight is not developed. In none of the 16 [textbooks in the field of deviance] is there an extensive discussion of how power operates in the designation of deviance. Instead of a study of power, of its concrete uses in modern, corporate America, we are offered rather fascinating explorations into the identities and subcultures of "deviants," and misplaced emphasis on the middle-level agents of social control.

STATE POWER AND THE MEANING OF CRIME: CONTROLOLOGY

The theories of deviance and social reaction described in the last section began with explaining deviance itself, but increasingly focused on explaining the social reaction to the deviance and the power of the react-

---

For a very different (and more conventional) analysis, see Valerie Jenness and Kendall Broad, *Hate Crimes: New Social Movements and the Politics of Violence*, Aldine de Gruyter, New York, 1997. See also Jenness, "Social Movement Growth, Domain Expansion, and Framing Processes," *Social Problems* 42(1): 145–70 (1995).

[53]Alexander Liazos, "The Poverty of the Sociology of Deviance: Nuts, Sluts and 'Preverts,'" *Social Problems* 20(1): 103–20 (summer 1972), especially p. 115. Since Liazos made this comment, several books have been published in the area of deviance that focus on power relations. See Pat Lauderdale, ed., *A Political Analysis of Deviance*, University of Minnesota Press, Minneapolis, 1980; and Edwin M. Schur, *The Politics of Deviance: Stigma Contests and the Uses of Power*, Prentice Hall, Englewood Cliffs, NJ, 1980. See also Ruth-Ellen Grimes and Austin Turk, "Labeling in Context: Conflict, Power and Self-Definition," in Marvin D. Krohn and Ronald L. Akers, eds., *Crime, Law, and Sanctions*, Sage, Beverly Hills, CA, 1978, pp. 39–58; and the readings in H. Laurence Ross, ed., *Law and Deviance*, Sage, Beverly Hills, CA, 1981.

ing groups to make the deviant definitions stick. One group of theorists took this trend all the way to its logical end point, so that they no longer attempted to explain deviance at all and focused all their attention on the groups who defined other people as deviant. They evolved the view that criminal justice agencies are part of a much broader range of social control mechanisms, including welfare, mental health, education, and the mass media, all of which are used by the state for the purposes of controlling "problem" populations. In 1979, Ditton introduced the term "controlology" to refer to this group of theories.[54]

The foundation of this group of theories was built by Michel Foucault, a French philosopher.[55] In his work *Madness and Civilization*,[56] Foucault argued that seemingly more humane mental institutions had replaced the apparently more coercive prisons in modern societies as the central instrument of state control. This movement was packaged and sold by the state as a more humane, enlightened, reasonable response to deviance, but Foucault argued it was actually a way to expand the scope of state control and the subtlety with which that control could be operated.

In his later book *Discipline and Punish*,[57] Foucault expanded his argument by focusing on the earlier development of prisons in the 1700s. Foucault argued that prisons arose at that time to replace a vast system of torture and execution, in which state power was manifested primarily through public spectacles in which havoc was wreaked on the body of the condemned person. That system of torture and execution did not include extensive safeguards, such as we have today, to ensure that these punishments were not carried out on innocent people. The fundamental idea, according to Foucault, was not specifically to punish or deter criminals, but to manifest state power. If it turned out that the person was innocent, it only demonstrated that state power was absolute and that no one was safe from it.

But for a variety of reasons, in the 1700s, this type of exhibition of state power began to cause problems. In particular, instead of making the crowds docile and afraid, these public spectacles became the occasion for riots against the arbitrary injustice of the state. Therefore, the

---

[54]Jason Ditton, *Controlology: Beyond the New Criminology,* Macmillan, London, 1979.

[55]These comments are based on Erich Goode, *Deviant Behavior* 4th ed., Prentice Hall, Englewood Cliffs, NJ, 1994, pp. 132–38.

[56]Michel Foucault, *Madness and Civilization: A History of Insanity in the Age of Reason,* Mentor, New York, 1967.

[57]Michel Foucault, *Discipline and Punish,* Vintage, New York, 1979.

state transformed the way it exerted its control over the people. Instead of public spectacles, the infliction of punishments was moved behind high walls, hidden from public view. Instead of being directed at the body of the offender through physical torture and execution, state control was redefined as "rehabilitation" and directed at the souls and minds of offenders.

This constituted a shift in the direction of the looking. Under the old system of torture and execution, the state put on a spectacle with the body of the accused, at which the crowd looked. The crowd then went away with a knowledge of the massive, overwhelming power of the state. Under the new system of imprisonment, the state prevented the crowd from seeing anything with its high walls. At the same time, the state looked into the soul of the prisoner, discovered the evil and sickness that was lurking there, and rooted it out.

Garland later criticized Foucault's analysis for having a great many historical inaccuracies,[58] but the themes that Foucault identified persisted nevertheless in a broad range of works, including Garland's. Goode identified these themes as follows.[59] First, social control itself, and state control in particular, is an important topic for scientific theory and research. It is not sufficient to say, as many people do, that the state's efforts to control deviants are appropriate and functional and natural and should be viewed as a given in every society. Second, the state attempts to maintain its legitimacy by packaging its control efforts so that they appear to be reasonable, humane, and necessary. But always hidden within this "velvet glove" is an iron fist whose ultimate goal is to control troublesome populations. In particular, there are always specific groups who pursue their own economic and political agendas in the context of these social control functions, usually at the expense of other, less powerful groups. Third, the broad range of social control activities all ultimately are directed and manipulated by the state, even when some aspects of them, such as the mass media, are technically outside state jurisdiction. Fourth, these various state control mechanisms therefore have a general unity, despite their appearance of diversity. That is, ultimately all the various state control mechanisms mentioned above work in a coherent way to achieve a widespread control over the entire society.

In some ways, contrologists have more in common with the Marxist

---

[58]David Garland, *Punishment and Welfare: A History of Penal Strategies,* Gower, Aldershott, England, 1985.

[59]Goode, op. cit., pp. 134–36. See also David Garland, "'Governmentability' and the Problem of Crime," *Theoretical Criminology* 1(2): 173–214 (1997).

criminologists who will be discussed in Chapter 14. On the other hand, beginning with Foucault, these theorists have focused very strongly on the meaning that criminals and deviants have for the dominant groups who exert state control over them, and the meaning of the diverse actions that these dominant groups take to control these troublesome people. This leads them to focus heavily on the thinking and words of the dominant groups—what controlologists call the "universe of discourse."[60] And in many ways, their thinking originated in the social reaction argument that those who define others as deviant must have more power than the deviants themselves, and that they may not be doing this for the benefit of society generally but rather for the benefit of themselves personally. In that sense, these theorists more appropriately are placed in this chapter rather than in the chapter on critical criminology.

IMPLICATIONS AND CONCLUSIONS

Theories that focus on the meaning of crime seem inevitably to end up discussing the issue of power. Tittle's comment on Katz's work suggests that issues of power are embedded in this type of explanation, although they are not explicitly brought out. The controlologists described in the previous section most directly focus on the relative power of deviants and the groups who define them as such. On the other hand, they do so in the context of a fairly Marxist orientation that focuses strongly on the state and its subservience to economically powerful groups.

A more general approach to the role of power in the definition of crime would simply argue that the general concept of social reaction combines and confuses two separate phenomena: the official reaction of the social control agencies and the personal reaction of particular individuals and groups in society. Individuals and groups construct behavioral norms based on their own moral values and personal self-interests, and they react to specific behaviors as deviant when those behaviors violate their norms. These individuals and groups then compete among themselves in an attempt to have their norms enforced by the official social control agencies. Their success in this competition depends directly on the degree of power they possess and are willing to use. Official policies are the result of the conflict and compromise process among these groups. To the extent that the group is successful in having its norms enforced by the social control agencies, it arrogates to itself the right to

---

[60]Goode, p. 134.

speak in the name of the entire society. But the mere fact that one group has sufficient power to define another group as deviant does not imply that there is any broad consensus on the matter (there may or may not be) and does not preclude the possibility that the other group may be able to reverse the power distribution in the future. This is the approach taken in conflict criminology, which is the subject of the next chapter.

CHAPTER THIRTEEN

Conflict Criminology

Throughout the long history of thinking about human societies, social theorists have repeatedly presented two starkly contrasting views.[1] Consensus theorists place *a consensus of values* at the very center of human societies—i.e., shared beliefs about what is good, right, just, important, or at least excusable. Conflict theorists, in contrast, place *conflicts of interests* at the very center of human societies—i.e., competitions over money, status, and power. These contrasting views have very different implications for the role of the organized state, and therefore for the nature of crime and functions of criminal justice.

Consensus theorists recognize that there inevitably will be at least some value conflicts among different individuals and groups in every human society. In addition, there inevitably will be conflicts of interest, as individuals and groups seek their own benefits without regard to what is good or right or just or appropriate or even excusable. But consensus theorists argue that the role of the organized state is to mediate these conflicts and to represent the common values and common interests of the society at large. Values ultimately determine interests, since it is in everyone's interests to have societies that are governed in accordance with goodness and righteousness and justice.

Conflict theorists, on the other hand, argue that interests ultimately determine values. Beliefs about goodness and righteousness and justice tend to be thin films that conceal personal gains and losses, personal

---

[1] A history of the consensus-conflict debate, going back to Plato and Aristotle, can be found in Thomas J. Bernard, *The Consensus-Conflict Debate: Form and Content in Social Theories,* Columbia University Press, New York, 1983.

costs and benefits. Even sincere people tend to believe that, if something benefits them personally, then it probably is good and right and just, and if something harms them personally, then it probably is bad and wrong and unjust. In the real world, conflict theorists argue that the organized state does not represent common interests, but instead represents the interests of those with sufficient power to control its operation. As a result, more powerful people are legally more free to pursue self-interests, while less powerful people who pursue self-interests are more likely to be officially defined and processed as criminal. The result is an inverse relation between power and official crime rates: The more power that people have, the less likely they are to be arrested, convicted, imprisoned, and executed, regardless of their behavior. And vice versa.

EARLY CONFLICT THEORIES: SELLIN AND VOLD

In 1938, Thorsten Sellin presented a criminology theory focused on the conflict of "conduct norms."[2] Conduct norms are cultural rules that require certain types of people to act in certain ways in certain circumstances. In simple, homogeneous societies, many of these conduct norms are enacted into law and actually represent a consensus in the society. But in more complex societies, there will be overlap and contradiction between the conduct norms of different cultural groups. Sellin defined "primary cultural conflicts" as those occurring between two different cultures.[3] These conflicts could occur at border areas between two divergent cultures; or, in the case of colonization, when the laws of one culture are extended into the territory of another; or, in the case of migration, when members of one cultural group move into the territory of another. "Secondary cultural conflicts" occur when a single culture evolves into several different subcultures, each having its own conduct norms. In each of these cases law would not represent a consensus of the various members of the society, but would reflect the conduct norms of the dominant culture.

Twenty years after Sellin wrote, George B. Vold presented a group conflict theory in the original edition of the present book.[4] Vold's theory was based on a "social process" view of society as a collection of groups held together in a dynamic equilibrium of opposing group interests and efforts. In Vold's theory, groups in society more or less continuously

---

[2]Thorsten Sellin, *Culture Conflict and Crime,* Social Science Research Council, New York, 1938, pp. 32–33.

[3]Ibid., pp. 63, 104, 105.

[4]George B. Vold, *Theoretical Criminology,* Oxford University Press, New York, 1958, pp. 203–19.

struggle to maintain, or to improve, their place in an ongoing interaction and competition with other groups. These social interaction processes grind their way through varying kinds of uneasy adjustment to a more or less stable equilibrium of balanced forces, called social order or social organization. Social order therefore does not reflect a consensus among the groups, but reflects instead the uneasy adjustment, one to another, of the many groups of varying strengths and different interests. Conflict is therefore one of the principal and essential social processes in the functioning of society.

This social process view of human societies is associated with a view of human nature which holds that people are fundamentally group-involved beings whose lives are both a part of and a product of their group associations. Group are formed when people have common interests and common needs that can best be furthered through collective action. New groups are continuously formed as new interests arise, and existing groups weaken and disappear when they no longer have a purpose to serve. Groups become effective action units through the direction and coordination of the activities of their members, and they come into conflict with one another as the interests and purposes they serve tend to overlap, encroach on one another, and become competitive. Conflict between groups tends to develop and intensify the loyalty of group members to their respective groups.

The conflicts among organized groups are especially visible in legislative politics, which is largely a matter of finding practical compromises between opposing interests. But the conflicts themselves exist in the community and in the society long before they become visible in legislative politics. As groups in the society line up against one another, each seeks the assistance of the organized state to help them defend their rights and protect their interests against the opposing groups. This general situation of group conflict gives rise to the familiar cry "There ought to be a law!"—essentially the demand by one of the conflicting groups that the power of the organized state be used to support them in their conflict with the other groups. Naturally, the other groups, against whom the proposed law is directed, oppose its passage. Whichever group interest can marshal the greatest number of votes in the legislative process will determine whether or not there will be a new law to promote the interests of the one group and to hamper and curb the interests of the other groups.

Once the new law has been passed, those who opposed the law in the legislature are more likely to violate the law, since it defends interests and purposes that are in conflict with their own. Those who promoted the law, in contrast, are more likely to obey it and to demand that the criminal justice agencies enforce it against violators, since the law defends interests and purposes they hold dear. In other words, those who produce legislative majorities win control of the criminal justice power of the state and decide the policies that determine who is likely to be officially defined and processed as criminals.

Thus the whole process of lawmaking, lawbreaking, and law enforcement directly reflects deep-seated and fundamental conflicts between group interests and the more general struggles among groups for control of the police power of the state. To that extent, Vold described criminal behavior as the behavior of "minority power groups"—that is, groups that do not have sufficient power to promote and defend their own interests and purposes in the legislative process.

Pointing to the fundamental conditions of life in organized political society, Vold's group conflict theory suggested that a considerable amount of crime is intimately related to the conflicts of groups. For such situations, the criminal behavior of the individual is best viewed in the context of the course of action required for the group to maintain its position in the struggle with other groups. A sociology of conflict is therefore the basis for understanding and explaining this kind of criminal behavior.[5] On the other hand, Vold argued that group conflict theory was strictly limited to those kinds of situations in which the individual criminal acts flow from the collision of groups whose members are loyally upholding the in-group position. Such a theory does not explain many kinds of impulsive and irrational criminal acts that are quite unrelated to any battle between different interest groups in organized society.

CONFLICT THEORIES IN A TIME OF CONFLICT: TURK, QUINNEY, AND CHAMBLISS AND SEIDMAN

Ten years after Vold wrote his group conflict theory, the United States was embroiled in enormous social and political turmoil surrounding the civil rights movement and the Vietnam War. The criminal law and the criminal justice system supported some groups against others in these political conflicts, and many people came to believe Vold's argument that crime is the behavior of "minority power groups." This perception

---

[5]Vold relied primarily on Simmel's sociology of conflict. See *The Sociology of Georg Simmel*, translated and with an introduction by Kurt H. Wolff, The Free Press, Glencoe, IL, 1950; also Simmel's *Conflict* (trans. by Kurt H. Wolff) and *The Web of Group Affiliations* (trans. by Reinhard Bendix), The Free Press, Glencoe, IL, 1955. Simmel's work is analyzed in Lewis A. Coser, *The Functions of Social Conflict*, The Free Press, Glencoe, IL, 1956. See also Bernard, op. cit., pp. 111–42.

suddenly brought conflict theory to the forefront of criminology, and three important conflict theories were published in three successive years.

In 1969, Austin Turk proposed a "theory of criminalization" that attempted to describe "the conditions under which . . . differences between authorities and subjects will probably result in conflict, (and) the conditions under which criminalization will probably occur in the course of conflict. . . ."[6] Turk argued that the organization and sophistication of both authorities and subjects affect the likelihood of conflict between them.[7] Authorities are presumed to be organized, since organization is a prerequisite for achieving and retaining power. Conflict is more likely when subjects are organized, since group support makes an individual less willing to back down. Turk defines "sophistication" as "knowledge of patterns in the behavior of others which is used in attempts to manipulate them." More sophisticated subjects will be able to achieve their goals without precipitating a conflict with the superior powers of the state, and less sophisticated authorities will have to rely more strongly on overt coercion to achieve their goals rather than more subtle, alternative tactics.

Given these conditions that affect the likelihood of conflict between authorities and subjects, Turk discusses the conditions under which conflict is more likely to result in the criminalization of the subjects. The primary factor, Turk argues, will be the meaning that the prohibited act or attribute has for those who enforce the law (i.e., the police, prosecutors, and judges).[8] To the extent that these officials find the prohibited act or attribute very offensive, it is likely that there will be high arrest rates, high conviction rates, and severe sentences. The second factor will be the relative power of the enforcers and resisters.[9] In general, criminalization will be greatest when the enforcers have great power and the resisters are virtually powerless. The third factor is what Turk calls the "realism of the conflict moves," and it relates to how likely an action taken by the subjects or authorities may improve the potential for their ultimate success. Turk states that unrealistic conflict moves by either party will tend to increase criminalization, which is a measure of the overt conflict between the two groups.

---

[6]Austin Turk *Criminality and Legal Order,* Rand McNally, Chicago, 1969, p. 53.

[7]Ibid., pp. 58–61.

[8]Ibid., pp. 65–67.

[9]Ibid., pp. 67–70.

In 1970, Richard Quinney published his theory of "the social reality of crime."[10] Relying on Vold's group conflict theory, Quinney argued that the legislative process of defining criminal laws and the criminal justice process of enforcing criminal laws occur in a political context in which individuals and groups pursue their own self-interests. But where Vold focused on conflicts among organized interest groups, Quinney discussed conflicts among "segments" of society. Segments are said to be people who share the same values, norms, and ideological orientations, but who may or may not be organized in defense of those commonalities.[11] Some segments, such as business and labor, have been organized into interest groups for many years, but other segments, such as women, poor people, and homosexuals, have organized themselves only recently. There are also segments of society that have only minimal organization, such as young people, and segments that have virtually no organization at all, such as prisoners and the mentally ill. Because of this difference, Quinney used conflict theory to explain all crime instead of merely some of it. Vold specifically excluded "impulsive, irrational acts of a criminal nature that are quite unrelated to any battle between different interest groups in organized society."[12] Quinney, on the other hand, would hold that irrational and impulsive people represent a segment of society with common values, norms, and ideological orientations, even if this segment is not organized into any interest group.

Relying on Sutherland's differential association theory, Quinney argued that different segments of society have different normative systems and different patterns of behaviors, all of which are learned in their own social and cultural settings. The probability that individuals will violate the criminal law depends, to a large extent, on how much power and influence their segments have in enacting and enforcing the criminal laws. In more powerful segments of society, people are able to act according to their own normative standards and behavioral patterns without violating the law. But when people in less powerful segments do the same thing, their actions are legally defined and officially processed as criminal.

Finally, Quinney argued that conceptions of crime are created and communicated as part of the political process of promoting particular

---

[10]Richard Quinney, *The Social Reality of Crime*, Little, Brown, Boston, 1970. Quinney summarizes his theory in six propositions on pp. 15–23.

[11]Ibid., p. 38.

[12]Vold, op. cit., p. 219.

sets of values and interests.[13] Political agendas are readily apparent when, for example, consumer and ecology groups argue that the real criminals are corporate executives, or when community organizers in inner-city neighborhoods argue that the real criminals are the absentee landlords and greedy storeowners. But these conceptions of crime often are not taken very seriously because the groups promoting them do not have much political power. Conceptions of crime promoted by individuals and groups with a great deal of power, however, often are widely accepted as legitimate by other people in the society. "The social reality of crime," according to Quinney, is that powerful individuals and groups promote particular conceptions of crime in order to legitimize their authority and allow them to carry out policies in the name of the common good that really promote their own self-interests.

In 1971, Chambliss and Seidman published a conflict analysis of the functioning of the criminal justice system entitled *Law, Order, and Power*[14] These authors note that consensus and conflict theories provide radically different versions of how the criminal justice system actually functions. Therefore they examined the day-to-day functioning of that system in order to determine which of the two theories is correct. Specifically, they sought to discover whether the power of the state (as embodied in the criminal justice system) is "a value-neutral framework within which conflict can be peacefully resolved," or whether, as conflict theory would have it, "the power of the State is itself the principal prize in the perpetual conflict that is society."[15]

The criminal justice process begins with the legislative activity of lawmaking. Consensus theory describes this process as "a deliberative assembly of one nation, with one interest, that of the whole, where, not local purposes, nor local prejudices, ought to guide, but the general good, resulting from the general reason of the whole."[16] As Vold and Quinney

---

[13]This argument relies particularly on Peter L. Berger and Thomas Luckmann, *The Social Construction of Reality,* Doubleday, Garden City, NY, 1966.

[14]William J. Chambliss and Robert B. Seidman, *Law, Order, and Power,* Addison-Wesley, Reading, Mass., 1971. Other conflict analyses of criminal justice published about the same time include Stuart L. Hills, *Crime, Power, and Morality: The Criminal Law Process in the United States,* Chandler, New York, 1971; Richard Quinney, *Critique of Legal Order,* Little, Brown, Boston, 1973; Erik Olin Wright, *The Politics of Punishment,* Harper & Row, New York, 1973; Clayton A. Hartjen, *Crime and Criminalization,* Praeger, New York, 1974; Barry Krisberg, *Crime and Privilege,* Prentice-Hall, Englewood Cliffs, NJ, 1975; and Harold E. Pepinsky, *Crime and Conflict,* Academic Press, New York, 1976.

[15]Chambliss and Seidman, p. 4.

[16]Edmund Burke, *Works,* H. J. Bohn, London, 1893, p. 447; quoted in Chambliss and Seidman, op. cit., p. 63.

had done earlier, the authors argue that "every detailed study of the emergence of legal norms has consistently shown the immense importance of interest-group activity, *not 'the public interest,'* as the critical variable in determining the content of legislation."[17] Chambliss and Seidman maintain that "the higher a group's political and economic position, the greater is the probability that its views will be reflected in the laws."[18]

Chambliss and Seidman then turn to appellate court decisions that have the effect of creating law. These are decisions in "trouble cases" where no law clearly applies or where more than one law seems to apply. Appellate courts are said to be "the institution *par excellence* for which society most carefully cherishes the idea of value-neutrality."[19] Originally judges referred to "natural law" to support their decisions in trouble cases, but it later became apparent that the natural law really embodied their own personal values.[20] Later justifications were phrased in terms of preexisting laws and the principles embodied in those laws,[21] but dissenting opinions in the same cases have also been justified in terms of preexisting laws and principles. Still later, legal scholars concluded that appellate court decisions inevitably must be based on value judgments about what is "best" for society.[22] Roscoe Pound attempted to state the common values that would underlie judicial decisions, but his formulation did not meet with widespread acceptance and was criticized for primarily reflecting his own personal values.[23] Therefore Chambliss and Seidman conclude that, in the last analysis, judges must rely on their personal values when they make decisions in trouble cases.[24]

Chambliss and Seidman give a number of reasons why the personal values of appellate judges will be primarily oriented to the wealthy rather than the poor.[25] As law students, future appellate judges largely are trained by the "casebook" method which focuses on issues raised in earlier court cases. Those issues predominantly relate to the needs and concerns of the wealthy. As young lawyers, future appellate judges tend to focus on cases involving the wealthy, since those clients are able to

[17]Ibid., p. 73.
[18]Ibid., pp. 473–74.
[19]Ibid., p. 75.
[20]Ibid., pp. 125–28.
[21]Ibid., pp. 128–31.
[22]Ibid., pp. 131–45.
[23]Ibid., pp. 141–42.
[24]Ibid., p. 151.
[25]Ibid., pp. 95–115.

pay high legal fees. As trial judges, future appellate judges have achieved a socially prominent position and can be expected to socialize with the wealthy and powerful and become attuned to their needs. Promotion of trial judges to the appellate level is inevitably tied in one way or another to the political process, so that trial judges who deal appropriately with the politically powerful are more likely to be promoted. Thus there are many subtle pressures encouraging appellate judges to carefully consider issues related to powerful and wealthy people. At the same time, there are organizational pressures to restrict the amount of litigation before the court to prevent overloading the docket. These pressures, together with the fact that appellate cases depend in part on the ability of the defendant to pay for the cost of the litigation, mean that the majority of case law concerns issues relating only to the wealthy and powerful. Chambliss and Seidman conclude that appellate court decisions overwhelmingly reflect the needs and desires of the wealthy and powerful.

Finally, Chambliss and Seidman examine the day-to-day functioning of criminal justice agencies to see if their functions reflect the arguments of consensus or conflict theories. Their analysis focuses on the bureaucratic nature of those organizations and their connections to the political structure.[26] Law enforcement agencies, like all normally functioning bureaucracies, tend to engage in goal-substituting behavior. That is, in an agency's day-to-day functioning, "the official goals and norms of the organization" tend to be replaced by policies and activities that "maximize rewards and minimize the strains on the organization." This goal substitution is more extensive in criminal justice agencies than in other bureaucracies because criminal justice agents have much greater discretion and because there are fewer official or unofficial penalties for engaging in goal-switching behavior. Chambliss and Seidman then argue that, because law enforcement agencies depend on political organizations for their resources, they can maximize their rewards and minimize their strains if they process those who are politically weak and refrain from processing those who are politically powerful. They conclude that "it may be expected that the law-enforcement agencies will process a disproportionately high number of the politically weak and powerless, while ignoring the violations of those with power."

Based on their reviews of the legislative process, of appellate court decisions, and of the functioning of law enforcement agencies, Chambliss and Seidman conclude that both in structure and in function the law

---

[26]The theory is summarized in six points on ibid., p. 269.

operates in the interests of power groups. The public interest is represented only to the extent that it coincides with the interests of those power groups.[27]

BLACK'S THEORY OF THE BEHAVIOR OF LAW

Only five years later, in 1976, Donald Black published a sociological theory entitled *The Behavior of Law*, in which he attempts to explain variations in the quantity and style of law.[28] The theory shares some similarities with, although it is much broader than, the conflict theories described above. Black argues that the quantity of law (i.e., governmental social control) varies in time and place—i.e., there is more law at some times and places and less law at other times and places. Reporting a crime, making an arrest, deciding to prosecute, deciding to convict, sentencing someone to prison, and sentencing someone to death all represent more law, while not taking these actions represents less law. Black also argues that law varies in its style. Black mostly discusses penal law, in which law is enforced by a group against an offender. But law can also be compensatory, in which victims demand payment in reparation for harm done. Law can be therapeutic, in which law acts on behalf of a deviant. Finally, law can be conciliatory, in which various parties work together to resolve imbalances.[29]

Black explores five social dimensions of social life—stratification, morphology, culture, organization, and social control. Stratification is the "vertical distance between the people of a social setting" and is best measured by the difference in average wealth between each person or groups and every other person or group, or by the difference between the lowest and highest levels of wealth.[30] Morphology is the "horizontal aspect of social life, the distribution of people in relation to one another, including their division of labor, networks of interaction, intimacy, and integration."[31] Culture is the "symbolic aspect of life, including expressions of what is true, good, and beautiful. . . Examples are science, technology, religion, magic, and folklore. . . Culture includes aesthetic life of all sorts, the fine arts and the popular, such as poetry and painting, clothing . . . architecture, and even the culinary arts."[32] Organization is the

---

[27]Ibid., p. 503.

[28]Donald Black, *The Behavior of Law*, Academic Press, New York, 1976, pp. 3–4.

[29]Ibid, pp. 4–5.

[30]Ibid., p. 13.

[31]Ibid., p. 37.

[32]Ibid., p. 61.

"corporate aspect of social life, the capacity for collective action."[33] Finally, social control "is the normative aspect of social life. It defines responds to deviant behavior, specifying what ought to be . . . Law is social control . . . but so are etiquette, custom, ethics, bureaucracy, and the treatment of mental illness."[34]

Within each dimension Black forms hypotheses about law. In the case of stratification, Black argues that the higher a person is in on the ladder of stratification, the more the person is able to invoke law on his or her behalf. In addition, the further apart two people are in terms of stratification, the more law the higher ranked person can exercise over the other. For example, if a corporate executive claims to be victimized by a street person, more law will be exercised against the street person than if the executive claims to be victimized by another corporate executive or if the street person claims to be victimized by the corporate executive. Black's arguments about stratification are what make his theory comparable to the other conflict theories described above.

However, Black goes on to discuss variations in the quantity and style of law that are related to four other societal characteristics. Morphology concerns the relational distance between people, or the degree to which they participate in each other's lives. Black argues that the relationship between law and relational distance is curvilinear: "Law is inactive among intimates, increasing as the distance between people increases but decreasing as this reaches the point at which people live in entirely separate worlds."[35] Hermits rarely need or use law since they live in an entirely separate world, and married couples do not invoke law against each other unless their intimacy with each other breaks down. Law is greater, says Black, when the relational distance is somewhere between intimacy and isolation.

One of Black's hypotheses concerning culture is that law is greater in a direction toward less culture than toward more culture, and furthermore, that the amount of cultural distance linearly affects the amount of law. Using education as a measure of culture, for example, if an offender is less educated than the victim, more law will be invoked to address the victimization, and the most law of all will be used when the difference in education between the offender and the victim is greatest.[36] On the other hand, if the offender is more educated than the victim, less law

---

[33]Ibid., p. 85.

[34]Ibid., p. 105.

[35]Ibid., p. 41.

[36]Ibid., pp. 65–66.

will be used to address the victimization, and the least law of all will be used when the difference in education between the offender and victim is greatest.

Similarly, Black argues that law varies directly with organization. If offenders are more organized than their victims (e.g., if the offender is a corporation and the victim is an individual), less law will be used to address the victimization. In addition, the most law will be used when the organizational distance between the offenders and victims is the greatest. But if the offenders are less organized than the victims (e g , the offender is an individual and the victim is a corporation), the reverse is true: More law will be used to address the victimization, and the most law will be used when the organizational distance between the victims and offenders is greatest. Black uses these propositions to explain relatively light sanctions directed toward white-collar offenders.

Finally, Black argues that law will be greater where other forms of social control are weaker. All in all, across the five social dimensions, Black forms over twenty hypotheses about how law varies in quantity and style. His evidence for each is primarily anecdotal, including anthropological examples from a variety of sources, but he does not perform any systematic test of the hypotheses.

In his preface to *The Behavior of Law*, Black states: "This book does not judge the variation of law, nor does it recommend policy of any kind. Rather, it is merely an effort to understand law as a natural phenomenon. . . ."[37] But in a later book on the subject, *Sociological Justice*,[38] Black does judge variations in the quantity and style of law as being "wrong" in some sense. He therefore recommends three types of policy reforms to reduce social variation in law: legal cooperatives, desocialization of law, and starvation of law. In the first reform, people would join subsidized legal cooperatives to reduce corporate advantages in the legal system. Each co-op would consist of a variety of people so that relations among the co-ops themselves would be relatively equal. Informal social control might come about within the co-ops, as those who cause the group expensive legal costs may be expelled. Of course, this could also work to perpetuate social variations in law if groups are quick to expel undesirable individuals. Black's second reform would make social information about offenders unavailable to criminal justice system actors handling cases. For example, jurors would not be allowed to actually see

---

[37]Ibid., p. x.
[38]Donald Black, *Sociological Justice*, Oxford University Press, New York, 1989.

offenders, witnesses, or victims. All testimony would be done electronically, so that evidence would be stripped of social characteristics such as dialect or education. Black's third proposal is to "starve" the law. Basically, he argues that if the law has only the barest minimum in resources, then people will be forced to rely on other mechanisms for dealing with conflicts, such as conflict resolution. While there are serious flaws with each of these proposals, the book's purpose is noble: to eliminate social factors from the behavior of law.[39]

An initial attempt to test Black's theory raised conceptual questions about the "seriousness" of an offense. Gottfredson and Hindelang found that variation in Black's social dimensions did not significantly predict variation in the quantity of law, which instead was predicted primarily by the seriousness of the offense.[40] Black responded that describing a crime as "serious" is itself influenced by the five social dimensions and that, in practice, the term "serious" means that the action receives a large quantity of law.[41] Gottfredson and Hindelang responded that if this is true, Black's theory cannot be tested unambiguously.[42] The confusion around how to deal with seriousness has hampered subsequent attempts to test Black's theory, and to date, there remains no comprehensive, accepted test.[43]

On the other hand, some recent research looks at relationships between actors, rather than looking at absolute social status without regard to relative position. For example, one study of court disposition patterns uses Hagan's structural criminology as a theoretical point of departure, and employs some of Black's propositions, in attempting to show how the relationship between victim and offender may influence criminal justice reaction to behavior. Jamieson and Blowers found a greater probability of dismissal of cases with less organized victims, especially when the suspected offenders were more organized.[44] This finding is consis-

---

[39]See Thomas J. Bernard, "Review Essay: Donald Black's *Sociological Justice*," *The Critical Criminologist* 3(2): 7–8, 13–14 (Summer 1991).

[40]Michael Gottfredson and Michael Hindelang, "A Study of the Behavior of Law and Theory and Research in the Sociology of Law," *American Sociological Review* 44: 3–18 (1979).

[41]Black, "Common Sense in the Sociology of Law," *American Sociological Review* 44: 18–27 (1979).

[42]Gottfredson and Hindelang, *American Sociological Review* 44: 27–37 (1979).

[43]But see Larry Hembroff, "Testing Black's Theory of Law," *American Journal of Sociology* 93: 322–47 (1987); and Gloria Lessan and Joseph Sheley, "Does Law Behave?," *Social Forces* 70: 655–78 (1992). For a discussion of this issue, see Thomas J. Bernard, "The Black Hole—Sources of Confusion for Criminologists in Black's Theory," *Social Pathology* 1(3): 218–27 (Fall 1995).

[44]Katherine Jamieson and Anita Neuberger Blowers, "A Structural Examination of Misdemeanor Court Disposition Patterns," *Criminology* 31(2): 243–62 (1993).

240 Theoretical Criminology

tent with Hagan's idea that power differentials—one being organization—may influence reaction to behavior, and with Black's proposition that law varies with organization.

Black does not mention conflict theory in any of his works on the behavior of law; nor has his work been identified as conflict theory elsewhere. Yet, some of the core propositions of his theory are consistent with conflict notions, in that they imply that more powerful social actors have more ability to use law against less powerful actors. Black's theory probably has not been conceived as a conflict theory for at least two reasons. First, Black simply states his propositions as purely sociological laws, without imputing either individual or structural motivation. Conflict theory assumes disproportionate treatment has a purpose attached to it—namely, to protect the interests of the more powerful. Second, Black's theory is much broader than conflict theory. Conflict theory generally pertains to power relations, whereas Black's theory pertains to differences across several types of social relationships, some involving power and some not.

A UNIFIED CONFLICT THEORY OF CRIME

In this section we attempt to bring together some of the most important concepts from the various conflict theories to create an integrated or unified theory. The following conflict theory is derived principally from the theories of Vold, Quinney, and Chambliss and Seidman presented in this chapter.[45]

VALUES AND INTERESTS IN COMPLEX SOCIETIES

1. A person's *values* (i.e., beliefs about what is good, right, and just, or at least excusable) and *interests* (i.e., what rewards or benefits the person) are generally shaped by the conditions in which the person lives.

2. Complex, highly differentiated societies are composed of people who live under very different conditions.

3. Therefore, the more complex and differentiated the society, the more that people within the society have different and conflicting values and interests.

---

[45]Earlier versions can be found in Thomas J. Bernard, "The Distinction Between Conflict and Radical Criminology," *Journal of Criminal Law and Criminology* 72(1): 362–79 (spring 1981), and in the second, third, and fourth editions of the present book.

PATTERNS OF INDIVIDUAL ACTION

4. People tend to act in ways that are consistent with their values and interests. That is, they tend to act in ways that they think are good, right, and just, or at least excusable. They also tend to act in ways that benefit themselves personally.

5. When values and interests conflict, people tend to adjust their values to come into line with their interests. Over time, people tend to believe that the actions that benefit them personally are really good, right, and just, or at least excusable.

6. Because the conditions of one's life (and therefore one's values and interests) tend to be relatively stable over time, people tend to develop relatively stable patterns of action that benefit them personally and that they believe are good, right, and just, or at least excusable.

THE ENACTMENT OF CRIMINAL LAWS

7. The enactment of criminal laws is part of a general legislative process of conflict and compromise in which organized groups (and, to a much less extent, private individuals) attempt to promote and defend their values and interests.

8. Specific criminal laws usually represent a combination of the values and interests of many different groups rather than the values and interests of one particular group. Nevertheless, the greater a group's political and economic power, the more the criminal law in general tends to represent the values and interests of that group.

9. Therefore, in general, the greater a group's political and economic power, the less likely it is that the group's relatively stable patterns of action (i.e., actions which benefit group members personally and which they believe are good, right, and just, or at least excusable) will violate the criminal law, and vice versa.

THE ENFORCEMENT OF CRIMINAL LAWS

10. In general, the more political and economic power that people have, the more difficult it is for official law enforcement agencies to process them, and the less political and economic power that people have, the easier it is for official law enforcement agencies to process them, when their behavior violates the criminal law.

11. As bureaucracies, law enforcement agencies tend to process easier rather than more difficult cases.

12. Therefore, in general, law enforcement agencies tend to process individuals with less, rather than more, political and economic power.

THE DISTRIBUTION OF OFFICIAL CRIME RATES

13. Because of the processes of criminal law enactment and law enforcement described above, the distribution of official crime rates in every society (i.e., arrests, convictions, imprisonments, executions) will tend to be the inverse of the distribution of political and economic power in that society, independent of any other factors (e.g., social, psychological, or biological factors affecting the behavior of offenders or the behavior of criminal justice agents).

This united conflict theory presents a theoretical chain that begins with general social structural characteristics, moves through the processes by which individuals in similar social structural locations learn similar patterns of behavior, and concludes by relating those patterns of behavior to the processes of enacting and enforcing criminal laws in order to explain the distribution of official crime rates.[46] Because it combines and interrelates a theory of criminal behavior with a theory of the behavior of criminal law, this theory is described as a "unified theory of crime."

TESTING CONFLICT CRIMINOLOGY

Conflict criminologists generally are able to demonstrate that broad patterns in crime and criminal justice are consistent with the arguments and predictions of their theories. But other possible explanations also exist for the same patterns. The major problem with testing conflict criminology is distinguishing between conflict explanations and the other possible explanations.

For example, "macro-level threat theory" argues that when minorities pose an increasing threat to the status quo, the overall level of police activity increases and the police activity itself is directed more at the minorities.[47] Research on this theory commonly tests hypotheses such as: An increase in the relative proportion of African Americans in a city will result in an increase in the number of police officers and the number of arrests. A positive association between percentage of minorities and police activity or strength is typically viewed as support for this type of conflict criminology.

---

[46]Akers, ibid., pp. 61–68, makes a similar argument about structural sources of behavior and social processes of learning those behaviors. The present argument extends the theoretical chain to the distribution of official crime rates.

[47]For a broad review of many different types of social threat theory, see Allen Liska, *Social Threat and Social Control*, SUNY Press, Albany, NY, 1992.

However, non-conflict explanations are also compatible with the same findings.[48] If crime occurs disproportionately in poor and minority areas, then potential victims, who themselves are poor and members of minorities, may ask for greater police protection. Also, these same minorities may have other social problems and may need a variety of social services, at least some of which ultimately are provided by the police. The greater police attention therefore may reflect the political strength of community residents, not their political weakness. Research to date has had a very difficult time distinguishing the threat hypothesis from non-conflict interpretations of the same findings.[49]

In addition, other types of conflict criminology do not assume a threat hypothesis but focus instead on routine bureaucratic factors. For example, when considering whether to make an arrest, a police officer may conclude that conviction is unlikely because of the political and economic power of the offender. The officer then may be reluctant to do all the work (e.g., fill out all the forms) to process an official arrest, even if there are strong grounds for the arrest. On the other hand, a police officer may be quite solicitous of powerful victims who request the arrest of an offender, and they may make that arrest even if conviction seems unlikely and the grounds for arrest are not very strong. Thus, variation in police arrest decisions, especially with offenses that are less serious, may reflect the degree of political and economic power of offenders and victims but be unrelated to any macro-level threat.

Similar problems of interpretation arise with the attempt to explain variations in imprisonment rates. In 1999, for example, there were 3,408 African American males in prison for every 100,000 population, compared to 417 European American males,[50] a ratio of over eight to one. The question is whether a conflict-type theory explains these patterns, or whether they are explained by other, very different theories.

Often, this question is phrased in terms of *differential offending* vs. *differential processing*. That is, how much of these differences in imprisonment rates are explained by more frequent and more serious offending by African American males, and how much is explained by the fact that, for one reason or another, African American males are processed

---

[48]David Greenberg, R. C. Kessler, and Colin Loftin, "Social Inequality and Crime Control," *Journal of Criminal Law and Criminology* 76: 684–704 (1985).

[49]For a discussion, see, Mitchell B. Chamlin and John K. Cochran, "Race Riots and Robbery Arrests: Toward a Direct Test of the Threat Hypothesis," *Social Pathology* 6(2): 83–101 (2000).

[50]Allen J. Beck, "Bureau of Justice Statistics Bulletin: Prisoners in 1999," U.S. Department of Justice, Washington, DC, 2000, Table 14.

differently by the criminal justice system. Another way to phrase this same question is: To what extent are criminal justice decisions, particularly at sentencing, influenced by *non-legal variables* such as race and class, as opposed to *legally relevant variables* such as the seriousness of the present offense and the length of the prior record?

In the 1960s and early 1970s, many researchers concluded that African Americans were sentenced more harshly than European Americans. But Hagan found that, for the most part, these early studies did not control for seriousness of present offence or length of prior records.[51] Once studies began to control for such factors, the effect of race largely disappeared. In addition, Hagan argued that actual amount of disparity found in these early studies (e.g., the number of days served in jail) was fairly small.

After reviewing the research on this subject, Walker and his colleagues have reached the conclusion that the influence of extra-legal variables at any particular decision point in the criminal justice system is small.[52] However, they also argue that there is more extra-legal influence at some stages of the criminal justice system than at others, more in some jurisdictions than in others, and more for some types of crime than for others.

More important, they point out that criminal justice involves a sequence of decisions, with each decision determined at least in part by earlier decisions. These effects tend to accumulate as a person moves through the system and can become quite large. For example, the effect of race on sentencing is small, since most sentencing is determined by legally relevant variables. But African Americans are more likely to be sentenced to prison because they are less likely to retain private attorneys.[53] In addition, African Americans tend to be given longer prison sentences because they are less likely to make bail, which reduces their ability to provide an effective defense.[54] Thus, although race has only a small effect on sentencing, race also affects the ability to to hire a private attorney and make bail, and those then have a separate affect on sentencing. The total effect of race on sentencing should therefore include

---

[51]John Hagan, "Extra-legal Attributes and Criminal Sentencing: An Assessment of a Sociological Viewpoint," *Law and Society Review* 8: 357–383 (1974).

[52]Samuel Walker, Cassia Spohn, and Miriam DeLone, *The Color of Justice: Race, Ethnicity, and Crime in America,* 2nd ed. Wadsworth, Belmont, CA, 2000. For a different conclusion, see William Wilbanks, *The Myth of a Racist Criminal Justice System,* Brooks/Cole, Monterey, CA, 1987.

[53]Cassia Spohn, J. Gruhl, and Susan Welch, "The Effect of Race on Sentencing: A Re-examination of an Unsettled Question," *Law and Society Review* 16: 72–88 (1981–82).

[54]Alan Lizotte, "Extra-Legal Factors in Chicago's Criminal Courts: Testing the Conflict Model of Criminal Justice," *Social Problems* 25: 564–580 (1978).

the effect of race on these earlier decision points. Thus, if all these racial effects are added up, the total effect of race on sentencing is fairly large.

This accumulation of effects has been well documented in the processing of juveniles.[55] Small differences in the handling of poor and minority children tend to accumulate as children move through the system, result in large overall effects. These differences are generally attributed, in one way or another, to prejudicial attitudes by juvenile justice agents. Moore, however, raises the possibility that at least some of these differences may not be due to prejudice at all.[56] Rather, he suggests that fewer family and community resources are available to help poor and minority children, so that even in the complete absence of prejudice by juvenile justice agents, such children and their families are disproportionately subjected to official processing. Indeed, Moore suggests that the entire overrepresentation of minorities in juvenile justice may not be the result of prejudice at all, but rather "the result of real differences in family and community capacity."[57] Moore describes this factor as "the most troubling possibility."

Like Moore's findings in juvenile justice most of the accumulated small effects in the adult criminal justice system, it would seem, do not result from race prejudice but instead from the routine operations of the system as it relates to social class. Wealthy African Americans, such as O. J. Simpson, are able to marshal much the same resources as wealthy European Americans to impede and prevent their being officially defined and processed as a criminal.[58] This is consistent with conflict criminology's focus on political and economic power, which is more directly related to class than to race.

---

[55]E.g., Belinda McCarthy and Brent L. Smith, "The Conceptualization of Discrimination in the Juvenile Justice Process," *Criminology* 24: 41–64 (1986); Barry Krisberg et al., "The Incarceration of Minority Youth," *Crime and Delinquency* 32: 5–38 (1987); Carl E. Pope and William H. Feyerherm, "Minority Status and Juvenile Justice Processing: An Assessment of the Research Literature," *Criminal Justice Abstracts* 22: 327–35 and 527–42 (1990) Donna M. Bishop and Charles S. Frazier, "The Influence of Race in Juvenile Justice Processing," *Journal of Research in Crime and Delinquency* 25: 242–63 (1988); and Bishop and Frazier, "Race Effects in Juvenile Justice Decision-Making," *Journal of Criminal Law and Criminology* 86: 392–413 (1996).

[56]Mark Harrison Moore, *From Children to Citizens. The Mandate for Juvenile Justice*, Springer-Verlag, New York, 1987, p. 112.

[57]See also Jennifer Calnon and Thomas J. Bernard, "Discrimination Without Prejudice," unpublished manuscript. Calnon and Bernard argue that even in the total absence of prejudice, many formal criminal justice policies produce differences in outcomes related to race and class but unrelated to the individual's offending behavior. They describe this effect as "discrimination without prejudice" and conclude that criminal justice policies that produce "discrimination without prejudice" are a much larger and more troubling problem than race or class prejudice by criminal justice agents.

[58]E.g., see Gregg Barak, ed., *Representing O. J.: Murder, Criminal Justice, and Mass Culture*, Harrow and Heston, Guilderland, NY, 1996.

All of the above concerns the routine operations of the criminal justice system in enforcing the criminal laws. Beyond that are the definitions found in the criminal laws themselves, particularly the types of actions that are defined as criminal and the types of criminal actions that are defined as more or less serious. Another words, beyond the enforcement of criminal laws lies their enactment. A concrete example can be found in the debate over sentencing for crack vs. powder cocaine.[59] Both are forms of the same drug, but 5 grams of crack gets the same mandatory sentence in federal law as 500 grams of powder. Crack cocaine is predominantly used by the poor and African American; powder cocaine is predominantly used by the rich and European American. The difference in sentencing may reflect an overall tendency to define the illegal actions of poor and minority individuals as "more serious" than the illegal actions of wealthy and majority individuals. Tonry goes even further, arguing that the entire war on drugs was "foreordained to affect disadvantaged black youths disproportionately" and that it required "the willingness of the drug war's planners to sacrifice young black Americans."[60]

Tonry's conflict-oriented interpretation of the drug war can be contradicted by other, non-conflict interpretations of the same set of facts. For example, differences in mandatory sentencing for crack vs. powder may reflect differences in the extent to which they are associated with violent crime. However, empirical tests of these alternate interpretations are difficult to arrange.

Despite this pervasive difficulty with testing conflict-type interpretations, it seems undeniable that political and economic power have at least some impact on the enactment and enforcement of criminal laws, and therefore on the resulting distribution of official crime rates. The real question seems to be the extent of that impact. Does the distribution of power shape the overall distribution of official crime rates? Or is the effect of power only slight and marginal, operating around the edges of real crime?

IMPLICATIONS AND CONCLUSIONS

Theories of conflict criminology imply that greater equality in the distribution of power among groups in society should result in greater equality in the distribution of official crime rates.[61] Groups that presently

---

[59]Kathryn K. Russell, *The Color of Crime*, New York University Press, New York, 1998.

[60]Michael Tonry, *Malign Neglect*, Oxford, New York, 1995, p. 123.

[61]Bruce A. Arrigo and Thomas J. Bernard, "Post Modern Criminology in Relation to Radical and Conflict Theory," *Critical Criminology* 8(2): 39–60, 1997.

have high official crime rates should have lower rates as they use their newly acquired power to legally pursue and defend their values and interests. Groups that presently have low official crime rates should find themselves with higher rates as their ability to pursue and defend their values and interests is increasingly hindered by other groups. Despite these increases, there should be an overall reduction in total amount of crime in the society, reflecting reductions in overall levels of conflict as the power of groups is equalized.[62]

Within the context of conflict theory, the specific process by which a redistribution of power can be achieved is through the establishment of organized groups by which the presently unorganized aggregates of individuals are able to pursue and defend their values and interests.[63] This process bears a resemblance to the policy implication of control theory, since it entails bonding previously isolated individuals to groups that will interact with other groups according to mutually agreed-upon rules. The difference is that control theory generally implies that the individual should be bonded to "conventional" groups, whereas conflict criminology implies that the individual should be bonded to other individuals who have similar values and interests and who occupy similar social structural locations. To the extent that particular individuals are considered deviant, the groups that best represent their values and interests will also be considered deviant. The view that the best solution to social conflict lies in the representation of diverse aggregates of individuals by an equally diverse number of organized groups under conditions of relative equality is the reason why conflict theory in general is most comfortable with pluralist democracy as a form of government.[64]

Conflict criminology asserts that there is a general tendency for power and official crime rates to be inversely related. In the context of that assertion, it is interesting to consider Lord Acton's famous observation: "Power corrupts, and absolute power corrupts absolutely." Power may corrupt, but official criminalization requires that there be some greater power able to define that corruption as criminal. Otherwise, no matter how corrupt the action is, it either will not be defined as a crime in the criminal law, or the person will not be processed as a criminal through the criminal justice system. Absolute power may corrupt absolutely, but people with absolute power are never officially defined as criminals.[65]

---

[62]This conclusion is consistent with research that shows that reductions in economic inequality are associated with reductions in violence. See above, Chapter 5.

[63]Ralf Dahrendorf, *Class and Class Conflict in Industrial Society*, Stanford University Press, Stanford, CA, 1959, pp. 225–27.

[64]Dahrendorf, op. cit.; Coser, *The Functions of Social Conflict*.

[65]See Thomas Hobbes, *Leviathan*, E. P. Dutton, New York, 1950, Chapter 18, p. 148.

CHAPTER FOURTEEN

Marxist and Postmodern Criminology

The term "critical criminology" has been described as "an umbrella designation for a series of evolving, emerging perspectives" that are "characterized particularly by an argument that it is impossible to separate values from the research agenda, and by a need to advance a progressive agenda favoring disprivileged peoples."[1] This chapter focuses on two of these emerging critical perspectives—Marxist criminology and postmodern criminology.[2] Feminist criminology, a third perspective that sometimes is also described as critical criminology, is discussed in the next chapter on gender and crime.

Like the conflict theories presented in the last chapter, critical theories share the view that inequality in power is causally related to the problem of crime. But conflict theory largely ignores the sources or origins of power, while critical perspectives make specific arguments on that issue. Marxist theories generally locate power in ownership of the means of production, while postmodern theories locate it in the control

---

[1]Martin D. Schwartz and David O. Friedrichs, "Postmodern Thought and Criminological Discontent: New Metaphors for Understanding Violence," *Criminology* 32: 221–46 (1994), p. 222. For overviews of critical criminology, see Raymond J. Michalowski, "Critical Criminology and the Critique of Domination: The Story of an Intellectual Movement," *Critical Criminology* 7(1): 9–16 (1996); and Bruce A. Arrigo, "Introduction: Some Preliminary Observations on Social Justice and Critical Criminology," in Arrigo, ed., *Social Justice, Criminal Justice*, West/Wadsworth, Belmont, CA, 1999, pp. 3–9.

[2]Readable chapters on other types of "critical" theories in criminology can be found in Arrigo, op. cit.

over language systems.[3] Both perspectives imply that the crime problem can only be solved if power arrangements are changed.

These are "radical" theories in the sense of Latin word (*radix*) for root.[4] Getting to the root of the problem of crime, according to these perspectives, requires social change at the most fundamental level. Ultimately, these perspectives focus on ideals such as social justice and attempt to determine how contemporary societies can achieve those ideals. The focus on "what ought to be" rather than "what is," on the ideal rather than the real, is what most distinguishes these theories from mainstream criminology, including conflict theory.[5]

Critical theories are difficult to summarize for two reasons. First, their complexity leads to profound disagreements among different theorists within the same area. Second, theorists in these areas may frequently change their own positions as their thinking develops. Thus, one theorist may take one position at one time and a different position only a short time later. Consequently one can only summarize some of the major themes, but a great many arguments must be left out.

OVERVIEW OF MARX'S THEORY

Karl Marx (1818–83) wrote in the immediate aftermath of the massive social changes brought about by the Industrial Revolution.[6] In one lifespan (approximately 1760–1840), the world as it had been for a thousand years suddenly changed. Marx attempted to explain why those profound changes had occurred when they did, and to give some sense of what was coming next. His theory linked economic development to social, political, and historical change, but it did not deal with the problem of crime in any significant way.

---

[3]Werner Einstadter and Stuart Henry, *Criminological Theory*, Harcourt Brace, Fort Worth, 1995, chs. 10–12. For a discussion of the relationships among conflict, Marxist, and postmodern criminology, see Bruce A. Arrigo and Thomas J. Bernard, "Postmodern Criminology in Relation to Radical and Conflict Criminology," *Critical Criminology* 8(2): 39–60, 1997.

[4]For a discussion of "radical" criminology, see Michael J. Lynch, Raymond Michalowski, and W. Byron Groves, *A New Primer in Radical Criminology: Critical Perspectives on Crime, Power and Identity*, 3rd ed., Criminal Justice Press, Monsey, NY, 2000, pp. 3–15.

[5]E.g., see Thomas J. Bernard, "Foreword," in Bruce A. Arrigo, ed., *Social Justice, Criminal Justice*, West/Wadsworth, Belmont, CA, 1999.

[6]This account of Marx's theory is taken from Thomas J. Bernard, *The Consensus-Conflict Debate: Form and Content in Social Theories*, Columbia, New York, 1983, pp. 95–98. Other overviews of Marx's theory as it relates to criminology can be found in David Greenberg, *Crime and Capitalism*, Mayfield, Palo Alto, CA, 1980, pp. 13–17; Richard Quinney, *Class, State and Crime*, 2nd ed., Longman, New York, 1980, pp. 13–17; Lynch, Michalowski, and Groves, op. cit., ch. 2; and Lynch and Paul Stretesky, "Marxism and Social Justice," pp. 14–29 in Arrigo, *Social Justice, Criminal Justice*, op. cit.

The principal conflict that Marx presented in his theory, and on which the theory is based, was the conflict between the material forces of production and the social relations of production.[7] The term *material forces of production* generally refers to a society's capacity to produce material goods, and includes technological equipment and the knowledge, skill, and organization to use that equipment. The term *social relations of production* refers to relationships among people. These include property relationships, which determine how the goods produced by the material forces of production are distributed—that is, who gets what.

The development of the material forces of production is relatively continuous throughout history, since it consists in the development of technology, skills, etc. The social relations of production, however, tend to freeze into particular patterns for long periods of time. When first established, the social relations enhance the development of the material forces of production, but as time goes by they become increasingly inconsistent with the material forces and begin to impede their further development. At some point, the social relations change abruptly and violently, and new social relations are established that once again enhance the development of the material forces of production.

Marx used this general model to explain the profound changes that had just occurred in European societies. When the social relations of feudalism were first established, they were progressive in the sense that they were necessary for the further development of the material forces of production. After a thousand years, however, the material forces of production had developed extensively, but the social relations had hardly changed at all. At that point the social relations of feudalism were hindering the further development of the material forces of production. The massive changes of the Industrial Revolution reflected a sudden and violent restructuring of the social relations of production. The new social relations—bourgeois capitalism—were progressive in the sense that they were necessary for the further development of the material forces of production.

Having analyzed the causes of the recent violent and abrupt social changes in Europe, Marx used the same basic analysis to predict what would happen next. The material forces of production would continuously develop under capitalism, but the social relations would remain relatively fixed, just as they had under feudalism. Over time, the social relations of capitalism would therefore increasingly become a hindrance

---

[7]A summary of this argument is found in Karl Marx, *Critique of Political Economy* (1859), English translation, International Library, New York, 1904, pp. 11–13.

to the further development of the material forces production. Ultimately, Marx predicted, there would be a sudden and violent restructuring of the social relations in which socialism would replace capitalism.

Marx was fairly specific on why he thought this restructuring would happen. The logic of capitalism is "survival of the fittest," with the "fittest" gobbling up the "less fit." As Marx phrased it: "One capitalist always kills many."[8] By this process, property is increasingly concentrated into fewer and fewer hands, and former capitalists are transformed into wage laborers who work for someone else instead of having other people work for them. At the same time, increasing mechanization in business and industry means that fewer workers are needed, so that there is an increasing pool of underemployed and unemployed workers. With so many workers available who want jobs, those who have jobs can be paid low wages because others will work for even less.

Thus, Marx argued, capitalist societies tend to polarize into two conflicting groups. One group consists of people who, as they gobble up their competitors, own an increasing portion of the property in the society. Over time, this group grows smaller and richer. The other group, consisting of employed and unemployed wage laborers, keeps getting larger and poorer, as mechanization increases unemployment and real wages decrease because the supply of labor exceeds the demand for it.

This polarization, one group growing smaller and richer, the other growing larger and poorer, is what Marx called the "contradiction" in capitalism; as it becomes more extreme, it acts as a great hindrance to the further development of the material forces of production. Thus, a revolutionary restructuring of the social relations of production is inevitable at some point. To end the cycles of overproduction and depression that plague capitalism,[9] Marx believes that restructuring should entail the establishment of collective ownership of the means of production and the institution of centralized planning.

MARX ON CRIME, CRIMINAL LAW, AND CRIMINAL JUSTICE

Marx did not discuss at length the problem of crime or its relation to the economic system, although he did address the subject in several pas-

---

[8]Karl Marx, *Capital*, vol. 1, International, New York, 1967, p. 763.

[9]See, in general, Karl Marx, *Critique of the Gotha Programme*, International, New York, 1970. See also D. Ross Gandy, *Marx and History: From Primitive Society to the Communist Future*, University of Texas Press, Austin, 1979, pp. 72–95.

sages.[10] Two of Marx's arguments in these passages have been particularly important in later Marxist theories of criminal behavior.

First, Marx argued that it was essential to human nature that people be productive in life and in work. But in industrialized capitalist societies, the large numbers of unemployed and underemployed people unproductive and become demoralized; thus they are subject to all forms of crime and vice. Marx called these demoralized people the *lumpenproletariat*.[11]

Second, Marx argued against the classical philosophy, dominant in his day, that all people freely and equally joined in a social contract for the common good, and that the law represented a consensus of the general will.[12] Marx maintained that this view ignored the fact that unequal distribution of wealth in a society produced an unequal distribution of power. Those with no wealth have no power in the formation of the social contract, whereas those with great wealth can control it to represent their own interests. Thus Marx did not see crime as the willful violation of the common good, but as "the struggle of the isolated individual against the prevailing conditions."[13] This conclusion is sometimes called Marx's *primitive rebellion* thesis, since it implies that crime is a primitive form of rebellion against the dominant social order, one that eventually may develop into conscious revolutionary activity.

Marx also wrote several passages analyzing the historical origins of criminal laws and criminal justice agencies. While still a follower of the philosopher Hegel, the young Marx wrote several articles on the crime of the theft of wood in Germany around 1840.[14] Traditionally, the nobility had the right to hunt and chase in the forest, while the peasants had the right to collect forest products such as wood. In the early 1800s, however, the value of wood increased dramatically because of a boom in shipbuilding, railroad building, and so on. A number of laws were passed that took away the traditional rights of the peasants and defined

---

[10]For discussions of Marx's views of crime, see Ian Taylor, Paul Walton, and Jock Young, *The New Criminology*, Harper and Row, New York, 1973, pp. 209–36. Original passages from Marx and Engels can be found in Maureen Cain and Alan Hunt, eds., *Marx and Engels on Law*, Academic Press, New York, 1979; or Paul Phillips, *Marx and Engels on Law and Laws*, Barnes and Noble, Totowa, NJ, 1980.

[11]Paul Q. Hirst, "Marx and Engles on Law, Crime, and Morality," in Ian Taylor, Paul Walton, and Jock Young, eds., *Critical Criminology*, Routledge and Kegan Paul, London, 1975, pp. 215–21.

[12]Karl Marx and Friedrich Engles, *The German Ideology*, Lawrence and Wishart, London, 1965, pp. 365–67.

[13]Ibid., p. 367.

[14]Peter Linebaugh, "Karl Marx, the Theft of Wood, and Working Class Composition," in David Greenberg, *Crime and Capitalism*, pp. 76–97. See also Greenberg's comments on pp. 60–63 and 484.

the taking of wood from the forest as a crime. The enforcement of these laws then became a major function of criminal justice agencies, and in some locations almost three-quarters of criminal prosecutions were for forest crimes such as the taking of wood. On the basis of his Hegelian philosophy, Marx argued that the "true" state would uphold the rights of all citizens, whereas these laws only represented the interests of the forest owners.[15]

Marx later argued in *Capital* that the economic basis of capitalism rested on a similar theft of the traditional rights of the peasants.[16] Prior to capitalism, most peasants were independent producers with hereditary rights to the use of state-owned, church-owned, or commonly held lands. Through a variety of legal means, the peasants' rights to these lands were terminated, their traditional ways of earning a living were declared illegal, and the lands they had used were turned over to private capitalists. Deprived of their traditional means of living, many peasants then became beggars and vagabonds or formed roving bands of robbers. All these methods of earning a living were also defined as criminal, so that peasants were virtually forced by the criminal law to become wage laborers working for the capitalists. Marx documented that, whenever given a choice, peasants attempted to remain independent producers rather than become wage laborers. Thus, he argued, the economic basis of capitalism had been established by a theft of the grandest scale imaginable, a theft accomplished through the coercive power of the criminal law.

THE EMERGENCE OF MARXIST CRIMINOLOGY

An early Marxist criminologist, Willem Bonger, provided an extensive theory of crime in his book *Criminality and Economic Conditions*, published in 1916.[17] Bonger argued that the capitalist economic system encouraged all people to be greedy and selfish and to pursue their own benefits without regard for the welfare of their fellows. Crime is concentrated in the lower classes because the justice system criminalizes the greed of the poor while it allows legal opportunities for the rich to pursue their selfish desires. Bonger argued that a socialist society would ultimately eliminate crime because it would promote a concern for the

---

[15]Marx later rejected idealistic Hegelianism, stating "The philosophers have only *interpreted* the world in various ways; the point, however, is to change it." Greenberg, p. 484.

[16]Karl Marx, *Capital*, quoted in Greenberg, pp. 45–48. See also Greenberg's comments on pp. 38–39.

[17]Willem Bonger, *Criminality and Economic Conditions*, Little, Brown, Boston, 1916; reprinted by Agathon, New York, 1967. See the excellent introduction by Austin Turk in the abridged edition, Indiana University Press, Bloomington, 1969.

welfare of the whole society and would remove the legal bias that favors the rich.

After the mid-1920s Marxist criminology virtually disappeared from the English-speaking world,[18] but reappeared in the 1970s in connection with the radical social climate of the times.[19] These versions of Marxist criminology tended to portray criminals in terms of Marx's *primitive rebellion* thesis—that is, criminals were engaged in crime as an unconscious form of rebellion against the capitalist economic system. The 1970s also produced *instrumentalist* views of the criminal justice system—i.e., the enactment and enforcement of criminal laws are solely the instruments of a unified and monolithic ruling class that conspires to seek its own advantage at the expense of other groups.

These simplistic views of criminals and criminal justice were criticized almost immediately by others as misinterpretations of Marx's thought.[20] Block and Chambliss, for example, criticized the early theories for their simplistic portrayal of the ruling class as a unified and monolithic elite; for the argument that the enactment and enforcement of laws reflects only the interests of this ruling class; and for the argument that criminal acts are a political response to conditions of oppression and exploitation.[21] Greenberg pointed out that these theories ignored studies that showed a widespread consensus on legal definitions of crime; that underprivileged people are most frequently victims of crime by other underprivileged people, so that they have an interest in the enforcement of criminal laws; and that it is unrealistic to expect that crime will be eliminated in socialist societies.[22] Greenberg later described these theories as primarily political statements rather than genuine academic arguments about the nature of crime.[23] When the politics of the New Left collapsed, "leftists who retained their political commitments dug in for the long haul." Some turned to community organizing while others turned to Marxist theory to deepen their understanding of

---

[18]Greenberg, op. cit., p. 1.

[19]See, for example, Richard Quinney, *Critique of Legal Order*, Little, Brown, Boston, 1973; Richard Quinney and John Wildeman, *The Problem of Crime*, 2nd ed., Harper & Row, New York, 1977; and Taylor, Walton, and Young, *The New Criminology*, op. cit.

[20]Hirst, op. cit.; also R. Serge Denisoff and Donald McQuarie, "Crime Control in Capitalist Society: A Reply to Quinney," *Issues in Criminology* 10(1): 109–19 (spring 1975).

[21]Alan A. Block and William J. Chambliss, *Organizing Crime*, Elsevier, New York, 1981, pp. 4–7. For a much harsher but less substantive criticism of these early theories, see Tony Platt, "Crime and Punishment in the United States: Immediate and Long-Term Reforms From a Marxist Perspective," *Crime and Social Justice*, Winter 1982, pp. 38–45.

[22]David F. Greenberg, "On One-Dimensional Criminology," *Theory and Society* 3: 610–21 (1976).

[23]Greenberg, *Crime and Capitalism*, pp. 6–10.

the broader social processes. Greenberg concludes: "By the mid-1970s, a specifically Marxian criminology began to take shape."[24] This new and rigorous Marxist criminology attempts to relate criminal behavior and crime policies to the political economy of the particular societies in which they occur, and it relies primarily on historical and cross-cultural studies for support, since only in such studies can societies with different political economies be compared.

MARXIST THEORY AND RESEARCH ON CRIME

In this more rigorous Marxist criminology, the simplistic instrumentalist view of criminal law and criminal justice has given way to a more complex structuralist view.[25] In this view, the primary function of the state is not to directly serve the short-term interests of capitalists, but rather to ensure that the social relations of capitalism persist in the long run. This goal requires that many different interests be served at different times, in order to prevent the rise of conditions that will lead to the collapse of capitalism. Thus, on any particular issue, including the enactment and enforcement of criminal laws, the actions of the state may serve other interests besides those of the owners of the means of production. Nevertheless, the owners of the means of production can still be described as a ruling class in that the organized state serves their economic interests in the long run. Moreover, the owners have an excessive amount of political power in comparison to other groups, with a disproportionate ability to get the state to serve their interests in the short run.

Within the context of this structuralist view, Marxists have often focused on the harmfulness of the behaviors of the ruling class in their pursuit of economic self-interest, and on the failure of the criminal law and criminal justice agencies to officially define and process those harmful behaviors as criminal. For example, Reiman argues that, in terms of property losses, physical injuries and deaths, the public's victimization by the ruling class is much greater than their victimization by street criminals.[26] Using government figures, he estimates the cost of street crime in the United States at about $18 billion per year, while the cost of corporate crime is closer to $1 trillion. In addition, about twice as many people die and eleven times more people are injured because of illegal workplace conditions as die from criminal homicides or are injured in

---

[24]Ibid., p. 10

[25]A useful summary of the instrumentalist vs. structuralist views of the state and the legal order is found in Lynch, Michalowski, and Groves, op. cit., ch. 3.

[26]Jeffrey Reiman, *The Rich Get Richer and the Poor Get Prison*, Allyn and Bacon, Boston, 1998.

criminal assaults. Reiman also argues that the continuing failure of criminal justice agencies to control street crime actually serves the long-term
interests of the ruling class. When the public is in a state of constant anxiety about lower-class crime, attention is diverted away from the public's
much greater victimization by the wealthy and powerful.[27]

This Marxist argument is similar to the conflict theory argument, described in the last chapter, about the ability of high power groups to
shape the enactment and enforcement of criminal laws so that their own
behaviors are not defined and processed as criminal. The difference be
tween the two types of theories is that Marxists generally argue that
there is some objective basis for determining what is (or what should be)
a crime. Marxist and other radical criminologists have therefore explored a wide range of "socially injurious" behaviors that are not officially defined or processed as criminal because they are committed by the
powerful against the powerless. These include "violations of human
rights due to racism, sexism, and imperialism; unsafe working conditions; inadequate child care; inadequate opportunities for employment
and education; substandard housing and medical care; crimes of economic and political domination; pollution of the environment; price-
fixing; police brutality; assassinations; war-making; violations of dignity;
denial of physical needs and necessities; and impediments to self-deter-
mination, deprivation of adequate food and blocked opportunities to
participate in relevant political decisions."[28] Most of these actions are
not defined as criminal at all; when they are defined as criminal, the laws
are rarely enforced; when enforced, the punishments are usually minimal compared to punishments routinely imposed on street criminals
whose actions cause less objective harm.

The focus on the socially harmful actions of the ruling class initially
led Marxists to ignore or romanticize lower-class street crimes.[29] For
example, in 1973, Taylor, Walton, and Young argued that deviant behavior should be considered authentic human action rather than the product of individual or social pathology.[30] That is, deviance is a manifesta-
tion of human diversity, and the criminalization of deviance is a societal
need unrelated to the quality of the behavior. These authors concluded:
"The task is to create a society in which the facts of human diversity,
whether personal, organic or social, are not subject to the power to

---

[27]See also the radical perspectives on police, courts, and corrections in Lynch, Michalowski, and
Groves, op. cit., chs. 8–10.

[28]See the discussion of the definition of crime in Lynch, Michalowski, and Groves, op. cit., ch. 4.

[29]Platt, op. cit., p. 40.

[30]Taylor, Walton, and Young, op. cit.

criminalize."[31] It was to create such a society that these authors turned to Marxism.

However, Marxists who worked in lower-class communities quickly found that lower-class crime, which was primarily directed against other lower-class people, was indeed a serious problem. Therefore, beginning about 1980 or so, Marxists began to propose explanations of lower-class crime that moved away from Marx's primitive rebellion thesis and moved back towards his arguments about the lumpenproletariat. That is, instead of implying that lower-class crime was "authentic human action" in one form or another, the behavior came to be described as the pathological consequences of the social structure of advanced capitalism.[32]

These explanations are quite similar to explanations found in more traditional criminological theories, except that they link their basic concepts to a broader view of political-economic systems and the historical processes in which those systems change.[33] Some of these Marxist theories propose causal arguments similar to those found in strain[34] and control[35] theories, but most are similar to traditional criminology theories that describe criminal behavior as socially learned. That is, Marxist theories generally argue that criminal behaviors are the result of social learning by normal individuals in situations structured by the social relations of capitalism. This view is consistent with the view found in Marxist theory that, in general and in the long run, individuals act and think in ways that are consistent with their economic interests.

For example, Chambliss took this approach in his analysis of organized crime in Seattle.[36] He argued that at one time most of the goods

---

[31]Ibid., p. 282.

[32]For example, Richard Quinney (*Class, State and Crime,* op. cit., pp. 59–62) described street crimes as crimes of "accommodation" to capitalist social relations in the sense that they are the actions of people who have been brutalized by the conditions of capitalism. These criminals reproduce the exploitative relations of capitalism in their own criminal activities—that is, they treat their victims the way they themselves have been treated. Quinney's description relies on Marx's arguments about the lumpenproletariat, as described above.

[33]See chapters 5–7 in Lynch, Michalowski, and Groves, op. cit. See also W. Byron Groves and Robert J. Sampson, "Traditional Contributions to Radical Criminology," *Journal of Research in Crime and Delinquency* 24(3): 181–214 (1987).

[34]E.g., see Mark Colvin and John Pauly, "A Critique of Criminology: Toward an Integrated Structural-Marxist Theory of Delinquency Production," *American Journal of Sociology* 89(3): 513–51 (1983). See also Mark Colvin, *Crime and Coercion: An Integrated Theory of Chronic Criminality,* St. Martin's Press, New York, 2000, which extends the earlier argument but also moves back in the direction of a traditional strain theory.

[35]E.g., see David O. Friedrichs, "The Legitimacy Crisis: A Conceptual Analysis," *Social Problems* 27(5): 540–55 (1980).

[36]William J. Chambliss, *On the Take: From Petty Crooks to Presidents,* Indiana University Press, Bloomington, IN, 1978.

and services provided by organized crime were legal. For various historical reasons, these goods and services were declared illegal but the demand for them did not disappear. Chambliss then pointed out that in our political system politicians have a strong need to generate funds in order to run for office, and that, at the same time, they control the conditions under which laws against illegal goods and services are enforced. This situation creates very strong pressure for a coalition between politicians and organized crime figures, and Chambliss claimed that he found such a coalition at the heart of organized crime in Seattle. Chambliss was fairly pessimistic about the possibilities for reform to eliminate such crime, except to argue that decriminalization would be helpful. He did note that most reforms merely replaced the people in key positions but did nothing about the basic political-economic forces (demand for illegal goods and services, need for money by politicians) that gave rise to organized crime in the first place. As a result, the new reform people respond to the same forces and therefore tend to take the same kinds of actions done by the corrupt politicians they replaced.

In his later book with Block, Chambliss generalized some of his arguments, relating various types of crime to the political-economic systems of societies in which they occur.[37] Block and Chambliss argued that every political-economic system contains contradictions that cannot be resolved without changing the fundamental structure of the society. Crime in a society is essentially a rational response to those contradictions. The problem with crime-control policies in general is that they attempt to deal with the symptoms without changing the basic political-economic forces that generate those symptoms.[38]

Despite their focus on changing the larger political-economic forces of capitalist society, some Marxist criminologists have attempted to take a more limited approach to the current problems of crime. Called "left realists," these criminologists recognize that crime causes serious problems for working-class citizens and that criminal justice agencies can respond to those problems even if the capitalist economic system is not overthrown.[39] These criminologists have therefore made a variety of policy recommendations that are not much different from the recommendations of mainstream (if liberal) criminologists.[40] In particular, this includes the implementation of decentralized, community-based polic-

---

[37]Block and Chambliss, op. cit.

[38]Greenberg, *Crime and Capitalism*, pp. 23–25.

[39]See, for example, Jock Young, "Ten Points of Realism," in Jock Young and Roger Matthews, eds., *Rethinking Criminology*, Sage, London, 1997; Matthews and Young, eds., *Issues in Realist Criminology: A Reader*, Sage, Thousand Oaks, CA, 1992.

[40]Lynch, Michalowski, and Groves, op. cit., pp. 216–19.

ing.[41] Community residents often favor repressive, get-tough police policies, and the challenge of the left realist criminologists is to get the community to approach the crime problem in the larger context of oppressive economic conditions and to enlarge their perceptions of the various ways in which they are victimized. Other similar policy recommendations include prosecuting white collar offenders,[42] reforming prisons,[43] regulating (as opposed to criminalizing) street prostitution,[44] and addressing the major health, housing, and educational needs of inner cities as a long-term strategy for dealing with the drug problem.[45] These and other mid-range policy responses to crime attempt to reduce the economic marginality, social alienation, and political oppression that characterize class-based capitalist societies.

OVERVIEW OF POSTMODERNISM

Modernism is associated with what is described in Chapter 1 of this book as the naturalistic approach, including the view that science is an objective process directed toward predicting and controlling the world.[46] Most criminology is modernist in this sense, except that the spiritualistic approaches discussed in Chapter 1 might be described as *pre*modernist since they were the dominant ways of thinking about the world prior to the rise of the modernism.

*Post*modernist theories attempt to move beyond modernism by arguing that all thinking and all knowledge are mediated by language, and that language itself is never a neutral medium.[47] Whether or not people are aware of it, language always privileges some points of view and disparages others. For example, modernism privileges scientific thinking by holding that it has special validity and objectivity in comparison to

---

[41]John Lowman and Brian Maclean, eds., *Realist Criminology: Crime Control and Policing in the 1990s*, University of Toronto Press, Toronto, 1992; and Richard Kinsey, John Lea, and Jock Young, *Losing the Fight Against Crime*, Blackwell, Oxford, 1986.

[42]David O. Friedrichs, *White Collar Crime in Contemporary Society*, Wadsworth, Belmont, CA, 1995.

[43]Roger Matthews, "Developing a Realist Approach to Prison Reform," pp. 71–87 in Lowman and MacLean, op. cit.

[44]John Lowman, "Street Prostitution Control," pp. 1–17; and Roger Matthews, "Regulating Street prostitution and Kerb-Crawling: A Reply to Lowman," pp. 18–22 in *British Journal of Criminology* 32, spring 1992. See also John Lowman, "The 'Left Regulation' of Prostitution," pp. 157–76 in Lowman and MacLean, op. cit.

[45]Elliott Currie, "Retreatism, Minimalism, Realism: Three Styles of Reasoning on Crime and Drugs in the United States," pp. 88–97 in Lowman and MacLean, op. cit.

[46]Anthony Borgman, *Crossing the Postmodern Divide*, University of Chicago Press, Chicago, 1992.

[47]See Dragan Milovanovic, *A Primer in the Sociology of Law*, Harrow and Heston, Albany, New York, 1994, pp. 143–45, 155–84.

other types of thinking. Postmodernists, in contrast, do not give scientific thinking a special position, and describe it instead as being neither more nor less valid than other types of thinking. To a certain extent, postmodernists even attack scientific thinking because they attempt to deconstruct privileged points of view—i.e., they identify implicit assumptions and unsupported assertions that underlie the ways in which the point of view of scientific thinking is legitimized and other points of view are disparaged. At the same time, postmodernists seek out the disparaged points of view in order to make them more explicit and legitimate.[48] The goal is not simply to tear down one point of view and replace it with the other, but rather to come to a situation in which different grammars can be simultaneously held as legitimate, so that there is a sense of the diversity of points of view without assuming that one is superior and the others are inferior.

Schwartz and Friedrichs point out that postmodernism is difficult to summarize because "there seems to be an almost infinite number of postmodern perspectives."[49] In addition, Schwartz has pointed out the difficult writing style of many postmodernists, stating that even after reading them several times, "I really do not know what the hell they are talking about."[50] Both these problems are related to postmodernism itself since it holds that linear thought processes, statements about cause and effect, syllogistic reasoning, objective analyses, and other standards of scientific thinking, are no more valid than other forms of thinking. Thus, to the extent that one tries to summarize postmodern thought in some logical, coherent, systematic fashion, one contradicts postmodern thought itself. Nevertheless, at least some postmodern theorists have attempted to make such summaries while acknowledging the self-contradictory nature of the effort.[51]

---

[48]Because of this tendency to attack privileged lines of thinking, post-modernism in general, and deconstruction in particular, has been criticized as nihilistic and relativistic. See Einstadter and Henry, *Criminological Theory*, op. cit., p. 298. Some postmodernists do emphasize these nihilistic, deconstructive, and oppositional approaches, but others emphasize the affirmative, reconstructive, and prospective aspects that incorporate constitutive methods. For applications to criminology, see Stuart Henry and Dragan Milovanovic, *Constitutive Criminology: Beyond Postmodernism.* Sage, London, 1996.

[49]Schwartz and Friedrichs, "Postmodern Thought and Criminological Discontent," op. cit., p. 222. These authors also mention the possibility that "much of what has been published is only a pretentious intellectual fad."

[50]Martin D. Schwartz, "The Future of Criminology," pp. 119–24 in Brian MacLean and Dragan Milovanovic, *New Directions in Criminology,* Collective Press, Vancouver, 1991.

[51]For example, Bruce Arrigo ("The Peripheral Core of Law and Criminology," *Justice Quarterly* 12[3]: 447–72 [1995]) comments on the "delicious irony" in attempting to summarize this perspective (pp. 449–50). See similar comments by Schwartz and Friedrichs, op. cit., pp. 222–23; and Einstadter and Henry, op. cit, p. 281.

Central to postmodernism is the view that modernism in general, and science in particular, has led to increased oppression rather than to liberation:[52]

(Postmodernism) contends that modernity is no longer liberating, but rather has become a force for subjugation, oppression, and repression; this contention applies to social science itself, which is a product of modernity. Postmodernists are disillusioned with liberal notions of progress and radical expectations of emancipation . . . The forces of modernism (e.g., industrialism) have extended and amplified the scope of violence in the world. Even worse, according to the postmodern critique, the major form of response to this violence is through rational organizations (e.g., the court system and the regulatory bureaucracies) with great reliance on specialists and experts. Such a response simply reproduces domination, the critique suggests, in perhaps new but no less pernicious forms.

The postmodernist response is to expose the structures of domination in societies as a means of achieving greater liberation. The principal source of this domination, according to postmodernists, is control of language systems[53] because language structures thought—i.e., the words and phrases that people use to convey meaning are not neutral endeavors but support dominant views of the world, whether the people who use those languages know it or not.[54]

Postmodernists therefore examine the relationship between human agency and language in creating meaning, identity, truth, justice, power, and knowledge.[55] This relationship is studied through *discourse analysis,* a method of investigating how sense and meaning are constructed in which attention is paid to the values and assumptions implied in language Discourse analysis considers the social position of the person who is speaking or writing in order to understand the meaning of what is said or written. However, it is not an analysis of the social roles that people occupy. Rather, it considers how language is embedded in these roles and how that language shapes and forms the way people in these roles think and speak. Thus, these roles are considered as "discursive subject positions."

---

[52]Schwartz and Friedrichs, op. cit., p. 224.

[53]The following discussion relies heavily on Arrigo and Bernard, "Postmodern Criminology in Relation to Radical and Conflict Criminology," op. cit.

[54]Milovanovic, *A Primer in the Sociology of Law,* op. cit., pp. 143–45, 155–84; Bruce Arrigo, *Madness, Language, and the Law,* Harrow and Heston, Albany, NY, 1993, pp. 27–75.

[55]Henry and Milovanovic, *Constitutive Criminology,* op. cit., pp. 8 11, 26 44.

POSTMODERN CRIMINOLOGY

Within the context of this frame of reference, postmodern criminologists examine "the incommensurable fullness of all human actors (e.g., victims, criminals, police agents, correctional officials, courtroom administrators, judges, attorneys) in their contradictory being and becoming, especially as they participate in the irony and the serendipity of the social order."[56] For example, to understand fully what lawyers mean when they speak *as lawyers,* it is necessary to understand quite a bit about "lawyering" as a historically situated and structured position in society.[57] There are many other "discursive subject positions" in crime and criminal justice which come connected with their own language systems—e.g., those of police, juvenile gang members, drug dealers, corrections officers, organized crime figures, corporate and political offenders, court workers, shoplifters, armed robbers, and even criminologists.

Postmodernist criminologists point out that, once people assume one of these "discursive subject positions," then the words that they speak no longer fully express their realities, but to some extent express the realities of the larger institutions and organizations. Because people's language is somewhat removed from their reality, people are described as *decentered*—i.e., people are never quite what their words describe and always tend somewhat to be what their language systems expect or demand.[58]

For example, women who have been raped must present their stories to prosecutors, who then reconstruct and repackage the stories into the language of the courts—i.e., "legalese."[59] The woman may testify at the trial, but her testimony may not deviate from the accepted language system without jeopardizing the chances that the defendant will be convicted.[60] Even when the defendant is convicted, the woman who has been raped may leave the court with a deep and dissatisfying sense that her story was never fully told, her reality never fully seen, her pain never fully acknowledged. The language of the court system expresses and

---

[56]Arrigo, "The Peripheral Core," op. cit., p. 467. See also Dragan Milovanovic, *Postmodern Criminology,* Garland, New York, 1997; and Stuart Henry and Milovanovic, eds., *Constitutive Criminology at Work: Applications to Crime and Justice,* State University of New York Press, Albany, 1999. For an argument that critical criminologists should abandon postmodernism, see Russell Stuart, "The Failure of Postmodern Criminology," *Critical Criminology* 8(2): 61–90 (1997).

[57]Peter Goodrich, "Law and Language: An Historical and Critical Introduction," *Journal of Law and Society* 11: 173–206 (1984).

[58]Henry and Milovanovic, op. cit., 1996, p. 27.

[59]Milovanovic, *A Primer in the Sociology of Law,* pp. 145–50.

[60]Bruce A. Arrigo, "An Experientially-Informed Feminist Jurisprudence," *Humanity and Society* 17(1): 28–47 (1993).

institutionalizes a form of domination over the victim, and this is one reason that victims so often are dissatisfied with the courts.

A similar situation happens with defendants who are accused of crimes. Criminal defense lawyers routinely repackage and re-construct the defendant's story into legalese as part of constructing the defense. The lawyer does this because it is the only way to win the case, but the full meaning of the defendant's story is normally lost in the process. Less-experienced defendants may object because the story that is told in court has so little resemblance to what actually happened. But more sophisticated defendants know that this is how the game is played. Even if the defendant "wins" the case (i.e., is acquitted), there has still been a ritualistic ceremony in which the reality of the courts has dominated the reality of the defendant. Thus, independent of who wins the case, the language of the court expresses and institutionalizes the domination of the individual by social institutions.

Other postmodern analyses have demonstrated the way that official language dominates participants in the criminal justice process, so that the participants themselves experience the system as marginalizing, alienating, and oppressive. These include studies of jailhouse lawyers,[61] police officers responding to 911 calls,[62] and the experience of female lawyers in criminal courts.[63] In each case, one view of reality (i.e., that of the inmates, the police, and the female lawyers) is replaced by another (i.e., the language of the court or correctional system), thereby affirming and legitimizing the status quo.

Postmodernists describe the present situation as one in which discourses are either dominant (e.g., the language of medicine, law, and science) or oppositional (e.g., the language of prison inmates). The goal of postmodernism is to move to a situation where many different discourses are recognized as legitimate. One of the ways of doing that is to establish "replacement discourses" in which the language itself helps people speak with a more authentic voice and to remain continuously aware of the authentic voices of other people.[64] The goal is greater inclusivity, more diverse communication, and a pluralistic culture. To achieve these ends, postmodernists listen carefully to the otherwise excluded views in constituting the definition of criminal acts. They conclude that creating a society in which alternative discourses liberate citi-

---

[61]Dragan Milovanovic, "Jailhouse Lawyers and Jailhouse Lawyering," *International Journal of the Sociology of Law* 16: 455–75 (1988).

[62]Peter K. Manning, *Symbolic Communication: Signifying Calls and the Police Response*, MIT Press, Cambridge, MA, 1988.

[63]Arrigo, *Madness, Language, and the Law*, op. cit.

[64]Henry and Milovanovic, op. cit., p. 204.

zens from prevailing speech patterns will also legitimate the role of all citizens in the project of reducing crime. The result will be greater respect for the diversity of people in the entire society, less victimizing of other people by criminals, and less official punishment of criminals by agents of the larger society.[65]

Postmodernism exposes a basis for power and domination in societies that has been ignored in earlier conflict and Marxist theories. However, it has tended toward an "appreciative relativism"[66] and "communal celebration,"[67] which resemble early simplistic Marxist views of crime, especially to the extent that they "appreciate" or "celebrate" the actions of criminals when they victimize other people. This view contradicts the later "left realist" approach, which concludes that crime is a real social problem that needs to be addressed by real criminal justice policies. Pepinsky, however, argues that coercive social policies merely perpetuate the problem:[68]

Crime is violence. So is punishment, and so is war. People who go to war believe that violence works. So do criminals and people who want criminals punished. All these believe violence works because they also believe that domination is necessary. Someone who is closer to God, natural wisdom, or scientific truth has to keep wayward subordinates in line, or social order goes to hell.

Similarly, Quinney states:[69]

. . . the criminal justice system in this country is founded on violence. It is a system that assumes that violence can be overcome by violence, evil by evil . . . This principle sadly dominates much of our criminology . . . When we recognize that the criminal justice system is the moral equivalent of the war machine, we realize that resistance to one goes hand-in-hand with resistance to the other. This resistance must be in compassion and love, not in terms of the violence that is being resisted.

Ultimately, these criminologists have come to the conclusion that the violence of punishment can only perpetuate and increase the violence of crime. Only when criminologists and the public give up their belief in

---

[65]Arrigo and Bernard, op. cit.

[66]Einstadter and Henry, op. cit., p. 289.

[67]This term is used by Einstadter and Henry (ibid., p. 299, fn. 13) in reference to Borgman, op. cit.

[68]Harold E. Pepinsky, "Peacemaking in Criminology and Criminal Justice," in Pepinsky and Richard Quinney, eds., *Criminology as Peacemaking,* Indiana University Press, Bloomington, 1991, p. 301.

[69]Richard Quinney, "The Way of Peace," in Pepinsky and Quinney, ibid., p. 12

the effectiveness and appropriateness of violence can we reasonably expect criminals to do the same thing.

CONCLUSION

Most societies based on Marxism have now collapsed, which clearly suggests that economic systems based on Marxism have fatal flaws. However, the new nations that have emerged from the collapse of Marxist societies have experienced large increases in crime as they reestablished capitalism.[70] These increases suggest that there may be some validity to the claim within Marxist criminology that there is a link between crime and capitalism. At a minimum, criminologists might examine recent developments in the former communist countries to determine whether capitalism is causally related to certain types and levels of crime. If a relationship between political economy and crime rates does exist, it may be because, as was suggested in Chapter 5, capitalism tends to be associated with higher levels of economic inequality, and the inequality itself, rather than the capitalist economic system, causes crime.

Postmodernist criminology has many similarities to Marxist criminology, but shifts attention from economic production to linguistic production. Postmodernists draw attention to the uses of language in creating dominance relationships, a point of view that seems to have a great deal of merit in general and in the study of crime in particular.[71] In addition, the development of "replacement discourses" that are inclusive and accepting, instead of exclusive and rejecting, could have considerable benefits for criminology and may well be a method to reduce crime.[72]

However, postmodernists take a position of "appreciative relativism" that privileges all points of view equally and treats scientific discourse as having no more validity than any other language. This position may go too far for most criminologists, who hold to the validity of the basic scientific process despite all of its practical difficulties. Indeed, criminolo-

---

[70]See, for example, Aleksandar Fatic, *Crime and Social Control in "Central"-Eastern Europe*, Ashgate, Aldershot, U.K. 1997.

[71]The use of language in creating dominance relationships is a major focus of Bernard, *The Consensus Conflict Debate*, op. cit. The book attempts to show how social theories use certain language systems (the "form" of the theory) to construct ideas about who and what is legitimate in the society (the "content" of the theory). These ideas about legitimacy are then used to privilege certain people and to repress others in the society. The book shows that these patterned ways of constructing legitimacy go back as far as Plato and Aristotle and are the actual point at issue in what is known more recently as "the consensus-conflict debate."

[72]For example, Braithwaite's shaming theory, discussed in Chapter 17, makes some similar arguments about inclusive and exclusive uses of language in responding to deviance. However, he does so in the context of a traditional scientific approach, rather than a postmodern approach.

gists may look at postmodern criminology from a scientific perspective. One of its fundamental assertions is that violence begets violence, so that the violence of our present criminal justice policies will only increase the violence of criminals in our society. This, in the last analysis, is an empirical assertion that can be tested with scientific research—e.g., the violence of criminal justice policies in different states or nations could be compared to the crime rates of those states or nations. If the postmodernists are correct, there should be a clear relationship between violent criminal justice policies and violent crime.

CHAPTER FIFTEEN

Gender and Crime

Gender is the strongest and most consistent correlate of crime and delinquency.[1] With few exceptions (such as prostitution), males are much more likely to offend than females. Why this is so is not entirely clear, and recently this has become a more explicit focus within criminological theory and research.

This chapter opens with a discussion of feminist criminology, which has raised a variety of issues related to women's offending, women's victimization, and women's experiences in the criminal justice system. The chapter then focuses narrowly on theories related to offending. Traditional criminology theories, as described in the earlier chapters of this book, largely ignore women's offending. Feminist criminology therefore poses the question of the extent to which these theories can be "generalized" to explain women's offending. But the larger question is the extent to which criminology theories can explain the gendered nature of crime—the tendency for crime to be largely a male phenomenon. The chapter therefore examines recent explanations of why women's crime rates are so low, and why men's crime rates are so high.

THE DEVELOPMENT OF FEMINIST CRIMINOLOGY

Feminism is an extremely broad area of social theorizing that has applications to the field of criminology, although this certainly is not its major focus. Just as there are numerous branches of feminism, there are nu-

---

[1]For a review of data, see, Charles R. Tittle and Raymond Paternoster, *Social Deviance and Crime*, Roxbury, Los Angeles, 2000, pp. 316–24.

merous branches of feminist criminology, with numerous disagreements and shadings of meanings within those branches. What follows here is only a brief overview intended to give a sense of the area and to identify its major themes.

The initial feminist writings in criminology were critiques of tradition-al criminology theories for ignoring or heavily distorting a number of topics related to women offenders.[2] Traditional theories largely ex-plained the criminal behavior of men,[3] and the few theories that ex-plained the criminal behavior of women were simplistic and relied on stereotypical images.[4] In addition, most traditional criminology theories were gender neutral and therefore (in theory at least) applied equally to women as well as to men. They ignored the socially constructed rela-tions between men and women that are associated with the concepts of masculinity and femininity.[5] Consequently, these theories largely were unable to explain the gendered nature of crime (i.e., men commit the vast majority of crime). When the gendered nature of crime was ad-dressed, the theories tended to focus on supposed characteristics that implied women's inferiority and tended to reinforce their subordination to men in the larger society.[6] Traditional criminology theories also failed to address the differences in the ways women, versus men, were treated by the criminal justice system.[7] For example, women accused of sexual crimes were often treated more harshly than men accused of similar

---

[2]Dorie Klein, "The Etiology of Female Crime: A Review of the Literature," *Issues in Criminology* 8: 3–30 (1973); Carol Smart, *Women, Crime and Criminology: A Feminist Critique*, Routledge and Kegan Paul, Boston, 1976. These books are briefly reviewed in Sally S. Simpson, "Feminist Theory, Crime, and Justice," *Criminology* 27(4): 605–31, (1989); and in Kathleen Daly and Meda Chesney-Lind, "Feminism and Criminology," *Justice Quarterly* 5(4): 497–538, (1988).

[3]Eileen B. Leonard, *Women, Crime and Society: A Critique of Criminology Theory*, Longman, New York, 1982; Ngaire Naffine, *Female Crime: The Construction of Women in Criminology*, Allen and Unwin, Boston, 1987.

[4]These early theories included Cesare Lombroso and William Ferrero, *La Donna Delinquente* (1893), translated and reprinted as *The Female Offender*, Hein, Buffalo, NY, 1980; Willem Bonger, *Criminality and Economic Conditions*, Little, Brown, Boston, 1916; reprinted by Agathon, New York, 1967. W. I. Thomas, *The Unadjusted Girl* (1923), reprinted by Patterson Smith, Montclair, NJ, 1969; Sheldon Glueck and Eleanor Glueck, *Five Hundred Delinquent Women* (1934), reprint-ed by Periodicals Service, Germantown, PA, 1972; and Otto Pollock, *The Criminality of Women*, (1952), reprinted by Greenwood, Westport, CT, 1972. See the discussion in Meda Chesney-Lind and Randall G. Shelden, *Girls, Delinquency, and Juvenile Justice*, 2nd ed., West/Wadsworth, Bel-mont, CA, 1998, pp. 74–81.

[5]Daly and Chesney-Lind, op. cit.

[6]Smart, op. cit.; Frances Heidensohn, *Women and Crime*, New York University Press, New York, 1985. For a brief discussion with some examples, see James W. Messerschmidt, *Masculinities and Crime*, Rowman and Littlefield, Lanham, MD, 1993, pp. 2–4, or Messerschmidt, *Capitalism, Pa-triarchy and Crime: Toward a Socialist Feminist Criminology*, Rowman and Littlefield, Totowa, NJ, 1986, pp. 1–24.

[7]Jane R. Chapman, *Economic Realities and the Female Offender*, Lexington Books, Lexington, MA, 1980; Susan Datesman and Frank R. Scarpitti, *Women, Crime and Justice*, Oxford University Press,

crimes, but women accused of violent crimes were often treated more leniently. These differences in treatment led to differences in official crime rates (e.g., higher rates of sexual offenses but lower rates of violent offenses), which then affected the explanations of women's criminality by criminology theories. Finally, none of the existing criminology theories discussed the new roles that women were taking on in the larger society as part of what in the 1970s was called women's liberation, and how those new roles might impact women's participation in criminal activity.

The critiques that pointed to the many problems with traditional criminology theories were followed by two books on the subject of women and crime that appeared in 1975. In *Sisters in Crime: The Rise of the New Female Criminal*,[8] Freda Adler argued that women were becoming more aggressive and competitive as they moved out of traditional homebound social roles and into the previously largely male world of the competitive marketplace. Essentially, Adler believed that women were taking on what had been masculine qualities as they fought the battles that men had always fought. She argued that the same kind of transformation was occurring among criminals, where "a similar number of determined women are forcing their way into the world of major crimes . . ." Now, she argued, there were "increasing numbers of women who are using guns, knives, and wits to establish themselves as full human beings, as capable of violence and aggression as any man."

In that same year, Rita James Simon published *Women and Crime*.[9] Simon also described recent changes in the types and volume of crime committed by women, but argued that it was not because they were taking on masculine characteristics. Rather, as women moved out of traditional homebound roles, they encountered a much wider variety of opportunities to commit crime, particularly economic and white-collar crimes, which required access to other people's money in positions of trust.

Both Adler's and Simon's theories argued that liberation from traditional women's roles would increase crimes committed by women. The major difference between the two had to do with the prediction about the type of crime these new female criminals would commit: Adler's theory suggested a larger portion of this crime would be violent, whereas

---

New York, 1980; Clarice Feinman, *Women in the Criminal Justice System,* Praeger, New York, 1986. Some of the differences are reviewed in Simpson, op. cit. pp. 612–17.

[8]McGraw Hill, New York, 1975.

[9]Lexington Books, Lexington, MA, 1975. See also Simon and Jean Landis, *The Crimes Women Commit, the Punishments They Receive,* Lexington Books, Lexington, 1991.

Simon's theory suggested predominantly property and white collar crime. Later research indicated that Simon's opportunity thesis had more validity, but on the whole there was little evidence that this "new female criminal" existed at all.[10] In addition, Simpson suggested that these theories generated enormous interest among nonfeminist criminologists, and in some ways set back the cause of a feminist criminology because they "diverted attention from the material and structural forces that shape women's lives and experiences."[11] Because of this, other feminist criminologists argue that neither theory should be described as feminist criminology.[12]

SCHOOLS OF FEMINIST CRIMINOLOGY

After Adler's and Simon's contributions, criminological writings that focused on explaining women's participation in crime expanded dramatically. While there are many similarities and differences in these writings, certain categories have appeared in the literature as ways to group these writings to illustrate their range and variety. These are sometimes described as schools of feminist thought.[13]

Initially, many feminist writings in criminology could be described as a part of traditional criminology itself, filling in gaps and correcting the distortions of the past. As such, they were part of what came to be called *liberal feminism.*[14] This branch of feminism basically operated within the framework of existing social structures to direct attention to women's issues, promote women's rights, increase women's opportunities, and transform women's roles in society.

Soon, however, several strands of "critical" feminism arose that directly challenged the social structures within which liberal feminism operated. These strands looked at the much more fundamental questions of how women had come to occupy subservient roles in society and how societies themselves might be transformed. The first such strand is known as *radical feminism,* and its central concept is that of "patriarchy," originally a concept used by sociologists like Max Weber to de-

---

[10]Simpson, op. cit., p. 610.

[11]Simpson, op. cit., p. 611. Daly and Chesney-Lind (op. cit., p. 511) also point to the "limitations of the liberal feminist perspective on gender that informed their work."

[12]Allison Morris, *Women, Crime and Criminal Justice,* Blackwell, New York, 1987, p. 16. Daly and Chesney-Lind (op. cit., p. 507) agree with her conclusion.

[13]For an overview of the schools of feminism in criminology, see Meda Chesney-Lind and Karlene Faith, "What About Feminism?" pp. 287–302 in Raymond Paternoster and Ronet Bachman, eds., *Explaining Criminals and Crime,* Roxbury, Los Angeles, 2000.

[14]Alison Jaggar, *Feminist Politics and Human Nature,* Roman and Allanheld, Totowa, NJ, 1983.

scribe social relations under feudalism. Kate Millett resurrected the term in 1970 to refer to a form of social organization in which men dominate women.[15] Millett argued that patriarchy is the most fundamental form of domination in every society. Patriarchy is established and maintained through sex-role socialization and the creation of "core gender identities," through which both men and women come to believe that men are superior in a variety of ways. Based on these gender identities, men tend to dominate women in personal interactions, such as within the family. From there, male domination is extended to all the institutions and organizations of the larger society. Because male power is based on personal relationships, Millet and her fellow feminists concluded that "the personal is political."

Where Millett had placed the root of the problem in socialization into gendered sex roles, *Marxist feminists* combined radical feminism with traditional Marxism to argue that the root of male dominance lies in men's ownership and control of the means of economic production.[16] For Marxist feminists, patriarchy is tied to the economic structure of capitalism and results in a "sexual division of labor" in which men control the economy and women serve them and their sexual needs.[17] Much like Marxist criminology in general, Marxist feminist criminologists argue that actions which threaten this capitalist-patriarchal system are defined as crimes by the criminal law and the criminal justice system. Thus, women's actions that threaten male economic dominance are defined as property crimes, and women's actions that threaten male control of women's bodies and sexuality are defined as sexual offenses. Like other Marxists, some Marxist feminist criminogists take an instrumental view of the criminal law—law is a direct instrument of men's oppression—while others take a more complex structural view that looks to overall patterns through which law maintains the system of patriarchy.[18] Thus another source of women's criminality in this perspective is the frustration and anger they feel by being trapped in these limiting social roles.[19]

Finally, *socialist feminists* retained both the focus on social roles and economic production, but moved away from a rigid Marxist framework.

---

[15]Kate Millett, *Sexual Politics*, Doubleday, New York, 1970.

[16]See Michael J. Lynch, Raymond Michalowski, and W. Byron Groves, *The New Primer in Radical Criminology*, Criminal Justice Press, Monsey, NY, 2000, pp. 108–11.

[17]Polly Radosh, "Woman and Crime in the United States: A Marxian Explanation," *Sociological Spectrum* 10: 105–31 (1990).

[18]Dawn Currie, "Women and the State. A Statement on Feminist Theory," *Critical Criminologist* 1(2): 4–5 (1989).

[19]Radosh, op. cit.; Daly and Chesney-Lind, op. cit.

In particular, they argued that natural reproductive differences between the sexes underlie male-female relationships. Before birth control, women were much more at the mercy of their biology than men—menstruation, pregnancy, childbirth and nursing, menopause—all of which made them more dependent on men for physical survival. The biological role of women in pregnancy, birth, and nursing led to their taking major responsibility for raising children, who require extensive care for long periods of time. Ultimately, this care led to a sexual division of labor in which men worked outside the home and women worked inside it, thereby forming the basis for male domination and control over women.[20] According to socialist feminists, the key to an egalitarian society lies not so much in women taking ownership of the means of economic production, but in women taking control of their own bodies and their own reproductive functions. Once they have done that, they can move on to taking their rightful place in the larger society.

Liberal, radical, Marxist, and socialist feminisms are all widely recognized as separate strands of feminism, but several other strands are also sometimes mentioned.[21] One of these is *postmodern feminism.*[22] Smart, for example, discusses how discourse is used to set certain women apart as "criminal women."[23] Wonders argues that both postmodernism and feminism question the nature of justice in the context of storytelling and narrative, and that both tend to see "truth" as an opinion that benefits some at the expense of others.[24] Other feminists criticize postmodernism. Chesney-Lind and Faith question whether it is useful for women to dispute the notion of truth just at the point when women are gaining a voice in the knowledge production process.[25] Still others appear to reject postmodernism because they advocate feminist theory and research that adheres to standards of scientific objectivity.[26]

---

[20]Shulamith Firestone, *The Dialectics of Sex: The Case for Feminist Revolution*, William Morrow, New York, 1970.

[21]See, for example, Daly and Chesney-Lind, op. cit., p. 501; and Simpson, op. cit., p. 606.

[22]Chesney-Lind and Faith, op. cit., pp. 296–97.

[23]Carol Smart, *Feminism and the Power of Law*, Routledge, London, U.K., 1989 and "Feminist Approaches to Criminology or Postmodern Woman Meets Atavistic Man," pp. 70–84 in Loraine Gelshorpe and Allison Morris, eds., *Feminist Perspectives in Criminology*, Open University Press, Milton Keynes, UK, 1990. For a different postmodernist feminist view, see Christine Garza, "Postmodern Paradigms and Chicana Feminist Thought: Creating a Space and Language," *Critical Criminologist* 4(3/4): 1–2, 11–13 (1992).

[24]Nancy A. Wonders, "Postmodern Feminist Criminology and Social Justice," pp. 111–128 in Bruce A. Arrigo, *Social Justice, Criminal Justice*, West/Wadsworth, Belmont, CA, 1998.

[25]Chesney-Lind and Faith, op. cit., p. 297.

[26]E.g., Chesney-Lind and Faith (ibid., p. 298) call for "solid research- and theory-building" related to women's crime and victimization

Whether or not they adhere to postmodernism as a whole, many feminists now take an "appreciative relativism" stance within feminism that is similar to postmodernism. That is, they recognize and appreciate many different feminist voices as legitimate, and they refrain from analyzing, classifying, and ultimately picking apart those different voices.[27] In particular, feminist criminologists value multi-racial and multi-cultural voices that speak about women's experiences related to crime, victimization, and criminal justice.[28] This *multicultural feminism* focuses on the interlocking structures of domination: race, class, and gender.[29] Earlier feminism, dominated by middle-class European American women, tended to ignore the very different experiences of, for instance, poor African American women.[30]

GENDER IN CRIMINOLOGY

The problem of gender in criminology usually has been addressed in one of two forms. First, the *generalizability* problem focuses on whether traditional criminology theories, which were formulated to explain male criminal behavior, can be generalized to explain female criminal behavior. Second, the *gender ratio* problem focuses on explaining why women are less likely than men to engage in criminal behavior.[31]

Daly and Chesney-Lind suggest that the generalizability problem is the safe course of action for female criminologists who are just entering the field: "focus on the generalizibility problem and to use a domesticated feminism to modify previous theory."[32] While generalizability is "safer," the problem is that the traditional male-oriented criminology theories have limited value for explaining female criminality.[33] Daly and

---

[27]On the other hand, inclusion of diverse women's experience tends to weaken arguments about women's common experiences of oppression. See Dawn H. Currie, "Challenging Privilege: Feminist Struggles in the Canadian Context," *Critical Criminologist*, 3(1): 1–2, 10–12 (1991).

[28]Chesney-Lind and Faith, op. cit., p. 297–98. To some extent, the appreciative relativism of multi-cultural feminism contradicts the view of other feminists, who claim that feminist thinking is superior to male-dominated thinking, which they describe as biased, distorted, and lacking objectivity due in its loyalty to male domination. See Jagger, op. cit., p. 370. Also see Daly and Chesney-Lind, op. cit., pp. 499–500. Because it neither privileges nor disparages particular points of view, postmodernism itself would seem to suggest that male-dominated thinking is as legitimate as feminist thinking. To that extent, postmodernism is difficult to reconcile with feminism. See Einstadter and Henry, op. cit., pp. 299–300.

[29]Patricia Hill Collins, *Black Feminist Thought*, Unwin Hyman, Boston, 1990.

[30]See Sylvia Walby, *Theorizing Patriarchy*, Basil Blackwell, Cambridge, MA, 1990.

[31]Daly and Chesney-Lind, op. cit., pp. 514–20.

[32]Ibid., p. 518.

[33]Ibid., p. 514.

Chesney-Lind maintain that the theoretical concepts on which these theories are based "are inscribed so deeply by masculinist experience that this approach will prove too restrictive, or at least misleading" when applied to female crime.[34] On the other hand, after reviewing the literature, Smith and Paternoster conclude that it is premature to abandon these male-based theories entirely in the attempt to explain female offending.[35] Similarly, Kruttschnitt concludes that "the factors that influence delinquent development differ for males and females in some contexts but not others."[36]

Women criminologists who focus on the gender ratio problem, as opposed to the generalizability problem, have been more likely to utilize observations and interviews, and they "have displayed more tentativeness and a discomfort with making global claims" at the theoretical level. In contrast, the men criminologists who address the gender ratio problem have been bolder in making grand theoretical claims, and have tended to do empirical research that involved statistical analysis of quantitative data. Daly and Chesney-Lind state that women criminologists

. . . are more interested in providing texture, social context, and case histories: in short, in presenting accurate portraits of how adolescent and adult women become involved in crime. This gender difference . . . (is related) to a felt need to comprehend women's crime on its own terms, just as criminologists of the past did for men's crime.[37]

The problem for these women criminologists is that "global or grand theoretical arguments and high-tech statistical analyses are valued more highly by the profession." The women criminologists therefore run the risk that their approaches "will be trivialized merely as case studies, or will be written off as not theoretical enough."[38]

Chesney-Lind and Faith argue that gender must become a central concept in criminology theories.[39] Social class has been the central concept in many criminology theories in the past, yet many criminologists

---

[34]Ibid., p. 519.

[35]Douglas A. Smith and Raymond Paternoster, "The Gender Gap in Theories of Deviance," *Journal of Research in Crime and Delinquency* 24: 140–72, 1987.

[36]Candace Kruttschnitt, "Contributions of Quantitative Methods to the Study of Gender and Crime, or Bootstrapping Our Way Into the Theoretical Thicket," *Journal of Quantitative Criminology* 12: 135–61, 1996, p. 141.

[37]Ibid., p. 518.

[38]Ibid., pp. 519–20.

[39]Op. cit., pp. 289–90.

argue there is no direct relationship between class and crime.[40] In contrast, the relationship between gender and crime is strong and undeniable. Beyond that, Chesney-Lind and Faith argue that the gender ratio problem (why women are less likely, and men more likely, to engage in criminal behavior) can only be fully explained in the context of the sex-gender system (or patriarchy). While it varies from culture to culture, this system constructs gender categories out of biological sex, associates those gender categories with different roles or tasks in a division of labor, and then values men and their tasks over women and their tasks.[41] Ultimately, in order to explain the gender ratio problem, Chesney-Lind and Faith argue that criminologists will have to "theorize gender" in their theories of crime. That is, both women's and men's experiences as offenders and victims, as well as their divergent treatment in criminal justice systems, can only be fully understood in the context of the sex-gender system of patriarchy.[42]

Feminist criminology has raised a wide variety of issues related to women as offenders, women as victims, and women's experiences with the criminal justice system, and all these issues have implications for much existing criminological knowledge about men. The following sections, however, consider only the gender ratio problem. For most of the twentieth century, explanations of the gender ratio have focused on why women's crime rates have been so low, and these explanations are the subject of the next section. In effect, this approach assumes that male crime rates are the norm, and it attempts to explain why women's crime rates are different from that norm.[43] The opposite question—Why are men's crime rates so high?—is addressed later in this chapter.

WHY ARE WOMEN'S CRIME RATES SO LOW?

In the first half of the twentieth century, criminology theories generally explained all crime in terms of biological and psychological disorders. Such theories tended to assume that, because women commit less fre-

---

[40]For a recent discussion of the issue, see R. Gregory Dunaway, Francis T. Cullen, Velmer S. Burton, Jr., and T. David Evans, "The Myth of Social Class and Crime Revisited," *Criminology* 38: 589–632 (2000).

[41]Claire Renzetti and Dan Curran, *Women, Men and Society*, Allyn and Bacon, Boston, 1993.

[42]Chesney-Lind and Faith, op. cit., pp. 290.

[43]Maureen Cain, "Realist Philosophy and Standpoint Epistemologies for Feminist Criminology as a Successor Science," pp. 124–40 in Loraine Gelsthorpe and Allison Morris, eds., *Feminist Perspectives in Criminology*, Open University Press, Buckingham, U.K., 1990.

quent, less serious crime than men, women offenders must therefore have even more serious biological and psychological disorders than men offenders.[44] By the middle of the twentieth century, theories of men's criminality had turned to social explanations, such as the ecology, strain, differential association, control, and labeling theories discussed in earlier chapters. These theories, as originally proposed, had little or nothing to say about female offending.[45] Theories of women's criminality during these years remained almost entirely focused on individual pathology, and they tended to view women's offending as minor offending predominantly related to sexual activity. When women engaged in more serious offenses, it was often viewed as being the result of the influence of their male romantic partners.[46] Only with the rise of feminism was women's criminality viewed as an entity in itself and in the context of women's social situation.

Many of the recent theories look at variations in socialization, particularly as related to gender roles, arguing that females are socialized towards greater conformity and less risk-taking than males.[47] An alternate but related perspective is that females are more controlled than males, particularly in terms of direct controls such as surveillance and supervision.[48] Hagan and his colleagues combine both of these perspectives in power-control theory, which argues that parents control daughters more than sons and, that boys are therefore more likely to engage in risky behavior than girls.[49] This disproportional controlling behavior will be greatest in a patriarchal family, in which the father has more power than the mother because of his employment in the workforce. This contrasts with non-patriarchal families in which both parents have equal power because of their equal status in the workplace. Individual delinquency rates are thus viewed as the product of two levels of distribution of power—power relations in society (the workplace) and power relations in

---

[44]Peggy C. Giordano and Sharon Mohler Rockwell, "Differential Association Theory and Female Crime," pp. 3–24 in Sally S. Simpson, ed., *Of Crime and Criminality,* Pine Forge Press, Thousand Oaks, CA, 2000, p. 4.

[45]For a review see Chesney-Lind and Shelden, op. cit., pp. 81–91.

[46]Peggy C. Giordano and Stephen A. Cernkovich, "Gender and Antisocial Behavior," pp. 496–510 in David M. Stoff, James Breiling, and Jack D. Maser, eds., *Handbook of Antisocial Behavior,* John Wiley, New York, 1997.

[47]E.g., Margaret L. Anderson, *Thinking About Women,* 2nd ed., Macmillan, New York, 1988.

[48]E.g., Charles Tittle, *Control Balance,* Westview, Boulder, CO, 1995.

[49]The original work on power-control theory is by John Hagan, A.R. Gillis, and J. Simpson, "The Class Structure of Gender and Delinquency: Toward a Power-Control Theory of Common Delinquent Behavior," *American Journal of Sociology* 90: 1151–78 (1985). The theory is then presented in a larger theoretical context in John Hagan, *Structural Criminology,* Rutgers University Press, New Brunswick, NJ, 1989.

the family. Tests of power-control theory have found support for a variety of its arguments.[50]

Where power-control theory focuses on the greater controls of girls, other explanations consider female offending in the context of strain-type theories. Many theories have discussed the particular victimizations that women experience and have sought to link these to the particular types of offenses that women commit. Chesney-Lind and Faith state that "research consistently documents that victimization is at the heart of much of girls' and women's lawbreaking, and that this pattern of gender entrapment, rather than gender liberation, best explains women's involvement in crime."[51]

Still other theories have approached women's offending in the context of differential association theory. Giordano and Rockwell, for example, interviewed 127 girls in 1982, the total population in Ohio's only institution for female delinquents, and re-interviewed most of them again in 1995.[52] They found that "these women appear to have been literally 'immersed' in deviant lifestyles—where aunts, cousins, siblings, fathers, and mothers routinely engaged in violence and criminal behavior."[53] The authors presented anecdotal accounts to illustrate the family's influence on criminal definitions, as well as the direct and indirect learning of the behavior itself from family and extra-family influences. Also in the differential association tradition, Heimer and De Coster found that "boys are more violent than girls largely because they are taught more definitions favoring such behavior; girls are less violent than boys because they are controlled through subtle mechanisms, which include learning that violence is incompatible with the meaning of gender for them and being restrained by emotional bonds to family."[54] These authors conclude that "consistent with feminist arguments, gender differences in violence ultimately are rooted in power differences."[55]

More recently, some feminists have looked at female criminality in the context of "doing gender," an approach to gender which assumes

---

[50]John Hagan, *Structural Criminology*, chs. 7–9; Hagan, A. R. Gillis, and John Simpson, "Clarifying and Extending Power-Control Theory," *American Journal of Sociology* 95: 1151–78 (1990); Brenda Sims Blackwell, "Perceived Sanction Threats, Gender, and Crime," *Criminology* 38: 439–88 (2000).

[51]Chesney-Lind and Faith, op. cit., p. 299.

[52]Giordano and Rockwell, op. cit.

[53]Ibid., p. 22

[54]Karen Heimer and Stacy De Coster, "The Gendering of Violent Delinquency," *Criminology* 37: 277–318 (1999), p. 306.

[55]Ibid., p. 305.

that the feminine gender role is something that must be accomplished in the context of specific situations.[56] The feminine gender role itself may be dysfunctional in various ways, but the greater problem lies in over-conformity to the role generated by the need to prove something, to demonstrate femininity in specific contexts. This approach is associated with the multi-cultural feminism described above, since different racial and ethnic groups may have different norms for femininity. What are called "hegemonic" gender roles (breadwinner for males, housewife for females) are the masculinity and femininity defined by the dominant European American culture. Quoting Spender,[57] Simpson and Ellis describe this femininity as girls learn it in schools:

Simultaneously expected to behave and conform but not perform (at least not in subjects that "really" matter, like physics, mathematics, biology, chemistry, and so forth), "women learn that they are not as worthy, that they do not count as much, and that what competence they may have is usually restricted to a specialized sphere which does not rank high in the male scheme of values." The above view captures, for the most part, a hegemonic femininity.[58]

Simpson and Ellis then argue that this hegemonic femininity is more relevant to European American females, but less relevant to females who are expected to work, including African American females.

Others researchers also take the "doing gender" approach, but they examine the very different femininities of females involved in serious crimes. For example, Maher[59] describes the gendered division of labor in serious drug markets in Brooklyn, NY, while Miller[60] interviews women involved in armed robberies in St. Louis. These women operate in rigidly stratified gender hierarchies where women's roles are severely limited, and while their motives are similar to those of male offenders, their specific actions can only be understood in the context of that gendered environment.

---

[56]Candace West and Sarah Fenstermaker, "Doing Gender," *Gender and Society* 9: 3–37 (1995).

[57]Dale Spender, *Invisible Women*, Writers and Readers Publishing, London, 1982, p. 23.

[58]Sally S. Simpson and Lori Elis, "Doing Gender: Sorting Out the Caste and Crime Conundrum," *Criminology* 33: 47–81 (1995), p. 71.

[59]Lisa Maher, *Sexed Work: Gender, Race, and Resistance in a Brooklyn Drug Economy*, Clarendon, Oxford, UK, 1997

[60]Jody Miller, "Up It Up: Gender and the Accomplishment of Street Robbery," *Criminology* 36: 37–66, 1998; also "Feminist Theories of Women's Crime: Robbery as a Case Study," pp. 25–46 in Simpson, ed., *Of Crime and Criminality*, op. cit.

WHY ARE MEN'S CRIME RATES SO HIGH?

Heidensohn remarks that one of the lessons that should be learned from all the theory and research on women's offending is that "we have to ask a different question—not what makes women's crime rates so low, but why are men's so high?"[61] Chesney-Lind and Faith suggest that asking the question this way means that "suddenly men have a gender, not just women; and male behavior is no longer normalized."[62] Heidensohn describes this question as "stunning in its implications."

Before they were questioned by feminist criminologists, traditional criminology theories largely dealt with male offending and were largely tested with male populations. Nevertheless, most of these theories were gender neutral in their arguments and could not explain the differences between male and female offending (the gender ratio problem). The problem was that the causal factors proposed by these theories, such as economic inequality or social structural strain, did not appear to affect men and women differently. Thus, the theories themselves implied that men's and women's crime rates should be equal.[63]

A few of these traditional criminology theories proposed causal factors that are unequally distributed by gender. For example, testosterone levels, one biological factor associated with crime, are more concentrated in men than in women.[64] Few criminologists deny that such biological factors have some effect on gender differences in crime, but as discussed in Chapter 3 these effects themselves are not large. In addition, the very large within-gender differences in crime (i.e., some men commit a lot of crime and some men commit none) indicate that strictly biological factors can play only a limited role in criminology theories.[65]

Other traditional theories proposed causal factors that might be unequally distributed by gender, although this was not argued in the theory itself. For example, Hirschi's social control theory could explain the gender ratio problem if boys experience fewer social controls than girls. However, this argument is not actually part of the theory, and Hirschi

---

[61]Frances Heidensohn, "Gender and Crime:" pp. 761–98 in Mike Maguire, Rod Morgan, and Robert Reiner, eds., *The Oxford Handbook of Criminology,* 2nd ed., Oxford, New York, 1996, p. 791.

[62]Chesney-Lind and Faith, op. cit., p. 287.

[63]James W. Messerschmidt, *Masculinities and Crime,* Rowman and Littlefield, Lanham, MD, 1993, pp. 2–4.

[64]Ibid., Chapter 3.

[65]Tittle and Paternoster, op. cit., p. 364–65.

himself discarded all data on females before testing his theory.[66] As discussed above in the section on women's crime rates, recent testing on this assertion has produced mixed results.

Similarly, Gottfredson and Hirschi's theory of low self-control might explain the gender ratio problem if the standard child-rearing practices for boys, as compared to girls, are more likely to result in low self-control as a stable personality construct in adolescence and adulthood. Gottfredson and Hirschi agree that gender is a "major, persistent correlate" to crime.[67] After reviewing the research, they conclude that some gender differences in offending reflect "differences in opportunity variables or supervision," in that parents "seek to minimize opportunities for crime, especially for daughters." But they conclude that "there are substantial self-control differences between the sexes" and that explanations of gender differences in crime must include "differences in self-control that are not produced by direct external control." They speculate that gendered differences in self-control may originate in gendered differences in parental monitoring and punishment of deviant behavior of very young children, but then state that "it is beyond the scope of this work to attempt to identify all of the elements responsible for gender differences in crime."[68]

Finally, very few traditional criminology theories explicitly dealt with masculinity or the sex-gender system (patriarchy) as a causal factor in crime. Some theories of gang behavior, however, were an exception.[69] In his theory of lower class culture, Miller described a tenuous masculinity at the heart of gang behavior, which is a "one-sex peer group" of adolescent boys who mostly live in female-headed households.[70] Similarly, in his strain theory, Cohen argued that a boy's gang behavior "has at least one virtue: it incontestably confirms, in the eyes of all concerned, his essential masculinity. The delinquent is the rogue male."[71] Relying on

---

[66]Messerschmidt, op. cit., p. 3.

[67]Michael R. Gottfredson and Travis Hirschi, *A General Theory of Crime*, Stanford University Press, Stanford, 1990, pp. 144–49.

[68]Karen Hayslett-McCall and Thomas J. Bernard ("Attachment, Self-Control, and Masculinity: A Theory of Male Crime Rates," forthcoming in *Theoretical Criminology*) positively support this speculation, linking it to broader theories of masculinity.

[69]Miller, Cohen, and Cloward and Ohlin are quoted in Chesney-Lind and Shelden, op. cit., pp. 84–86.

[70]Walter B. Miller, "Lower Class Culture as a Generating Milieu of Gang Delinquency," *Journal of Social Issues* 14: 5–19 (1958). See the discussion in Chapter 9.

[71]Albert Cohen, *Delinquent Boys: The Culture of the Gang*, Free Press, New York, 1955, pp. 139–40. See the discussion of Cohen in Chapter 8.

Miller and Cohen, Cloward and Ohlin[72] stated in their strain theory that gang boys

have trouble forming a clear masculine self-image. . . . Engulfed by a feminine world and uncertain of their own identification, they tend to 'protest' against femininity. This protest may take the form of robust and aggressive behavior, and even of malicious, irresponsible, and destructive acts. Such acts evoke maternal disapproval and thus come to stand for independence and masculinity to rebellious adolescents.

These theories suggest that gang delinquency involves the process of "doing gender" as described in the feminist theories of female crime and delinquency. That is, the gang behavior itself is a means of demonstrating masculinity in the context of particular situations and particular cultural contexts. Messerschmidt has developed this view at considerable length, examining how the criminal behavior of men in different cultural contexts reveals an attempt to demonstrate the different masculinities associated with those contexts.[73]

In this approach, the masculine gender role is said to be the source of a variety of men's problems, including increased suicide, crime, health problems, and relationship problems. All of these problems, particularly relationships with women, are driving changes in the masculine gender role today. However, the greater problem is that most men experience themselves as not "living up to" gender role expectations and therefore as needing to "prove" their masculinity. Thus, men focus less on the gender role itself than on the process by which they attempt to live up to its demands. The exact behaviors by which men demonstrate "masculinity" then depends very much on the particular cultural and situational contexts in which they find themselves.

CONCLUSIONS

With regard to the explanation of female criminality, Miller concludes that "it is important to strike a balance between recognizing the signifi-

---

[72]Richard A. Cloward and Lloyd E. Ohlin, *Delinquency and Opportunity*, Free Press, New York, 1960. See the discussion in Chapter 8.

[73]Messerschmidt, *Capitalism, Patriarchy, and Crime*, op. cit. Messerschmidt, *Crime as Structured Action: Gender, Race, Class, and Crime in the Making*, Sage, Thousand Oaks, CA, 1997. See also Timothy Newburn and Elizabeth A. Stanko, *Men, Masculinities, and Crime*, Routledge, New York, 1991; Tony Jefferson, "Masculinities and Crime," in Maguire, Morgan, and Reiner eds., *The Oxford Handbook of Criminology*, op. cit., and Lee H. Bowker, *Masculinities and Violence*, Sage, Thousand Oaks, CA, 1998.

cance of gender and gender inequality but not to reduce everything to gender."[74] Similarly, Giordano and Rockwell conclude that "a truly comprehensive approach . . . inevitably would include attention to causal processes that appear gender specific (e.g., backgrounds of sexual abuse) and to those that appear to have applicability to both males and females (e.g., family histories that include exposure to criminal definitions and opportunities)."[75] These conclusions about the role of gender in criminology theories appear to be reasonable generally.

Crime is overwhelmingly a gendered activity, and the "gender ratio" may be considered the single most important fact that criminology theories must be able to explain. Traditional theories have largely failed to even consider this problem, much less explain it. It seems likely that the full explanation of the gender ratio will have to include some theories that are common to both genders and some that are specific to each gender. Beyond that, the full explanation of the gender ratio will have to include what feminists describe as the sex-gender system of patriarchy— the stratified system of gender roles and expectations by which women and men enact femininity and masculinity.

---

[74]Miller, "Feminist Theories," op. cit., p. 43.

[75]Giordano and Rockwell, op. cit., p. 22.

CHAPTER SIXTEEN

Age and Crime

Most theories in criminology focus on the relationship between crime and various biological, psychological or social factors, and they assume that these factors have the same effect on offenders regardless of their age. In contrast, developmental theories assume that different factors may have different effects on offenders of different ages. These developmental theories therefore explain crime in the context of the life course: i.e., the progression from childhood to adolescence to adulthood and ultimately to old age. For example, developmental theories may assert that some factors explain criminal behavior that starts in childhood or early adolescence, but other factors explain crime that starts in late adolescence or adulthood. Some factors explain the fact that a person begins to commit crime, while other factors explain whether the person continues to commit crime for a long time or quickly stops.

Some criminologists argue that these developmental theories do not contribute anything new to criminology, and that the standard theories that do not consider age and the life course are adequate to explain crime. A major debate about this issue was fully engaged by the mid-1980s. At its center was an argument about the relationship between age and crime. But the debate also was entangled in complicated arguments about criminal careers, since that concept refers to the development and progression of offending over time. The debate also involved a particularly fierce argument about the type of research needed to test criminology theories. We begin with a review of this debate and of some of the evidence that was marshalled to defend each side. We then discuss other developmental theories that have been recently proposed.

THE GREAT DEBATE: CRIMINAL CAREERS, LONGITUDINAL RESEARCH, AND THE RELATIONSHIP BETWEEN AGE AND CRIME

In 1986, the National Research Council's Panel on Research on Criminal Careers published a two-volume work entitled *Criminal Careers and "Career Criminals."*[1] The panel's research was based on ideas that had been brewing for some time. In 1972, a study in Philadelphia had concluded that 6 percent of juveniles accounted for 52 percent of all juvenile contacts with the police in the city and 70 percent of all juvenile contacts involving felony offenses.[2] These figures led to the idea that there was a small group of active "career criminals" who accounted for a very large portion of crime.[3] This conclusion in turn led to the idea that crime rates could be reduced dramatically by locking up these chronic offenders.[4] Subsequently, a great deal of money was poured into research that attempted to develop these ideas so they could form the basis for practical crime policies.

Although the distinction was unclear at first, the ideas of "career criminals" and "criminal careers" are very different. A *career criminal* is thought to be a chronic offender who commits frequent crimes over a long period of time. In contrast, the term *criminal career* does not imply anything about the frequency or seriousness of the offending. It simply suggests that involvement in criminal activity begins at some point in a person's life, continues for a certain length of time, and then ends. Many people have short and trivial "criminal careers"—they commit one or two minor offenses and then stop.

The Panel on Research on Criminal Careers introduced a new set of terms with which to describe criminal behavior in the context of a criminal career. *Participation* refers to whether a person has ever committed a crime—it can only be "yes" or "no." *Prevalence* is the fraction of a group of people (such as all those under 18 years of age) that has ever participated in crime. *Frequency* (symbolized by the Greek letter lamb-

---

[1] Alfred Blumstein, Jacqueline Cohen, Jeffrey A. Roth, and Christy A. Visher, *Criminal Careers and "Career Criminals"*, National Academy Press, Washington, DC, 1986.

[2] Marvin Wolfgang, Robert Figlio, and Thorsten Sellin, *Delinquency in a Birth Cohort*, University of Chicago Press, Chicago, 1972.

[3] The idea of a career offender dates much further back than the Wolfgang et al. study, but it was this study that spurred new enthusiasm in the area. See Michael Gottfredson and Travis Hirschi, "The True Value of Lambda Would Appear to Be Zero: An Essay on Career Criminals, Criminal Careers, Selective Incapacitation, Cohort Studies, and Related Topics," *Criminology* 24(2): 213–33 (1986).

[4] In actual fact, the Philadelphia study did not support this conclusion. See Thomas J. Bernard and R. Richard Ritti, "Selective Incapacitation and the Philadelphia Birth Cohort Study," *Journal of Research in Crime and Delinquency* 28(1): 33–54 (1991).

da) refers to the rate of criminal activity of those who engage in crime, measured by the number of offenses over time. *Seriousness*, of course, concerns the severity of one's offenses. *Onset* and *desistance* refer to the beginning and end of a criminal career, while *duration* refers to the length of time between onset and desistance.

The first major use of this new language system was to interpret the relationship between age and crime, which set off the great debate mentioned above. It has long been known that crime rates rise rapidly throughout the adolescent years, peak in the late teens or early twenties, and steadily decline from then on. The traditional view has been that the decline in this curve after about age 20 is due primarily to changes in frequency—i.e., the number of offenders remains the same but each offender commits fewer offenses. In contrast, career criminal researchers suggest that the decline is caused by a change in participation—i.e., the number of offenders declines but each remaining offender still engages in a high rate of offending. If these researchers are right, then those offenders who continue to commit crimes at high levels after their early 20s are "career criminals" who need to be incapacitated. On the other hand, if all offenders gradually commit fewer crimes, then none of them are "career criminals" in the sense of being a more frequent and chronic offender than the others.

This interpretation of the age-crime relationship also has another implication. Because some offenders always participate whereas others end their careers early, it may be necessary to develop different models for predicting participation and frequency. It may be that one set of factors influences whether someone participates in crime, whereas another set of factors affects the frequency and duration of their criminal acts.

Essentially, these factors represent the central contentions of the two sides in the great debate mentioned above. On the one side were the career criminal researchers, notably Alfred Blumstein, Jacqueline Cohen, and David Farrington, while on the other side most notably were Michael Gottfredson and Travis Hirschi.[5] Gottfredson and Hirschi

---

[5]This debate can be reviewed in a series of articles: Alfred Blumstein and Jacqueline Cohen, "Estimation of Individual Crime Rates from Arrest Records," *Journal of Criminal Law and Criminology* 70: 561–85 (1979); Travis Hirschi and Michael Gottfredson, "Age and the Explanation of Crime," *American Journal of Sociology* 89: 552–84 (1983); David Greenberg, "Age, Crime, and Social Explanation," *American Journal of Sociology* 91(1): 1–21 (1985); Gottfredson and Hirschi, "The True Value of Lambda Would Appear to Be Zero: An Essay on Career Criminals, Criminal Careers, Selective Incapacitation, Cohort Studies, and Related Topics," *Criminology* 24(2): 213–33 (1986); Blumstein, Cohen, and David Farrington, "Criminal Career Research: Its Value for Criminology," *Criminology* 26(1): 1–35 (1988); Gottfredson and Hirschi, "Science, Public Policy, and the Career Paradigm," *Criminology* 26(1): 37–55 (1988); Blumstein, Cohen, and Farrington, "Longitudinal and Criminal Career Research: Further Clarifications," *Criminology* 26(1): 57–73 (1988).

took the position that, independent of other sociological explanations, age simply matures people out of crime. The decline of crime with age therefore is due to the declining frequency of offenses among all active offenders, rather than declines in the number of active offenders. Because of this, Gottfredson and Hirschi argue that there is no reason to attempt to identify and selectively incapacitate "career criminals."

The debate on the relationship between age and crime led to a particularly ferocious dispute about the type of research that is required to test out these theories. Much prior research in criminology looked at aggregate crime rates—for example, burglary rates in a given city. But these aggregate rates say nothing about whether burglaries are committed by a small number of offenders who each commit a large number of burglaries or by a large number of offenders who each commit only a few. To answer this question, career criminal criminologists focused on the patterns of crimes committed by individual criminals over a period of time, rather than on aggregate crime rates within a particular location.[6] In particular, they tended to use "longitudinal research," which follows the same individuals over a long period of time. An early example of longitudinal research, as discussed in Chapter 3, was carried out by the Gluecks, who followed the lives of 500 delinquents and 500 nondelinquents over many years, attempting to assess why some juveniles become delinquent or criminal and others do not.[7]

In contrast, most other criminologists have used "cross sectional" research, which compares different individuals at the same time. For example, criminologists might examine a number of juveniles in a particular city, find out which juveniles commit the most offenses, and assess what types of factors are associated with those juveniles. Cross-sectional research is much cheaper than longitudinal research since it can be done at one time. Gottfredson and Hirschi argue that because the age-crime relationship is invariant, cross-sectional research is sufficient, and it is an unnecessary waste of resources to collect information about the same individuals over a long time period.[8] Other criminologists, howev-

---

[6]This was based on their view "that crime is committed by individuals, even when they organize into groups, and that individuals are the focus of criminal justice decisions" (Blumstein et al., op. cit., p. 12).

[7]Sheldon Glueck and Eleanor Glueck, *500 Criminal Careers* (New York: Knopf, 1930); *Juvenile Delinquents Grown Up* (Commonwealth Fund, New York, 1940); *Unraveling Juvenile Delinquency* (Harvard University Press, Cambridge, 1950); and *Delinquents and Nondelinquents in Perspective* (Harvard University Press, Cambridge, 1968).

[8]Michael Gottfredson and Travis Hirschi, "The Methodological Adequacy of Longitudinal Research on Crime," *Criminology* 25(3): 581–614 (1987).

er, believe that longitudinal data collection and analysis can be beneficial to the study of criminal behavior.[9] They argue that cross-sectional designs only allow the study of correlates of criminal behavior, whereas longitudinal designs allow for the study of causation because they can establish which factors came first. Longitudinal research also allows one to assess the extent to which prior behavior influences present and future behavior. Additionally, it allows assessment of whether different models are necessary to explain behavior at different points in the life course.

CRIMINAL PROPENSITY VS. CRIMINAL CAREER

After considerable thrashing about, the age-crime debate described previously boiled down to a debate between the "criminal propensity" and the "criminal career" positions. Gottfredson and Hirschi espouse the *criminal propensity* position. Essentially, they argue that some people are more prone to commit crime and other people are less prone, but everyone's propensity to commit crime is relatively stable over their life course after the age of about 8. That propensity might manifest itself in a variety of patterns of behavior, due to chance and circumstances, so that individuals with the same propensity might actually commit somewhat different amounts and types of crime. But because criminal propensity is essentially constant over the life course, it is unnecessary to explain such factors as age of onset of crime, duration of a criminal career, and frequency of offending. Actual variations in the amount of offending by given individuals then are explained primarily by their point on the age-crime curve. Everyone will follow the age-crime curve, in the sense that they all will have their greatest criminal involvement in their late teens and decline thereafter. But over the entire age curve, those with the lowest propensity always will have the lowest actual involvement with crime, while those with the highest propensity always will have the highest actual involvement. Thus, the age-crime curve, combined with variations in the propensity to commit crime, looks like Figure 16-1.

Gottfredson and Hirschi argue that the age-crime curve itself is invariant and does not require any explanation. Therefore, all that is required is to explain why different people have different criminal

---

[9]See, for example, Scott Menard and Delbert Elliott, "Longitudinal and Cross-Sectional Data Collection and Analysis in the Study of Crime and Delinquency," *Justice Quarterly* 7(1): 11–55 (1990).

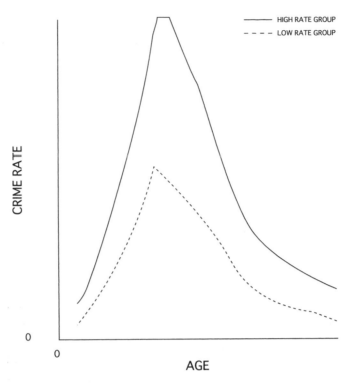

FIGURE 1 Hypothesized relation among age, propensity, and crime. (From Travis Hirschi and Michael Gottfredson, "Age and the Explanation of Crime," *American Journal of Sociology* 89[3]: 565 [1983]. Reprinted by permission.)

propensities.[10] And because criminal propensity does not vary over the life course, the explanation can be tested with cross-sectional research, and there is no need for the more expensive longitudinal designs. This is the context for their theory of low self-control, as presented in Chapter 10.

In contrast to the criminal propensity position in the *criminal career* position, which we have previously discussed. According to this position, different sets of variables may explain behavior at different points in the life course. Thus it is necessary to build separate models for age of onset, participation, frequency, duration, and desistance. To some extent, then,

---

[10]In *A General Theory of Crime* (Stanford: Stanford University Press, 1990) Gottfredson and Hirschi argue that the propensity toward crime is a product of low self-control, and allow for variation in the effect propensity has on actual behavior by introducing opportunity into their model. Low self-control only brings about criminal behavior when opportunities for such behavior are present. See Ch. 10.

the debate focused on whether the entire "criminal career" could be explained with a single causal theory (the "criminal propensity" position) or whether different causal processes were at work at different points in the life span (the "criminal career" position). In particular, the debate took on the focus of whether it was necessary to have separate causal models for participation and frequency, since those were the two crucial factors in the two contrasting explanations of the age-crime curve.

Once the age-crime relationship debate was established as one that set criminal propensity and criminal career positions against each other, researchers went to work attempting to garner support for one or the other position. Although the issue is not yet resolved,[11] there is some preliminary evidence supporting both positions.

Probably the strongest evidence for the criminal propensity position comes from Rowe, Osgood, and Nicewander, who fit a latent trait model to crime data.[12] A latent trait is a quality that is unobservable, but can be inferred through various measures. If it exists, then the inherent propensity to commit crime would be a latent trait because, for a given person, there is no way directly to observe it. The question, of course, is whether it exists at all. The way Rowe et al. decided to proceed was to make certain assumptions about the latent "criminal propensity" trait and then use those assumptions to predict how criminal activity would be distributed among offenders if such a trait actually existed. They then compared those predictions with the actual distribution of offenses that had been found in four different cities. Rowe et al.'s model was basically atheoretical in that it did not discuss where this latent propensity toward criminal behavior comes from. Instead it was just a test to see if such a propensity may exist. According to the propensity position, such a trait should account for differences in both one's likelihood to participate in criminal behavior and one's frequency of participation, since both of these outcomes stem from the same source. Applying their models to four different sets of data on individual behavior, Rowe et al. found solid support for the propensity position.[13]

---

[11]D. Wayne Osgood and David Rowe have recently attempted to lay out a detailed guide of how researchers may begin to competitively test the propensity and criminal career positions, in "Bridging Criminal Careers, Theory, and Policy Through Latent Variable Models of Individual Offending," *Criminology* 32(4) 517–54 (1994).

[12]David Rowe, D. Wayne Osgood, and W. Alan Nicewander, "A Latent Trait Approach to Unifying Criminal Careers," *Criminology* 28(2): 237–70 (1990). These researchers define propensity in terms of the relative stability of causal factors (p. 241).

[13]In each data set, there is a distribution of how many offenders committed zero, one, two, etc. offenses. For example, in Wolfgang's Philadelphia cohort, 65 percent of the cohort committed zero offenses, whereas 2.3 percent were responsible for nine or more. Rowe et al.'s study assumes that

In contrast, Simons and his colleagues also tested a latent trait model and found support for the criminal career view.[14] Youths who exhibited antisocial behavior in late childhood tended to receive lower quality parenting and schooling and to have more associations with delinquent peers. These three factors then increased delinquency in early adolescence. If these three events did not happen, however, there was no increase in adolescent delinquency. These findings suggest that these youths did not have a latent antisocial trait, but that adolescent delinquency was a product of developmental events in the life course. In addition, Monkonnen looked at age-specific violent offending in New York City from 1773 to 1874 and from 1976 to 1995.[15] In the earlier time period, violent offending peaked between ages 20 and 30, while in the recent time period there was a much younger peak and a much flatter rate of offending from the early 20s onward. Monkkonnen concluded that the age distribution of recent violent crime is a new phenomenon in history. His conclusion challenges Gottfredson and Hirschi's argument about the invariant relationship between age and crime.

On the other hand, O'Brien and his colleagues studied age-specific homicide rates from 1960 to 1995.[16] In the 1990s, youths age 14–17 were two to three times more likely to commit homicides than similarly aged youths in the 1960s and 1970s, while people 25 years and older in the 1990s were less likely to commit homicide than similarly aged people in the 1960s and 1970s. O'Brien et al. argued that, given the high total number of births at the time and the high portion of births to unwed mothers, the high rate of violence resulted from the few resources that were available when these youths were small children. This pattern of violence persisted and was relatively stable as this particular group of juveniles aged. This finding supports Gottfredson and Hirschi's propensity

latent propensities are normally distributed, that the relationship between one's propensity to engage in crime and rate of offending (lambda) is exponential, and that the relationship between lambda and observed offending can be modeled with a Poisson distribution (a probabilistic distribution of relatively rare events occurring over a continuum of time). Combining these probabilistic relationships, the authors produced frequency distributions that were very similar to actual distributions of offenses in data sets from Philadelphia, London, Richmond (Calif.), and Racine (Wis.). While this modeling represents strong support, it also should be noted that the validity of such modeling depends on the validity of the assumptions described above.

[14]Ronald L. Simons, Christine Johnson, Rand D. Conger, et al. "A Test of Latent Trait versus Life-Course Perspectives on the Stability of Adolescent Antisocial Behavior," *Criminology* 36(2): 217–43 (1998).

[15]Eric H. Monkkonnen, "New York City Offender Ages," *Homicide Studies* 3(3): 256–70 (1999).

[16]Robert M. O'Brien, Jean Stockard, and Lynne Isaacson, "The Enduring Effects of Cohort Characteristics on Age-Specific Homicide Rates," *American Journal of Sociology* 104(4): 1061–95 (1999).

position, in which the propensity toward crime is established at an early age and then simply follows the age-crime curve over time.[17]

THE TRANSITION TO DEVELOPMENTAL CRIMINOLOGY

Criminologists are still testing the propensity and criminal career positions against each other, and the issues involved in the argument are becoming increasingly complex.[18] In general, however, researchers are less likely to regard these two positions as polar opposites. For example, Nagin and Land found support for both the criminal career and propensity positions, and suggested that "a moratorium should be called on strong either-or theoretical positions on the nature of criminal careers . . ."[19] In addition, there is a developmental criminology forming, one which has strong roots in developmental psychology and which treats crimes as social events in the life course.[20] As these new developmental theories are being created and evaluated, the great debate between criminal careers and criminal propensity is becoming less important.

This is not to say that the work on criminal careers is irrelevant to developmental criminologists. On the contrary, these theorists have largely adopted the terminology of the criminal career paradigm. For example, in their review of the developmental literature, Loeber and Le Blanc organize the material around activation, aggravation, and desistance,[21] concepts that are similar to the core concepts of the criminal career paradigm. Activation refers to the continuity, frequency, and diversity of

---

[17]Ibid., pp. 1087–88.

[18]For example, see Raymond Paternoster, Charles W. Dean, Alex Piquero, et al., "Generality, Continuity, and Change in Offending," *Journal of Quantitative Criminology* 13(3): 231–66 (1997); Alex Piquero, Raymond Paternoster, Paul Mazerolle, et al., "Onset Age and Offense Specialization," *Journal of Research in Crime and Delinquency*, 36(3): 275–99 (1999); and Robert Brame, Shawn Bushway, and Raymond Paternoster, "On the Use of Panel Research Designs and Random Effects Models to Investigate Static and Dynamic Theories of Criminal Offending," *Criminology* 37: 599–641 (1999).

[19]Daniel Nagin and Kenneth Land, "Age, Criminal Careers, and Population Hetergeneity: Specification and Estimation of a Nonparametric, Mixed Poisson Model," *Criminology* 32(3): 357 (1993).

[20]One of the first attempts to direct research away from the criminal career debate and towards a developmental perspective was made by John Hagan and Alberto Palloni, "Crimes as Social Events in the Life Course: Reconceiving a Criminological Controversy," *Criminology* 26(1): 87–100 (1988). These authors suggest that criminologists should broaden their focus from criminal behaviors to anti-social behaviors, substitute the idea of "social events" for "criminal careers," and look at the causes and consequences of those behaviors in both the short and the long run.

[21]Rolf Loeber and Marc Le Blanc, "Toward a Developmental Criminology,", pp. 375–473 in Michael Tonry and Norval Morris, eds., *Crime and Justice: A Review of Research* (vol. 12), University of Chicago Press, Chicago, 1990; Le Blanc and Loeber, "Developmental Criminology Updated," pp. 115–98 in Michael Tonry, ed., *Crime and Justice: A Review of Research* (vol. 23), University of Chicago Press, Chicago, 1998.

criminal activities. It consists of acceleration (increased frequency), sta-bilization (continuity over time), and diversification (of criminal activi-ties). Aggravation is a developmental sequence that escalates in serious-ness over time. Desistance refers to a decrease in the frequency of offending, a reduction in its diversification (specialization), and a reduc-tion in its seriousness.

In the following sections we review two developmental theories which each contribute a different twist.[22] Thornberry's interactional the-ory explores the relationship between past and present criminal behav-ior, shows how causal processes of delinquent behavior are dynamic and how different forces shape each other over time, and shows that causal influences may depend on the period of an individual's life. Sampson and Laub's longitudinal study pays special attention to the tension be-tween stability and change perspectives in developmental psychology and criminology. They argue that although prior behavior is a strong de-terminant of present and future behavior, turning points in individuals' lives do exist, and change (both positive and negative) can occur at any point in a developmental sequence.

THORNBERRY'S INTERACTIONAL THEORY

Thornberry's interactional theory combines control and social learning theories (see Chapters 9 and 10), attempting to increase their collective ability to explain delinquent behavior.[23] To Thornberry, these theories are flawed by their reliance on unidirectional causal structures. He at-tempts to develop a model in which concepts from these theories affect each other over time, reciprocally, and in which actual delinquent be-havior also reciprocally affects the theoretical concepts. Also, Thornber-ry believes that the contributing causes to delinquent behavior will change over an individual's life course.

Interactional theory is based mostly on control theory, viewing social constraints as the primary cause of delinquency. However, reduced so-cial constraints may free up behavior, but delinquency still "requires an

---

[22]Two other important developmental theories are by G. R. Patterson, Barbara DeBaryshe, and Elizabeth Ramsey, "A Developmental Perspective on Antisocial Behavior," *American Psychologist* 44(2): 329–35 (1989); and Terrie Moffitt, "Adolescence-Limited and Life-Course-Persistent Anti-social Behavior: A Developmental Taxonomy" *Psychological Review* 100(4): 674–701 (1993). Mof-fitt's theory is briefly described in Chapter 4.

[23]Terrence Thornberry, "Toward an Interactional Theory of Delinquency," *Criminology* 25(4): 863–87 (1987). An earlier version of this section is found in Thomas J. Bernard and Jeffrey Snipes, "Theoretical Integration in Criminology," in Michael Tonry, ed., *Crime and Justice: A Review of Re-search*, Vol. 20, University of Chicago Press, Chicago, 1996, pp. 314–16.

interactive setting in which (it) is learned, performed, and reinforced."[24]
The theory is comprised of six concepts from control and social learning
theory: attachment to parents, commitment to school, belief in conventional values, association with delinquent peers, adoption of delinquent
values, and engagement in delinquent behavior. Three models are offered, for early adolescence (11–13), middle adolescence (15–16), and
late adolescence (18–20). The division of a theory into different models
for different phases in this manner is one of the distinguishing characteristics of developmental theory.

Thornberry's main goal in interactional theory is to sort out the debate
between control and social learning theorists: the former argue that
delinquent behavior affects the peers one attaches to; the latter argue
that one's peer associations affect delinquent behavior. Thornberry argues that peer associations may affect behavior, but behavior in turn can
influence one's selection of peers. In interactional theory, concepts from
control theory are the most important contributors, because delinquency will probably not occur unless social constraints are reduced. Thus,
the greater one's attachment to parents and commitment to school, the
less likely one is to engage in delinquent behavior. Belief in conventional values is influenced by both attachment and commitment, and it affects delinquent behavior indirectly, through its reciprocal influence on
commitment to school. Delinquent behavior negatively influences attachment and commitment. It also influences belief in conventional values, indirectly through its influence on attachment. As Thornberry says,
". . . while the weakening of the bond to conventional society may be an
initial cause of delinquency, delinquency eventually becomes its own indirect cause precisely because of its ability to weaken further the person's bonds to family, school, and conventional beliefs."[25]

Also included in Thornberry's interactional theory are hypotheses
about how models of delinquency might vary over the adolescent time
period. Generally, the models for early, middle, and late adolescence are
not very different; however, he does note a few expected disparities.[26] In
middle adolescence, attachment to parents is expected to play a smaller
role, since the adolescent is more involved in activities outside the
home. Also, delinquent values are expected to exert a more important
influence on commitment, delinquent behavior, and association with
delinquent peers than they do in early adolescence, since these values

---

[24]Thornberry, op. cit., p. 865.

[25]*Ibid.*, p. 876.

[26]*Ibid.*, pp. 877–82.

have had more time to solidify. In late adolescence, two variables are added to the model: commitment to conventional activities such as employment, college, and military service, and commitment to family, such as marriage and having children. These variables essentially supplant attachment to parents and commitment to school, since they are more relevant during this time period in an individual's life.

A variety of these arguments have been tested with longitudinal research, with generally supportive results.[27] Thornberry reviewed 17 longitudinal studies and concluded that "across all the studies, the overwhelming weight of the evidence suggests that many of the presumed unidirectional causes of delinquency are in fact either products of delinquent behavior or involved in mutually reinforcing causal relationships with delinquency behavior."[28] For example, with respect to variables from control theory, Thornberry found almost no relationship at all between delinquency and attachment to parents. This finding was quite surprising, and Thornberry speculated that tests from earlier ages (all these studies were done in middle adolescence) might reveal such a relationship. There were fairly strong interactive relationships between delinquency and beliefs ("belief in conventional values, at least during the midadolescent years, influences and is influenced by delinquent conduct,") and commitment ("investments in conformity—school and employment—reduce delinquency and crime, but delinquent behavior feeds back upon and attenuates attachment to school and involvement in work.")[29] With respect to social learning variables, Thornberry found that "the strongest and most consistent reciprocal relationship is observed for delinquent peers and delinquent behavior," where the causal effects are approximately equal in both directions.[30] That is, the effect of delinquent behavior on delinquent peers seems to be about the same as the effect of delinquent peers on delinquent behavior. Thornberry concludes that ef-

---

[27]In particular, see Terrence Thornberry, Alan Lizotte, Marvin Krohn, and Sung Joon Jang, "Testing Interactional Theory: An Examination of Reciprocal Causal Relationships among Family, School, and Delinquency," *Journal of Criminal Law and Criminology* 82 (1991), pp. 3–35, and "Delinquent Peers, Beliefs, and Delinquent Behavior: A Longitudinal Test of Interactional Theory", *Criminology* 32(1): 47–83 (1994). Like tests of the propensity vs. criminal career debate (see above, footnote 18), tests of the interactional theory require longitudinal data and therefore raise complex methodological issues. See Sung Joon Jang, "Age-Varying Effects of Family, School, and Peers on Delinquency," pp. 643–85, a comment by Janet L. Lauritsen, "Limitations in the Use of Longitudinal Self-Report Data," pp. 687–94, and Jang's rejoinder "Different Definitions, Different Modeling Decisions and Different Interpretations," pp. 695–701, in *Criminology* 37 (1999).

[28]Terence P. Thornberry, "Empirical Support for Interactional Theory," pp. 198–235 in J. D. Hawkins, ed., *Delinquency and Crime: Current Theories,* Cambridge University Press, New York, 1996, p. 229.

[29]Ibid., p. 230.

[30]Ibid., p 231.

fective policies to prevent delinquency can only be constructed if causes are accurately separated from effects in the correlates of delinquency, and this separation can only be accomplished by longitudinal research in the context of a developmental theory of delinquency.

SAMPSON AND LAUB'S AGE-GRADED THEORY OF INFORMAL SOCIAL CONTROL

Perhaps the most important early study of delinquency was begun in the 1930s by Sheldon and Eleanor Glueck, who compared 500 persistent delinquents and 500 proven non-delinquents.[31] The two groups were matched on age, general intelligence, ethnicity, and residence in under-privileged areas, and then compared to determine the factors most related to juvenile delinquency. Even though the Gluecks collected remarkable data on these youths, their analys of the data was limited by the methods available at the time and therefore has been criticized as inadequate by today's standards.

In 1985, John Laub located the original Glueck data, and he and Robert Sampson spent several years reconstructing and reanalyzing it in order to respond to many of the methodological criticisms. From their reanalysis came a major developmental study in which the authors developed a longitudinal theory of delinquency and crime, and used both quantitative and qualitative methods to support their arguments.[32] The theory has three components: the first explains juvenile delinquency, the second explores behavioral transitions as juveniles become adults, and the third explains adult criminal behavior.

According to Sampson and Laub, juvenile delinquency is directly explained by what they call "family context" factors. The family context factors that are most likely to produce delinquent behavior are erratic and threatening discipline by parents, lack of supervision by the mother, parental rejection of child, and child's emotional rejection of parents. These family context factors are themselves influenced by what Sampson and Laub call "background structural factors, including household

---

[31]Sheldon Glueck and Eleanor Glueck, *Unraveling Juvenile Delinquency*, Harvard University Press, Cambridge, MA, 1950.

[32]Robert Sampson and John Laub, *Crime in the Making: Pathways and Turning Points Through Life*, Cambridge: Harvard University Press, 1993. See also Laub and Sampson, "Turning Points in the Life Course: Why Change Matters to the Study of Crime," *Criminology* 31(3): 301–326 (1993); and Sampson and Laub, "Crime and Deviance in the Life Course," *Annual Review of Sociology* 18: 63–84 (1992). A good summary and overview is found in Laub, Sampson, and Leana C. Allen, "Explaining Crime Over the Life Course," pp. 97–112 in Raymond Paternoster and Ronet Bachman, eds., *Explaining Criminals and Crime*, Roxbury, Los Angeles, 2001.

crowding, family disruption (e.g., single parent family), family size, low family income, high residential mobility, foreign-born parents, mother's employment outside the home, and criminality by either or both parents. These background structural factors affect delinquency through their effect on the family context factors, such as erratic and threatening discipline.[33] These background structural factors may also result in weak attachment to school, poor performance in school, and attachment to delinquent siblings and delinquent friends. All these factors in turn increase the likelihood of delinquent behavior.[34]

The remainder of Sampson and Laub's theory concerns *stability* and *change* in the life course. They try to make sense of the apparent paradox that the best predictor of adult criminal behavior is childhood antisocial behavior and juvenile delinquency, but that most delinquents do not become criminals as adults.[35]

Stability in offending over the life course—i.e., the tendency for juvenile offenders to become adult offenders—is generally recognized as a common phenomenon and several attempts have been made to explain it. Gottfredson and Hirschi, for example, attribute stability in offending to a stable individual trait they call low self-control,[36] while Nagin and Paternoster focus on the causal influence of the earlier offending itself, arguing that it makes the later offending easier.[37] Sampson and Laub, in contrast, argue that stability is a result of what they call "cumulative continuity," a term which means that delinquent behavior, as well as being processed by the justice system, "closes doors" for the juvenile in a variety of ways. Delinquent behavior increases the likelihood of school failure, severs the juvenile's social bonds to school, friends, and family, and jeopardizes the development of future adult social bonds such as employment and marriage. All of these increase the potential for adult criminal behavior. This cumulative continuity, Sampson and Laub

---

[33]Sampson and Laub, *Crime in the Making*, pp. 65–71.

[34]Ibid, pp. 101–106.

[35]For example, Lee Robins ("Sturdy Childhood Predictors of Adult Antisocial Behaviour: Replications from Longitudinal Studies", *Psychological Medicine* 8: 611 [1978]) stated that "Adult antisocial behaviour virtually *requires* childhood antisocial behaviour [yet] most antisocial youths do *not* become antisocial adults." See also Moffitt, op. cit, p. 676.

[36]Gottfredson and Hirschi, *A General Theory of Crime*, op. cit.; for comments on the "cumulative continuity" argument, see Travis Hirschi and Michael Gottfredson, "Control Theory and the Life-Course Perspective," *Studies on Crime and Crime Prevention* 4: 131–43 (1995).

[37]Daniel Nagin and Raymond Paternoster, "On the Relationship of Past and Future Participation in Delinquency," *Criminology* 29: 163–90 (1991). This article describes the "state dependence" perspective.

argue, is independent of social class, background, family, and school factors.[38]

Despite the evidence of considerable stability in offending over the life course, Sampson and Laub also argue that *change* is common: juvenile delinquents often do not become adult criminals; adult criminals often stop committing crimes. Sampson and Laub argue that, for adults, the quality and strength of social ties is the strongest influence on whether one will engage in criminal behavior. Relationships with a spouse, job stability and commitment, dependence on an employer, and other such factors reduce the likelihood of criminal behavior. These factors are described as *social capital*[39]—the investment one has in social relationships with law-abiding people that help one to accomplish one's goals through legitimate means. Even though earlier juvenile delinquency negatively influences the ability to acquire adult social capital, the development of social bonds as an adult reduces the likelihood of crime, independent of childhood experiences. A former delinquent is disadvantaged by the past but not totally constrained by it.

Sampson and Laub's analysis of the Gluecks' data found general support for their developmental theory.[40] The strongest effects on delinquency were the family, school, and peer factors, which were influenced somewhat by the background structural factors. These background structural variables did not have much direct effect on delinquency, instead influencing delinquency through their effect on these informal social control variables. As expected, childhood delinquency was an important predictor of adult criminal behavior. Independent of one's past, the development of strong social bonds as an adult reduced the likelihood of crime and deviance.

One prime turning point in possible criminal behavior is marriage. In later research using the same Glueck data, Laub, Nagin, and Sampson found that marriage reduces delinquency and crime, and that the positive effect of marriage is gradual and cumulative over time.[41] They interpret these findings to mean that a good quality marriage functions as an informal social control that leads to desistance from crime. Using a

---

[38]Ibid., pp. 123–125. A similar argument is found in Moffitt, op. cit.

[39]James Coleman, "Social Capital in the Creation of Human Capital," *American Journal of Sociology* 94: 95–120 (1988).

[40]Sampson and Laub, op. cit., pp. 247–249. For a review of other empirical support for the theory, see Sampson, Laub, and Allen, op. cit., pp. 104–07.

[41]John H. Laub, Daniel S. Nagin and Robert J. Sampson, "Trajectories of Change in Criminal Offending," *American Sociological Review* 63(2): 225–38 (1998).

different data set, Warr found a similar effect for marriage, and also found that marriage resulted in a dramatic decline in the time spent with friends, particularly with delinquent friends.[42] Thus, he argued that the decline in crime associated with marriage is explained by changes in peer associations.

Current crime policies focus on locking up offenders for long periods of time—the incapacitation policies associated with career criminal research described at the beginning of this chapter. Sampson and Laub's study suggests that this policy may significantly increase crime and delinquency in the future.[43] Lengthy incarceration cuts off the social bonds, such as marriage and jobs, that are turning points which lead to desistance from crime. If Sampson and Laub are right, then lengthy incarceration would tend to be associated with continued criminality after release. Beyond that, the imprisonment of young males is associated with poor future employment prospects, which in turn is associated with families where fathers are absent, which then is associated with higher rates of delinquency in the children in these families.[44] Sampson and Laub find the extremely high rate of incarceration of African American men especially troubling.

They suggest that crime policy focus on prevention instead of incapacitation. Rather than locking up offenders after crimes have been committed, it would be better to address the causal sequence described in their book, including policies to address both the structural background and the family context factors described by their theory. These policies would be difficult to implement and would have to take into account the linkages among crime policies, employment, family cohesion, and the social organization of inner-city communities. But implementation of the policies would have much greater potential for reducing crime and delinquency in the long run than simply locking up offenders.

CONCLUSIONS

Developmental theories suggest that a single theory does not work well when to explain crime and delinquency. Instead, we need different theories to explain crime and delinquency at different points in the life course. In addition, interactive theories suggest that certain factors may

---

[42]Mark Warr, "Life-Course Transitions and Desistance from Crime," *Criminology* 36(2): 183–216 (1998).

[43]Sampson, Laub and Allen, op. cit., pp. 107–09.

[44]Sampson and Laub, *Crime in the Making*, op. cit., p. 255.

cause criminal behavior but that those same factors may also *be caused by* criminal behavior.

Future criminology theories probably will have to have both developmental and interactive characteristics. This means that future criminology theories probably will be more complex than past theories, but they will be better able to describe the complexity of crime and therefore better able to formulate effective policy responses.

Developmental and interactive theories assume that people change over time and that they respond to changes in their environments. These changes imply that, while there may be considerable stability in offending over the life course, there is no unchangeable propensity to commit crime. Future theories of crime will probably assume that there are always turning points at which individuals, no matter how much crime and delinquency they have committed in the past, can move into a conventional, law-abiding lifestyle. The search for such turning points will be important to future crime policies.

On the other hand, there are and will continue to be persistent, high-rate offenders who account for a large portion of crime. As of now, policies to identify and incapacitate these offenders have largely failed.[45] Two reasons for this failure are that serious offenders seem to commit fewer offenses than previously thought, and it is difficult to distinguish serious from low-rate offenders. As a result, incapacitation policies have locked up a very large number of low-rate offenders for very long periods of time. The declining crime rates of the 1990s may be one result of these policies, but in the future we may find that these policies have the long-term effect of generating crime.

Future crime policies are likely to turn away from incarceration and toward prevention, focusing on preventing the early childhood experiences that generate crime and delinquency in the long run. We do not yet know the exact sequence of events that ends with a person committed to a life of crime. But we do know much more now than we did twenty years ago, and we are likely to know even more in the relatively near future. At the present time, developmental theories are the basis for enormous funding by agencies that sponsor criminology research. In particular, the Project on Human Development in Chicago Neighborhoods, funded jointly by the MacArthur Foundation and the National Institute of Justice,[46] is expected to cost around $80 million. This project

---

[45]Franklin E. Zimring and Gordon Hawkins, *Incapacitation,* Oxford University Press, New York, 1995.

[46]Felton J. Earls and Christy A. Visher, *The Project on Human Development in Chicago Neighborhoods: A Research Update,* NIJ Research in Brief, Department of Justice, Washington, DC, 1997.

looks at the influence of communities and neighborhoods on individuals.[47] It also looks at individual change over time, and examines the multiple pathways that people can take into and out of antisocial, delinquent, and criminal behavior. The study is unique in that it will look at
how the changing relationship between an individual's development and
his or her community's development may affect the likelihood to engage
in delinquency or crime. The study is expected to be complete in 2003.

---

[47]See the discussion of Sampson's theory of informal neighborhood social control in Chapter 7.

CHAPTER SEVENTEEN

Integrated Theories

As the preceding chapters amply demonstrate, there are a very large number of theories in criminology.[1] Most criminologists believe that the way to reduce the number of theories is through the "falsification" process. According to this view, different theories make contradictory predictions that can be tested with research. Theories whose predictions are inconsistent with the data are falsified and can be discarded, thereby reducing the total number of theories.

Other criminologists, however, believe that for a variety of practical reasons, the falsification process has failed to work. These criminologists turn to integration as a way to reduce the number of theories. They argue that the different theories do not contradict each other, but instead focus on different aspects of the same phenomenon about which they make different predictions. These theories can therefore be combined through integration into a smaller number of larger theories. These criminologists also argue that the combined theories will be more powerful in the sense that they can explain more of the variation in crime. Integration is an alternative to falsification as a way to reduce the number of theories in criminology.

Since most theories integrate at least some previously existing material in their arguments, there is no firm and fast line between integrat-

---

[1] Earlier versions of portions of this chapter are found in Thomas J. Bernard and Jeffrey B. Snipes, "Theoretical Integration in Criminology," in Michael Tonry, ed., *Crime and Justice: A Review of Research*, vol. 20, University of Chicago Press, Chicago, 1996, pp. 301–48; and in Bernard, "Integrating Theories in Criminology," pp. 335–46 in Raymond Paternoster and Ronet Bachman, eds., *Explaining Criminals and Crime*, Roxbury, Los Angeles, 2001.

ed theories and other theories. In order to facilitate further discussion of integration in criminology, we present here several different theories that can reasonably be described as integrated theories.

ELLIOTT'S INTEGRATED THEORY OF DELINQUENCY AND DRUG USE

In 1979, Elliott, Ageton, and Cantor offered an early version of an integrated theory that explicitly combined strain, control, and social learning perspectives to explain delinquency and drug use.[2] In 1985, Elliott, Huizinga, and Ageton provided a more complete version of that integrated theory, and Elliott also defended theoretical integration as a process.[3] These efforts at integration, and the responses to them by those who opposed integration, set off a rather large debate about theoretical integration in criminology.

Elliott and his colleagues integrated criminology theories in two steps: first they integrated strain theory with social control theory, then they integrated the combined strain/control theory with social learning theory. In their view, strain theory argues "that delinquency is a response to actual or anticipated failure to achieve socially induced needs or goals (status, wealth, power, social acceptance, etc.),"[4] while social control theory argues that the strength of an individual's bonds to conventional society is inversely related to the probability that the individual will engage in delinquent behavior. Sources of weak social controls include inadequate socialization in the family and social disorganization in the community or society. Elliott and his colleagues integrated strain and control theories by arguing that the probability of delinquency should be highest when an individual experiences *both* more strain *and* less control. In addition, they argued that social disorganization, which is said to decrease social controls, should also increase strain. Finally, Elliott et al. argued that strain itself should reduce social control.

After integrating strain and control theories, Elliott et al. incorporated the social learning theory which argues that delinquency is affected by the balance between the rewards and punishments associated with both conforming and deviant patterns of socialization. Adolescents re-

---

[2]Delbert S. Elliott, Suzanne S. Ageton, and Rachelle J. Cantor, "An Integrated Theoretical Perspective on Delinquent Behavior," *Journal of Research in Crime and Delinquency* 16: 3–27 (1979).

[3]Delbert S. Elliott, David Huizinga, and Suzanne S. Ageton, *Explaining Delinquency and Drug Use*, Sage, Beverly Hills, CA, 1985; Delbert S. Elliott, "The Assumption that Theories Can Be Combined With Increased Explanatory Power," pp. 123–49 in Robert F. Meier, ed., *Theoretical Methods in Criminology*, Sage, Beverly Hills, CA, 1985.

[4]Elliott et al., 1985, p. 14.

ceive rewards and punishments for their behavior primarily from families, schools, and peers. Families and schools almost always reinforce conventional or law-abiding behaviors. In contrast, peer groups are much more likely to reinforce deviant behavior, although this influence varies quite a bit among different adolescents. Elliott et al. therefore argued that the amount of exposure to delinquent attitudes and behaviors within the peer group is the primary factor that affects the probability of delinquent behavior.

At this point, the authors found it necessary to modify control theory to take into account the type of group with which the individual bonds. Control theory holds that the content of socialization always favors conformity, and therefore only the strength of socialization is necessary to explain crime and delinquency (i.e., weak socialization leads to deviance). In addition, control theory holds that there are no strong bonds within deviant groups, since deviance itself is purely self-interested behavior. Thus, deviant groups (e.g., juvenile gangs) are sets of people who are purely self-interested, and the group stays together only to the extent it furthers the self-interests of each group member. In contrast, social learning theory holds that the content of socialization can favor either deviance or conformity, and that individuals can form strong bonds to deviant social groups. Elliott and his fellow authors integrated these two theories by hypothesizing that deviant behavior is most likely when there are strong bonds to deviant groups and weak bonds to conventional groups, and least likely when there are strong bonds to conventional groups and weak bonds to deviant groups.

The third step in integrating strain, control, and social learning theories is to propose a single line of causation that includes variables from all three theories (see Figure 17-1). Strain, inadequate socialization, and

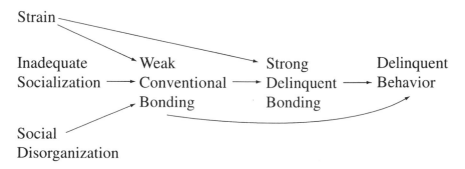

FIGURE 1   From Delbert S. Elliott, David Huizinga, and Suzanne S. Ageton, *Explaining Delinquency and Drug Use,* Sage, Beverly Hills, CA, 1985, p. 66.

social disorganization are all said to lead to weak conventional bonding. These failures then lead to strong delinquent bonding which, in turn, leads to delinquent behavior. Strain can also directly affect strong delinquent bonding, as at least some strain theories argue, but Elliott et al. argued that most of the effect of strain operates through the weak conventional bonding. In addition, weak conventional bonding can directly affect delinquent behavior, as control theories argue, but Elliott et al. argued that most of its effect operates through the strong delinquent bonding.

The authors identified the integrated model with the social control rather than the social learning perspective, reasoning that the control perspective is more general and can explain deviance across levels of explanation, and that it is more sociological in that it places great importance on the role of institutional structures in controlling deviant behavior. They then supported their model with longitudinal data from the National Youth Survey. They found *no* direct effects of strain and social control concepts on delinquent behavior. Instead, most of the variance in delinquent behavior was explained by bonding to delinquent peers.

THE FALSIFICATION VS. INTEGRATION DEBATE

In a response to Elliott et al.'s 1979 paper, Hirschi argued forcefully against integration as a strategy in criminology.[5] He stated that most criminology theories are contradictory because their assumptions are incompatible. Theories therefore must be tested on their own for internal consistency and explanatory power, or against other theories. Theories can only be integrated if they essentially argue the same thing, and most criminology theories do not. Hirschi concluded that, for criminology theories, "separate and unequal is better."

In the more complete version of the integrated theory, published in 1985, Elliott et al. responded to Hirschi's arguments against integration. They began by arguing that the "oppositional tradition" in criminology had failed. This tradition refers to the falsification process by which the different theories are tested against each other. Elliott et al. also argued that any individual theory can explain only 10 to 20 percent of the variance in illegal behavior: "Stated simply, the level of explained variance attributable to separate theories is embarrassingly low, and, if sociologi-

---

[5]Travis Hirschi, "Separate but Unequal Is Better," *Journal of Research in Crime and Delinquency* 16: 34–38 (1979).

cal explanations for crime and delinquency are to have any significant impact upon future planning and policy, they must be able to demonstrate greater predictive power."[6]

In a separate article, Elliott argued that theoretical competition is generally pointless because most of the time the different theories explain different portions of the variance in crime.[7] There are multiple causes of crime, and so different theories that incorporate different causal factors aren't necessarily incompatible. Elliott concluded that criminologists should synthesize such theories to achieve a greater explanation of deviant behavior, rather than allow them to remain in competitive isolation.

In a later article, Hirschi then expanded on his argument against integration, sardonically discussing the fall of the "oppositional tradition" and the recent movement toward theoretical integration.[8] He acknowledged that criminology theory has failed to advance despite the prevalence of theory competition. But he did not see integration as a solution to this problem. In particular, he objected to the changes in control theory that integrationists such as Elliott make when they integrate it with other theories. Hirschi argued that integrationists ignore the fact that the different criminology theories are incompatible, and plod ahead anyway. This is not the integration of existing theories, he maintains, but the creation of new theories.

BRAITHWAITE'S THEORY OF REINTEGRATIVE SHAMING

Despite Hirschi's protests, the trend toward integration continued. In 1989, the same year that Hirschi expanded his argument against integration, John Braithwaite published his theory of reintegrative shaming, which draws on labeling, subcultural, opportunity, control, differential association, and social learning theories.[9] Rather than combining arguments from earlier theories, as Elliott and his colleagues did, Braithwaite created a new theoretical concept—reintegrative shaming—and showed how that concept organizes the arguments of a large number of other theories.

---

[6]Elliott et al., 1985, p. 125.

[7]Elliott, "The Assumption that Theories Can Be Combined" op. cit.

[8]Hirschi, "Exploring Alternatives to Integrated Theory," pp. 37–49 in Steven F. Messner, Marvin D. Krohn, and Allen E. Liska, *Theoretical Integration in the Study of Deviance and Crime*, SUNY Press, Albany, 1989.

[9]John Braithwaite, *Crime, Shame, and Reintegration*, Cambridge University Press, Cambridge, U.K., 1989.

Braithwaite describes shaming as "all social processes of expressing disapproval which have the intention or effect of invoking remorse in the person being shamed and/or condemnation by others who become aware of the shaming"[10] He divides shaming into two types: stigmatization (when the shaming brings about a feeling of deviancy in the shamed) and reintegration (when the shamers ensure that they maintain bonds with the shamed). Reintegrative shaming occurs when violators are shamed into knowing what they did is wrong but are none the less allowed reentry into the conforming group. The core argument of Braithwaite's theory is that reintegrative shaming leads to lower crime rates, whereas stigmatizating shaming leads to higher crime rates. Braithwaite uses this argument to explain many different types of crimes involving victimization, but he does not use it to explain victimless crimes.

Braithwaite then describes how other criminology theories relate to this core argument.[11] Individuals with more social bonding are more likely to receive reintegrative shaming and are thus less likely to commit crime. Labeling theory is drawn upon to explain stigmatization, and once an individual is stigmatized, he or she is more likely to participate in a deviant subculture, and thus more likely to commit crime. Braithwaite's theory also acts on a structural level. Greater urbanization and mobility (from social disorganization theory) lessen the chance that "societal communitarianism" will exist. Communitarianism, or interdependency among individuals in a culture, tends to be associated with reintegration, while its absence leads to stigmatization and its consequent blockage of legitimate opportunities, formation of subcultures, presence of illegitimate opportunities, and higher crime rates.

Uggen offered several criticisms of Braithwaite's theory, to which Braithwaite responded by exploring its potential problems.[12] In addition, Makkai and Braithwaite found support for the relationship between reintegrative shaming and criminal behavior in the case of nursing-home compliance with the law.[13] However, this was the only

---

[10]Ibid., p. 100.

[11]For a more recent discussion about how shaming integrates criminology theories, see Braithwaite, "Reintegrative Shaming," pp. 242–51 in Paternoster and Bachman, op. cit.

[12]See Christopher Uggen, "Reintegrating Braithwaite: Shame and Consensus in Criminological Theory," *Law & Social Inquiry* 18: 481–500 (1993); John Braithwaite, "Pride in Criminological Dissensus," *Law & Social Inquiry* 18: 501–12 (1993); Uggen, "Beyond Calvin and Hobbes: Rationality and Exchange in a Theory of Moralizing Shaming," *Law & Social Inquiry* 18: 513–16 (1993).

[13]Toni Makkai and John Braithwaite, "Reintegrative Shaming and Compliance with Regulatory Standards," *Criminology* 32: 361–85 (1994); and "The Dialectics of Corporate Deterrence," *Journal of Research in Crime and Delinquency* 31: 347–73 (1994).

link that the research examined, and so the larger relationship between shaming and concepts from other theories remains unexplored.

Despite this limited discussion and testing, the theory has been linked to the much larger "restorative justice" movement, which responds to crime by attempting to restore victims, offenders, and communities to their condition prior to the crime. In the context of restorative justice, reintegrative shaming refers to restoring offenders to their condition before the offense. To a considerable extent, restorative justice is a normative theory—it describes how the world ought to be. In contrast, reintegrative shaming is an empirical theory—it asserts that reintegrated offenders are less likely to reoffend than stigmatized offenders. Braithwaite went on to review a very large empirical literature on restorative justice and found the results quite encouraging.[14] Beyond integrating a large number of criminology theories about offender behavior, Braithwaite has integrated empirical and normative theories about criminal justice responses to criminal behavior.

TITTLE'S CONTROL BALANCE THEORY:

In 1995, Charles Tittle proposed a general theory of deviance that integrates essential elements from differential association, Merton's anomie, Marxian conflict, social control, labeling, deterrence, and routine activities theories.[15] He first argues that each theory is defensible in its own terms, but that each is incomplete in that it does not answer questions which the other theories are designed to answer.[16] He then argues that an adequate theory must be able to explain a broad range of deviant behaviors, must fully account for those behaviors, must be precise in its causal arguments (e.g., including statements about when those processes operate with greater or lesser force and the time intervals between causes and effects), and must explain the entire causal chain and not simply start with preexisting causes that themselves are not explained.[17]

Like Braithwaite, Tittle then proposes a new concept around which to integrate the propositions from earlier, simpler theories: control bal-

---

[14]Braithwaite, "Restorative Justice: Assessing Opptimistic and Pessimistic Accounts," pp. 1–127 in Michael Tonry, ed., *Crime and Justice: A Review of Research*, vol. 25, University of Chicago Press, Chicago, 1999.

[15]Charles R. Tittle, *Control Balance: Toward a General Theory of Deviance*, Westview Press, Boulder CO, 1995. See also Tittle, "Control Balance," pp. 315–34 in Paternoster and Bachman, op. cit; and Raymond Paternoster and Charles Tittle, *Social Deviance and Crime*, Roxbury, Los Angeles, 2000, pp. 549–77.

[16]Tittle, *Control Balance*, op. cit., pp. 1–16.

[17]Ibid., pp. 17–53.

ance. His central assertion is that "the amount of control to which an individual is subject, relative to the amount of control he or she can exercise, determines the probability of deviance occurring as well as the type of deviance likely to occur."[18] This view accepts the premise of traditional control theories (like Hirschi's) that controls are the central concept in explaining conformity.[19] However, it contradicts those theories by asserting that control also is a central motivating factor that explains deviance: people who are controlled by others tend to engage in deviance to escape that control, while people who exercise control over others tend to engage in deviance in order to extend that control.[20] In this theory, then, conformity is associated with "control balance" rather than with control itself. That is, people are likely to engage in conforming behavior when the control they exert over others is approximately equal to the control that others exert over them. This pattern results in a U-shaped curve with the most deviance being committed by those who have the greatest control and those who have the least.[21]

Tittle defines deviance as "any behavior that the majority of a given group regards as unacceptable or that typically evokes a collective response of a negative type."[22] But rather than explaining deviance as a single construct, he divides it into six types: predation, exploitation, defiance, plunder, decadence, and submission.[23]

Predation involves direct physical violence or manipulation to take property, and includes such behaviors as theft, rape, robbery, fraud, and homicide. Exploitation is indirect predation, where the exploiter uses others to do the "dirty work." Examples are contract killings, price-fixing, and political corruption. Defiance occurs when individuals revolt against norms or values by engaging in such acts as violating curfews, vandalism, political protests, and "sullenness by a marital partner." Acts of plunder are typically undertaken by people without much of a social

---

[18]Ibid., p. 135.

[19]Ibid., p. 142.

[20]Ibid., p. 143. Tittle defines "being controlled" as "a continuous variable conveying the extent to which expression of one's desires or impulses is potentially *limited* by other people's abilities (whether actually exercised or not) to help, or reward, or hinder, or punish, or by the physical and social arrangements of the world." He defines "exercising control" as "a continuous variable reflecting the degree to which one can limit other people's realization of their goals or can escape limitations on one's own behavioral motivations that stem from the actions of others or from physical or social arrangements."

[21]Ibid., p. 183.

[22]Ibid., p. 124.

[23]Ibid., pp. 137–41.

conscience, are considered to be particularly heinous, and include such behaviors as destroying fields to hunt for foxes, pollution by oil companies, and unrealistic taxes imposed by occupying armies. Decadence refers to behavior that is unpredictable and viewed by most as irrational; examples are group sex with children and sadistic torture. Acts of submission involve "passive, unthinking, slavish obedience to the expectations, commands, or anticipated desires of others."[24] Examples are eating slop on command or allowing one's self to be sexually degraded. One may question whether several of the acts described in these categories are deviant (such as eating slop on command). According to Tittle, the theory explains more than deviance: It explains submission, decadence, and the other categories. Thus, an act may be submissive and not necessarily deviant but still be explained by theory.[25]

There are four primary concepts employed in control balance theory: predisposition, provocation, opportunity, and constraint. Predisposition toward deviant motivation includes one's desire for autonomy and his or her control ratio, which is the "amount of control to which the person is subject relative to the amount that he or she can exercise."[26] Tittle deems one's desire for autonomy as relevant to predisposition, but notes it varies very little across individuals. Varying more dramatically across individuals is the control ratio. Within each individual, may be fairly stable overall, but can also vary from situation to situation, since different contextual circumstances may arise the balance of control.

Provocations are "contextual features that cause people to become more keenly cognizant of their control ratios and the possibilities of altering them through deviant behavior . . ."[27] Examples include verbal insults or challenges. Constraint refers to the likelihood that potential control will actually be exercised (compared to the control ratio, which refers to potential control and not actual control). Finally, opportunity is defined in the traditional manner, relating to the circumstances under which it is feasible to commit a given act. For example, it is difficult to rape if there are no people present, or it is difficult to burglarize with no dwellings around.

The causal processes comprising control balance theory are fairly complex, so we shall limit this discussion to the core theoretical mecha-

---

[24]Ibid., p. 139.

[25]Ibid., p. 140.

[26]Ibid., p. 145.

[27]Ibid., p. 163.

nisms. Deviant behavior occurs when one attempts to alter his or her control ratio, whether temporarily or permanently. Thus, deviance serves a purpose for the person committing it. When the amount of control exercised is roughly the same as the amount of control one is subjected to, control balance occurs, and the probability of deviance is low. But when the ratio is not balanced (in either direction), the likelihood of deviance increases at a rate proportional to the degree of imbalance. Motivation drives the likelihood of deviant behavior, and motivation is influenced strongly by the control balance ratio. Other variables, such as provocations, constraint, and opportunity also converge in influencing the actual probability of deviance occurring, but one's motivation (and predisposition toward motivation) are the most important contributing factors to deviance.

Control balance theory explains type of deviance in addition to likelihood of deviance. Those with a balanced ratio are likely to conform. Those who have a higher ratio of autonomy to repression (are more likely to exercise control than to be controlled) are likely to engage in exploitation (minimal imbalance), plunder (medium imbalance), or decadence (maximum imbalance). Those who have a lower ratio of autonomy to repression (are more likely to be controlled than to exercise control) are likely to engage in predation (marginal imbalance), defiance (moderate imbalance), and submission (extreme imbalance). One question that immediately comes to mind is why the most serious forms of deviance (such as predation) are coupled with the slightest imbalances. Tittle explains this by saying that when control deficits are small, people will be able to commit more serious acts of deviance without as much fear of controlling response than if they had larger control deficits. People with marginal control deficits will usually be deterred from deviant acts, but when they do commit them, according to Tittle, they will be more serious in nature. People with more extreme control deficits will be "less able to imagine that such behavior will escape controlling responses from others,"[28] and thus their deviance will take less serious forms (such as submission and defiance). Similarly, people with control surplus (more autonomy than repression) will commit acts of deviance with seriousness that is in proportion to how controlled they are. Individuals with only a slight advantage will feel more limited in the extent to which they can exercise control, and will commit less serious acts (exploitation, compared to plunder and decadence).

---

[28]Ibid., p. 187.

Tittle's theory is too recent to have been subject to much criticism or testing.[29] Our brief summary of it masks its complexity as well as Tittle's exertion in building a neatly structured theory. Much of his book is devoted to detailing the requisites of a good theory and showing how most criminological theories lack some of the features of solid theory. He then builds control balance theory with these features in mind (breadth, comprehensiveness, precision, and depth) and provides an important chapter that discusses the contingencies of control balance theory (under what conditions might certain causal mechanisms not work). Tittle's theory does a nice job of explaining deviance committed by several segments of society, including both skid-row bums and political and corporate criminals.

VILA'S GENERAL PARADIGM

One of the broadest and most complex approaches to integration is taken by Brian Vila.[30] According to Vila, if a theory is to be general enough to explain all criminal behavior, it must be ecological, integrative, developmental, and must include both micro-level and macro-level explanations. An ecological theory considers the interconnection of individuals and their physical environment. A developmental theory allows for changes in the causes of crime as well as changes in crime itself over time, particularly as related to the age of the individual. Integrative theories allow for the inclusion of factors from multiple disciplines and from multiple theories. Finally, theories that use concepts at more than one level of explanation recognize that within-person variation, variation in social structure, and variation in the person-structure interaction all can affect individual behavior. Vila reviews a number of theories that meet at least two of these conditions, but shows that no theory to date meets all of them. Therefore, he calls existing criminology theories "partial theories."

---

[29]For discussions and criticisms, see the symposium on control balance theory, with contributions by James R. Short, Joachim J. Savelsberg, and Gary Jensen, and a response by Tittle, in *Theoretical Criminology* 3: 327–52 (1999). For a first empirical test, see Alex R. Piquero and Matthew Hickman, "An Empirical Test of Tittle's Control Balance Theory," *Criminology* 37: 319–41 (1999).

[30]Brian Vila, "A General Paradigm for Understanding Criminal Behavior: Extending Evolutionary Ecological Theory," *Criminology* 32(3): 311–60 (1994). Vila's theory is an extension of Lawrence E. Cohen and Richard Machalek, "A General Theory of Expropriative Crime," *American Journal of Sociology* 94: 465–501 (1988). Cohen and Machalek only attempted to explain expropriative crimes, such as theft and embezzlement, whereas Vila tries to explain all crime. Vila does not describe his approach as a theory; rather, he describes it as a paradigmatic model from which theory should develop.

Vila argues that biological factors must be included in any theory[31] so he criticizes developmental theories such as Sampson and Laub's[32] for ignoring their role. Not only must individual genetic traits be considered in a general theory, but intergenerational transmission of these traits must be considered as well. For this reason, the effect of biological factors may be lagged over lengthy periods.

Vila also criticizes existing theories for not allowing macro-level correlates of crime (such as social disorganization) to vary over time. Because macro-level contributors are dynamic, an individual's position in society is in flux. Ecological contributors to crime, such as opportunities provided by one's physical environment, also have the potential to change over an individual's lifetime.

Vila stresses the *interaction* of ecological, micro, and macro causal factors. For example, macro and micro factors might interact in the effect of cultural beliefs on parental style; macro and ecological factors might interact in the effect of sociocultural heterogeneity on opportunities for crime; and micro and ecological factors might interact in an individual attempting to modify his or her local environment. When allowing for both causal directions to occur across the three types of factors, the result is six types of two-way interaction terms.

A central assumption of the model is that all crime involves the seeking of resources. Expropriative crimes (such as theft and fraud) are aimed at acquiring material resources. Expressive crimes (such as sexual assault and drug use) are aimed at obtaining hedonistic resources. Economic crimes (such as illegal gambling and narcotics trafficking) are aimed at obtaining monetary resources. Political crimes (such as terrorism) are aimed at obtaining political resources. All crimes are committed with one or more of the following strategic styles: force, stealth, and fraud. The extent to which a person develops these styles depends on the interaction between biological, sociocultural, and developmental factors. All these affect the motivation toward crime, which is determined by how many resources a person has and how much that person desires. But only when an opportunity also exists to commit crime will the motivated individual commit a crime.

On one hand, Vila's paradigm is frustratingly general. The sense one gets is that everything affects everything and that these effects are con-

---

[31]Ibid., pp. 328–30.

[32]Robert J. Sampson and John H. Laub, *Crime in the Making: Pathways and Turning Points Through Life*, Harvard University Press, Cambridge, MA, 1993. See the discussion of this theory in Chapter 16.

tinuously changing over time. On the other hand, it is intuitively appealing, because criminality is so much more complex than any of the major criminological theories allow for. Vila's evolutionary ecological paradigm incorporates the complexity of human behavior, but the question remains whether social scientists are capable of testing theories as complex as this.

Despite the difficulty of testing such a complex theory, the theory has rather straightforward policy implications focused on "nurturant strategies" that prevent crime rather than respond to it—such as with punishment, deterrence, or incapacitation—after it has occurred.[33] These strategies include policies to improve the early life experiences of young children and to channel the development of older children and adolescents, particularly through education, so they have a better "environmental fit" with the conventional social world. Vila estimates that if such strategies were implemented, the effects might not be seen for ten to fifteen years, and it might take as many as three or four generations to see a substantial decrease in serious crime. Nevertheless, he argues that there is strong empirical support for the effectiveness of these strategies.

BERNARD AND SNIPES'S APPROACH TO INTEGRATING CRIMINOLOGY THEORIES

Bernard and Snipes attempt to address Hirschi's arguments against integration while avoiding theories, like Vila's, that seem too complex to test.[34] Rather than offering an entirely new integrated theory, they present a new interpretation of existing criminology theories that, they maintain, accurately represents the content of those theories and at the same time allows both broad integration and empirical testing. Ultimately, their approach is based on an argument about the proper role of theory in the scientific process. The following points summarize their argument.

First, criminologists should focus on variables and the relationships among variables, rather than on theories themselves. Hirschi had argued that criminologists sometimes treat variables as if they were "owned by" theories—for example, attachment sometimes is treated as if it was owned by Hirschi's social control theory—so that evidence of a

---

[33]See the "Roundtable: Human Nature and Crime Control," with an article by Vila, comments by Lawrence E. Cohen, David P. Farrington, James C. Howell, Kenneth C. Land, Steven D. Levitt, Richard Machalek, Linda Mealey, Peter J. Richerson, Anthony Walsh and Lee Ellis, Franklin E. Zimring, and Marinus H. van Ijzendoorn, with a response by Vila, in *Politics and the Life Sciences* 16: 3–55 (1997).

[34]Bernard and Snipes, op cit.

relationship between attachment and crime is interpreted as evidence of the validity of Hirschi's theory. Bernard and Snipes go further than Hirschi by arguing that the only important question is this: What variables are related to crime, and in what ways? That is, they focus on whether and how attachment is related to criminal behavior, and they consider the question of the validity of Hirschi's theory to be unimportant. In fact, they view this question as counterproductive because it leads to endless debates that waste everybody's time.

Second, Bernard and Snipes argue, criminology theories should be evaluated in terms of their usefulness to the scientific process, not in terms of their validity. In the scientific process, theory interprets the results of past research and charts the course of future research. That is, theory explains the relationships among variables that research has already observed, and theory directs research to look for new relationships among variables that have not yet been observed. After its publication in 1969, Hirschi's social control theory was quite useful to criminologists in exactly this way. But social control theory is not nearly as useful to criminologists today. Even Hirschi himself now uses a new theory (low self-control) to interpret the results of past research and chart the course of future research. Bernard and Snipes argue that usefulness to the scientific process is the proper standard by which a scientific theory should be evaluated, not whether the theory is valid.

Third, criminology researchers should shift from the goal of falsifying theories to a risk-factor approach that deals in structured probabilities. The whole integration debate, as described earlier in this chapter, starts with the argument that falsification has failed as a process for reducing the number of criminology theories. The problem with falsification is that it requires "all or nothing" conclusions—the theory is either verified or falsified—based on competitive testing and statistical significance. But crime is so complex that it seems like every theory is true at least some of the time; therefore, no theory can ever truly be falsified.[35] In contrast, the risk factor approach allows for graduated conclusions—the factors identified by some theories explain a lot of the variation in crime, while the factors identified by other theories explain only a little. This approach is consistent with the focus on variables and the relationships among variables, recommended above. And where the falsification approach is competitive—if one theory is true, then others must be false—the risk factor approach is integrative—many factors may influence crime, some with larger effects than others.

---

[35]See Thomas J. Bernard, "Twenty Years of Testing Theories: What Have We Learned and Why?" *Journal of Research in Crime and Delinquency* 27: 325–47 (1990).

Fourth, Bernard and Snipes agree with Hirschi that contradictory theories cannot be integrated with each other. However, they disagree with Hirschi's conclusion that criminology theories contradict each other. In particular, Bernard and Snipes argue that Hirschi's social psychological interpretation of criminology theories in terms of strain, control, and cultural deviance is incorrect because it seriously distorts the arguments of so-called strain and cultural deviance theories.[36] They then propose an interpretation of these two types of theories in which the causal chain moves from social structural conditions to cultural ideas to criminal behaviors.[37]

Fifth, consistent with the risk factor approach, Bernard and Snipes argue that criminology theories should be interpreted and classified in terms of their location of independent variation and direction of causation.[38] This approach highlights the policy implications of the theory by focusing on what the theory proposes as causes of crime (i.e., the location of independent variation). In contrast, criminology theories are often criticized because, even though they are intuitively appealing, their policy implications are unclear.

Bernard and Snipes argue that, when considered in this way, there are two main types of criminology theories: "individual difference" theories and "structure/process" theories.[39] Individual difference theories reflect the common-sense observation that *some people are more likely than others to engage in crime, regardless of the situation they are in.* These theories therefore attempt to identify individual characteristics that cause differences in probabilities of criminal behavior. Structure/process theories reflect another common-sense observation: *Some situations are more likely to generate higher crime rates regardless of the characteristics of the people who are in them.* These theories therefore attempt to identify the characteristics of situations that cause differences in crime rates.

---

[36]Ibid, pp. 324–330.

[37]These structural interpretations are presented in Chapters 8 and 9.

[38]Ibid., p. 330. This is usually described in terms of "levels of explanation." In general, levels of explanation refers to the theory's dependent variable. Most criminology theories either explain the behavior of individuals or the rates and distributions of criminal behavior in societies. A few other theories explain the behavior of groups. Stating what the theory explains (i.e., the dependent variable) is more to the point than talking about the theory's level of explanation.

[39]This approach is comparable to the one taken in Albert J. Reiss and Jeffrey A. Roth, eds. *Understanding and Preventing Violence,* vol. 1, National Academy Press, Washington, DC, 1993, ch. 3. See also Robert J. Sampson and Janet L. Lauritsen, "Violent Victimization and Offending: Individual-, Situational-, and Community-Level Risk Factors," pp. 1–114 in Reiss and Roth, eds. *Understanding and Preventing Violence,* vol. 3, National Academy Press, Washington D.C., 1994. Bernard and Snipes's approach is also quite comparable to what Cressey (1960) described in terms of epidemiology and individual behavior.

Thus, individual difference theories use variations in characteristics of individuals to predict probabilities that the individual will commit crime. This type of theory, according to Bernard and Snipes, is based on three implicit assertions. First, differences in the probability of engaging in crime are explained by differences in individual characteristics. Second, these individual characteristics may be explained by interactions with others within the environment, but the environment itself is explained, not by social structural characteristics, but by the characteristics of the persons within it. Third, since crime is explained by individual characteristics, criminals themselves are assumed to be different from noncriminals in some measurable ways.

In contrast, structure/process theories explain variations in the rates and distributions of criminal behavior with variations in social structural characteristics, as manifested in the structured environment to which individuals respond.[40] These theories generally include two kinds of arguments: Structural arguments link structural conditions to the rates and distributions of criminal behavior within a society, while process arguments explain why "normal" (see definition below) individuals who experience those structural conditions are more likely to engage in that behavior. This type of theory is based on three implicit assertions. First, crime is a response of individuals who are freely choosing and whose choices are constrained by the immediate environment. Second, the immediate environment is structured, in that its characteristics are causally related to the broad structural features of social organization. And third, criminals are normal in that they are similar to noncriminals in the processes by which they interact with the immediate environment and in the motives that direct their responses to the environment.

Based on their interpretation of theories as being either individual difference or structure/process, Bernard and Snipes argue that the competitive testing of criminology theories is almost always inappropriate and that the integration of theories is almost always possible.[41] In effect, almost all criminology theories control for, rather than deny, the variation explained by other theories. Thus, the competition among criminology theories is almost entirely empirical, not theoretical. The important question is: How much does each theory contribute to explaining criminal behavior or rates of crime, relative to the other theories?

---

[40]This definition is close to that of Ronald Akers, in *Deviant Behavior: A Social Learning Approach*, Wadsworth, Belmont, 1985.

[41]Bernard and Snipes, op. cit., pp. 338–343.

CONCLUSION

Some criminologists may argue that taking a risk-factor approach which focuses on variables rather than on theories will turn criminology into an atheoretical, policy-driven enterprise. Our view, in contrast, is that this is a practical approach in which theory assumes its proper role in the scientific process. This approach will allow criminology to increase the explanatory power of its theories and identify practical policy implications that ultimately may reduce crime.

In the next chapter, we present an overall assessment of criminology theories based on our integration model. The chapter therefore serves two purposes. First, it provides a conclusion to the entire book by presenting an interpretive overview of all the different theories in this book. Second, it provides a concrete illustration of our approach to interpreting and integrating criminology theories.

CHAPTER EIGHTEEN

Assessing Criminology Theories

The different chapters in this book have presented and discussed many different types of theories in criminology. At the end of each chapter, there was a brief assessment of the extent to which the theories in that chapter contributed to our understanding of crime. In this chapter, we present an overall assessment of the extent to which criminology theory, taken as a whole, contributes to our understanding of crime.

The basis for this assessment is our own model for interpreting and integrating criminology theories, as presented at the end of the last chapter.[1] This model includes a classification system that focuses on the sources of independent variation within the theory, rather than on the theoretical arguments per se. It describes two types of theories: individual difference theories that assert a relationship between the characteristics of individuals and the probabilities that those individuals will engage in criminal behavior, and structure/process theories that assert a relationship between the characteristics of societal units and the rates and distributions of crime within those units. In this concluding chapter, we add a third type: theories of the behavior of criminal law. These theories seek to explain why some people and behaviors, and not others, are defined and processed as criminal.[2]

---

[1]Thomas J. Bernard and Jeffrey B. Snipes, "Theoretical Integration in Criminology," *Crime and Justice: A Review of Research* 20: 301–48 (1996).

[2]Theories of the behavior of criminal law were not discussed in the Bernard and Snipes article due to space considerations (ibid., p. 343). However, integrating these theories with the others is discussed in Thomas J. Bernard, "A Theoretical Approach to Integration," pp. 137–59 in Steven F. Messner, Marvin D. Krohn, and Allen E. Liska, eds., *Theoretical Integration in the Study of Deviance and Crime*, State University of New York Press, Albany, NY, 1989.

SCIENCE, THEORY, RESEARCH, AND POLICY

As described in the first chapter of this book, the theories assessed here all take a naturalistic and scientific approach to the problem of crime. The scientific approach focuses on relationships among observable phenomena. Therefore, in this chapter, we do not consider theories that take a spiritualistic approach to the problem of crime. This does not mean we think spiritualistic theories are invalid. But our approach is scientific, and our overall goal in this chapter, and in this book in general, is to advance criminology as a science.

Within the scientific approach, our focus is on identifying the causes of crime. By interpreting theories in terms of their arguments about causes of crime, the policy implications of the theory become apparent.[3] At the same time, assessing theories in terms of their policy implications draws attention directly to the purported causes of crime within these theories. In the past, many criminology theories have been intuitively appealing but have not been particularly clear in their arguments about the causes of crime or their implications about the policies that might respond to crime.[4] In his famous aphorism, Lewin said that nothing is as practical as a good theory. In the context of that aphorism, this chapter can be interpreted as assessing the extent to which criminology theories are "good theories" in the sense that they have practical policy implications.

In Chapter 1, we said that there are four criteria for inferring causation in science: correlation (the two phenomena must vary with each other), theoretical rationale (there must be a good reason to believe that the one phenomenon causes the other), time sequence (the causal phenomenon must come first in time), and the absence of spuriousness (both phenomena must not be caused by something else). Of these four criteria, the most troublesome are time sequence and the absence of spuriousness. Many factors are correlated with crime, and it is almost always possible to present theoretical rationales for why these factors may cause crime. But many of these factors may be correlated with crime at the same times and in the same places, such as in high-crime inner-city neighborhoods. In this situation, establishing time sequence and the absence of spuriousness can be very difficult. That is, it can be hard to figure out which factors in these situations *cause* crime, which factors *are*

---

[3]For an example of crime policies that are informed by criminology research, see "Critical Criminal Justice Issues: Task Force Reports for the ASC to Attorney General Janet Reno," *The Criminologist* 20(6): 3–16 (Nov./Dec., 1995).

[4]See Jack Gibbs, "The Methodology of Theory Construction in Criminology," ppp. 23–50 in Robert F. Meier, ed., *Theoretical Methods in Criminology*, Sage, Beverly Hills, CA, 1985.

caused by crime, and which factors *are caused by the same factors that also cause crime.*[5]

For many of the factors discussed below, criminology researchers simply have not fully sorted out the issues. But in this assessment, we present what we believe are reasonable, if tentative, conclusions about the factors that actually cause crime, and in what ways.

In this chapter, we do not make the traditional distinction between classical and positivist theories in criminology. We initially made that distinction in the first two chapters because it is deeply embedded in views of the field. But we argued in Chapter 2 that classical theories really are scientific theories that focus on the effects of punishment policies on crime rates. We also described contemporary classical approaches in Chapter 11, including deterrence, rational choice, and routine activities theories. These are all scientific theories that propose relations among observable variables. Therefore, we regard the distinction between classical and positivist theories as artificial.

A more fundamental distinction is found in the different approaches initially taken by Quetelet and Lombroso, as described in Chapter 2. Quetelet initially looked at different areas of France and tried to determine which social characteristics were associated with higher or lower crime rates in those areas. Lombroso initially looked at criminals and tried to determine which individual characteristics were associated with more or less criminal behavior. By the end of their careers, both theorists had incorporated elements of the other's approach in their explanations of crime, which clearly indicates that these two approaches are not incompatible. Rather, they are entirely separate questions: Why are some people more or less likely to engage in crime than others, and why do some social units have higher or lower crime rates than others? These questions constitute the basis for what we call individual difference theories and structure/process theories.

Individual difference theories assume that some people are more likely than others to engage in crime, regardless of the situation they are in. These theories therefore attempt to identify the individual characteristics that cause differences in criminal behavior. *Structure/process* theories assume that certain types of social situations generate high crime rates regardless of the characteristics of the people in those situations. These theories therefore attempt to identify the social characteristics that cause differences in crime rates. There is no contradiction between

---

[5]This is the problem of multicollinearity, as discussed Chapter 5.

these two types of theories—they simply represent distinct scientific problems.[6]

INDIVIDUAL DIFFERENCE THEORIES

Many of the theories we have reviewed, particularly in the early chapters of this book, focused on characteristics of individuals which are thought to increase or decrease the probabilities that an individual will engage in crime. In reviewing these characteristics, it is important to keep in mind two points. First, none of these characteristics absolutely determines that the person will engage in crime. Most people with these characteristics do not engage in crime at all—it is just that people with these characteristics are somewhat more likely than other people to engage in crimes.[7] Second, while these characteristics may increase the probability that a particular individual will engage in crime, they may have no effect on overall crime rates. This conclusion is similar to the situation with unemployment. Certain factors may increase the probability that an individual will be unemployed—e.g., poor education, motivation, and job skills. Most often, however, increases in unemployment rates are not caused by increases in the number of people with these characteristics. Instead, they are caused by societal characteristics that have nothing to do with the characteristics of individuals—e.g., interest rates, budget deficits, trade deficits, stock market prices. Similarly, increases in crime rates normally are not caused by increases in the number of people who have these characteristics. (Factors associated with increases and decreases in crime rates are reviewed in the next section.) With these two points in mind, we now review the individual difference theories discussed in the various chapters in this book.

While Lombroso's theories connecting crime to physical appearance are clearly false, the "body type" theories of Sheldon and the Gluecks are more difficult to assess. There seems to be some correlation between body type and likelihood of engaging in criminal behavior. How-

---

[6]This approach is roughly comparable to the one taken in Albert J. Reiss and Jeffrey A. Roth, eds. *Understanding and Preventing Violence,* vol. 1, National Academy Press, Washington, DC, 1993, ch. 3. See also Robert J. Sampson and Janet L. Lauritsen, "Violent Victimization and Offending: Individual-, Situational-, and Community-Level Risk Factors," pp. 1–114 in Reiss and Roth, eds., *Understanding and Preventing Violence,* vol. 3, National Academy Press, Washington, DC, 1994.

[7]See, for example, David P. Farrington, "Early Predictors of Adolescent Aggression and Adult Violence," *Violence and Victims* 4: 79–100 (1989). This article gives percentages for a very large number of characteristics of those who engage in adolescent aggression, teenage violence, and adult violence, and who have been convicted of a violent crime.

ever, we believe that this correlation probably is mediated by some other variables, such as personality or motivation. We conclude that physical appearance, in itself, is never actually a cause of crime, and therefore we suggest that theories focusing on physical appearance be abandoned.

A different situation exists with certain biological variables. In general, twin and adoption studies support the notion of a biological and hereditary impact on human behavior. But aside from these narrowly focused research designs, we are unable to measure the effect of hereditary factors on the probability of engaging in criminal behavior. If genetic research examining specific identifiable risk factors continues to develop at its current rate, it is possible that it may eventually contribute to an overall theory of individual differences.

Other studies of specific biological characteristics suggest some modest causal impacts on the likelihood of committing crime, including neurotransmitter imbalances such as low serotonin, hormone imbalances such as extra testosterone, central nervous system deficiencies such as frontal or temporal lobe dysfunction, and autonomic nervous system variations such as unusual reactions to anxiety. In addition, alcohol intake at least temporarily increases the likelihood of engaging in crime, as do many illegal drugs. Other biological factors seem to have long-term effects on the likelihood of criminal behavior, including ingesting some toxins such as lead, suffering certain types of head injuries, and pregnancy or birth complications.

All these have been linked—at least tenuously—to antisocial, deviant, or criminal behavior. However, the processes by which these variables are linked to criminal behavior are not well understood. One major problem lies in determining the direction of causation. For example, high testosterone levels may increase the likelihood of participating in crime, but it is also possible that participation in crime increases testosterone. In addition, testosterone may act on some third variable, such as social integration, which then causes crime. Thus, it is unclear whether high testosterone itself has a causal impact on crime.

Despite these many questions, it seems reasonable at this point to conclude that causal relationships exist between these biological characteristics and the probability of engaging in criminal behavior. If this is the case, then there are a variety of policy interventions that could reduce crime—e.g., prescribing lithium carbonate to increase serotonin levels. The major danger with such policy interventions is that they can be applied to offenders who have normal biology. For example, a very small portion of offenders may have low serotonin levels but, given the political nature of public policies, a very large portion of offenders could end up receiving lithium carbonate.

With respect to psychological factors, there are clear correlations between low IQ scores and the likelihood of committing crime. The question is whether there is some sense in which low intelligence itself causes crime. This question is complicated by several empirical issues, which are reviewed in Chapter 4. For example, intelligence itself cannot be directly measured, and the principle measure of intelligence—IQ scores—may instead measure reading ability or the motivation to succeed at academic tasks. The issue is also complicated because the suggested causal paths between low intelligence and crime imply that low intelligence itself is not the causal factor. For example, one such causal path is through school failure. If this is the case, then school failure rather than low intelligence is the actual cause of crime. Given appropriate teaching techniques, children with low intelligence could succeed in school and would be no more likely to engage in crime than other children. At the same time, children with high intelligence can experience school failure for a variety of reasons, and then may be more likely to commit crime. Similarly, it has been suggested that low intelligence affects crime through the failure to learn higher cognitive skills, such as moral reasoning, empathy, or problem solving. But high intelligence children can fail to learn these cognitive skills for a variety of reasons, in which case they may be more likely to engage in crime. And delinquent children, who on the average score only eight IQ points lower than non-delinquent children, could be taught these cognitive skills with a little extra effort, much as children with learning disabilities are taught reading and math. If this were done, then low intelligence children would be no more likely to commit crime than other children. Again, the source of independent variation does not seem to lie in low intelligence itself, but in other factors. For these empirical and theoretical reasons, at this point we tentatively conclude that intelligence itself has no independent causal impact on crime.

In the past, results from personality tests have suggested that certain "personality types" are associated with an increased likelihood of committing criminal and delinquent behavior. But much of the time, these results seem to consist of applying fancy psychological labels to criminals. These fancy labels add nothing to our knowledge about the person or to our ability to do anything to reduce the criminal behavior. There may be some personality characteristics associated with an increased risk of engaging in criminal behavior, but research to date has not clearly determined what those are. At present, the best candidate may be impulsivity, which recent research consistently links to antisocial or criminal behavior. Impulsivity may be linked to other individual characteristics—e.g., Gottfredson and Hirschi argue that people who are impulsive, insensitive, physical (as opposed to mental), risk-taking, short-sighted, and nonverbal will have higher probabilities of committing crimes, while Moffitt pointed to impulsivity combined with "negative emotionality," in which people experience emotions such as anger and anxiety in a wider range of situations than other people. In addition, Walters described eight specific thinking patterns characterized by "a global sense of irresponsibility, self-indulgent interests, (and) an intrusive approach to interpersonal relationships."

At this point, we conclude that all these characteristics are at least somewhat linked to increased tendencies to commit crime. If this is the case, then various cognitive or cognitive-behavioral therapies might be able to change these patterns of responses, thus reducing the tendency to commit crime. Psychologists have also generally concluded that earlier childhood problem behaviors and poor parental child management techniques, such as harsh and inconsistent discipline, are both associated with increased likelihood of later criminal and delinquent behavior. If this is the case, then policy implications would focus on training parents in effective child-rearing techniques, and early cognitive-behavioral interventions with problem children.[8]

The above individual differences are derived from biological and psychological theories in criminology, but implications about individual differences can also be found in some sociological theories. For example, Akers's and Sutherland's theories suggest that people who associate with others who are engaged in and approve of criminal behavior are more likely to engage in it themselves. Agnew's strain theory suggests that people are more likely to engage in crime when they experience negative emotions, such as disappointment, depression, fear, and anger, because they are unable to escape from relationships and situations in which they are not treated the way they want. Various cultural theories suggest that certain shared cognitions may be associated with increased likelihood of committing crimes—e.g., the lower class "focal concerns" of trouble, toughness, smartness, excitement, fate, and autonomy, or the exaggerated sense of "manliness" found in subcultures of violence. Hirschi's control theory suggests that people who are more attached to others, more involved in conventional activities, have more to lose from committing crime, and have stronger beliefs in the moral validity of the law, are less likely to engage in criminal and delinquent behavior. These positive characteristics can be phrased in the reverse to indicate characteristics that

---

[8]See, for example, Peter W. Greenwood, Karyn E. Model, C. Peter Rydell, and James Chiesa, "Diverting Children from a Life of Crime," Rand Corporation, Santa Monica, CA, 1996.

increase the probability of committing crime. It also appears, from perceptual deterrence research, that individuals who perceive less risk of being punished are more likely to engage in criminal behavior. Finally, "lifestyle" theories suggest that certain characteristics increase the likelihood that a person will be a victim of crime: frequently being away from home, especially at night; engaging in public activities while away from home; and associating with people who are likely to commit crime.

While all these factors seem to be associated with an increased probability of committing crime and delinquency, they cannot fully explain either the age or gender distribution of crime. Gottfredson and Hirsch argue that the age distribution of crime, with crime peaking in late adolescence and early adulthood, is invariant and therefore exists separate from all the above factors. In contrast, developmental theories suggest that age interacts with the above factors, affecting individuals somewhat differently at different ages. The developmental interpretation is more modest than Gottfredson and Hirschi's age-invariance hypothesis, so we tentatively conclude that it more likely is correct. The gender distribution of crime, with males much more likely to offend than females, can be partially explained by the fact that males are disproportionately likely to experience at least some of these factors, as compared to females. On the other hand, it seems likely that a major portion of males' increased probability of committing crime and delinquency cannot be explained by any combination of the above factors, but only by the stratified system of gender roles and expectations associated with the terms "masculinity" and "femininity." In particular, masculinity as a gender role seems to be independently associated with an increased probability of engagement in crime and delinquency.

To summarize, the following characteristics are associated with increases in the probability of committing criminal behavior.

1. A history of early childhood problem behaviors and of being subjected to poor parental childrearing techniques, such as harsh and inconsistent discipline; school failure and the failure to learn higher cognitive skills such as moral reasoning, empathy, and problem solving.

2. Certain neurotransmitter imbalances such as low seratonin, certain hormone imbalances such as high testosterone, central nervous system deficiencies such as frontal or temporal lobe dysfunction, and autonomic nervous system variations such as unusual reactions to anxiety.

3. Ingesting alcohol, a variety of illegal drugs, and some toxins such as lead; head injuries; and complications during subject's pregnancy or birth.

4. Personality characteristics such as impulsivity, insensitivity, a physical and nonverbal orientation, and a tendency to take risks.

5. Thinking patterns that focus on trouble, toughness, smartness, excitement, fate, and autonomy; and a tendency to think in terms of short-term rather than long-term consequences.

6. Association with others who engage in and approve of criminal behavior.

7. Weak attachments to other people, less involvement in conventional activities, less to lose from committing crime, and weak beliefs in the moral validity of the law.

8. A perception that there is less risk of punishment for engaging in criminal behavior.

9. Masculinity as a gender role.

All these factors somewhat differently affect individuals at different ages. In addition, the following set of differences seems to increase the probability that a person will be a victim of crime:

10. Frequently being away from home, especially at night; engaging in public activities while away from home; and associating with people who are likely to commit crime.

The competition among these different theories is largely empirical, over which factors explain more or less of the variation in crime. Certainly the relative contribution of each characteristic is often debated. As in some recent integrated theories, it is important to recognize interactive causes in explaining crime. One particularly important area of interaction may be in the area of biosocial theory. This recognizes the independent impact of biological and social variables, as well as the interaction between them. The point is that certain biological characteristics may have a large impact on crime under some social circumstances, but little or no impact under others. Another interaction is between age and various factors; these factors have different effects on people at different ages.

Integrating the various individual difference theories must be done with careful attention to the way in which the theories may fit together, especially with respect to causal order. The point is to clearly identify the sources of independent variation and to eliminate other variables. The actual sources of independent variation become clear when one considers policy recommendations derived from these theories. For example, as mentioned above, high testosterone levels may not actually increase criminal behavior, but instead may reduce social integration, which then increases criminal behavior. If this is true, then administering drugs to reduce testosterone will not reduce crime unless steps also are taken to increase social integration. At the same time, increasing social integration may reduce crime whether or not testosterone levels are reduced. In addition, certain subcultural beliefs may be causally related to crime, but those beliefs may themselves be caused by structural conditions. If that is true, then policies directed at changing the beliefs will be ineffective, since the beliefs will be continually regenerated by the structural conditions that generated them in the first place. Policies therefore must be directed instead at changing the structural conditions that generate those beliefs.

STRUCTURE/PROCESS THEORIES

In contrast to individual difference theories, we have also discussed a wide range of structure/process theories, especially in the later chapters of this book. These theories assume that some situations are associated with higher crime rates regardless of the characteristics of the individuals within them. The theories therefore attempt to identify variables in the situation itself that are associated with higher crime rates.

In discussing these theories, it is important to keep several points in mind. First, these theories tend to be complex and descriptive, and it is sometimes hard to determine the proposed causes of crime. To the extent that is true, the policy recommendations of the theory will be vague. Second, these theories often have been interpreted and tested at the individual level. Such testing necessarily involves some variation of the "ecological fallacy,"[9] and it has led to considerable confusion about the theories themselves. Third, situations with high crime rates often have a large number of variables, all of which are correlated with each other and all of which are correlated with crime—e.g., poverty, inequality, high residential mobility, single parent families, unemployment, poor and dense housing, the presence of gangs and illegal criminal opportunities, inadequate schools, and a lack of social services. It can be extremely difficult to determine which (if any) of these variables is causally related to high crime rates, and which have no causal impact on crime at all.[10] Finally, the number and complexity of these theories means that many are left out or shortchanged in the following discussion. For all these reasons, our summary of structure/process theories may evoke more disagreement and dissatisfaction than the summary of individual difference theories we have just presented.

In spite of these daunting problems, we offer the following interpretation and assessment. In each case, we first assert that some structural

---

[9]W. S. Robinson, "Ecological Correlations and the Behavior of Individuals," *American Sociological Review* 15: 351–57 (June, 1950).

[10]See the discussion of multicollinearity in Chapter 5.

characteristic is associated with some rate or distribution of crime. This is the "structure" portion of a structure/process theory. We then provide a brief description of the supposed reasons why normal people in this structural situation may demonstrate a greater probability of engaging in crime than people in other situations. This is the "process" portion of a structure/process theory.

Economic modernization and development are associated with high property crime rates. Originally, Durkheim argued that the process by which normal people within this structural situation would engage in high rates of crime involved normlessness associated with rapid social change, but now that argument appears to be incorrect. Rather, the process probably involves changes in the routine activities in which people engage, and in the wider range of opportunities for crime that exist in a developed society. In particular, as societies develop, people spend more time away from their homes, which exposes both them and their homes to victimization. In addition, people own much more property that is both valuable and portable and therefore can be stolen. Property crimes tend to increase until the society is quite highly developed, and then to hold steady at that very high level. The process involved in stabilizing those crime rates probably involves the increasing effectiveness of countermeasures, such as target hardening, surveillance, alarm systems, and neighborhood watches. Since modernization probably is not a reversible process, these countermeasures are the only policy implications associated with this line of theory.

Economic modernization and development are not strongly associated with higher rates of violence. Many undeveloped societies are extremely violent and at least some developed societies have little violence. However, at least in its initial stages, economic development tends to be associated with a great deal of economic inequality, and economic inequality is associated with high rates of violence. Thus, there is usually at least an initial burst of violent crime at the beginnings of economic development. Societies that retain a great deal of economic inequality after they are developed also tend to retain high rates of violent crime.

The association between economic inequality and high violent crime is sometimes asserted as a structural argument without any discussion of the process by which people who live in situations with high economic inequality come to commit high levels of violent crime. Other times, process arguments involving feelings of frustration or relative deprivation are presented. The policy implications of such structural arguments involve reducing economic inequality to decrease the levels of violence in the society as a whole. Of course, this policy could also reduce the overall rate of economic growth in the society. If that is the case, it would be necessary to balance the gains associated with violence reduction against the losses associated with slower economic growth before implementing this policy.

In addition, societies whose cultures have a strong emphasis on the goal of material success and only a weak emphasis on adhering to legitimate means will tend to have higher rates of instrumental crime than other societies. This is particularly true if the noneconomic institutions in a society (families, schools, jobs, and even politics) are all strongly affected by and even subservient to the needs of the economic system. If such societies also have social structures that unequally distribute the legitimate means among social groups, then the rates of instrumental crime will be distributed inversely to the distribution of the legitimate means. Finally, illegitimate means of achieving material success often develop in situations with few legitimate means. This includes delinquent and criminal gangs comprised of youths who aspire to make lots of money but have little expectation of being able to do so by legitimate means. Once illegitimate means develop, then rates of instrumental crime in those situations further increase. However, in areas where there are neither legitimate nor illegitimate means to achieve material success, there may also be high rates of violent crime.

In a separate but comparable behavior trend, people in general and adolescents in particular seek to gain social status among their peers. People who are unable to achieve status according to conventional criteria tend to band together, create new criteria for distributing status, and then distribute status to themselves according to those new criteria. This process may take different forms (e.g., computer nerds), but in high-crime neighborhoods with a strong cultural demand for material success but no legitimate opportunities to achieve that success, there may be a tendency to give status on the basis of the commission of criminal acts.

There has been a controversy about the processes by which these structural situations generate high crime rates. The traditional view has been that people in these situations feel high frustration, and that the frustration itself generates higher crime rates. A more recent view is that people simply have a tendency to act in ways that are consistent with their self-interests, and that they therefore pursue material success or status by whatever means are available. In this second view, it does not matter whether people in these situations feel frustrated or not.

Policy implications of these theoretical arguments include changing the culture by reducing the emphasis on achieving material success and increasing the emphasis on adhering to legitimate means of gaining self-satisfaction. One way to do this would involve strengthening noneconomic institutions (families, schools, jobs, and politics), so that they are not so strongly influenced by the needs of the economic system. Another way is to attempt to arrange things so that social status is achieved by following the legitimate means. This change, of course, would be quite tricky. In addition, policy implications involve changing social structures by equalizing the distribution of legitimate opportunities to achieve material success. This change also can be quite tricky, as illustrated in the failures of the War on Poverty. Attempts to deal directly with illegitimate opportunity structures (e.g., illegal drug networks) will probably fail without first dealing with the larger culture and structure.

At the neighborhood level, particularly under conditions of economic development and economic inequality, with cultures emphasizing economic success and structures limiting access to it, crime is associated with social disorganization. High crime neighborhoods tend to have three structural characteristics: high unemployment, frequent residential mobility, and high family disruption. The process by which these structural characteristics result in high crime rates involves anonymity, lack of relationships among neighbors, and low participation in community organizations. Ultimately, this process means that neighbors are unable to achieve common values and goals—a condition described as social disorganization. The neighborhood then spirals into decay and crime. Policy implications of this theory include a variety of measures directed at changing the structural conditions that give rise to this situation. It may also be possible directly to address the issue of neighborhood anonymity; however, without addressing the structural conditions that generate this anonymity in the first place, such policies are unlikely to reduce crime.

Other shared cultural ideas, besides those involving the value of material success, can also be causally related to crime. In particular, when cultures and subcultures include ideas that justify the use of violence in a wide variety of situations, then one can expect high rates of violent crime. Some of these cultural or subcultural ideas may be structurally generated. For example, the structural conditions of unemployment and racial discrimination may generate a subcultural code of the street in which violence is the expected response to a variety of situations. This code ultimately reflects the hopelessness and alienation that inner-city residents feel when confronting joblessness and racism. If subcultural ideas are structurally generated, then policy responses that attempt to deal directly with the ideas will fail. Instead, policy must address the structural conditions that generate the ideas in the first place. Other cultural or subcultural ideas may be unrelated to current structural conditions. For example, the exaggerated sense of "manliness" among Southern white males seems unrelated to any current structural conditions, and policy responses may best address these ideas by other means, for example through the media.

The media, of course, may also serve to disseminate cultural ideas that are favorable to law violation. Both the techniques and rationalizations to commit crime can be repeatedly presented in a favorable light. This is particularly true for violent crime. In addition, the media can create the impression that violence, even when it is legal, is the primary method for resolving interpersonal conflicts. When the media and other cultural institutions promulgate such views, one can expect high rates of violence and crime in the society. The process by which violent crime rises involves social learning, which includes direct learning of techniques and rationalizations, and indirect learning of the consequences that criminal behaviors have for others. Policy implications include encouraging or requiring the media more consistently to present images favorable to obeying the law and resolving interpersonal conflicts by non-violent methods.

Societies that rely on stigmatizing shaming, in which the bonds to the shamed person are permanently broken, tend to have higher crime rates than those that rely on reintegrative shaming, in which the bonds to shamed persons are maintained and those persons are welcomed back into the community. The process involves the limitation of legitimate opportunities and the establishment of subcultures. Societies with a control balance (i.e., where people exert approximately as much control over others as is exerted over them) will tend to have less crime than those with a control imbalance (i.e., where some people exert a great deal of control over others while other people have little or no control over anything). The process here involves a natural tendency for people to extend their control over others. Whether societies engage in stigmatizing or reintegrative shaming, and whether or not they have a control balance, may be affected by a variety of other societal characteristics, such as economic inequality.

Marxist criminologists have argued that capitalism itself is a cause of crime. While the explosion of crime in the new nations of the former Soviet Union seems to support this notion, we tentatively conclude that this is not the case. Rather, crime probably is caused by the other conditions described above, all of which may be associated with capitalism: economic development, economic inequality, a cultural emphasis on material success combined with structural limitations on access to legitimate means of achieving that success, neighborhood social disorganization, the dissemination of cultural values that approve of the use of violence in a wide variety of situations, the use of stigmatizing shaming, and the presence of control imbalances.

Criminal justice policies in a jurisdiction also clearly influence crime rates within that jurisdiction. Research on deterrence suggests that crackdowns achieve a temporary deterrent effect that rapidly decays but which may also extend beyond the point at which the crackdown itself terminates. It also appears that increases in the objective certainty of punishment tend to be associated with decreases in crime rates. On the other hand, most of the research on increases in the severity of punishments indicates that it has little or no deterrent effect; at this point somewhat more research suggests that increases in severity, especially when severity levels are already high, actually result in increases in crime (e.g., the "brutalization" effect).

To summarize, the following structural arguments describe societal characteristics that seem to be associated with higher crime rates. Each structural argument is followed by a brief description of the processes said to operate in those structural situations, processes that result in people in those situations, regardless of their individual characteristics, demonstrating an increased tendency to commit crime.

1. Economic modernization and development is associated with a rise in property crime rates. Property crime tends to increase until the society is quite highly developed, and then to hold steady at a high level. The processes that result in this pattern of crime involve changes in routine activities and in criminal opportunities, which eventually are balanced by the increasing effectiveness of countermeasures.

2. Economic inequality is associated with a rise in rates of violence. Such violence may involve feelings of frustration and relative deprivation.

3. Cultures that emphasize the goal of material success at the expense of adherence to legitimate means are associated with high rates of utilitarian crime; an unequal distribution of legitimate means to achieve material success is associated with an inverse distribution of utilitarian crime; in situations without legitimate means to economic success, the development of illegitimate means is associated with increased utilitarian crime while the lack of such development is associated with increased violent crime; in these situations, the inability to achieve status by conventional criteria is associated with status inversion and higher rates of non-utilitarian criminal behavior. The processes involved in these structural patterns involve either frustration or the simple tendency to engage in self-interested behavior.

4. Neighborhoods with high unemployment, frequent residential mobility, and family disruption tend to have high crime rates. The processes involve neighborhood anonymity that results in social disorganization.

5. Media dissemination of techniques and rationalizations that are favorable to law violation are associated with increased rates of law violation. The process involves direct learning of techniques and rationalizations, and indirect learning of the consequences that criminal behaviors have for others.

6. Joblessness and racism can generate an inner-city code of the street that promulgates normative violence in a variety of situations. The process includes feelings of hopelessness and alienation among inner-city residents and the generation of an oppositional subculture as a means of maintaining self-respect.

7. Increases in the objective certainty of punishments are associated with reductions in crime rates, but increases in the objective severity of punishments seem to be associated either with no changes or with increases in crime rates. In addition, crackdowns on certain types of crime are associated with short-term reductions in the rates of those crimes that may extend beyond the life of the crackdown policy itself.

8. Societies that stigmatize deviants have higher crime rates than those that reintegrate deviants. The process involves blocked legitimate opportunities and the formation of subcultures.

9. Societies in which some people control others have higher crime rates than societies in which people control and are controlled by others in approximately equal amounts. The process involves people's natural tendency to expand their control.

As presented in this summary, the various structure/process theories do not seem to be incompatible with each other. It certainly may be true, and it is even quite likely, that some of the above arguments are false, but that is an empirical question about each particular assertion. Empirical support for one of these arguments does not imply lack of support for any other argument. To that extent, depending on their empirical support, all these structural arguments can be integrated into a single theory that describes the characteristics of societies with high or low crime rates.

Finally, there is no contradiction between these structure/process theories and the individual difference theories reviewed earlier. Nothing in the structure/process theories contradicts the assertion that there are some people who are more likely to engage in crime regardless of their situation. Similarly, nothing in the individual difference theories contradicts the assertion that there are some situations in which people, regardless of their individual characteristics, are more likely to engage in crime. These are separate assertions, and both types of theories can be integrated in a larger theory of criminal behavior.

THEORIES OF THE BEHAVIOR OF CRIMINAL LAW

A number of arguments are made in various chapters of this book that have implications about how the criminal law itself behaves. These arguments are quite separate from arguments about the types of people who are likely to commit crime, or the types of situations that are likely to have high crime rates.

For example, Durkheim and Erikson argued that, in mechanical societies, law defines the moral boundaries of the society by excluding and punishing criminals and other deviants. In normal times, societies need a relatively constant level of punishment to maintain social solidarity. But when social solidarity is threatened, the punishment function can be expected to expand, regardless of the level of crime. This particular theory could be used to explain the fact that, in the last ten years or so, crime rates in the United States have been declining but incarceration rates have tripled. Durkheim's theory would suggest that this great expansion of incarceration is motivated by a threatened sense of solidarity in the larger society, rather than by the threat of crime itself.

Sutherland argued that the state responded to the victimizing behaviors of lower-class people with criminal sanctions, but responded to the victimizing behaviors of white-collar people with regulations and civil violations. The theory focused on the ability of white-collar groups to define the norms about what constitutes crime. Therefore, for Sutherland, variation in the enactment and enforcement of criminal laws, rather than variations in victimizing behavior, explained the class distribution of official crime rates.

Non-Marxist conflict theories make a similar argument, but focus on interests rather than values or norms. According to this theory, people in both legislatures and criminal justice agencies act in ways that are consistent with their interests, where those interests are shaped by social structure. Evaluative ideas (including values and norms) also are shaped by interests, so that ultimately they influence what people think is right and wrong, good and bad, just and unjust, criminal and legal. According to these interests, legislators and criminal justice agents are likely to define the behaviors typical of low power groups as criminal, and the behaviors typical of high power groups as legal, independent of the actual harm the behaviors cause to life or property.

Conflict theory argues that the enactment and enforcement of criminal law is shaped by the distribution of political power. This power is one element—stratification—in Black's much broader theory of the behavior of law. Black also argues that law is shaped by four other factors: morphology, organization, culture, and social control. Essentially, these characteristics define what is seen as "more serious" or "less serious" crimes. For example, Black would argue that crimes committed by an individual against an organization are seen as "more serious," and thus as deserving greater punishment, than comparable crimes committed by an organization against an individual. Similarly, crimes committed by a person without culture against a person who is highly cultured are generally seen as more serious, and thus deserving greater punishment, than comparable crimes committed by a person with high culture against a person who entirely lacks culture.

Finally, Marxist theories argue that, regardless of any other interests that are served by the criminal law, that law must serve the economic interests of the owners of the means of economic production. If the criminal law harms their economic interests, then the owners can simply move the means of production to a jurisdiction where their interests will be served. Thus, people who enact or enforce criminal laws that harm the economic interests of the owners of the means of production will find that they have impoverished themselves. This consequence effectively gives the owners of the means of production veto power over the content of criminal law.

In addition to these explicit theories, many theories of criminal behavior contain implicit theories about the behavior of criminal law. For example, Gottfredson and Hirschi[11] describe "the nature of crime" as acts that involve simple and immediate gratification of desires but few long-term benefits, are exciting and risky but require little skill or planning, and generally produce few benefits for the offender while causing pain and suffering to the victim. They derive this "natural definition" from an analysis of the characteristics of ordinary crime. While this argument is phrased in terms of a natural law philosophy, it actually makes an implicit assertion about the behavior of criminal law enactment and enforcement agencies. Specifically, if Gottfredson and Hirschi are right, then legislators and criminal justice agents must generally define and process "low self-control" acts as criminal, but not "high self-control" acts. This is no longer a philosophical statement but an empirical assertion.

From the point of view of a scientific criminology, there are advantages to translating Gottfredson and Hirschi's philosophical statement about the nature of crime into an empirical assertion about the behavior of criminal law: Empirical assertions can be tested with research. For example, it is clear that at least some actions that are high self-control are defined and processed as criminal. Reversing Gottfredson and Hirschi's statements, high self-control actions are complex and involve

---

[11]Michael Gottfredson and Travis Hirschi, *A General Theory of Crime*, Stanford University Press, Stanford, CA, 1990, pp. 15–44, 89–91.

delayed gratification of desires and few short-term benefits, are dull and safe while requiring considerable skill and planning, and generally produce large benefits for the offender while causing little pain and suffering to the victim. These are the characteristics of several types of white-collar crimes. If we are making empirical assertions about the behavior of criminal law, then we can examine why some low self-control actions are not defined and processed as criminal, while some high self-control actions are. It is more difficult to do that in the context of philosophical arguments about the nature of crime. Like the rest of criminology, theories of the behavior of criminal law must move beyond philosophical statements and become scientific, so that their assertions are subject to empirical testing.

Summing up, the following are some assertions about the behavior of criminal law.

1. When social solidarity of a society is threatened, criminal punishment increases independent of whether crime increases.

2. The enactment and enforcement of criminal laws reflect the values and interests of individuals and groups in proportion to their political and economic power.

3. In addition to stratification, the quantity of law that is applied in particular cases is influenced by morphology, culture, organization, and the extent of other forms of social control.

4. Regardless of what other interests are served by the criminal law, it must serve the economic interests of the owners of the means of economic production.

5. Actions that involve simple and immediate gratification of desires but few long-term benefits, are exciting and risky but require little skill or planning, and generally produce few benefits for the offender while causing pain and suffering to the victim, are more likely to be defined and processed as criminal than other actions.

These assertions about the behavior of criminal law are not necessarily incompatible with each other. If some of these assertions are supported by empirical research, that support does not necessarily imply lack of support for other assertions. For example, it may be true that low self-control behaviors are more likely to be defined and processed as criminal, but it may also be true that people who lack political and economic power are more likely to be defined and processed as criminal. If both assertions were true at the same time, then low self-control people who have very little power would have higher official crime rates than low self-control people who have a lot of power.

Theories of the behavior of criminal law do not contradict theories of criminal behavior. More than anything else, they ask a different question: Why are some behaviors and people, and not others, defined and processed as criminal? However, that separate question has implications for theories that address the causes of the behaviors that are officially defined and processed as criminal. For example, Gottfredson and Hirschi's theory of criminal behavior (criminals have low self-control) implies a theory of the behavior of criminal law (law enactment and enforcement officials define and process low self-control actions as criminal, but not high self-control actions). To the extent that their theory of the behavior of criminal law is wrong, then their theory of criminal behavior is also wrong because low self-control behavior would not be the same as criminal behavior.

Ultimately, criminologists must come up with a theory that simultaneously explains the behavior of criminal law and the behavior of individual criminals. This could be described as a "unified theory of crime."[12] If Gottfredson and Hirschi's implicit theory of the behavior of criminal law is made explicit, then theirs is a unified theory of crime, since it includes coordinated explanations of why certain behaviors are defined and processed as criminal and why certain people engage in those behaviors. The relevant question then becomes the empirical adequacy of the theory: Both Gottfredson and Hirschi's theory of how criminal law behaves and their theory of why individual criminals behave the way they do must be consistent with the observed data.

CONCLUSION

In the past, crime policies often have been the product of political ideology: conservatives favored some policies while liberals favored others. Neither liberals nor conservatives were particularly interested in research on whether their favored policies actually worked. Instead, they often seemed to take the position that "my mind is made up, don't bother me with the facts."

Today, both liberals and conservatives increasingly rely on criminology theory and research to support their recommendations about crime policy. As described throughout this book, and particularly as summarized in this chapter, this theory and research suggests that the world is not as simple as either liberals or conservatives had portrayed it. Instead, some liberal policies seem to reduce crime while others do not,

---

[12]See Bernard, "A Theoretical Approach to Integration," op. cit. See also the "unified conflict theory of crime" in Chapter 13.

and some conservative policies seem to reduce crime while others do not.

Based on this research, liberals and conservatives are now tending to agree on at least some crime control policies.[13] For example, at the moment both liberals and conservatives seem to favor the prevention policies that focus on early childhood. To some extent, liberals may favor these policies because they help rather than punish people, while conservatives may favor these policies because they strengthen families. But both liberals and conservatives are aware that the empirical research shows that these policies are quite effective in the long run. Thus, to some extent, criminological theory and research are superseding political ideology as the source for crime policy.

In the future, criminology theory and research, rather than political ideology, will be the major source of crime policy. The whole point of science, as stated in the first chapter of this book, is to gain control over our world. As criminologists increasingly identify variables that are causally related to crime, crime policies increasingly will address those variables. We will gain increasing control over our world, and we will use that control to reduce crime. Some criminologists may warn against moving in this direction, fearing that the costs associated with this increased control will outweigh the benefits that will come from the reduced crime. But regardless of these warnings, it seems clear that criminology and crime policy in the larger society are moving in this direction.

---

[13]See, for example, the report to the United States Congress prepared for the National Institute of Justice by Lawrence W. Sherman, Denise Gottfredson, Doris MacKenzie, et al., *Preventing Crime: What Works What Doesn't, What's Promising*, U.S. Department of Justice, Washington, DC, 1997.

Index